J.B. Priestley's Yorkshire

J.B. Priestley's Yorkshire

Compiled and
Introduced
by W.R. MITCHELL

The Dalesman Publishing Company Ltd
Clapham, Lancaster, LA2 8EB

First published 1987

ISBN: 0 85206 913 8

Cover photographs. Front, top — J.B. Priestley, in January, 1975 **(Telegraph and Argus).** *bottom — Hubberholme Church* **(painting by Geoffrey M. Holdsworth).** *Back — J.B. Priestley painting near Ribblehead* **(Marie Hartley).**

The publishers acknowledge the co-operation of A.D. Peters & Co Ltd and William Heinemann Ltd in the production of this book.

Obituary

You saw a man of stature:
A burly bulk of a man,
A homely hulk of a man –
Nay, even more than that
You saw a paradox of a man,
A pipe-loving Puck of a man!
For he whose very voice and stance,
Each attitude, gesture, and mannerism,
Declared his downright Yorkshireness,
This portly personification
Of the old-style West Riding,
Having dwelt mainly amidst strangers,
Had spent a lifetime's strength and skill
In squeezing from the presses of the years
The elusive essence of our unique
Englishness!

Charles Bragg

Printed in Great Britain by Fretwell & Cox Ltd.
Healey Works, Goulbourne Street, Keighley, West Yorkshire BD21 1PZ.

Contents

J.B. Priestley, photographed at Muker in Swaledale ***(W.R. Mitchell).***

An Introduction

J. B. PRIESTLEY died in August, 1984, after a long life and a short illness. He, who was for long fascinated by the theme of time, defied to an advanced age its worst ravages on the human mind and frame. John Boynton Priestley – to give him his "Sunday name" – was born in Bradford in September, 1896, being the only son of a schoolmaster who took a lively interest in the town's affairs. J.B. grew up in the heady atmosphere of a self-confident town, basking in a rich Edwardian twilight: he tucked away in his mind aspects of the wool trade, memories of some outrageous characters, the atmosphere of music and concert hall and the spirit of an idealistic type of Socialism that hoped to bring about change by persuasion and the evidence of an old system's decay rather than by revolution. JB joined the Army at the age of 19. Never again would he live in his native North Country, yet the mark of those West Riding years was with him for life: and to the mill town memories he would add the complimentary recollections of the Yorkshire Dales, where in due and proper course he would have his last resting place, his ashes buried in the yard of Hubberholme church.

JB's literary output was prodigious – over 80 books, articles and essays, criticism, biography, autobiography, short stories, film and television scripts, plus a number of plays that added lustre to the English stage. (He thought of himself primarily as a dramatist). He was fond of saying that as a young man he was never encouraged to write anything. "The West Riding, where I grew up, had a genius for discouragement as stony as its walls!" He became a Jack-of-all-literary-trades who achieved mastery in most of them. He was never pretentious. "Deliberately," he said, "I aim at simplicity and not complexity in my writing. No matter what the subject in hand might be, I want to write something that at a pinch I could read aloud in a bar-parlour." He never sat down at a typewriter with a blank mind and a blank sheet of paper, hoping for inspiration. He had already thought out what he wanted to record. Writing was just the manner of its recording. JB was a one-draft man!

His wanderlust took him to some of the most dramatic settings on earth, but he had tucked at the back of his mind clear impressions of the Bradford of his boyhood and of the dale country lying to the north of the Aire Gap. Closer at hand were the Moors, beginning at Dick Hudson's inn at Eldwick. For many Bradfordians, life in the stone canyons formed by the mills and warehouses was tolerable, only because from time to time they could savour their own little wilderness, with its peat-flavoured air and a big sky which sometimes was blue.

I have known J. B. Priestley's books since boyhood. Some of them were arranged on the bookshelf in my grandfather's home in one of the little industrialised villages lying off the Aire Valley. Grandfather, a Methodist local preacher, Sunday School teacher and also Socialist in the old-fashioned sense, liked JB's direct manner and the originality of expression. He would say that there was not a dull sentence in any of his work. Every writer has his "off" days, but I knew what grandfather meant. It has been a special pleasure to look through the writings of JB and select items of Yorkshire interest for this anthology.

I first met him 30 years ago when he was visiting the Dales, with his wife Jacquetta, to gather information and impressions for an article in *Life International.* I can picture him now, his stocky form at rest in our most comfortable chair. There was that sagging face, the steady eyes set under beetling brows, and the mouth into which a briar pipe fitted as of ancient right. JB had turned up unexpectedly at our house in the Dales market town of Settle; he courteously refrained from smoking. (When the pipe was operating at full blast, it was like a chimney at a West Riding mill in which there was a rush order for cloth). JB was then 70 years of age and in good spirits. Someone had written of him that he had so many chips on his shoulder that if you were to gather them up there would be material for a good fire. Some critics misunderstood his Yorkshireness: he *was* rather dour, somewhat withdrawn, but could be fulsome and entertaining in the right company. He was always impatient of what he considered to be foolish talk.

It pleased me, looking at him on that day 30 years ago, to reflect briefly on some of his literary output. Here was one of literature's great all-rounders, a man who was not only supremely talented but was for ever experimenting. Success first came to him in 1929, when he was 35 years of age, with the publication of his picaresque long novel, *The Good Companions.* Who could have foreseen, in those days of industrial

J.B. Priestley and his son, Tom, photographed in June, 1938.

depression, when people were lamenting – as they have always done – the death of the novel, that this amiable, rambling story would become a runaway best-seller? JB had previously concentrated on essays and criticism; he might justifiably have followed *The Good Companions* with a similar sort of block-buster. Yet he abhored the notion of being in a rut, and deliberately wrote *Angel Pavement* as something totally different from anything he had done before.

The Thirties which for millions were a time of poverty and despair, and for all thinking people were a morally troublous time, with the rise of the Nazi movement in Germany, were for JB a glowing time professionally. In 1932, he made an impressive debut as a playwright with *Dangerous Corner.*

He wrote that play in a mere 10 days. In 1934, he offered us a special sort of travel book, *English Journey,* in which he did not concentrate on the romantic, glamorous places in the land and presented aspects of contemporary life. All was not gloom, even in the depressed 1930s. He ventured into his beloved dales. He heard the story of the daleswoman who had stopped visiting Kettlewell – a village of modest size, and remote enough never to be noisy – because, as she explained to a friend: "I can't stand t'racket." To catalogue JB's output would be to invite writer's cramp, but of special interest to me is the film script for *Sing as We Go,* featuring Gracie Fields against the backdrop of Lancashire milldom. One of my favourite plays, *When We Are Married,* is a characterful assessment of family life in the West Riding during that lingering Edwardian twilight. The play includes that choice description of the gluttonish fellow, who was "digging his grave with his knife and fork." To read JB's wartime radio broadcasts – *Postscripts* – is infinitely less satisfying than it was to hear him deliver them. His mellow, well modulated voice resounded through the nation on Sunday evenings, after the nine o'clock news. He spoke in grim times, in the midst of a war of which no one knew the outcome. He spoke of simple but enduring things, and his talks were great morale-builders. They appealed to the heart as well as the intellect.

The pre-1914 Bradford in which young Priestley formed vivid impressions of North Country life.

On the visit to Settle, to which I have referred, JB apologised for arriving just before lunch on baking day. Could I recommend a cafe (but nowhere "posh") where he and his wife might have a meal? I suggested a place frequented by dentists and bank clerks, and when we met again, an hour later, I inquired about the meal. It was "not so bad". (Curiosity led me to visit that cafe a few days later, and I was amused to find a *Good Companions* flavour about the place. That day, the menu, which was propped against a sauce bottle, featured "plumbs and custard").

JB and I were on familiar, much-loved ground when we conversed about the Yorkshire Dales, which he once described as "the most satisfying – and perhaps the most beautiful – countryside I know." This from a man who had been round the world and had seen many of the sights, "from Lake Louise in the Rockies to Tahiti to the volcanoes of southern Chile, from Rainbow Bridge in Utah to Japan's Inland Sea to Marrakesh and the Grand Atlas." He enjoyed meeting dalesmen and listening to the Norse character of their speech. These men, he once said "are rather like minor Ibsen characters." They were good people, not yet corrupted by tourism. "They have produced singularly few artists and writers – unlike the industrial West Riding – but for some mysterious reason they have given England, in more than one century, some of her most famous physicians. Perhaps they had to leave their native air, sharp but sustaining, to find an adequate number of patients."

At Séttle, I introduced him to Tot Lord, a major Dales character, who was quick to open up his museum of prehistoric bones and stones for our scrutiny. We approached the house through an overgrown garden, where the plant life included a palm tree. On the verandah stood a wicker table, wicker chairs – and the bleached skull of an elephant. It was rather like strolling on to the set of a film featuring one of Somerset Maughan's eastern tales. JB smiled wrily. During that tour of Tot's museum, I whispered to a local man: "To really understand these objects, we should try to get into the mind of Early Man." JB was listening. He retorted: "The great thing for civilisation today is to get out of the mind of early man!" Somehow, we squeezed into my tiny car for a crossing of Buckhaw Brow to the *Dalesman* offices at Clapham, where I introduced JB to the founder, Harry J. Scott, who already knew him well by repute and through correspondence. The two men talked and smoked pipes. (JB was the proud possessor of well over 50 pipes at the time). When I rejoined them, visibility in Harry Scott's office was down to a few feet!

There were times when JB and his Yorkshire friends conversed, Yorkshire fashion, in monosyllables; on other occasions the flow of words was unstoppable. Stanley Parker, a friend of JB who met him on his visit to Bradford, in 1941, apologised for taking up so much of the great man's time. "Don't worry," said JB. "I wouldn't have done it if I hadn't been too tired to go to bed. You get to the stage, you know, when it's less of an effort to go on talking than it is to stop." Stanley Parker met him in the foyer of a Bradford hotel on that same visit. Knowing that JB did not like to waste time, he decided to keep talk to a minimum. "By the way . . ." said Parker, as JB took up a pen to sign the register. JB began to speak. As the clock struck one, the pen was still poised in mid-air. When the clock struck two, JB had put it down again and was gesticulating wildly. At three, he had picked it up again. By twenty past three – after much talk – he had signed. "It had taken him three hours and twenty minutes to sign a hotel register!"

I met JB in his favourite Wensleydale. It was a bright morning, with a curlew-busy sky. JB was staying at the *Rose and Crown,* Bainbridge. For a time I stood outside the hotel. From a partly opened window came the machine-gun patter of JB's typewriter and pipe smoke drifted from the window, rising to join the cumulus clouds above the dale. We arranged to meet at Muker, in Swaledale, where he resumed his talk about the Dales. I heard about his walking tour in 1919, shortly after his demobilisation from the Army, and the four or five articles he had been commissioned to write for *The Yorkshire Observer* at the rate of "a guinea a time". JB added: "You could buy a lot of beer and ham-and-eggs and cut plug for a guinea then." He had walked "out of the iron and blood and misery of war into wonderland, still magically illuminated by memories of my boyhood."

JB always marvelled at the astonishing variety of scene to be found in the Yorkshire Dales. "A day's walking will seem to bring you to extremes of desolation and village cosiness . . . And the play of light and the endless shifting of colour and tones are an enchantment." He was particularly sensitive to "colour and tones" when I met him, for in his car were some artist's materials. For 10 years he had painted, and his favourite medium was gouache. "You do need a bit of sunlight to bring out the colours of the Dales . . . I only paint on holiday and I get very cross when I can't do it. I've only done one sketch since I came, which makes me angry . . ." He looked to the Dales for interesting skies, actually preferring those that were cloudy. It was a small boy from an upland farmer, during an art lesson, who was unimpressed by the blue-and-white sky the teacher painted for him. "Wear I come from, miss", he declared, "t'cloud's is mucky!" In JB's native Bradford, industrial smoke had filtered out the best of the sunlight. He once referred to Bruddersford's shifting canopy of smoke and the effect of sunlight upon it as "a peculiar alternation of dim gold and grey gloom."

In due course, JB's Dales article appeared in *Life International.* It was an example of a writer enjoying himself without showing off; he commented wittily on the less obvious facets of Dales landscape and Dales life. He had noticed how few people there were in the Dales, and on the evidence that

The "other Yorkshire" — Conistone, in Wharfedale, at sheep-clipping time. To have a day in the Dales was the overwhelming desire of many Bradfordians in summer ***(Robert Rixon).***

existed for a much higher population in the past. "The churchyards up there are crowded with the tombstones of people who died in their later 80s. These lives were saved by air fit to breathe, food fit to eat and the challenge of wild weather." He had been happy in the company of old friends, including Marie Hartley and Joan Ingilby, who welcomed him to their home at Askrigg. He had sought and found Dick Chapman, a native of the dale who retired here after many years of teaching in Bradford, and who demonstrated to a delighted JB how to catch crayfish in the river Ure.

As his 90th birthday aproached, Central Television arranged with his son, Tom, to prepare a programme in which the two would yarn about this and that. Extracts from JB's writings would be read by a distinguished actor. In the film, we saw the aged but still genial JB enjoying himself and we had a rare insight into his early life. But first we watched him strike a match so that he might talk and smoke. Was ever a match struck with more telling effect? We waited for the smoke to clear, for the bowl of the briar to glow, for the smoker to talk. He had enjoyed every minute of his writing career and "I've been reasonably successful . . ." He thought of himself as being "more a writer than I am a human being." Father and son glanced through leaves in a photograph album. "That is a picture of one of my grandfathers," said JB, indicating a bearded man. He smiled, adding: "Come to think of it, he looks like everybody's grandfather!"

JB had undoubtedly mellowed. No longer did he feel inclined to project a blunt Yorkshireness as part of his image. He had been only 26 years old, with one published book, *Brief Diversions,* when he had taken up the literary life full-time as a freelance. (At that time his wife was expecting a child and they had only about £50 in the bank; he just had to succeed!). Long before television existed to give a character the prospect of instant stardom, JB had to painstakingly build up a reputation and to write incessantly. He was successful. Looking back, when he was 89, he could ponder on the ranch in Arizona on which he had stayed, on the houses in Highgate and the Isle of Wight which he owned, on occasions when he dined at the Savoy Grill with such as Sir Hugh Walpole and Sir Cedric Hardwicke, and on meetings with Elgar, whose music gave him great pleasure.

For the last 20 years of his life, his home was Kissing Tree House, Alveston, in the Shakespeare Country. He enjoyed its rural setting and the daily walks he could undertake along quiet, hedge-fringed roads. Susan Cooper, who interviewed him at Alveston for *The Sunday Times Magazine,* thought he had the look of a gentler Merlin: "benevolent but brooding, unpredictable, as much unlike his image as Alveston is unlike a Yorkshire wool town."

Bradford no longer lies beneath a "long smudge of smoke", as it did when it was the setting of some of JB's early novels. Now the city has a futuristic appearance, especially at night, in the orange glare of sodium chloride street lighting. The enormous Victorian town hall, the design of its tower based on one in Italy, still rises at the heart of the place – like a gothic exclamation mark. Those famous "mountaineering" trams have gone. So have the people with outrageous West Riding manners. Their descendants share the pavements of Bradford with families whose forbears came from Pakistan to work in the West Riding mills.

JB was aware of the sheer hard work carried out in the Dales as well as in the heavy industries of the towns. "In Swaledale, which now looks a rather austere Arcadia, it was lead-mining, which began in earliest times and did not end until about 80 years ago, by which time there were miles of perilous underground levels, often reached by rough wooden ladders. What men have done, century after century, just to keep body and soul together!"

He was not religious in the orthodox sense, yet in April, 1986, by special faculty, his ashes were buried in the churchyard at Hubberholme, beside the infant river Wharfe. A memorial tablet at Hubberholme, made of Hopton Wood stone, bears the following inscription: "J.B.Priestley, O.M., 1894-1984. Author and Dramatist, whose ashes are buried nearby. He loved the Dales and found 'Hubberholme one of the smallest and pleasantest places in the world'". The plaque was unveiled by Jacquetta, his widow, whose love for the Yorkshire Dales matches in depth that shown by JB.

We gathered at Hubberholme on a grey day. It was theoretically spring, but winter lingered on in the wizened state of the vegetation, in the chilliness of the air and the patches of snow in the ancient joints of the fells. Few farmers were able to attend the service; it was a difficult lambing time and any ewes at the topmost farms were without sufficient milk to nourish the lambs. These needed special attention. At Hubberholme, the contralto voices of the ewes mingled with the high-pitched cries of their offspring. Inside the church, a stray shaft of sunlight picked out some of the fine details of the ancient "rood" loft, the pews made by Thompson, wood-carver of Kilburn, and the stained glass, some of it featuring everyday sights in the dale, sights familiar to JB on his many visits to the district.

Tom Priestley, his son, said that central to much of JB's writing was a feeling of duality, of a dream. There was ordinary living – and something else: a quality that was hard to define, but "something beyond". You could be aware of this "other country" if you looked in the right place and with the right frame of mind. Tom Priestley gave us some attractive word pictures of JB, and especially his love of painting the winter scene and sky. He had dabbed in the clouds with a finger charred from pushing tobacco into his pipe and dented from constant typing over the years. JB had travelled all over the world, but Hubberholme remained his favourite spot. He enjoyed its smallness, the great age of its buildings – and the peacefulness of this place. "Here there is space and beauty. The elements seem to be balanced; the earth seems to touch the sky . . ."

And there was JB's own vision of eternity, in his "Dream of the Birds", a piece read with joy in this small place where the large and restless spirit of one of our great writers had found its last home:

. . . But now the gear was changed again and time went faster still, and it was rushing by at such a rate that the birds could not show any movement but were like an enormous plain sown with feathers. But along this plain, flickering through the bodies themselves, there now passed a sort of white flame, trembling, dancing, then hurrying on; and as soon as I saw it I knew that this flame was life itself, the very quintessence of being; and then it came to me, in a rocket-burst of ecstacy, that nothing mattered, nothing could ever matter, because nothing else was real, but this quivering and hurrying lambency of being. Birds, men or creatures not yet shaped and coloured, all were of no account except so far as this flame of life travelled through them. It left nothing to mourn over behind it; what I had thought was tragedy was mere emptiness or a shadow show; for now all real feeling was caught and purified and danced on ecstatically with the white flame of life. I had never felt before such deep happiness as I knew at the end of my dream of the tower and the birds . . .

After a memorial service to J.B. Priestley at Hubberholme in Upper Wharfedale. Mrs. Priestley is third from the left ***(David Hyde).***

THE ANTHOLOGY

A Yorkshireman's Traits

The Yorkshireman tends to extremes. He can be the prince and paragon of good fellows; he is often the emperor of all the louts. Sometimes he is too apt to atone for his blunt manners by sharp practice, which adds naught to his popularity. Nothing could be ampler than his hospitality; yet, often, a grain of courtesy added would double its value. He is too fond of straddling his legs; standing with his back to the world as if it were his own fireside and jingling the loose half-crowns in his pocket, an attitude not to my taste. "I'm a Yorkshireman," he will say, as if the mere fact of being born at the foot of the Pennine Hills excused a man from the courtesies and amenities of civilised life. Alas! perhaps it does now, since he had ridden rough-shod over other people's feelings so many times after declaiming his birth.

He has been told so often that he is a "hard-headed man" with "no nonsense about him" that he is apt to make a pose of it, acting up to the part to the best of his ability. So that if you tell him that he has a feeling for beauty, a passion for music, maybe, or a liking for the bold loveliness of hill and dale and moorland, he will take it as an insult. He would rather be thought of as a good man of affairs and what affairs some of them are! than a lover of beauty, a searcher for truth, one beloved of the gods and men. So he cannot grumble if he is often take in at his own rating, and incurs the shrugging contempt of folks who have not half his appreciation of the good things of the world.

Anyone who comes to know the Yorkshireman intimately will soon discover that he possesses an understanding, a heart, and an immortal soul, although he is so apparently ashamed of those priceless possessions.

In his attitude to strangers we see the Yorkshireman at his worst. Civilisation came late into these parts, and he cannot understand why a man should dress and speak differently from himself. There is more rudeness in his streets than one could meet in a day's march in the South and West of England. Yet there is no real harm in his attitude; no ill-will to others; it is merely a touch of the "Tony Lumpkin" in his composition.

In his conversation he is too much given to vague grumbling and dissatisfaction; he will never admit prosperity, but is always ready to "rail on Lady Fortune in good, set terms"; you gather from his talk that he is a much-tried, ill-treated man, who only just contrives to hold his own in a hard and cruel world. But that is only his outward manner; he really wishes you to think he is making his way, despite difficulties. "Yon's doing well," as he grudgingly admits of certain of his contemporaries.

And there are thank Heaven! great compensations, solid traits which go along with this type of character. If he is not overburdened with imagination and fancy, on the other hand he is not fickle and vacillating, and does not develop hysteria. He does not, like some folks, set up idols third-rate actresses and adventurers to cheer himself hoarse over them, and then depose and replace them, with others equally worthless, all within a few weeks' time. He is not given to "mafficking"; nor does he take kindly to hat-touching and carriage-door holding. He is no snob and hanger-on, but is, if anything, too independent, liking, above all things to plant his feet firmly upon the earth and "go his own gait." Neither lending nor borrowing are to his taste and he never proffers help nor asks for it. As a lover he cuts no great figure, but he shapes well as a husband, and, best of all, as a father, as I myself can testify, he has not his equal in the length and breadth of the land.—*Article in the "Yorkshire Observer", May 1919.*

Bruddersford in its Setting

There, far below, is the knobbly backbone of England, the Pennine Range. At first, the whole dark length of it, from the Peak to Cross Fell, is visible. Then the Derbyshire hills and the Cumberland fells disappear, for you are descending, somewhere about the middle of the range, where the high moorland thrusts itself between the woollen mills of Yorkshire and the cotton mills of Lancashire. Great winds blow over miles and miles of ling and bog and black rock, and the curlews still go crying in that empty air as they did before the Romans came. There is a glitter of water here and there, from the moorland tarns that are now called

Forster Square in the 1930s. ***(Metropolitan Bradford Libraries).***

reservoirs. In summer you could wander here all day, listening to the larks, and never meet a soul. In winter you could lose your way in an hour or two and die of exposure perhaps, not a dozen miles from where the Bradford trams end or the Burnley trams begin.

Here are Bodkin Top and High Greave and Black Moor and Four Gates End, and though these are lonely places, almost unchanged since the Doomsday Book was compiled, you cannot understand industrial Yorkshire and Lancashire, the wool trade and the cotton trade and many other things besides, such as the popularity of Handel's *Messiah* or the Northern Union Rugby game, without having seen such places. They hide many secrets. Where the moor thins out are patches of ground called "Intake," which means that they are land wrested from the grasp of the moor. Over to the right is a long smudge of smoke, beneath which the towns of the West Riding lie buried, and fleeces, tops, noils, yarns, stuffs, come and go, in and out of the mills, down to the railways and canals and lorries. All this too, you may say, is a kind of Intake.

At first the towns only seem a blacker edge to the high moorland, so many fantastic outcroppings of its rock, but now that you are closer, you see the host of tall chimneys, the rows and rows of little houses, built of blackening stone, that are like tiny sharp ridges on the hills. These windy moors, these clanging dark valleys, these factories and little stone houses, this business of Intaking, have between them bred a race that has special characteristics. Down there are thousands and thousands of men and women who are stocky and hold themselves very stiffly, who have short upper lips and long chins, who use emphatic consonants and very broad vowels and always sound aggressive, who are afraid of nothing but mysterious codes of etiquette and any display of feeling.

If it were night, you would notice strange constellations low down in the sky and little golden beetles climbing up to them. These would be street lamps and lighted tramcars on the hills, for here such things are little outposts in No Man's Land and altogether more adventurous and romantic than ordinary street lamps and tramcars. It is not night, however, but a late September afternoon. Some of its sunshine lights up the nearest of the towns, most of it jammed into a narrow valley running up to the moors. It must be Bruddersford, for there, where so many roads meet, is the Town Hall, and if you know the district at all you must immediately recognise the Bruddersford Town Hall, which has a clock that plays *Tom Bowling* and *The Lass of Richmond Hill.* It has been called "a noble building in the Italian Renaissance style" and always looks as if it had no right to be there.

Yes, it is Bruddersford. Over there is the enormous factory of Messrs. Holdsworth and Co., Ltd, which has never been called a noble building in any style but nevertheless looks as if it had a perfect right to be there. The roof of the Midland Railway Station glitters in the sun, and not very far away is another glitter from the glass roof of the Bruddersford Market Hall, where, securely under cover, you may have a ham tea or buy boots and pans and mint humbugs and dress lengths and comic songs. That squat bulk to the left of the Town Hall is the Lane End Congregational Chapel, a monster that can swallow any two thousand people who happen to be in search of "hearty singing and a bright service." That streak of slime must be the Leeds and Liverpool Canal or the Aire and Calder Canal, one of the two.

There is a little forest of mill chimneys. Most of them are only puffing meditatively, for it is Saturday afternoon and nearly four hours since the workpeople swarmed out through the big gates. Some of the chimneys show no signs of smoke; they have been quiet for a long time, have stayed there like monuments of an age that has vanished, and all because trade is still bad. Perhaps some of these chimneys have stopped smoking because fashionable women in Paris and London and New York have cried to one another, "My dear, you can't possibly wear that!" and less fashionable women have repeated it after them, and quite unfashionable women have finally followed their example, and it has all ended in machines lying idle in Bruddersford. Certainly, trade is still very bad. But as you look down on Bruddersford, you feel that it will do something about it, that it is only biding its time, that it will hump its way through somehow: the place wears a grim and resolute look.– *"The Good Companions" (1929).*

Bradford – A Lost World

Bradford is not one manufacturing town out of many, a place to be visited and sketched; it is not really a town at all; it is a vast series of pictures, in time and space; it is an autobiographical library; it is a hundred thousand succeeding states of mind; it is my childhood and youth; it is a lost world.

Of all the cities, towns, and large villages in England, Bradford is the most contradictory, the most paradoxical. Never was there such an odd civic mixture. Bradford itself is ugly and forbidding, and yet within the easiest reach of its Town Hall Square is some of the loveliest country in England. When you are in the town, you feel, as you glance round at the hills bristling with dark chimneys, that you will never see a green field again, and yet you have only to take a tram or bus or two and you find yourself on a moor top, with not a tall chimney in sight, surrounded by wild stuff that has hardly changed since the Domesday Book was compiled. What other city in England has such lovely country near it? I cannot think of one. Bradford is the dark ugly place where you can take a threepenny tram to Arcadia. There's an oddity for you.

That is only a beginning. Bradford is a very provincial city. It is not even on the main line of a railway system. It is folded away in its own narrow smoky valley. No place of its size seems to have less of a metropolitan or cosmopolitan air. When you are in Bradford you are very much in the West Riding of Yorkshire, and if you don't like it, you can lump it. A town so situated, and with such a parochial atmosphere, ought to be known to nobody who lives further away than Morecambe. Is Bradford unknown, then? Not a bit of it. It happens to be one of the most widely known towns in the whole world. I myself have seen the name "Bradford" in the queerest and most out-of-the-way corners. Wherever good cloth is valued there Bradford is known. Bradford has never merely dealt with this place and that, but has dealt with the whole wide world, putting a best coat and waistcoat on the planet itself. Moreover, Bradfordians themselves are great travellers, or certainly were once. They packed their bags in Heaton or Horton Bank Top and could be discovered unpacking them in Russia and India, South America and Australia. If cloth could be bought and sold, if there was growing wool on a sheep's back, then in that place, no matter

Workaday Bradford — Corner of Cheapside.

where it might be, you had a chance of finding a man who liked to spend his leisure in Peel Park or Shipley Glen.

I suppose that in no European country can there ever have been a city of Bradford's size with fewer well-educated men in it. There is nothing in Bradford to attract to it a number of professional men. It has no law courts, no university, and Masters of Arts must be hard to find in its streets. In most cities you get a sort of aristocracy of old business families, who send their sons to public schools and universities before offering them junior partnerships in the firms. There have been such families in Bradford, but remarkably few of them. It is not a city of old-established family businesses. Men have made money quickly in Bradford, but when they have made it they have generally taken care to remove themselves and their families at least twenty miles from Forster Square. Not a few highland lairds and south-country landowners are really Bradford wool merchants, heavily disguised. Thus, though Bradford in its time has been a rich city, it has never had the atmosphere of wealth and whatever small refinements go with the possession of money.

Yet Bradford people are, I fancy, unusually intelligent, and know about twenty times as much as they often pretend to know. Perhaps before the War, which robbed us of a very intelligent section of the community, the large foreign one, and also robbed us of a very large number of exceptionally fine young men, the level of intelligence in the place was rather higher than it is now. It may have very few official Masters of Arts, but it has always had a great many unofficial Masters of Arts. I may be mistaken, but I have a feeling that the number of people in Bradford who sing, play the piano or violin, draw and paint, collect geological specimens or wild flowers, listen knowingly to birds, act in serious plays, ransack the Free Libraries for good books, and travel intelligently, is unusually high, and would make the figures supplied by some other and more imposing cities look very small indeed. Those streets of blackened stone can breed a grim determination to get the best out of life.

The city is, indeed, the oddest mixture. What it has not got, either in its people or its stones, is charm-not a glimmer of it. It is a better place for men than for women. But if it has offered me some of the stupidest people I have ever known, it has also offered me some of the very best, the kindest, the most loyal, the soundest characters. I believe that most of its citizens are romantics at heart, having a curious, glum, and grumpy romanticism all their own. It offers little or nothing to artists of any kind, but on the other hand it keeps on breeding them, doing a not ignoble export trade in them. Out of the strong comes forth sweetness. It does not surprise me that the most delicate and wistful of all modern composers, Delius, should come from a family settled in Bradford, and equally it does not surprise me that the average Bradford citizen is not at all proud of the fact. That is part of the oddity of the place and its people.

What will happen to it and them, so provincial and yet so cosmopolitan, so surly and yet so kind, so grim and yet so humorous? Will Bradford recover its old prosperity or will it fall gradually into decay? I don't know, and I don't believe anybody knows. All that I know is that it is one of the queerest of towns and one of the most lovable.–*"Heaton Review" (1931).*

Gateway to the Moors

If you go from Bradford to Bingley, from Bingley to Eldwick, then up the hill from Eldwick, you arrive at Dick Hudson's. Mr Hudson will not be there to greet you, because he has been dead this long time. But the old grey inn that stands on the edge of the moors is called by his name and by no other. Even the little bus that runs up there now has "Dick Hudson's" boldly painted on its signboard. And there's a pleasant little immortality for you. "We'll go," they say to one another in Bradford, and have said as long as I can remember – "we'll go as far as Dick Hudson's." If you start from the other end, climbing the moorland track from Ilkley, you will inevitably come to Dick Hudson's when you finally drop down from the high moor, and if the hour is right, you will inevitably have a pint of bitter at Dick's.

That is what I did, the other day. I returned, after years of southern exile, to the moors, and began by having two pints at Dick's. And I was mightily relieved to find it still there, the same old grey building, the same cool interior, still smelling of good beer and fried ham; for at any moment now, they may begin monkeying with the old place, turning it into an ice-cream parlour or some such horror.

If you live in Bradford, Shipley, Keighley, you kindle at the sound of Dick Hudson's. That is not merely because you have been so often refreshed there, but chiefly because you know it is the most familiar gateway to the moors. The moors to the West Riding folk are something more than a picnic place, a pretty bit of local countryside. They are the grand escape. In the West Riding towns you have something to escape from, for industrial mankind has done its worst there. But the moors are always, waiting for you, and you have only to leave the towns for an hour or two, climbing the hills, to see them dwindle into a vague smoulder and a sheen of glass roofs in the valleys, then vanish, and perhaps be forgotten.

The moors are there, miles and miles of countryside that has not changed for centuries, and you have only to squeeze through the little hole in the wall, just beyond Dick Hudson's, to take your fill of them. It does not matter who you are, for they are yours while you are there, and the richest wool man in the town can claim no more right in them than you can. Once through that hole in the wall, you have escaped miraculously; and if you were a favoured lad in a fairy tale you could have no better luck, no more elaborate transformation worked for you, for one afternoon. So if you are a stranger to those parts and should visit them, do not let the black streets, the monotonous rows of little houses almost set on end, the trams that drone away between factories, the whole grim paraphernalia of old-fashioned industrialism, depress you too much, but please remember that the winds that suddenly swoop down on the sooty slates have come over leagues of moorland and still have the queer salty tang in them.

Well, I had my pints at Dick Hudson's, went through the little hole in the wall, and climbed on to the moor, as I had so many times before and yet had not done for many a year. It was a weekday and very quiet. The sun was hot and seemed to smite these uplands, bruising every blade and blossom so that they sent out sharp odours. Once more I seemed to be walking on the roof of England. The singing larks only rose a little way from the ground, as if they were high enough now. The winds came sliding or shooting over the top, at no more than shoulder height, and there was in them the old magical scent, earthy enough and yet with always something of the sea in it, that strange saltiness.

Against the brown hillsides I saw the tender green of the young bracken. There, once more, were the tumbled rocks, floating in and out of the great cloud shadows; the ruined byres and the mysterious stone walls; the granite dust of the moorland path glittering in the sunlight. I heard again the baaing of the moorland sheep, like complaining voices coming from great hollows. Everything there was as it had always been.

Down in the valleys, among the streets I once knew so well, they were putting up new buildings and tearing down old ones, they were going into bankruptcy or starting afresh, old men were dying and young men were

Thornton Heights, near Bradford **(Clifford Robinson).**

marrying, and nothing was standing still. The life of the town was hurrying away from the life that I once knew, and down there, among the stalwarts that had so suddenly and strangely grown bent, grey and old, and the babies that had so suddenly and strangely shot up into young men and women, I was rapidly becoming a man from another place, a stranger. But up there, on the moors, there were no changes at all. I saw what I had always seen, and there was no sense that did not receive the same old benediction.

Yet it was not the same. I sat down on the smooth springy grass, with my back against a rock, and as I smoked my pipe in that high lonely place, I tried to disentangle it all. I was happy to be there again, and not a sight, a sound, an odour, that returned to me failed to give me pleasure, and yet in this happiness there was the strangest melancholy. It was as if there was between me and these dear and familiar sights and sounds a sheet of glass. I felt as if I had only to pluck the ling and heather at my side for it to wither and crumble in my hand. I might have been a man on parole for one golden afternoon from some distant internment camp. There were no tears in my eyes, but I will swear my mind knew the salt glitter of them. If I had spoken to a fellow-traveller then, he would have concluded that I was a man who had once known great happiness in these parts and had then gone into some sad exile. And he would have been wrong.

I am happier now than ever I was when I used to come to these moors week in and week out, when I was on the easiest and friendliest terms with them, and every rock and clump of heather spoke to me in my own language. When I walked these moors then, or stretched myself on the grassy carpet in the sun, hour after hour, I spent my time dreaming of the happiness that would be mine when I should be as I actually am now. I do not say that I was really unhappy in those days, for I was a healthy youngster with plenty of things to do and with many good friends, but I was certainly restless and dissatisfied and apt to be sulkily despondent in a world that did not appear to appreciate my unique merit. I thought I was a fine fellow then, but nevertheless I had not acquired that armour of conceit which begins to protect our self-esteem later in life, that armour which compels some elderly members of my profession to move so ponderously. I could be snubbed then, could retire in haste, all hot and pricking, from many a company. There is no doubt whatever that I am happier now.

What hocus-pocus, what sentimental attitudinising, was it then that made me feel so melancholy, the other afternoon on the moors? I was not an exile at all. If I want to live near the moors and visit them every day, there is nothing to prevent me. I could go there, and stay there, to-morrow, if I really wanted to. I know very well that I don't want to, that I would much rather live where I do live. I am well aware of the fact that the moors would bore me very soon and that I get more out of them by visiting them now and again than I ever would by living near them. Like most people, I have lost several persons very dear to me, but, there again, to be honest, I must confess that there is nobody who is associated with the moors in my mind who is now lost to me. The only possible person is that other, younger self, who had trod these very paths so often; but then, I do not mourn him.

Let the young cub perish. First youth has gone, it is true, but I do not see that there is anything specially admirable in early youth. I have strength and vigour, a sense of fun and a sense of wonder, still with me, and I have not the slightest desire to be nineteen again. All this I pointed out to myself, as I sat against that rock and watched the great purple cloud-shadows drift across the moorland, but that feeling of melancholy remained and would not budge. It was like one horn, amid the happy tumult of a full orchestra, ceaselessly sounding a little theme of despair. If the moors were real, then I was a ghost. If I was real, then all this sober richness of bracken and heather and tumbled rock and blue sky was a mirage, a bubble landscape that one determined forefinger could prick so that it gave a wink and then vanished for ever.

I returned, a man in a puzzling dream, but also a hot and thirsty man, to Dick Hudson's. – *"Four-in-Hand" (1934)*.

J.B.P. about 1943 **(A. Royden Willetts).**

Old Bradford. Above — The car has now displaced the horse as a common form of transport but in an earlier picture (below, at the entrance to Manningham Park) no one looks twice at a tram. Right: Wrought ironwork at Cartwright Hall ***(Derek G. Widdicombe).***

Above: Manningham Lane. Below: Bradford's first trolleybus, photographed near Laisterdyke in about 1911 ***(Metropolitan Bradford Libraries).***

St. George's Hall, Bradford, an expression of part of Bradford's rich musical life and a place well-known to the aspiring Priestley.

The wool industry was represented in the very heart of the city in the form of substantial and stylish buildings. Right: Sunshine brightens up the back streets of Bradford ***(Clifford Robinson).***

J.B. receives an honorary degree from Lord Wilson at the University of Bradford in July, 1970.

Visitors to Bilberry Glen

Once he had passed the first crest, he was fairly on the moors, which shimmered and blazed round him for miles. Haliford might have been at the bottom of the sea. Not a single mill chimney in sight. He might have just walked into an older century. The only buildings still in view were a few distant farmhouses or taverns-cum-tearooms, not to be missed because of their whitewashed walls. There were a few coloured specks of people here and there, and he could still hear the cars groaning and hooting despairingly away on the main road. His path came into a broader one, which set out bravely across the bare tableland, as if it knew exactly where it wanted to go. He went with it.

He had been this way several times before. Quarter of an hour's walking, this way, would bring him to a sharp dip in the moorland, a valley with a good stream dashing through it and plenty of rocks, and a tea-room or two, known as Bilberry Glen. (You could pick bilberries there, dye your mouth dark purple with them, or hurry them home by the basketfull to make pies. It was like eating a fine day on the moors when you had bilberries.) There would be people, of course, lots of them, but after a full hour's solitude, he felt ready for people again. Besides, the Glen was a fine place to lounge about in, and you could be certain of some tea there.

Very soon, the path began descending, past huddles of grey rock, where, in the shade, young couples were sprawling, half-asleep or negligently fondling one another or taking sticky chocolate out of silver paper. He turned right where the path divided, taking the one that led to the bottom of the Glen, so that he could follow the stream up towards the tea-rooms at the top. The water, now broadening into pools, now rippling over toothy littly rocks, had attracted most of th people in the Glen to its side, and they and their children, who were paddling and screaming to one another and pretending to fish, were thick around it at the bottom. Two fattish men, their trousers well rolled up above their mottled legs, were amusing a large group of their friends, well provided with paper bags and beer bottles, by jumping and splashing. Three young men, higher up, were throwing stones at a tin can, and not hitting it, perhaps because they were keeping an eye on three young women, who said things to one another in low voices, laughed a lot, and rolled about and showed a great deal of stocking.

Their neighbours were four middle-aged women, very carefully dressed in dark clothes, perched on the edge of a dumpy rock, passing a small paper bag of boiled sweets to one another and talking in lugubrious flat voices. Wherever Haliford people are enjoying themselves, there are always these sad middle-aged women, even gloomier than they are at home, and Edward, who did not even try to understand what life might possibly look like to a middle-aged woman, was always puzzled by them.

There were other people, too, scolding their children, snoring in the shade of a rock, throwing stones into the water, holding warm hands or snatching sticky kisses, talking about illnesses or house rents, yawning and wondering what time it was. Their presence did not improve the Glen, but it did not spoil it, for there was room under the wide sky for them all; and the sunlight, the glint and blue shadow of the rocks, the flashing stream, the patches of smooth grass that lay about like vivid green rugs, all remained to soften and mellow the most raucous voices and the most idiotic antics. – *"They Walk in the City" (1936).*

Writing "The Good Companions"

This idea of a picaresque long novel aroused about as much enthusiasm as a stuffed walrus at an exhibition of watercolours. The long novel was out of fashion, expensive to print, hard to sell. The picaresque was out too, except perhaps as an excuse for fancy dress. Then my next move made matters worse. For I decided that this story should be about a concert party – or pierrot troupe. I knew nothing about concert parties and had to mug them up a bit. I also visited a few towns, never large cities, and stayed a few nights in theatrical digs. (Afterwards I had scores of letters from pro telling me I must have spent years touring.) This decision, I was told, was fatal. The monster I was planning would now be "a back-stage novel", which readers, it appeared, had always disliked.

That was not all. I had found a title that was no good. "No, old boy; think again." I did, once I had finished the book, so that my desk was littered with sheets on which I had scribbled possible alternatives. But it was no use, the white elephant would have to be called *The Good Companions*. Not that this title was thought to be too sentimental. That came later, when the advertisers, the calendar publishers, the photographers, with their pretty groups of puppies and kittens, saw what could be done with it. No, at that time, before the book was out, the title was thought to be too odd. This seems incredible, I know, but it is the honest truth.

The Good Companions was no sugary commonplace when I first put the words together; all that, I repeat, came later. What also came later, so that I suffered under it for the next twenty years, was the habit, which every speaker seemed to mistake for a new and bright idea, of referring to me in public as a good companion. Many a chairman, as he turned towards me with an arch look, a coy smile, must have been astounded by the glare he got. For while among friends and in the mood I am amiable enough, even high-spirited on occasion. At no time have I made any claims to good companionship. I merely gave my novel the same name as the concert party whose adventures it described.

True, the story had a cosy fairy-tale atmosphere, which incidentally I have never tried to reproduce, although so many people, almost with tears in their eyes, have begged me to make the attempt. (Writers should never give in to such people.) The background might be contemporary and realistic, as I have already said, but what happened in front of it did suggest one of the cosier fairy tales. There are two reasons for this. The first, and less important, is that unless an author has made up his mind never to give way, a large picaresque novel lures him into this atmosphere. The second reason I understand now but was not ever conscious of at the time. I had had the War, in which almost every man I had known and liked had been killed. Then, just as life was opening out, there came a period of anxiety, overwork, constant strain, ending tragically. Later, when that time was further away, I would be able to face it, not only in memory but in my work, where it can all be found in one place or another. (The Russians consider me an interesting writer but far too pessimistic for socialist realism. This is at least nearer the truth than the Jolly Jack nonsense of silly journalists here.)

But first I had to find some release, give myself a holiday of the spirit while writing this novel of 250,000 words. Certainly if I had been entirely committed to novel-writing-and, as I have already suggested, I never have been – I might have taken the opposite course, dredging it all up in autobiography thinly disguised as fiction. That might have been more healing, but temperamentally I am opposed to this almost direct use of personal experiences in so-called creative work, I must find, at some remove from them, characters and action symbolic of my own thought and feeling. So in *The Good Companions* I gave myself a holiday from anxiety and strain and tragic circumstance, shaping and colouring a long happy daydream. And because a lot of other people then must have felt in need of such a holiday, so long a daydream, the elephant suddenly turned into a balloon.

Though the leading booksellers had been given page proofs to read, the total advance sale was only about 3,000 copies. The book cost 10s. 6d., a stiff price for a novel in 1929. Moreover, the slump had arrived. My publishers, Heinemann, having to face the expense of setting up a book of this length, risked printing 10,000 copies. If the reviews were helpful – then, we thought, 7,000 or even 8,000 might be sold. I quote these figures to show what nonsense was written and talked afterwards about a shrewd author, astute publishers, booksellers who knew their customers.

The bóok came out in July and for weeks nothing much happened. Then in autumn the balloon went up. The book had to be printed and bound all over the place, and all kinds of vans were hired to deliver it. Towards Christmas the daily sale was more than the total advance had been. This was all very exciting of course, but I was too busy to make many public appearances as a successful author: I was hard at work on another long novel, *Angel Pavement.* – *"Margin Released" (1962).*

Women at the Mill

The women and girls who worked in the mills then were no models of feminine refinement. Sometimes, when I finished earlier than usual at the office and walked home, the route I preferred took me past one of the largest mills in the district, often just when the women were coming out. I would find myself breasting a tide of shawls, and something about my innocent dandyism would set them screaming at me, and what I heard then, though I was never a prudish lad, made my cheeks burn. and it was still the custom, in some mills if not in that particular one, for the women to seize a newly-arrived lad and "sun" him, that is, pull his trousers down and reveal his genitals.

But all this not unwholesome and perhaps traditional female bawdiness – there was a suggestion of mythology, ancient worship, folklore, about that queer "sunning" ritual – was far removed from cynical whoring. There was nothing sly, nothing hypocritical, about these coarse dames and screaming lasses, who were devoted to their own men, generally working in the same mill, and kept on "courting", though the actual courtship stage was over early, for years and years until a baby was due, when they married. They may not have lived happily ever afterwards, but they saved themselves from some unpleasant surprises. – *The Swan Arcadian, in "Margin Released" (1962).*

A woman weaving cloth at a tappet loom (as seen on a memorial in Bradford).

A Return to the North

We were now in the true North country. One glance at the people, with their stocky figures and broad faces, humorous or pugnacious, told you that. On the road to Barnsley the stone walls began, settling any possible doubts. The North of England is the region of stone walls. They run from the edges of the towns to the highest and wildest places on the moors, firmly binding the landscape, unbroken and continuous from every tram terminus to the last wilderness of bog and cloud. No slope is too steep for them. No place is too remote. They will accurately define pieces of ground that do not even know a rabbit and only hear the cry of the curlews. Who built these walls, why they were ever thought worth building, these are mysteries to me. But when I see them, I know that I am home again; and no landscape looks quite right to me without them. If there are not a few thousand leagues of them framing the bright fields of asphodel, it will be no Elysium for me.

Along this road to Barnsley the sun flared hugely before finally setting. All the western edges of the slag-heaps were glittering. I saw in one place a great cloud of steam that had plumes of gold. In another, we passed under a vast aerial flight of coal trucks, slowly moving, in deep black silhouette, against the sunset. It would not have made a bad symbolical picture of the end of one phase of industrial England. When we looked down upon Barnsley, we saw it for a moment dimly ranged about an ebony pyramid of slag. When we stopped in the town for tea, the sun had gone and the air was nippingly cold. In the café where I ate my toasted tea-cake a young man was being funny to his girl about somebody's bad elocution. (I suspect that the somebody was a local big-wig.) 'He said "lor" for "law", said the young man, 'and "dror" for "draw". Honestly he did. "We will now dror to a conclusion," he said. Yes, really.' And as they were in that stage of courtship in which each finds the other's least remark a miracle of apt speech, they were very happy, two refined but humorous souls in a wilderness of clods.

It was almost dark when we left Barnsley for Huddersfield. The hills were now solidly black; their edges very sharp against the last faint silver of the day. They were beginning to take on, for me, that Wordsworthian quality which belongs to the North. The factories might be roaring and steaming in the valleys, their lighted windows glaring at us as we passed, but behind were those high remote skylines, stern enough and yet still suggesting to me a brooding tenderness:

> The silence that is in the starry sky,
> The sleep that is among the lonely hills.

A road well lighted and of immense width led us into Huddersfield, which is not a handsome town but yet is famous in these parts for the intelligence and independence of its citizens. Whether they really deserve this reputation I have never been able to discover, though I know the place fairly well. We climbed from Huddersfield, on our way to Bradford, to the heights of Shelf. The familiar nocturnal pageant of the West Riding was all round us. This is the region of mountaineering trams; you see them far away at night, climbing the hills, like luminous beetles. You will go through mile after mile of streets, climbing all the time, and then suddenly arrive at a stretch of open country that seems nearly as wild and cold as Greenland. From such heights you look across at hills that are constellated and twinkling with street lamps. If the towns in the West Riding were as brilliantly illuminated as Los Angeles, they would run excursions from London so that people could see these patterned hills at night. Even as it is, the spectacle has a never-failing charm. We ran down from Shelf, which is a place as mysterious to me as it probably is to you, into the centre of Bradford, then climbed another hill and reached our destination.

I was back in my old home, and, journey or no journey, there I intended to stay for the next six or seven days.—*"English Journey" (1934).*

Bradford assurance, with everything built to last.

Haliford's Rise and Decline

Haliford, in the West Riding of Yorkshire, is a textile town. A hundred years ago it was of no importance at all; merely a little market town, with a few small mills dotted about the hillsides. It grew steadily during the Fifties and Sixties; then came the Franco Prussian War – a godsend – and Haliford made money, or rather, some people there made a lot of money and the others were able to buy an extra joint of meat now and again and perhaps risk an annual four days' holiday at the seaside; and after that, in spite of a slump or two towards the end of the century, the town grew and prospered, until at last there came the Great War – and what a godsend that was – and Haliford men still at home and with their wits about them began to make fortunes, and slaved away trying to get rid of their excess profits, and the town, though a little lacking in brisk young manhood, reached its peak.

It started slipping and sliding down the other side, towards nobody knows what, early in the Nineteen Twenties. The world seemed to take a sudden dislike to Haliford and its undeniably excellent products. Now, most of the mills have begun to look old. Some of them – grim black stone boxes though they are – have even begun to look pathetic. You feel – as they say round there – that they are "past it." In the watery sunlight of the Pennines, their windows sometimes look like the eyes of a blind beggar. The tall chimneys that are still smoking do it now in a leisurely fashion, like retired men making a morning pipe last as long as possible. Many of the chimneys have stopped smoking, not having known the heat of a furnace for years. The air above Haliford ought to be clear by this time, but somehow the old haze still lingers, perhaps out of kindness to the bewildered townsfolk below, who would feel naked without it.

– *"They walk in the City"* (1936)

Down-to-Earth Bradford

Bradford is one of those cities and towns that are products of nineteenth-century Industrialism. In 1801 it had a population of about 13,000. In 1901 its population had risen to nearly 280,000. (The only town in the country that grew faster was Middlesbrough.) It was very fortunately placed for its own staple trade of worsted and woollen manufacturing. It was near some large coal-fields, and what was even more important, it had an excellent supply of soft water free from lime, good for both washing wool and dyeing it. All the processes of worsted manufacture – combing, spinning, weaving, dyeing and finishing – are carried on in Bradford. It also deals in alpaca, mohair and silk. Indeed, there is nothing that can be spun and woven that does not come to Bradford. I remember myself, as a boy, seeing there some samples of human hair that had been sent from China: they were pigtails that had been cut off by Imperial command. And there used to be one factory in Bradford that specialised in dolls' hair, those crisp curls you find in the nursery cupboard.

When I was a rebellious lad, I used to think that a wool office – and I was sent to one for a season – was the very symbol of the prosaic; but now I see that I was wrong. Revisiting them again, I saw that these offices, with their bins of samples, bluewrapped cylinders of hair, are really romantic. Take down some of those greasy or dusty samples and you bring the ends of the earth together. This wool was lately wandering about on our own South Downs. This comes from the Argentine, this from Australia. The dust and dried dung that falls out of this packet comes from the desert. Here, in this blue paper, is hair clipped from the belly of a camel. These wools and hairs will be sorted, scoured, combed, the long strands forming Tops, the short Noils, and these Tops and Noils, if they are not used locally, may be exported all over the place, from Finland to Spain. What they will end as, God only knows. Their adventures are terrific. Do the Bradford wool men, with their broad faces and loud voices, ever think about these things? I fancy they do, but they never mention them in public. Their talk is all of prices. You might think, to hear them, that they cared for nothing but "t'brass". Don't you believe them.

It was after 1830 that Bradford began growing rapidly and piling up wealth. Apart from its natural advantages and the general state of trade, there was another reason for this, and that is that during the early and midVictorian periods, a number of German and GermanJewish merchants, with German banks behind them, came to settle in the town. Many of these merchants were men of liberal opinions, who knew they could be happier outside Germany. The results of this friendly invasion were very curious. Bradford became – as it still remained when I was a boy there – at once one of the most provincial and yet one of the most cosmopolitan of English provincial cities. Its provincialism was largely due to its geographical situation. It is really in a backwater. The railway main lines went to Leeds, ten miles away, and not to Bradford, with the result that Leeds, though it has never had the worldwide reputation of Bradford, is a larger city and of much greater local importance. It was Leeds, and not Bradford, that became the great marketing centre of West and Mid-Yorkshire. Leeds has a university and law courts; Bradford has not. I have always thought that there must be proportionately fewer university graduates in Bradford than in any other large town in England.

Then again, the wool business was so much a local trade that a man might spend all his life in it, unless he happened to be sent out buying or selling, and never meet anybody but his neighbours. A city that has mixed trades will probably have some of its corners rubbed off; it must work with other places; but Bradford, with its one trade, was all corners, hard provincial angles. There was no mistaking a Bradford man. Morover, Bradford was, and still is, on the edge of the moors, hardly more than a tram-ride from wild Pennine country. A man might spend his mornings in the Wool Exchange and then spend his evenings among moorland folk, who would not do badly as characters in the medieval Wakefield Nativity Play. Wuthering Heights are only just round the corner.

The town did not gently fade away into regions decorated by landed proprietors and gentleman farmers. John Ball's old gibe, "When Adam delved and Eve span, Who was then the gentleman?" had no application to Bradford, where everybody was busy spinning. A few were rich, and a great many were very poor, working from morning until night for miserable wages; but they were all one lot of folk, and Jack not only thought himself as good as his master but very often told him so. Bradford was not only provincial but also fiercely democratic. (The Independent Labour Party was born there.) If, having made some big lucky gambles in wool, you made a fortune there and determined to retire and set up as an English gentleman, you never stayed in Bradford, where everybody was liable to be sardonic at your expense; but bought an estate a long way off, preferably in the South.

Yet at the same time – and this is what gives the place its odd quality – Bradford was always a city of travellers. Some of its citizens went regularly to the other side of the globe to buy wool. Others went abroad, from Belgium to China, selling yarn and pieces. They returned to Market Street, the same sturdy Bradfordians, from the ends of the earth. You used to meet men who did not look as if they had ever been further than York or Morecambe, but who actually knew every continental express. They would go away for months, keeping to the most complicated time-tables. When they returned they did not give themselves cosmopolitan airs; it was very dangerous in Bradford to give yourself any airs, except those by tradition associated with solid wool men. And then there was this curious leaven of intelligent aliens, chiefly German-Jews and mostly affluent. They were so much a part of the place when I was a boy that it never occurred to me to ask why they were there. I saw their outlandish names on office doors, knew that they lived in certain pleasant suburbs, and obscurely felt that they had always been with us and would always remain.

That small colony of foreign or mixed Bradfordians produced some men of great distinction, including a famous composer, two renowned painters, and a wellknown poet. (In Humbert Wolfe's *Now a Stranger* you get a glimpse of what life was like in that colony for at least one small boy.) I can remember when one of the bestknown clubs was the *Schillerverein*. And in those days a Londoner was a stranger sight than a German. There was, then this odd mixture in pre-war Bradford. A dash of the Rhine and the Oder found its way into our grim runnel – "t'mucky beck." Bradford was determinedly Yorkshire and provincial, yet some of its suburbs reached as far as Frankfurt and Leipzig. It was odd enough. But it worked.

The war changed all that. There is hardly a trace now in the city of that GermanJewish invasion. Some of the merchanting houses changed their names and personnel; others went out of business. I liked the city better as it was before, and most of my fellow Bradfordians agree with me. It seems smaller and duller now. I am not suggesting that these GermanJews are better men than we are. The point is that they were different and brought more to the city than bank drafts and lists of customers. They acted as a leaven, just as a colony of typical West Riding folk would act as a leaven in Munich or Moscow. These exchanges are good for everybody. . . .

–*"English Journey"* (1934)

High Tea with the Resurrectionists

It may have been a splendid gathering but it was certainly a very odd meal. Inigo remembered other high teas but none higher than this. The forms were a solid mass of eaters and drinkers, and the tables were a solid mass of food. There were hams and tongues and rounds of cold beef and raised pies and egg salads; plates heaped high with white bread, brown bread, currant teacakes, scones; dishes of jelly and custard and blanc-mange and fruit salad; piles of jam tarts and maids of honour and cream puffs and almond tarts; then walnut cake, plum cake, chocolate cake, coconut cake; mounds of sugar, quarts of cream, and a steady flood of tea. Inigo never remembered seeing so much food before. It was like being asked to eat one's way through the Provision and Cooked Food departments of one of the big stores. The appetite was not tickled, not even met fairly; it was overwhelmed.

The sight of these tables drove hunger out of the world, made it impossible to imagine it had ever been there. Inigo ate this and that, but he hardly knew what he was eating, he was so warm, so tightly wedged in, so amazed at the spectacle. The Second Resurrectionists were worthy of the colossal meal spread before them. This highest of high teas had met its match. If they had all been forty years in the wilderness, they could not have dealt with it more manfully. They were not your gabbling, laughing eaters; they did not make a first rush and then suddenly lose heart; they did not try this and taste that. No, they were quiet, systematic, devastating;

they advanced steadily in good order from the first slice of ham to the last slice of chocolate cake; and in fifty minutes the tables were a mere ruin of broken meats, the flood of tea a pale and tepid trickle.

Inigo, who retired early from the conflict, though he had to stay where he was, with Mr Timpany steaming on one side and Freda delicately grilling on the other, looked on with wonder and admiration. Across the table were two middle-aged women with long yellow faces, almost exactly alike, and a little round man who had no teeth and whose nose and chin came within an inch of one another as he worked away. It did not look as if three such persons would be able to do more than skirt the fringes of a high tea, but actually they walked right through and emerged unruffled at the other end. Above their heads, high on the opposite wall, was yet another of Mr Grudy's crimson placards, which began: *And the light of a candle shall no more at all in thee.* Inigo stared, now at the people, now at the placard.

It was all very odd, absolutely.—*"The Good Companions" (1929).*

A West Riding Wool Man

The secret of Joe Ackworth, whom I soon came to like enormously, was that he played for all it was worth, day and night, a character part. This character performance, almost always on identical lines, was common then among a certain class of Bruddersford wool men. Oftern they were men whose work took them away a good deal, for Bruddersford men went all over the world then; and they must have decided that if they could not be cosmopolitan then they would be as aggressively provincial as possible, and would deliberately exaggerate every West Riding trait, broadening their accent, often assuming a brutal insensitiveness and pugnacity, and pretending they cared about nothing but money and eating and drinking and fat cigars. (W.H.Hudson somewhere describes meeting one of them, who, he discovered to his surprise, came every year to a certain place to listen to the nightingales.) Joe Ackworth was this type. Behind his bellowing and blustering, he was far more sensitive, far more aware of other people's feelings, than the genteel and mincing Croxton.

He had a passion, among other things, for roses, which flourished in the heavy clay soil of Bruddersford; and he spent a great deal of his spare time and money growing roses, and experimenting with new varieties, and every year he sent a selection of them to the famous Saltaire Rose Show.

He was also, as I found out soon to my astonishment, a knowledgeable reader, especially of history and solid fiction; and it was he who lent me Mrs Garnett's translations of the great Russian novelists. "Summat to get yer teeth into'ere, lad," he said of them. "They wrote about life, them chaps did – an' no bloody fairy tales for school – kids. ah went to Russia one time – just the once, that's all – an' if ever they get properly started an' get rid o' their Grand Dukes an' suchlike – they'll mak' some of us sit up, Russians will. You mark my words, lad,' And I did, and remembered his prophecy afterwards. – *"Bright Day" (1946).*

The Fallen Titan

I met one man I was glad to meet, for it proved, as I thought it would, a most odd and illuminating encounter. I was introduced to him on the ground floor of a very dingy warehouse, where he was doing an odds-and-ends sort out business in various textile commodities. He was a man who had been a legend up there ever since the war. I have never heard of him before the war, but afterwards I hardly ever heard about anybody else. He was easily the richest man the West Riding had recently produced, and he was also a character. (And still is.) Nobody knew how much he was worth, at the time when he was bestriding the whole wool trade like a Colossus, but I gather that it was betweeen five and ten millions. His operations were vast and mysterious, and did not stop at wool business, combing and spinning mills, and the like, but at last even including West End theatres, in which he lost a lot of money finally by speculation and by putting on expensive musical comedies. There was a wonderful crop of stories about him, in the usual West Riding vein, but the only one I remember that pleased me went something like this; at the time when he still controlled this staggering array of properties, extending from remote industrial villages in Yorkshire to Shaftesbury Avenue, but when the slump was just beginning, somebody asked hime how things were, and he replied:"Nay, out of all t'lot, there's nowt paying but eighteen milk bee-asts Ah've got up i' North Yorkshire."

This story may not be true, but I can certainly imagine the man I met making this reply. He was a tall, well-covered man, with a face at once forceful and droll, like that of a comic pirate. I have not the least idea whether he was a good financier or a bad one, a mediocre man who was lucky for a season or a clever man who was ultimately unlucky, but I do know that he was-and is-a character. I have never understood exactly what happened to all his combines and properties. Apparently the whole pagoda-like edifice collapsed, leaving him-and I will swear, with a droll look-among the ruins. He did not go bankrupt and he had the sense and courage-unlike so many of these financial Napoleons-not to blow his brains out. He began all over again, in a small way; and there he was, on the ground floor of a dingy warehouse. It is quite probable that if I had met him when he was a multi-millionaire, I should have disliked him; but as an ex-multi-millionaire-not, I imagine, the easiest of situations-he seemed to me very good company. It is a pity he could not write a perfectly frank autobiography . . .

I wish I could have complimented him upon bringing out of his crazy vanished Eldorado so much humour and courage, two notable West Riding qualities. But we never pay compliments in Bradford. We are, as we readily admit, not good at expressing our feelings, which only means, of course, that we are bad at expressing our pleasant feelings, for I have noticed that we give tongue to the other kind with great frequency and force. I feel that now is the moment when I should put down some memorable concluding sentence of praise about the whole of the West Riding and its people; and of course I cannot do it. But then I am one of them, and they are the very people who will understand why I cannot do it. So-well, I'm off. Behave thi'sen, lad!—*"English Journey" (1934).*

A Funeral at Haliford

Haliford Verrey was now sitting with the driver at the front of the hearse and exchanging remarks with him in a sort of ventriloquial fashion, each man freely expressing himself, and perhaps telling a good story, while keeping a straight and professionally woeful face. Mrs Fielding and Mr Verrey between them had spared neither expense nor trouble to make the late Mr Fielding's final passing as hideously impressive as possible, and if they had been a couple of mad tragic Elizabethan dramatists, a Webster and Tourneur, they could hardly have worked more cunningly.

Only Death, with his dreadful raven-black trappings, his coffins, his tributes of sickly-smelling lilies, his yawning graves, his massive marble or granite tombstones, is welcomed with such pageantry and poetic symbolism in places like Haliford, where all the rites and ceremonies that belong to Life are merely shuffled through and have drearily dwindled. But Death still commands and receives his due of costume and ritual. The very poor save their shillings and pence, freely denying themselves, against his coming. It is the only poetry left them . . .

Nobody spoke in the car. It is a good four miles from Sutcliffe Place to Haygarth Cemetery, and they travelled at the regulation funeral paçe: he had plenty of time to think. Also, to watch the men they passed solemnly raising their hats. How pleased his father would have been if a few of them had raised their hats so respectfully to him when he was alive!

At the main building in the cemetery – which seemed a pleasant spot this fine morning, with birds singing everywhere, and a richer green, fed by the bones below, on all sides – they got out of their car, and stood apart from the group of further relatives and friends of the family who had not gone to the house. Mr Verrey and his assistant came and beckoned, and then they headed a slow procession to the open grave, where the assistant, apparently afraid of their missing the least sensation, almost pushed them to the very edge. The minister from Mrs Fielding's chapel, a broad gloomy Scotsman much more at home now than he was when trying to preside gaily over a tea and concert, conducted the service, pronouncing the beautiful words of our despair and hope very slowly and distinctly, as if for the benefit of the unbelievers present. One of them, Edward, was now clenching his hands until his nails hurt him, though he did not realise until afterwards, when there was no longer a coffin to stare at, down there in the clay, how deep they had gone into his flesh.

They returned to the main building again, and now people began talking, as if they felt life flowing back into them once more. It was queer looking at the people. There were relatives he had not seen for years and years; strange figures out of the dimming epic of his childhood, figures from half-forgotten Christmases, fantastic and incredibly old great-aunts and uncles that had once seemed like giants, looming in corners during old Boxing Day family parties, and now almost shrunk into dwarfs. One or two of them spoke to him, but only until they could command the attention of his mother, who was much in demand as the chief character of the funeral.

The only person who really talked to him was not a relation at all, but an old friend of his grandfather's, Jonathan Crabtree, the owner of a small woolcombing mill just outside Haliford. Edward was surprised to see him there. He did not appear to know anybody or want to know anybody, and, in defiance of all possible conventions, he had lit his pipe, which, like himself, was old, short, gnarled and tough. He was one of those West Riding men of the old school who know very well that they are characters, and enjoy – more and more as they get older – playing the character parts allotted to them.

"An' you'll be Edward, Ah'm thinking," he said, after giving Edward a sharp poke on the shoulder, coming very close and puffing very strong smoke in his face. "Ah well, yer father's not lived so long after *his* father, yer grandfather, lad, has he? Ah said to me-sen, nobbut a few weeks sin', when Ah saw him at t'club, that he wor looking poorly then, but Ah nivver thought it'ud finish him so quick. But he nivver had staying power, yer father hadn't. He worn't man yer grandad wor, nowt like, though Ah'm saying nowt agen him 'cos Ah liked him a lot better nor a lot o'fowk did."
– "They Walk in the City" (1936).

Jess Oakroyd's Homecoming

Having been away from England for the last few months and as far afield as the South Seas, I knew nothing about the Bradford Pageant until a few weeks ago, when I was returning home by way of Canada. I had to stay for a day or two in Toronto, and there I met an old acquaintance of mine. As a matter of fact, I met several, for it is an odd thing that no matter into what part of the world you go you meet Bradford men. I cannot begin to set down the names of the remote places in which Bradford men have popped up, imperturbably puffing away at their pipes. But why should I say that it is an odd thing? It is not. Bradford's staple trade has sent Bradfordians all over the world to buy, to sell, and to advise. It used to be a sore point with us that Bradford was not on the main line of the Midland or Great Northern Railways. But — good heavens! — Bradford has been on the main line of the world's commerce for a long, long time now. There are links between all the dandies, from Berlin and Paris to New York and Buenos Aires, and that Conditioning House of ours in Canal Road. And that, when you think about it, is a romantic fact.

Well, I met this old acquaintance of mine in Toronto. He had come into the city from a small town, Pittford Falls, Ontario. He was looking very well, though perhaps he was a trifle stouter and not quite so ruddy as he used to be. After a minute or two I remembered his name, which has a familiar Yorkshire ring about it. He was one Oakroyd. And it was he who told me about the Pageant. He had asked me when I was sailing for England, and when I had told him he had made haste to tell me that he was himself sailing very soon.

"Ay," he remarked, very complacently, sucking at his pipe, 'I'm off to t'Pageant. Eh, didn't yer knaw? Nay lad, yer knaw nowt. Ay, they're having a Pageant, an' a right big do an' all, t'biggest we've ivver had."

I asked him to tell me all about it. He did, and from a very capacious inside coat pocket he produced some very exciting literature on the subject. I glanced at it. Romans . . . Domesday Book . . . Cistercian monks . . . the first Woolsack . . . Siege of Bradford . . . Bolling Hall ghosts . . . Luddites. It was tremendous. Mr. Oakroyd noticed that I was suitably impressed..

"Champion," he declared, with a rather marked proprietary air. "I'm capped yer know nowt about it. I thowt yer might ha' been one o' t'performers like. Yer wouldn't mak' a bad Roman — wi' that gurt head o' yours — or happen one o' t'monks, for you're putting on weight rarely, lad — it mun be these big pies you've been having aht here."

"Are you in it?" I asked, for there was something very complacent and almost patronising about him.

"Nar that's tellin'," he replied, looking very deep and knowing. "But what made yer ask, lad?"

I don't know. I seem to remember you had something to do with the stage at one time. Or was it somebody else?"

"Nay, it wor me all right," he said stoutly. "An' I should think I had summat to do wi' t'stage. Yer can learn me nowt about that sort o' business. Knaw it from A to Z, lad. Been in t'road i' my time, I can tell yer."

"And you're in it?"

"I'm saying nowt," he retorted, with the air of a man saying a great deal.

I looked at the list of scenes again. Then I looked at Mr. Oakroyd, who smoked away and looked at nothing. "I'm trying to find your part," I told him. "Perhaps you're the Bolling Hall ghost."

"Happen I am, and then again, happen I'm not." He left it at that, but after a pause he took his pipe out, frowned at the stem, and then looked at me. "But I'll tell yer what it is, lad. It's a champion idea, this is. An' I'll tell yer for why. This 'ere Pageant — as yer can see for yersen — shows we go right back a bit, history like. A lot o' fowk think we nobbut started day afore yesterday, but this piece 'ull learn 'em summat. T'wool trade's been on t'go a long time."

"Everything's been on a long time in England," I said, troubled by a slight feeling of homesickness.

"That's right. An' you miss it 'ere, yer knaw, yer right miss it. I'm saying nowt agen this place — it's treated me right well — but it's a bit empty like, d'yer see, lad. It's nobbut just startin'. Whereas, t'owd shop — well, it's t'owd shop. An' mind yer, we've not finished yet. Don't get that idea i' yer head. Yer'll see. Onnyhow, lad, if yer go — look out for me. Ay, an' Sam Oglethorpe an' all."

"What! Is he in it, too?"

"By gow, he is that. An' what d'yer think Sam is? Yer'd nivver guess, not if yer tried from nar till Christmas. Well, I'll tell yer, but keep it dark. Sam's one o' t'monks — an he's shaved off his mustache o' purpose." And Mr. Oakroyd suddenly let out a bellow of laughter.

I didn't believe him, of course. I cannot believe that Mr. Oglethorpe is appearing at Peel Park as a Cistercian monk. I don't believe that Mr. Oakroyd is taking part in the Pageant either. In fact, I began to doubt if there was a Pageant, in spite of the fact that I had had a mass of its literature in my hand. But I know now that there is a Pageant, that Bradford will be *en fête* in July, and that the romance that lies behind our staple industry will take shape and colour and music to itself in Peel Park. I have always said that Bradford is at heart a romantic city. And now, apparently, it is boldly throwing off any prosaic disguise it may have worn. Bottom the Weaver re-enters the enchanted wood. A great industry and an ancient township now turn to drama and poetry. Below those hills where the smoke fades into the bloom of the moors, the happy highways of my boyhood, the trumpets sound. —*Brochure of the Bradford Pageant* (1931).

A worthy of old Bradford ***(W.R. Mitchell).***

David Hockney preparing a sketch of J.B. Priestley.

Bradford, as it was in 1891.

When We are Married

J.B.'s famous play, published in 1938, and dealing with life in a small West Riding town before the 1914-18 war shattered the social fabric, is staged successfully to this day. It was described by the playwright as "a Yorkshire farcical comedy"; it introduced us to three local worthies and their ladies who meet 25 years after their "marriages" on the same day, to discover that perhaps they are not married after all — that the parson who performed the ceremonies was guilty of negligence. Our extract begins with this discovery:

HELLIWELL (*dazed and bitter*). Why—the bloody donkey!

(*He sits down, dazed, on the upper end of the settee* L. *He and* PARKER *and* SOPPITT *look at one another in silent consternation.*)

SOPPITT (*slowly, thoughtfully*). Why, if we've never been married at all, then—— (*He goes to the upper end of the settee* R.)

HELLIWELL. Don't start working it out in detail, Herbert, 'cos it gets very ugly—very ugly. There's that lad o' yours at Grammar School, for instance—I wouldn't like to have to give 'im a name now——

SOPPITT (*indignantly*). Here, steady, Joe——

HELLIWELL. Well, you see, it gets very ugly. Keep your mind off t'details.

PARKER (*bitterly*). .Silver wedding! (*He sits in the chair* C.).

HELLIWELL. Now don't you start neither, Albert.

PARKER (*solemnly*). Joe, Herbert, when them three poor women upstairs get to know what they really are——

HELLIWELL (*grimly*). Then t'balloon goes up properly. Talk about a rumpus. You'll 'ear 'em from 'ere to Leeds.

PARKER (*gravely*). Joe, Herbert, they mustn't know. Nobody must know. Why— we'd be laughed right out o' town. What— Alderman Helliwell— Councillor Albert Parker—Herbert Soppitt—all big men at Chapel, too! I tell you, if this leaks out—we're done.

HELLIWELL. We are, Albert.

SOPPITT (*horrified*). If once it got into the papers!

HELLIWELL (*even more horrified*). *Papers!* OH—Christmas!—it's got to be kept from t'papers.

(GERALD, *who has been leaving them to themselves to digest this news, now turns to them again, coming to* L.C.).

GERALD (*holding out his hand*). You'd better give me that letter, hadn't you?

PARKER, HELLIWELL (*together*). Oh, no! (*They both rise*).

(*They stand together as if protecting it.*)

PARKER (*holding it out*). This letter——

HELLIWELL (*snatching it*). Here——

PARKER (*angrily*). Nay, Joe— give it back——

HELLIWELL. I'm sorry, Albert, but I don't trust nobody wi' this letter but meself. Why—it's—it's dynamite!

GERALD. Yes, but it's addressed to me, and so it happens to be my property, you know.

SOPPITT. I'm afraid he's right there.

HELLIWELL (*turning on him, annoyed*). You would have to put that in, wouldn't you? Dang me, you're in this mess just as we are, aren't you?

PARKER (*severely*). Anyhow, *we've* a position to keep up even if you havn't, Herbert.

SOPPITT (*apologetically*). I was only saying he's right when he says it's his property. We had a case——

HELLIWELL (*aggressibely*). Never mind about that case. Think about this case. It's a whole truck-load o' cases, this is. (*He turns up* C.)

GERALD. My letter please.

(HELLIWELL *turns down to him.*)

HELLIWELL (*ingratiatingly*). Now listen, lad. I know you only want to do what's right. And we happened to be a bit 'asty with you, when you first came in. We didn't mean it. Just—a way o' talking. When Herbert Soppitt there gets started——

SOPPITT (*indignantly*). What — me!

PARKER (*severely*). You were 'asty, y'know, Herbert, you can't deny it. (*To* GERALD.) Mind you, I'll say now to your face what I've often said behind your back. You gave us best *Messiah* and best *Elijah* we've ever had at Lane End.

HELLIWELL. Easy, easy! Best i' Cleckwyke! And why? I've told 'em when they've asked me. "That young feller of ours is clever," I said. "I knew he had it in him," I said.

SOPPITT (*hopefully, rising*). Yes, you did, Joe. (*To* GERALD.) And so did I. I've always been on your side.

GERALD. I believe you have, Mr. Soppitt. (*To all three of them.*) You can keep that letter to-night — on one condition. That Mr. Soppitt has it.

SOPPITT (*eagerly, holding out his hand*). Thank you, Joe.

HELLIWELL (*uneasily*). What's the idea o' this: (*He backs up a little*).

GERALD. That happens to be the way I feel about it. Now, either give it back to me at once — or hand it over to Mr. Soppitt, who'll be answerable to me for it.

SOPPITT (*eagerly*). Certainly, certainly.

(HELLIWELL *silently and grudgingly hands it over.* SOPPITT *puts it carefully in his inside packet. The others watch him like hawks.* GERALD *moves to the window. There is a pause, then we hear a knocking from upstairs.*)

HELLIWELL Knocking. (*Not happily.*)

PARKER (*grimly*). I 'eard.

HELLIWELL. That means she's getting impatient.

SOPPITT. I expect Clara's been ready to come down for some time.

HELLIWELL (*bitterly*). They want to get on with the celebration.

PARKER (*bitterly*). Chat about old times.

HELLIWELL (*bitterly*). Nice game o' cards.

GERALD (*after a pause*). I'd better be going. (*He moves up to the door.*)

HELLIWELL (*hastily going up to him*). No, no. Take it easy.

PARKER. No 'urry, no 'urry at all. I expect Joe has a nice cigar for you somewhere.

HELLIWELL (*with forced joviality*). Certainly I have. And a drink of anything you fancy——

GERALD. No, thanks, And I must be going.

(HELLIWELL *brings him down.*)

HELLIWELL. Now listen, lad. We've admitted we were 'asty with you, so just forget about it, will you? Now you see the mess we're in, through no fault of ours——

(*He goes up for his cigars.*)

GERALD. I do. And it *is* a mess, isn't it? Especially when you begin to think——

PARKER (*hastily*). Yes, quite so, but don't you bother thinking. Just — (*rather desperately*) try an' forget you ever saw that letter.

HELLIWELL (*who now comes down* C. *with the cigars*). We're friends, the best of friends. Now you've got to have a cigar or two, lad — I insist — (*he sticks several cigars into* GERALD'S *outside pocket, as he talks*) and you're going to promise us — on your word of honour — not to tell anybody anything about this nasty business, aren't you?

(*All three look at him anxiously. He keeps them waiting a moment or two.*)

GERALD. All right.

(*They breathe again.* HELLIWELL *shakes his hand.*)

HELLIWELL. And you won't regret it, lad.

(*The knocking grom upstairs is heard again.*)

PARKER (*miserably*). 'Ear that.

HELLIWELL. It's wife again.

SOPPITT (*thoughtfully*). Curious thing about wives. They're always telling you what poor company you are for them, yet they're always wanting to get back to you.

HELLIWELL (*darkly*). That's isn't 'cos they enjoy your company. It's so they can see what you're doing.

PARKER. Well, what are we doing?

HELLIWELL (*sharply now*). Wasting time. (*To them.*) Now listen, chaps, we're in no proper shape yet to face t'wives. They'd have it all out of us in ten minutes, and then fat'll be in t'fire.

PARKER. I know. We've got to put our thinking caps on.

SOPPITT. I suppose Mr. Beech couldn't have been mistaken, could he?

PARKER. We might take that letter and get expert advice——

HELLIWELL (*hastily*). What! An' 'ave it all over the town.

PARKER (*quickly*). We might put a case — without mentioning names—

HELLIWELL (*with decision*). I know what we'll do. We'll nip down to t'club, 'cos we can talk it over there in peace an' quiet. Come on, chaps. Just as we are, straight down t'club. (*To* GERALD.) Now, young man, you promised. You won't go back on your word?

GERALD. No. You're safe with me.

HELLIWELL (*urgently*). Good lad! Now, wait till we've got off, then go out front way. Come on, Albert, Herbert, we've no time to lose an' we go this way — (*bustling them towards the exit* R. *through the conservatory*) straight to t'club.

(*They go out* R. GERALD *looks at his watch, smiles, lights a cigarette, then makes for the door, which has never been quite closed. When he opens it suddenly,* MRS. NORTHROP, *still holding a towel and a large glass dish, which she is wiping perfunctorily, is discovered just behind the door. She is in high glee and not at all abashed at being found there. She leans against the hinge of the door, and* GERALD *backs a little into the room.*)

GERALD (*with mock sternness*). Have you been listening?

MRS. NORTHROP (*who may have had a drink or two*). Listening! I should think I have been listening! I wouldn't have missed this lot even if it means 'aving earache for a week. None of 'em rightly married at all! Not one of 'em properly tied up! (*She begins laughing quite suddenly, and then goes off into peals of laughter, rolling against the door. The dish she holds seems to be in danger.*)

GERALD (*amused as he goes past her, out*). Look out — or you may break that dish.

MRS. NORTHROP (*calling to him*). Brek a dish! If I want to I'll brek a dozen, now.

GERALD. (*just off, challengly*). Not you! I dare you!

MRS. NORTHROP (*coolly*). Well, here's a start, any road.

(*She tosses the dish down and it smashes noisily in the hall. We hear* GERALD *give a laughing shout, then bang the front door.* MRS. NORTHROP *now starts laughing helplessly again, still leaning against the door.*)

Nay — dammit! — (*Laughing.*) Oh dear — oh dear — oh dear——

(*She is still roaring with laughter as—*

The CURTAIN *briskly descends.*)

A Bruddersford Christmas

In Bruddersford they celebrated the season in a huge, rich, leisurely style. Since then, in other places, I had begun to think that Christmas, starting in early November, was something largely invented by the Advertising and Gift departments of the stores, a commerial racket to boost the mid-winter trade in profitable lines. In those days before 1914, certainly in Yorkshire, there was far less of this standardized *Merrie Yuletide* salesmanship, but a great deal more hearty and widespread enjoyment of the season itself. Christmas arrived at the proper time, late on the twenty-fourth of December, but once it did arrive then it really was Christmas – and often with snow too.

Brass bands played and choirs sang in the streets; you went not to one friend's house but to a dozen; acres of rich pound cake and mince-pies were washed down by cataracts of old beer and port, whisky and rum; the air was fragrant and thick with cigar smoke, as if the very mill chimneys had taken to puffing them; whole warehouses of presents were exchanged; every interior looked like a vast Flemish still-life of turkeys, geese, hams, puddings, candied fruit, dark purple bottles, figs, dates, chocolates, holly, and coloured or gilded paper hats; it was Cockaigne and "the lost traveller's dream under the hill"; and there has been nothing like it since and perhaps there never will be anything like it again.

Christmas Eve, as was the pleasant custom then, was devoted to visiting friends. These were chiefly members of my aunt and uncle's whist-drive circle, and among them were some very rum characters. . . .There was Mr. Peckel, who was enormously stout, had a high whinnying voice, could perform astonishingly good conjuring tricks, and was terrified of his wife, who was tiny but very fierce. There was Mr Warkwood, who looked rather like Abraham Lincoln, read Herbert Spencer over and over again, and was such a determined individualist that he fought an unending battle with all tax-collectors. His wife was plump and jolly, never understood what her husband was talking about, and was famous for her pastry. There was Mr Dunster, a massive growling man, notorious for his rough tongue at the mill, but renowned too for his passion for and knowledge of wild flowers, which often took him for a thirty-mile walk over the moors. And if he had had a few whiskies, Mr Dunster solemnly rose to sing "Asleep in the Deep" in a terrifying bass voice . . .

But to describe these people in this brief and cold-blooded fashion, as if they were caged in a zoo, is all wrong. They existed in their own atmosphere, and it was an atmosphere of friendliness, affection, easy hospitality, and comfortable old jokes. No doubt they had troubles unknown to me then as a youth. Their world didn't seem as secure, rich, and warm to them as it has since appeared to me. Nevertheless, when all allowance has been made for my youth and ignorance, I am certain these people lived in a world, in an atmosphere, that I have never discovered again since 1914, when the guns began to roar and the corpses piled up. The gaiety, at Christmas Eve or any other time, has always seemed forced and feverish since then. My Uncle Miles and his friends weren't trying to forget anything. The haunting hadn't begun. The cruelty was still unrevealed; the huge heartbreak wasn't there. No irony in the bells and the carols. You could still have a Merry Christmas.

So we did. Perhaps Christmas Day itself wasn't quite as merry as Christmas Eve. Ancient relatives, many of them strange to me, arrived in Brigg Terrace for dinner at half-past one. Some of them seemed as fantastic to me as dinosaurs. There were bewhiskered great-uncles and creaking great-aunts, who bellowed genealogy across the table and afterwards, in the vast somnolence of the afternoon, heavy with plum-pudding and flavoured still with rum, loosened their incredible sets of false teeth and muttered and snorted. In the evening, yawning and rather bilious after so much rich cake and mince-pie, we played Newmarket for shells and coloured counters, and one terrible old great-aunt persisted in cheating. Throughout the day these ancients talked about me as if I were not there or could not understand English (and indeed their Yorkshire accent was sometimes so broad that I could hardly understand *them*). . .

On Boxing Day afternoon, when all Bruddersford seemed to be shut up in a huge cold cupboard, into which an occasional flurry of snow found its way, I went a long walk with my uncle, who needed one as much as I did. My uncle and aunt were going that night to the Dunsters', and when my uncle heard that Mr Ackworth had given me an invitation to a Boxing Day Party, he advised me to go. I couldn't sit at home and do nothing on Boxing Night, he said, and they would probably settle down to play whilst at the Dunsters'. So I put on my best suit, muffled myself up, and took the tram to the Wabley terminus. From there I climbed, through a whirl of snowflakes, up towards the edge of the Glen. I felt as if I were looking for Mr Ackworth and his party in the Antarctic.

"Good lad! Glad to see you," roared Mr Ackworth in the hall, helping me off with my heavy overcoat. "Got a bit o' good stuff i' this overcoat an' all. Ah'll bet your Uncle Miles chose that for you, didn't he? Well, you know one or two of 'em'ere, but not so many. Mostly neighbours. Introduce yourself, lad. Ah can't be bothered. 'Ere's the wite, though. Better be introduced to 'er or there'll be ructions. Annie, this is young Gregory Dawson who 'elps me in t'sample-room."

"How do you do?" said Mrs Ackworth in a very deep voice. She was a stately, rather handsome woman, who seemed to think that it was her duty to have dignity enough for both of them, with the result that she was not unlike a duchess in a George Edwardes musical comedy. 'Seasonable weather, isn't it?'

"Ay, an' what this lad needs is a drop o' summat to warm 'im up an' get 'im started," said Mr Ackworth, winking at me.

He took me into a little room full of books, told me to look around it, and then after a minute or two came back with a steaming glass of a very generous size. "Mulled old ale. Warm you up in a jiffy, lad. Now get it down."

It was the strongest stuff I had ever tasted up to that time, and it was hot and I drank it quickly. Then I found I had a great desire to giggle. Mr Ackworth, Mrs Ackworth, and their party that I had not yet seen, they all seemed to me exquisitely droll. Mr Ackworth led me across the hall into a drawing-room packed with people, most of them very hot and many of them very fat. The Bruddersford agent of the Canal Company, whom I recognized although at that moment he was blindfolded, was trying to pin a paper tail on to an outline of a donkey. And then I saw that the three Alington girls were there, Joan and Eva and Bridget. They smiled, and I made my way, through a solid but almost steaming ton or so of wool merchants and wives, to join them in their corner.

I was one of the magic circle. And this, I realized at once, was a wonderful party.

–"Bright Day" (1946).

Band Concerts in Lister Park

My father and his friends were always among the thousands in the tiers of chairs that curved round the bandstand, though not entirely enclosing it. They were concert-going as well as sitting in the open, smoking their pipes; they could be critical and were not to be brassed and cymballed into appreciation; and I have listened more than once to a close friend of my father's–a happy man who had a tiny business he could leave any time for expeditions and cricket matches, company and the discussion of fine points–explaining why the clarinets of the Scots Guards, his favourites, were superior to those of the Irish or the Coldstream.

High above the nearest rows of chairs, higher than the top of the bandstand itself, was a promenade, and there the youth of our part of Bradford–Lister Park not being far from where I lived–congregated densely, some of the lads and girls packed along the rails, looking down through the blue haze of smoke and catching what came to them of Coppélia or *Les Deux Pigeons,* and all the rest, past counting, on the move in a thick sluggish stream, in which, as I realised more than once, it was devilish hard to find the only face you wanted. This innocent parade was often condemned by deacons and elders, who seemed to think that because they had had enough of it, all sexual life, together with all dressing-up, display, showing off, pursuit and capture, should come to an end.

No doubt the young males were often merely predatory—though the worst of them never paraded in the park, but, like two older men I knew slightly, lurked elsewhere, bent on seducing half-witted housemaids—but the girls, wearing their best clothes and usually in arm-linked trios and quartets, must have known very well, in spite of their glad-eyeing, whispering and giggling, that it was here, not in the mill or the office, not even at home or at the chapel bazaar, they were engaged in the serious business of life. And the place and the hour were propitious for mating: a summer evening, trees and grass between youth and the dark narrow streets; the hills above the tree-tops fading into dusk; all the people, thousands and thousands of them, sitting, standing, or in the slow river of faces on the promenade; the lighted bandstand in the haze below, a glitter of instruments, the scarlet flash of a uniform, coming through the blue air, and music coming too, not recognisable, not attended to, a long way off, but music.

A good place, a good time, for the beginning of love.

—The Swan Arcadian, recalling 1911, in "Margin Released" (1962).

Second House at the Music Hall

Sometimes in company with my Uncle Miles, given a night off by Aunt Hilda, I would go to the second 'house' of the Imperial Music-hall, where in our worn plush seats in the dress circle, price one-and-sixpence, we would listen to Little Tich and George Robey, Vesta Tilley and Maidie Scott (a deliciously saucy comedienne), Jack and Evelyn (and he was a superb improvising droll), and a glorious comic with a round face and an impossible moustache and an indescribably ridiculous manner, one of the best comics I ever saw, who drank hard and died young, called Jimmy Learmonth.

We used to read of what seemed to us the fantastic salaries paid to these variety stars—a hundred pounds a week!—and a little did I realize then, or even wildly dream, that the time would come when I would work for and be thoroughly acquainted with players who would receive more than ten times those salaries and yet not possess one-tenth of the talent. Thus we progress.

Looking back soberly at those music-hall shows, and making every allowance for my youth and for the infectious enjoyment of Uncle Miles, I see now that in those noisy smoky halls, with their brassy orchestras, their plush and tarnished gilt, their crudely coloured spotlights raying down from the gallery, we were basking in the brilliant Indian Summer of a popular art, a unique folk art that sprang out of the gusto and irony, the sense of pathos and the illimitable humour of the English industrial people, bracing it out in their mills and foundries and dingy crowded towns; an art that flourished, withered, and decayed well within a man's lifetime, but that, before it lost all vitality, scattered its seeds, its precious seeds of rich warm humanity, all over the darkening world, and sent an obscure droll called Chaplin as far as California so that his flickering image could go out to conquer the earth.

—"Bright Day" (1946).

A Fight with Death

The Bruddersford Infirmary could not be mistaken for one of the local factories because it has no tall chimney. Otherwise there is little difference. It is a rambling ugly building, all in blackened stone and surrounded first by an asphalt courtyard, where the smuts drizzle ceaselessly, and then by tall iron railings that would not seem out of place around a prison. Through these railings a nurse may be seen occasionally, and as she flits across those grim spaces of stone and soot she looks like a being from another world, incredibly immaculate. Here, out of the sunlight, far from green shades and blue distances, where no birds sing, but where the lorries and steam-waggons come thundering down and the trams go groaning up the hill, here behind this rusting iron and walls thickened with black grime, the Bruddersfordians have a bout or two, a tussle, or a fight to a finish, with Death.

The last time Mr Oakroyd had visited the Infirmary was to see a friend of his from Higden's, a good many years ago. He could hardly remember what it looked like inside. He was familiar enough with the outside, for the place was not quarter of a mile from Ogden Street and for years he had walked past it nearly every day. This morning, however, even the outside seemed strange. His wife was somewhere inside it, behind one of those dark windows.

"Is it special?" asked the porter, "'cos this isn't visiting time, yer knaw."

"Well, I don't know fairly," said Mr Oakroyd. "I wer sent for, like, an' I've come a long way."

"If yer'll howd on a minute. I'll see. What's t'name again? All right. Yer can wait in there." And the porter, after pointing to a door, turned away.

There were several people in the bare little waiting-room. One of them was an enormously fat woman, wrapped in a shawl. The tears were streaming down her face, and she made no attempt to dry her eyes, but repeated over and over again, without any variation of tone: "They nivver owt to ha' let him come in, nivver."

On the other side was an oldish man, whose drooping face Mr Oakroyd dimly recognised. "Fower operations in eighteen months, that's what she's had," he was saying. "Fower operations." There was mournful pride in his voice. He looked round, nodded vaguely to Mr Oakroyd, and then began again: "Ay, fower operations."

The others there, including two children, said nothing at all. They just waited, and Mr Oakroyd had an obscure conviction that they had been waiting a long time. His heart sank. He wanted to go away.

The porter was standing at the door, beckoning to him. "Oakroyd, isn't it? That's Num-ber Twen-ty-sev-en, List-er Ward. Well, t'sister says she's very sorry but yer can't see 'er now but will you come again this afternoon."

"I see," said Mr Oakroyd, and immediately found himself invaded by a feeling of relief. He tried to be disappointed, told himself he must see her as soon as he could, but nevertheless he could not help feeling relieved. He had been in there only a few minutes, had not really been inside, but even so it was comforting to be back again in the bustle of Woolgate. Something dogged him, however, throughout his stroll through the main streets. He was like a chap out on bail.

He called again in the early afternoon, only to be told to return later. Then at last he was admitted. He climbed up four flights of stone steps and then found Lister Ward. A nurse met him at the entrance. "Let me see," she said, "you're for Number Seventeen—little Doris Smith—aren't you?"

When Mr Oakroyd told her he was wanting Number Twenty-seven, she seemed disappointed, and this made him all the more uncomfortable, as if he had no right to be there.

"Yes, I remember now," she said, looking all round him but not at him. "Sister said you could see her, didn't she? You're the husband, aren't you? She hasn't been asking for you. There's a son, isn't there? I thought I'd seen him. This way then, and don't make too much noise. This isn't the proper visiting day, and you mustn't disturb the others."

He crept after her in a fashion that would not have disturbed a fly. He tiptoed so gently that his legs ached. They had to go almost the whole length of the ward, and though he tried to see as little of it as possible, he could not help noticing some things. All the women were in bed and they all seemed to have something blue on; some were old, some very young; some asleep, some staring fiercely; and there were strange things, pulley arrangements, on some of the beds; and one or two were completely surrounded by screens. No moaning and groaning; not a sound; it was all as quiet as a waxwork show; all tidy and polished and still; very queer, frightening.

The nurse suddenly stopped. She turned round, looking right at him this time. "Your wife's very ill, you know," she whispered. "You must be very quiet with her. Don't mind if she's not very clear, wandering a little. Just a minute." She walked forward to a bed, and he heard her say: "Now Twenty-seven, your husband's come to see you." What else she said he did not know, but he saw her leaning over the bed, doing something, and then she stepped back and nodded to him. He tiptoed forward, feeling horribly clumsy, uncertain. One hand, held behind him, was tightening, tightening, until its nails were digging into the horny palm. Then he stood by the bedside, looking down into the face of Number Twenty-seven.

"Eh, lass," he said huskily. He tried to smile, but could only make a grimace. "Nay—nay." And there seemed nothing more he could say.

—The Good Companions" (1929).

Sunday Evening in Bradford

We got back to Bradford, that Sunday evening, between six and seven. It was dark and miserably drizzling. I asked to be dropped in the centre of the town. "But what are you going to do?" they cried, starting at me as if I had been suddenly shaken out of my wits. "I don't know," I told them. "I want to see what there is to do in Bradford on a wet Sunday night." "But there isn't *anything,*" they almost screamed. I replied firmly, and not without a suggestion of the heroic, that I must see for myself. So I was dropped in Market Street. At first it did not look too bad. There were plenty of lights about, and though of course there were no shops open, some of the larger establishments had left their windows uncovered and illuminated. There were signs too that the evening was clearing up. Such drizzle as remained was not troublesome. I heard music and discovered that a Salvation Army band was playing just round the corner; it was playing quite well too; and a considerable crowd had collected. So far as I could judge only the innermost ring of this crowd was in search of salvation; the others were listening idly to the music, smoking their pipes, and waiting until the pubs opened . . .

Although it was such a poor night, there were lots of people, mostly young men, hanging about the streets. What were they doing there? Some of them, no doubt, were waiting for girls, or hoping that in some miraculous

Market Street, in Bradford.

fashion they would quite casually make the acquintance of a pretty and amiable young woman. But most of them, I think, were not baffled amorists: they were there simply to pass the time. They had to do something with their Sunday evening. They might have attended at one of the many and various places of worship; but obviously they did not like places of worship. They might have stopped at home or visited a friend's house; but then it was probably neither comfortable nor convenient for them to stay at home or for their friends to stay at home . . .

Bluntly, the position is this: the good old-fashioned English Sunday—the Sabbath, as it is called by a great many people who do not seem to realise, first, that they are not Jews, and secondly, that anyhow they are a day out in their calculations—is still being imposed upon large numbers of people, especially younger people, who no longer want the good old-fashioned English Sunday, any more than they want the good old-fashioned English side-whiskers, thick underclothing or heavy meals. It is imposed upon them legally and by force, not by mere suggestion; and the reason that the imposition is still successful is that in most provincial towns the authority is largely in the hands of elderly men who are not in sympathy with the desires of newer generations. And what these elderly men do not want, nobody else shall have: their attitude is a thoroughly dog-in-the-mangerish one. For obviously there is nothing to prevent anyone from having a quiet Sunday night, church or chapel, then cold supper and an hour or two's reading, solemn talk or meditation at home, if he or she really wants to have one.

You can have a quiet Sunday evening of this kind in Paris or Buenos Aires. There has never been any talk of compulsory attendance on Sunday nights at dance and concert halls, theatres, cinemas, just as it has never been proposed when discussing local option—and this would be the only sporting conclusion—that in the event of the vote going against them, total abstainers should be compelled to take an agreed amount of wine and spirits. I myself happen to live in a city and in a certain state of life that leaves me free to spend my Sunday evenings at theatres, cinemas, concerts, restaurants, and so forth; but as it also happens that I have more time for these things during the week than most people and I like to spend Sunday quietly at home or with my friends, I rarely take advantage of this freedom, remaining as sedate on most Sundays as a Baptist deacon. But that seems to me no reason why I should impose restrictions on other people, with different tastes. I have the kind of Sunday I like: let them have the kind of Sunday they like . . .

It is time, however, we returned to Bradford on a Sunday night. The rain stopped, but it remained a wettish raw night. I explored all the centre of the city and discovered that there were one or two very small cafés open and then, from seven o'clock onwards, all the pubs, and nothing else. You could take your choice and either promenade up and down Darley Street, North Parade, Manningham Lane, or go into the nearest pub. Ever since I can remember, elderly citizens have been protesting against this practice of promenading on Sunday nights. They have always been disgusted by the sight of young people monkey-parading in this fashion. It is, however, these same elderly citizens who have seen to it that nearly all doors leading out of the street shall be locked against these young people. They cannot listen to plays or music, cannot see films, cannot even sit in big pleasant rooms and look at one another; so they walk up and down the street. No doubt some of them would always want to promenade—even on nights like this, though it seems incredible—but most of them would obviously prefer one of a dozen different ways of spending Sunday evening. They have, of course, to get on with their mating, whatever elderly persons may think of them; but they could easily do it in a much more civilised fashion than this of monkey-parading.

Having seen the promenaders, I thought I would try the only places of entertainment allowed to open—the pubs. The first one I visited was very quiet—it was still early—and in the lounge I entered there were only five or six hobbledehoys drinking glasses of bitter and elaborately chaffing the barmaid in the traditional style. Nothing wrong with the place except that it was dull and stupid. The next pub, a large gaudy affair, was doing better business. Its chief customers were either young men who stared, whispered, suddenly guffawed, and a number of youngish females who, if they were not women of the town, had certainly taken the most astonishing pains to disguise themselves as such, even to putting on the swollen greedy faces of the type. Nothing much was happening in there: an occasional guffaw, another order for drinks, a move from this little table to that, with the women of the town grimacing over their stouts and ports and missing nothing. This is not an attack on the place; I have not the least desire to see it closed; but I am puzzled to know why it should be open when so many obviously better places—the Civic Theatre, for example—are shut; I cannot see why playgoing, listening to music, watching films, even dancing, should be considered so much worse—or at least more secular—than sitting and boozing with prostitutes . . .

I then had a short walk and ventured into pub number three, a large establishment that seemed to be doing a very brisk trade. This time the lounge, which was crowded with people and thick with smoke, boasted some little coloured electric lights. That was all; nothing else, not even reasonable comfort; but it was enough, and every table, every seat, was taken. Fifteen shillings' worth of coloured lamps: this was gaiety, this was life; and so the place was selling beer, stout, port as fast as it could serve them, to patrons of both sexes. I do not think any of these people—and they were mostly young, pairs of boys, pairs of girls; with here and there an older couple—could be said to be really enjoying themselves; but at least they could look at one another, giggle a bit, talk when they found something to say, and admire the carnival splendour of the coloured electric lights. They did not want to go home, they did not want to walk up and down the streets, so here they were.

I endured about a quarter of an hour of it, then marched out to walk the two miles or so to my home.

—"English Journey" (1934).

YORKSHIRE DALES

The Finest Countryside

After I was demobilised from the army in the spring of 1919, the very first writing job I was given was to do some articles on a little walking tour in the Dales, and I went, treading on air, a civilian again, a free-lance journalist at last, through Upper Wharfedale and then roaming about in Wensleydale. I shall never forget beginning that little walking tour. I have never found again—no, not even in the romantic islands of the West Indies or the South Seas, not in the deserts of Egypt or Arizona—the sunlight that set all the dewdrops glittering about my path that morning. And though many places have disappointed me when I have returned to them, the Dales have never disappointed me.

I still consider them the finest countryside in Britain, with their magnificent, clean and austere outlines of hill and moor, their charming villages and remote white-washed farms, their astonishing variety of aspect and appeal, from the high gaunt rocks down to the twinkling rivers. As far as my present life is concerned, the Dales have only two faults: they are not easy to get at from London, to which I am anchored for a good part of my year; and they have never offered me yet a country house suitable in size and type and cost to a family like mine. But I believe that one day I shall return to their high hills and grey-green valleys and lovely peace. So please see that your new magazine fights to keep them all unspoilt.

—Introducing Vol. 1, No 1, of "The Yorkshire Dalesman" (1939).

A Wayfarer goes to Wensleydale

You must start from Buckden, along the high road, on a fine spring afternoon. Very soon you will have climbed to Cray (you have taken the right-hand turning, remember), where you will, doubtless, rest a moment to enjoy the sight and sound of innumerable little splashing, gurgling falls. Then up, and up, and up, until you have nearly reached the roof of the world. But you will never arrive there, because you again turn to the right, and gradually descend.

All this time you are in no other company but that of the calm, eternal hills and the wide sky. And in this one blessed hour you wish for nothing better; the strong, sane beauty of high places has caught your soul. You meet with no one along the road. The inevitable timid sheep, with its attendant lamb, awaits your coming, in its usual dazed fashion, and then flees, panic-stricken. You hear nothing but the faint sound of running water, the high, sweet unison of the larks, and a cuckoo, far away constantly repeating its notes of enchantment.

Now you have dropped into Bishopdale, among leafy lanes, the quiet homes of men, and the endless murmuring of little rivers. You are climbing again; you pass Thoralby with scarce a sigh, and, conquering the last hill, you darken the low doorway of the George and Dragon at Aysgarth.

There has been silence in the tap-room for about half an hour (I am still at the George and Dragon), for the quaintly-whiskered old fellow who sits at the end of the settle said that a certain absent party was "niver a judge o' baists." This terrible verdict has shattered all attempts at conversation for the time being, and I fear there will be no more words spoken at all here tonight. But why should we speak; we have quiet hearts, and I, for one, feel that the great peace of the dale at evening-time is something too precious to be lightly broken? And so, to bed.

This morning the dale was filled with clear sunlight, and the great hills were swept bare of all superfluous ornament and colour. I have passed through lanes white with blossom, through sunlit, daisied meadows; past Thornton Rust and Worton, quaint little places where the years must go by like a dream, until I reached the old cross at Askrigg, and hied me to the King's Arms. This is an hostelry of the true and ancient order, full of low stairways and surprising passages and corners. At the moment, I am in one of the kitchens among oak settles, carved tables, and great hanging hams. Someone in the next room is playing little lilting tunes upon a violin. But I noticed a seat in front of the old church, and there I will sit and smoke until lunch time.

"Take care that you turn by the old mill," said the elderly man at the other end of the seat. But I was full of dreams, and heeded him not.

Wensley, the quite small village which gave its name to the dale in which it stands ***(Arthur Gaunt).***

So that when I did look for the Mill Beck Force I missed my way and had to scramble down steep banks and over tumbled rocks. A waterfall some 70 ft or 80 ft in height cannot long be overlooked, however, and very soon I was sprawling on a rock at the bottom of the force. There I remained for the better part of the afternoon, shaded by the already thick foliage and cooled by the neighbouring showers of fine spray. There are, I am told, other fine waterfalls further up the stream; but I am not greedy, and Mill Beck Force, with its narrow, thickly-wooded ravine, gorgeous with innumerable varieties of wild flowers, gave me contentment enough for one sunny afternoon.

I possess an elaborate map, and after consulting it in a languid sort of way I have decided to journey along the road to Hawes. So tomorrow will find me in the opposite direction—it always does; this is the great charm of maps to me—and I shall be drifting about Leyburn Market-place, or inquiring for cheese at Wensley.

This Leyburn is a half-baked, hobbledehoy sort of place; neither town nor village, with leanings towards cafes and garages and other modern frivolities. Talking with a very old ploughman, who was sucking his pipe in the Market Square, I compared Leyburn unfavourably with Askrigg, about ten miles away, but the old fellow said, rather mournfully, that he had "niver been so far up," and he evidently regarded me as a much-travelled person.

Tonight is no ordinary night at Leyburn, for there is a "Grand Peace Tea and Concert" at the Town Hall. Numerous bills inform me that the "special attractions" are: "Ham and tongue; Mr So-and-So, the great Yorkshire tenor." Too late for the ham and tongue, I stayed away.

After all I had heard and read of Middleham Castle–it played a great and tragic part in the Wars of the Roses–I was sadly disappointed when I came in sight of the ruins. It must have been small, not very strong, and not particularly well built; it could be put in one corner of Alnwick, Bambrough, or Windsor.

The village of Middleham is pleasant and picturesque enough, however, and it produced to the deep satisfaction of the inner man, some very delectable rhubarb tart and cream. I have left Wensleydale proper for Coverdale now, and have passed near the ruins of Coverham Abbey, through Coverham village and Melmerby, until I reached straggling little Carlton. And here at Carlton I sit, taking my ease, for tomorrow I must climb between Buckden Pike and Great Whernside, dropping down into Kettlewell, and so home.

–JB's first published work on the Yorkshire Dales, a two-part article in the "Yorkshire Observer" (May 1919).

A Dales Journey

The Bradford folk have always gone streaming out to the moors. In the old days, when I was a boy there, this enthusiasm for the neighbouring country had bred a race of mighty pedestrians. Everybody went enormous walks. I have known men who thought nothing of tramping between thirty and forty miles every Sunday. In those days the farmhouses would give you a sevenpenny tea, and there was always more on the table than you could eat. Everybody was knowledgeable about the Dales and their walks, and would spend hours discussing the minutest details of them. You caught the fever when you were quite young, and it never left you. However small and dark your office or warehouse was, somewhere inside your head the high moors were glowing, the curlews were crying . . . Sunday morning . . . opened wonderfully, so a little party of us took a car into the country. It was plain from the very first that the local enthusiasm had not vanished.

Burnsall Bridge, Wharfedale ***(Clifford Robinson).***

All that had happened since the war was that it had taken a somewhat different form. Before we used to set out in twos and threes, in ordinary walking clothes, for our Sunday tramps. Now they were in gangs of either hikers or bikers, twenty or thirty of them together and all dressed for their respective parts. They almost looked German. We passed the hikers very early on our journey, and so I cannot say much about them, except to doubt whether this organised, semi-military, semi-athletic style of exploring the country-side is an improvement upon our old casual rambling method . . . We saw a good deal of the cyclists, passing troops of them all along the road up to Grassington; and I remember wondering exactly what pleasure they were getting from the surrounding country, as they never seemed to lift their heads from the handlebars, but went grimly on like racing cyclists. They might just as well, I thought, be going round and round the city. But perhaps they call an occasional halt, and then take in all the beauty with a deep breath. There was plenty to take in too, that morning.

We went to Ilkley, then through Bolton Woods to Burnsall and Grassington, and never have I seen that country so magnificent. The long dry summer had given it an autumnal colouring that was past belief. The morning was on fire. The dry bracken and the heather burnished the hill-tops; and all the thick woods beside the Wharfe were a blaze of autumn. The trees dripped gold upon us. We would look down russet vistas to the green river. We would look up, dazzled, to see the moorland heights a burning purple. If we had been ten years in a dark cell and newly released, we could not have stared at a world that seemed more extravagantly but exquisitely dyed. I have never seen Bolton Woods looking like that before, and hardly dare hope to see them like that again. It was their grand carnival, and it will riot and glow in my memory as long as I live.

Grassington came, where several water-colouring friends of mine, as well as a number of wool merchants from Bradford, have made their home;

and after that we slipped into Upper Wharfedale, which is narrower and less wooded and far more austere than the lower reaches. There are great limestone crags for walls there, and between them the valley is smooth and green. Half-way up we passed the pleasant village of Kettlewell . . . I remember a woman who lived in one of these remote farmhouses, a solid West Riding countrywoman and not one of your fanciful arts-and-crafts misses, who swore that she saw fairies dancing on the hillside. (Have these lonely folk keener senses than ours, or do they merely take to imagining things? It is still an open question, and not to be settled by a report from a committee because a committee would never see anything.) We reached Buckden, towards the head of the Dale, and a notable goal for Bradfordians, who have emptied the barrels at the inn there many a time; and then we turned left, towards the long remote valley of Langstrothdale, up which you may go to Hawes in Wensleydale. We stopped, however, at Hubberholme, a tiny hamlet that had a fine little old church and a cosy inn. There we stayed for lunch.

In the afternoon we returned down Upper Wharfedale, but then cut east and climbed up to Blubberhouses. The sun had disappeared; the day was cloudy and sagging, with imminent signs of rain. Now we got that other and familiar aspect of these moorlands, seeing them as a high, grey desolation, with the winds shooting over them, threatening to shatter the heavy clouds. The long stone walls and the few stone buildings did not suggest man's handiwork or his presence, but seemed to be natural outcroppings of the grey rock. Not a soul was about. A few birds went beating up against the wind and crying desolately, that was all. The country was Tibetan in its height and emptiness. It was impossible to believe that in half an hour we might have dropped into Harrogate and taken the waters. I tried to remember exactly where it was that, years before in this region, I had stumbled upon a genuine deserted village.

There it was, on the moors, with two small factories and several rows of cottages, and completely uninhabited. (Something, I believe, went wrong with the water supply.) I remember eating my sandwiches inside one of the cottages from which most of the roof was gone. I stared at the gaping doorways and the grass-grown street; and not even a mouse stirred. No village I saw in the war area, I think, gave the same complete picture of desolation as that empty shell of a moorland village did. And it was somewhere in these parts, though behind what misty ridge I could not remember.

The sagging clouds broke, and it rained good and hard, as it always does up there. We bounded down towards Otley, past the reservoirs, which were mysterious lakes in that fast scribble of rain, and ran on through Mehston to Baildon, where we found friends and tea . . .

—"English Journey" (1934).

Jacquetta Priestley, through whose enthusiasm J.B. had his interest in the glories of the Yorkshire Dales re-awakened.

Crossing the Wharfe at Bolton Abbey **(Bertram Unne).**

A hill farm in Wharfedale ***(John Edenbrow).***

Rood loft in Hubberholme Church, by the upper reaches of the Wharfe **(H. Lefevre).** *The church, river, flanking fells and the folk of the area gave J.B.P. endless delight, and it was in the little church that a service was held to his memory on an April day in 1986. At the same time a memorial was unveiled, the inscription on which reads . . . Remember J.B. Priestley, O.M. 1894 - 1984. Author and Dramatist whose ashes are buried nearby. He loved the Dales and found "Hubberholme, one of the smallest and pleasantest places in the World."*

Dalesfolk at Leyburn Market, Wensleydale ***(Clifford Robinson).***

J.B.P.'s novel "Lost Empires" was filmed by Granada as a seven-part dramatisation for television. Here Julia Parrot plays Vesta Tilley in the recruiting scene which opened Episode One.

Also from "Lost Empires". Tom Priestley (right), son of J.B. Priestley, visits the location for the Army sequences used for a Prologue. With him is Colin Firth, who plays the story's narrator, Richard Herncastle.

Everything Fit to be Seen

My own favourite country, perhaps because I knew it as a boy, is that of the Yorkshire Dales. For variety of landscape, these Dales cannot be matched in this island or anywhere else. A day's walk among them will give you almost everything fit to be seen on this earth. Within a few hours, you have enjoyed the green valleys with their rivers, fine old bridges, pleasant villages, hanging woods, smooth fields; and then the lonely heights, which seem to be miles above the ordinary world, with their dark tarns, heather and ling and harebells, and moorland tracks as remote, it seems, as trails in Mongolia. Yet less than an hour in a fast motor will bring you to the middle of some manufacturing town, which can be left and forgotten just as easily as it can be reached from these heights.

—Introduction to "The Beauty of Britain" (1935).

Pennine Desolation

These Yorkshire Dales are now a National Park. It covers 680 square miles, and if this does not seem very much, let me add that once there, because of the astonishing variety of scene and place and prospect, it seems a great deal, like another country. You can make a stately progress along the valleys, from one grey old bridge or church to another, eating your head off. (In Burnsall in Wharfedale, for a birthday dinner, we had smoked salmon, and none of your paper-thin slices neither, roast duckling, bilberry pie and cream, and an excellent *Châteauneuf du Pape.*) You can go roaring over the fells in a car or, much better if you have the legs for it, climb the moorland tracks from one dale to another. But if you try it in the winter, you could die up there and never be heard of again. It really *is* another country.

So far it is one of the more casual National Parks—no wardens and fuss, no bullying notices. The bounds have been drawn rather cunningly, to avoid cutting into large estates. It starts just beyond Skipton, in the south, to include the lower and leafier reaches of Wharfedale, and ends beyond Swaledale, at the remote head of Arkengarthdale and on the grim heights of Tan Hill.

I suggest we stay up there for a few moments. This is the place to take your friends from overseas who believe that England is overcrowded, an

Opposite page — The Unspoilt Dales. A study at Arncliffe, in Littondale ***(Clifford Robinson).***

endless suburbia. It is as awe-inspiring in its own fashion as Death Valley, California, where I have also painted *gouaches.* Just before you reach the inn at Tan Hill, you stare across the wilderness of Stainmore where not a house, not a man, not even a beast, can be seen. The wind howls; the sky darkens; but there is still plenty of colour left—blue fells in the far distance, brown and purple hills nearer, and nearer still a level waste, olive green, umber, jet black, with just two distant patches, bright but sinister, of emerald green. Why don't our film-makers, turning some tale of murder into colour, go up there?

Tan Hill Inn, a whitewashed 18th-century building, is one of the highest in England, 1700-odd feet above sea level. Under an ebony cloud, as I saw it, a kind of doomsday sky, I felt it was about three miles high and 500 miles from anywhere. Nevertheless, there used to be a few odd coal pits up here, worked since the Middle Ages, and the last one closing down only about 30 years ago. They have left nothing but a grim ruin here and there, heightening the look of desolation . . .

I don't recommend it to everybody. Riviera body-toasters are warned off. And if your eyesight is blurred and your mind closed to purity of line and splendour of colour, don't go. If the past written in stone means nothing to you, if you must be up-to-the-minute in concrete, high-duty alloys and plastics, happy with the skyscraper boys, don't go. If you find joy only in roaring across maps in very fast cars, don't go, for one of the old stone walls may kill you, and nobody up there will burst into tears.

The purity of line can be enjoyed every clear day because most of the high fells are not peaks but tablelands or long humpbacks, often subtly modulated. Romantic mountain scenery is not entirely lacking. The big fellows, Ingleborough and Penyghent and Whernside, may not reach 3000 feet, yet they can seem immense mountains, cobalt or indigo against a yellow-grey sky. And in Malhamdale, especially up at Malham Cove and Gordale Scar, painted by generations of romantic artists up to our own John Piper, the limestone country does mad and tortures itself. But what to my mind is most characteristic of the whole region is the exquisite line of the flatter but faintly curved fells, high moorlands not mountains.

Then there are the walls, grey in the limestone country, seemingly black where there is millstone grit, walls that trace and bind every changing shape or patch of colour. Either you love these dry-stone walls, triumphs of a vanishing craft, as I do, or you care nothing about them and might as well go and toast yourself elsewhere; so let us have no argument. They seem to me not only to bind both the fells and the pastures below but also the centuries themselves. They come curving out of the past. And there has been a lot of past here, even in the high places. Bronze Age folk, the Celtic Britons, the Romans, all were here, long before the curtain was raised on our national history. This is an old wild place. Walk from dale to dale over the top, or get out of your car on some seemingly desolate height, and as you smell the sweet moorland air and hear its birds crying, you are at one with your ancestors. Ancient memories seem to creep along your spine.

—*Article in "Sunday Times Magazine" (1964).*

Looking across the head of Malhamdale from the rim of Malham Cove ***(Derek Widdicombe).***

Some Favourite Dales

My own favourite among these wonderful valleys is Wensleydale, which unlike most of the others runs east-west instead of north-south. It has a central position, has perhaps more good villages, and because it is broad and has a high northern wall of fells, it seems to me to offer the most beautiful lighting effects. So Wensleydale would be my first choice. You can catch crayfish in the river there, as I have done—it was like playing a magical game of grab—under the expert direction of Dick Chapman, once a schoolmaster and now Water Bailiff of the Yore River of Wensleydale. He belongs to my generation and has all its optimism, fiery energy and enthusiasm. (All right, I may be bragging, but where among later generations do you find these qualities?)

Upper Wharfedale to the immediate south is another favourite of mine, a narrow grass-and-lime-stone valley. Its smallest place, Hubberholme—just a bridge, an inn and a church, all old—is sheer magic, not quite in this world. Lower Wharfedale, around Bolton Abbey and Barden Tower, is altogether gentler, a charm of deep woods and a sparkling river, but I prefer sterner stuff.

You get that in Swaledale, north of Wensleydale, which gives you at once a sense of remoteness and melancholy grandeur. Teesdale, further north still and beyond the national park itself, is grand and wild in its upper reaches, where the finest waterfall in England, High Force, can be found. Lower down, near Bowes, is the district once notorious for its "Yorkshire Schools" to which unwanted children were sent to be half-starved, bullied, and kept out of the way. These wretched boarding schools were already a scandal when Dickens savagely satirized one of them, as Dotheboys Hall, in *Nicholas Nickleby*. What is claimed to be the original of Dotheboys Hall, or what is left of it, is now a café, where boys may eat where once they starved.

Ribblesdale has some charming villages such as Stainforth, Langcliffe, and Austwick, and it is on the way to the huge dramatic effects at the head of Malhamdale, created by a great limestone fault. At the opposite and eastern side of the Dales in Nidderdale, not one of my favourites, but it is worth a visit just to see the ancient and spectacular town of Knaresborough with its steep river bank and immensely high bridge—a town unlike any other in Britain. Even so, I must confess that it is many years since I saw it last, whereas I am always finding my way back to Wensleydale, still as magical to me now as it was over half a century ago.

—Article in "Life International" (1966).

High Force, Teesdale ***(Gordon Wood).***

Sunshine and Shadows

Now we come to the beauty of these Dales. This is chiefly a matter of colour and light. Most of these fells have rock on them, but they are not composed outwardly of rock, unlike the Lake Districk peaks. On the other hand, they are not at all like the grassy rounded hills—the Downs—of Southern England. Their tops and broad upper slopes are mostly a patchwork of moorland grasses, the light brown marram, ling and heather, dark stretches of peat, and perhaps a few bogs, a bright but sinister emerald green. Below are streams and pastures and woods, an intense green in early summer and a blaze of russet and gold in autumn, of all the valleys.

Now let these tops, these slopes, these valleys, be seen through swift changes of sunlight and cloud, from thin white mists to the angriest purples and blacks, and you have a scene, forever shifting, that entrances any sensitive eye and drives any landscape painter, who has never time to capture it, almost out of his mind. At one moment the slopes of the fells will be smothered in gray cloud, and a few moments afterwards they will be there in the sunlight, looking like magic carpets.

The very last time I drove from Ribblesdale to Wensleydale, over the top past Ribblehead, Gayle Moor, Redshaw Moss, I was in cloud and mist, a gray world, most of the way. But then suddenly, in the far distance below, a small patch of cloud lifted to reveal the lost sunlight—and it was like staring at the fields of Paradise. No other place I have ever seen offers such an ever-changing panorama and pageant of colour and light.

Then there are the stone walls, thousands and thousands of them, running up the fells, lighter than the landscape in the southern half of the Dales, where limestone is used, darker in the northern half where they use millstone grit. These walls are there to keep cattle and sheep within reasonable bounds, but to the visitor they add a kind of binding to the slopes and a curious accent to the scene. Many of these "dry-stone" walls (that is, without any mortar or cement) must be hundreds of years old, but there they stand, defying the roughest winter weather, thanks to the ancient art, now in danger of being lost, of "dry-walling." It depends on having a marvellous eye for stones that will hold together.

A friend of mine once thought he could help an old Dalesman who was repairing a wall. He felt that he had an eye too for the right stones. But every stone he offered the old man was contemptuously rejected—"Nay, lad, that'll nivver do."

—*"Life International"*

Kettlewell, Upper Wharfedale.

Dales Scenery

For the most part there is nothing dramatic and determinedly picturesque about this Dales scenery, except perhaps in parts of Teesdale, at its northern limit, and at its western edge in Malhamdale. Here the water has gone underground and finally brought about various collapses of the softer limestone rock, creating such dramatic effects as Gordale Scar, Malham Cove and the innumerable "potholes", down which young men, braver or more foolish than I have ever been, go exploring, hauling one another up and down cavern after cavern, in mysterious limestone depths.

These Yorkshire Dales are . . . the most rewarding countryside I have ever known. Is this simply local patriotism or the memory of early enchanted days? It is not. To begin with, in no other region I have known is there such variety within so small a compass as there is here. In more grandiose regions you may spend a day going along one valley or climbing a single slope. You risk six hours of monotony and tedium for one half hour of splendid dramatic effects. In those six hours in the Dales, whether you are in a car or on foot, you have been offered a surprising and entrancing variety. You reach the top of a fell and at once you are in another country, not overcrowded England but a place that has hardly ever seen a man, has heard nothing but the crying of the moorland birds, the curlews and pewits . . .

On the high wilderness of Stainmore, for example, I have reached the Tan Hill Inn, a whitewashed 18th Century building, the highest inn in England and the only house in sight, on a stormy afternoon, with a huge ebony cloud darkening the whole wide scene. It was like Doomsday. And there are scores of these high bare stretches that seem 500 miles from anywhere. Yet just below, 20 minutes in a car perhaps or a couple of hours' sharp walking, are the valleys with their trout streams, their gray stone bridges and cosy villages, their richness of foliage, and each of them, each dale, with its own particular character and charm. You have come down from Wuthering Heights into Arcadia.

—*"Life International"*

Looking for Crayfish

I met Dick Chapman, once a schoolmaster and now Water Bailiff of the Yore that flows through Wensleydale. Mr Chapman belongs to my generation and has all its fiery energy and optimism. He showed me how to catch crayfish, not so much a sport as a magical game of grab. He gave me two of the wettest but most rewarding hours I have known for some time.

Everybody but me may have known about crayfishing. I must point out, though, that the crayfish described by my encyclopaedia, three or four inches long, were rejected by us, returned to the river as babies, the creatures we tossed into our pail being considerably larger. So here goes. You fasten the strong-smelling innards of fowls, as bait, to stones, which in turn are tied to six feet or so of string and a twig that stays on the bank.

After sinking eight or nine of these weighted baits, you hang about, rain-coated and gum-booted, for half an hour or more, getting wetter and wetter. Then you lower a net, gently manoeuvre each baited stone into it, pull the net out, and discover in it some bewildered crayfish, looking like small greeny-brown lobsters. Later you boil them—no sickening panic, no scream; ours passed out long before boiling point was reached—and then you take the flesh out of the big claws and the tail.

The flavour of ours was not strong, perhaps too mild and delicate, though somehow they filled the house with a fishy smell. I nibbled a few; then my hostess created a *Quiche Lorraine Ecrévisses Wensleydale.* I ate more than my share—hot that night, cold on a picnic lunch next day—but told myself I might be turning it into literature.

—*Article in "Sunday Times Magazine (1964).*

View across Wensleydale, near Askrigg ***(Geoffrey N. Wright).***

Fred Lawson: Dales Artist

Quite immodestly, I shall begin with myself—as a painter of sorts. I did not start until I was about 60 and never went near an art school or any kind of teacher. I tried both watercolour and oils at first, but found watercolours too difficult (I mean good ones of course; anybody can paint a bad watercolour) and oils, a more promising medium for me, too heavy and messy for hotel rooms and planes. I settled finally for gouaches, a stout workhorse of a medium, and have painted landscapes in gouaches from Leningrad to Lima, Peru, from Greece to Guatemala (a wonderful painting country), from the Ring of Kerry to Death Valley, California. I am a flibbertiggibet holiday painter, hardly ever doing anything at home, not touching a brush until I am looking at a strange landscape, far from home and therefore exciting. Fascination and excitement have to take the place, with me, of technique.

In all of this I am the very opposite of a fine professional painter like Fred Lawson. And indeed I think few professional artists have so closely identified themselves and their work with one region as Lawson. He lived in the Dales; he knew and loved the Dales (as well he might because there is no better countryside); and he drew and painted what he saw, year after year, all round him. Please notice that watercolour *The Road,* which I promptly bagged, some years ago, when I opened an exhibition of Yorkshire Artists at Heal's in London. It reduces a bumbling holiday amateur like myself to dispair.

To begin with, it was done on the kind of day when I abandon the job in disgust—heavy cloud, little colour, not a hope of using any of my fancier gouache paints. Yet look what Lawson has made of it, finding wonderful variety within the narrow range imposed on him by the scene and the day. Then notice something else—it is tremendously *alive.* (Compared with this, all my gouaches are so many frozen landscapes, done in coloured icecream). The vigour of it all—there in the trees and bushes, the clouds, the road—is a direct expression of the man himself. Finally, I think there is something else here, over and above the fine technique and the vigour and zest—there is love. This man, we can say, *loved* this countryside.

The last time I was up in the Dales I had the pleasure of seeing and listening to Fred Lawson. I was hoping to have that pleasure again, later this coming summer. But now—no such luck! There are a lot of men that I, like you, have seen too much of. There are a few I know I never saw enough of. One of them—because our paths rarely crossed—was Fred Lawson.

He was a rich mixture. First, a great solid lump of North-country character. Secondly, a fine sensitive artist with a style and manner so much his own that often I have recognised at once tiny reproductions of pen drawings as being his work. Thirdly, in a restless age he was one of those sensible and fortunate men who know where they want to be, where they want to work if they are painters, where heart and minds can be at peace.

But the last words can come from his clever daughter Sonia, herself a painter, who wrote in a letter to me: *We have lost someone who was a whole man, a real man, a rare thing.*

—Catalogue for Fred Lawson's First Retrospective Exhibition

J.B. Priestley, at the age of 89 years.

The Priestley Statue

Alfred H. Robinson, of Eccleshill, in correspondence with W.R. Mitchell:

The statue is, I think, a fine piece of work. The facial resemblance is remarkable, and I quite like the idea of Priestley's greatcoat billowing out behind him as in a Pennine wind. And, of course, the setting for the statue of an author is an ideal one — between the Central Library and the National Museum of Photography, Film and Television, and with the Library Theatre on one hand and the magnificently refurbished and extended Alhambra Theatre on the other.

There is one rather remarkable fact concerning the Priestley statue. Vera Brittain opens her book *Testament of Friendship* (a biography of her friend Winifred Holtby, published in 1940) with the sentence: "A hundred years hence, literary tourists will find in Yorkshire the opportunity for many pious pilgrimages to places hallowed by association with celebrated writers of this generation." She goes on: "Perhaps they will visit first the stocky pugnacious statue of J.B. Priestley which will then stand before the Alhambra Theatre in Bradford, where the dramatised version of *The Good Companions* celebrated its first night and Phyllis Bentley, eagerly arriving too soon, waited on the steps for 20 minutes in the bitter wind."

In view of the fact that one has only to change the word "before" to "beside", one can only regard that sculptural prophecy of almost half a century ago as a fantastically accurate one! When I drew Mrs. Priestley's attention to it, she commented that it was indeed "astonishing."

I'm glad that the bronze statue stands 9 feet high on a stone pedestal 7 feet high. I think statues should be more than life-size to be really effective.

Ian Judd, the sculptor, was born in London in 1947. From 1965 he worked as a graphic designer for some ten years, during which time he developed an interest in fine art. In 1976 he went to art college to study painting, but found himself drawn towards sculpture. Having set up a workshop in Hampshire during 1980, he earned a living as a signwriter and letter-cutter, at the same time making sculpture for exhibition and to commission.

In 1984 he moved to Yorkshire and a year later started a workshop in Leeds. In February of 1986 he began a stone sculpture of a "Mother & Child" for Wakefield Cathedral which was installed in June. He has recently moved his studio to Dean Clough in Halifax. "All I heard about J.B. Priestley seemed to point to a rather difficult gentleman, but reading his books convinced me otherwise. Those who knew him described a shy, humorous and amiable character who nonetheless wasn't afraid to speak his mind. It was this Priestley that I wanted to convey."

Jacquetta Priestley and the Priestley statue ***(Telegraph & Argus).***

*The Wharfe at Hubberholme **(John Edenbrow).***

One of the Pleasantest Places in the World

A short walk beyond Buckden, in Upper Wharfedale, is Hubberholme, one of the smallest and pleasantest places in the world. It consists of an old church, a pub, and a bridge, set in a dale among high moors. In summer, long after the snows have melted, there is rarely much water in the river, so that it glitters and winks; and a man who has been walking for an hour or two can loiter on that bridge for quite a time, waiting for the pub to open and staring at the river.

—*"The Other Place" (1953).*

France
Languedoc

A rock climbing guidebook to the La... France

Adrian Berry

All uncredited photos by Adrian Berry
Other photography as credited
Edited by Alan James and Stephen Horne
Printed by Latitude Printing
Distributed by Cordee (www.cordee.co.uk)

Published by ROCKFAX November 2011

www.rockfax.com
www.ukclimbing.com

We only use paper made from wood fibre from sustainable forests and produced according to ISO 14001 environmental standard

ISBN 978 1 873341 62 9

This page: An idyllic setting at Chaulet Plage in the Ardèche for climbing, swimming or just hanging out.
Cover: Unknown climber on *Pyromania* (7c+) - *page 109* - Gorge du Tarn.

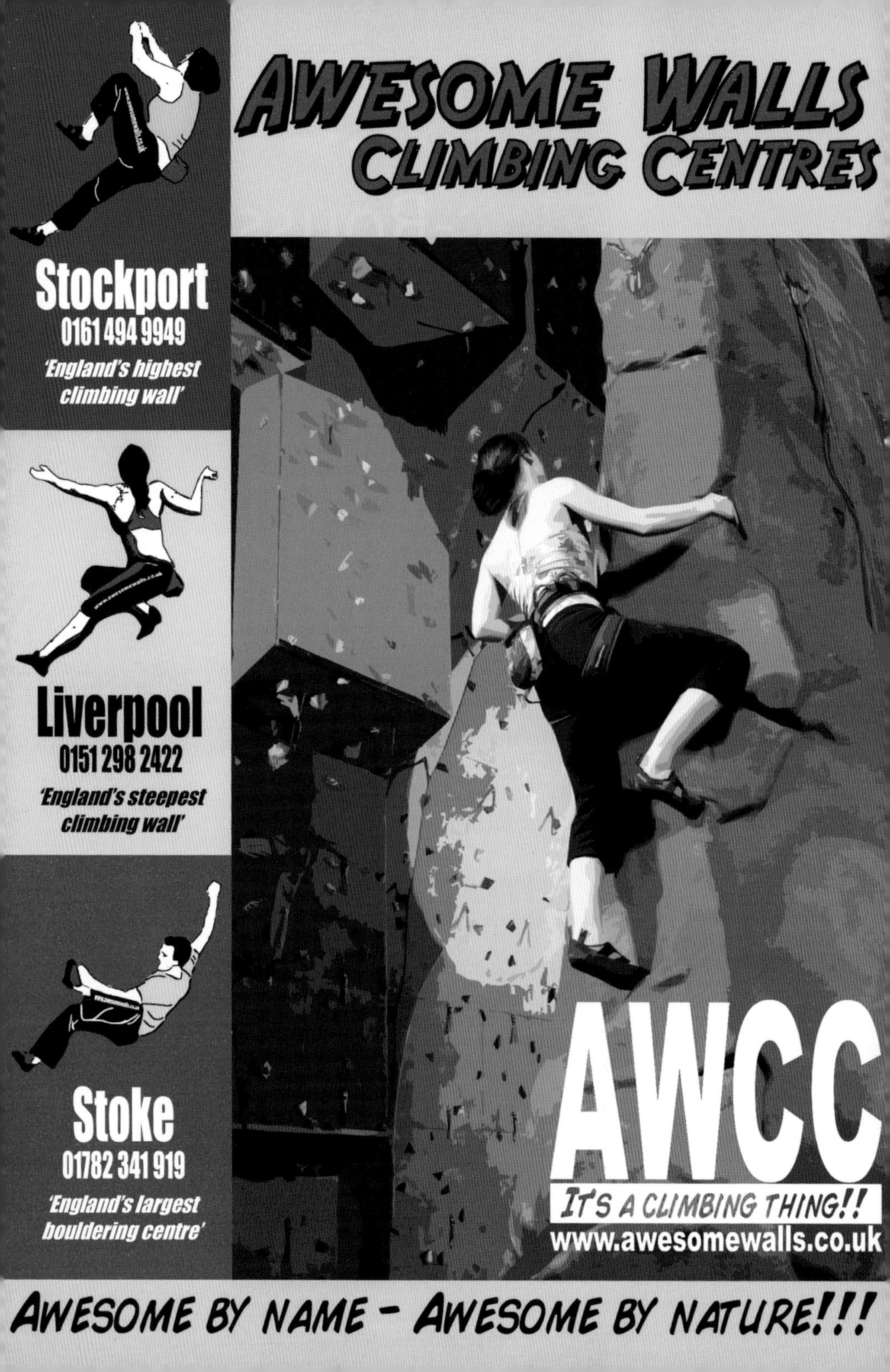
AWESOME WALLS
CLIMBING CENTRES
Stockport
0161 494 9949
'England's highest climbing wall'
Liverpool
0151 298 2422
'England's steepest climbing wall'
Stoke
01782 341 919
'England's largest bouldering centre'
AWCC
IT'S A CLIMBING THING!!
www.awesomewalls.co.uk
AWESOME BY NAME - AWESOME BY NATURE!!!

Andy Morris climbing at Nouveau Monde, Seynes.

Guidebook Footnote

The inclusion of a climbing area in this guidebook does not mean that you have a right of access or the right to climb upon it. The descriptions of routes within this guide are recorded for historical reasons only and no reliance should be placed on the accuracy of the description. The grades set in this guide are a fair assessment of the difficulty of the climbs. Climbers who attempt a route of a particular standard should use their own judgment as to whether they are proficient enough to tackle that route. This book is not a substitute for experience and proper judgment. The authors, publisher and distributors of this book do not recognise any liability for injury or damage caused to, or by, climbers, third parties, or property arising from such persons seeking reliance on this guidebook as an assurance for their own safety.

This is my second, and Rockfax's third guidebook to the climbing in the South of France. When I was working on my first guidebook to Haute Provence, the idea of going on a sport-climbing trip to France was surprisingly novel. I think I heard more of people jetting off around the world to sweat it out in places like Thailand or Nevada than packing the car and heading down to France. I think that this series of French guidebooks is succeeding in convincing people that they can save the airfare, the jet-lag, and the pollution and experience even better climbing somewhere that for most Europeans is rarely more than a day's drive away.

The more time I spend in France working on guidebooks, the more I am struck by the quality of what is available. For this book, I was already aware of places like the Gorge du Tarn, Seynes and Russan, but I was really in for a surprise and a treat when I dug a bit deeper and found so much more. I was awestruck by the Gorge de la Jonte, for example, somewhere only around the corner from the Tarn, and yet, for most climbers, there's so much more there to do. Another surprise was Orgon - I'd been to the Canal sector previously, and was in two minds as to whether to include it in this book, until I saw the rest of what it has to offer and realised it was a paradise for climbers looking for low to mid-grade climbs. The biggest surprise though, must have been Mont Gaussier, a place I'd never been, but one that I kept finding excuses to go back to, for just one more photo…

As with the other two books in the Rockfax France series, the goal is not just to promote France as a fantastic climbing destination, but also to give the wider picture on what is available there. As I mentioned already, crags like the Gorge du Tarn have been well-publicised by high-level climbers, for whom it is rightly a paradise, but for everyone else there are really much more suitable venues. La Jonte even has some brilliant trad routes!

This book also seeks to publicise an area that can be reached by climbers in northern Europe without necessarily flying. Over the two years it took to produce this book, airports were ignored, rides shared, and slowly, habits were changed. This guidebook has the train symbol on the maps, showing where the nearest railway station is located. The TGV is a fast way of getting to the south of France without worrying about paying for excess baggage. Also look into overnight sleeper-trains, where you wake up at your destination, pick up a car and get straight on the rock! There is no doubt that taking the train is far less damaging to the environment than flying and we hope that this book will help start a change in our behaviour for the better.

To get many of the photos you will see on these pages, I initiated 'Google-doc Climbing Trips' - where a collection of strangers can use the Internet to come together as friends, put on some colourful T-shirts and soak up the quality rock. These trips were a bit of a social experiment, but ultimately worked brilliantly. Although I will thank those who took part elsewhere for their contribution to this book, I'd also like to thank them here.

Finally, the title of this book was chosen to give an idea as to the area covered. You will find that there are many good areas in the Languedoc-Roussillon region (Vingrau for example) that didn't fit into the area we wished to cover. Conversely, quite a few of the areas covered are not in the Langedoc region - for example, the Ardèche is a part of Rhône-Alpes, and the Boffi is within the Midi-Pyrénées. Great climbing areas don't strictly follow political boundaries!

Adrian Berry, October 2011

Johannes Seiler on the tricky first pitch of *Keep cool Raoul* (6c+) - *page 163* - Gorge de la Jonte.

Simon 'Sol' Oliver on the first of many pitches that make up *Aquo es Quicon* (6a) - *page 163* - at the Gorge de la Jonte.

Access

All the areas covered by this book are well-publicised and popular and, unless indicated otherwise, you can assume there is a right of access. These rights have often been hard-won, and they should be respected since they can be lost in an instant by the thoughtless behaviour of one individual. One notable exception to this is the Gorge du Tarn - see page 100.

Park considerately - don't block access, and be prepared to climb elsewhere if there's nowhere to park.

Stick to the approach paths - avoid short-cuts through someone's private land.

Keep the noise down at the crag - crags are often in areas popular with walkers who are keen to get away from all that.

Take your rubbish home with you - better still, make space for some of other people's rubbish, and remember that everything you bring to the crag is rubbish if you leave it there, even orange peel takes around two years to decompose, is it really that much of a chore to carry it home?

Local Guidebooks

Nearly all the areas covered by this guidebook are detailed in locally available publications. Local guidebooks include more routes and may well be more up-to-date and, if you particularly like an area in this book, it would be well worth tracking down the local information.
In the introduction to each section, the current (as of 2011) local guidebook is featured so you know what it looks like. You can usually get hold of these from bookshops or the tourist information office, or, if there is a climbing shop in the area, then that is a good place to look.

It is not the policy of Rockfax to replace local guidebooks, but rather to introduce climbers to the areas covered by this book. Typically climbers who may be unaware of the wealth of climbing and who are unable to acquire information via local sources. Rather than competing with local guidebooks, we expect that the increased number of visitors will lead to more sales of quality local guidebooks and a general boost to the local economy.

Not what we want to see - recently some popular crags in the Gorge du Tarn were closed due to fears of litigation by the landowner. Photo: Olivier Obin

Feedback - Online Route Database

The database at **www.rockfax.com** contains a listing of every route in the book, with the opportunity for you to log comments and vote on grades and star ratings. This information is essential to help us ensure complete and up-to-date coverage for all the climbs. We can then produce updates and make sure we get it right in subsequent editions. To make this system work we need the help of everyone who climbs in the areas covered by this book, so if you think you have found a badly-graded route, or discovered a hidden gem that we have only given a single star to, let us know about it. Your general comments on all other aspects of this book are also welcome.

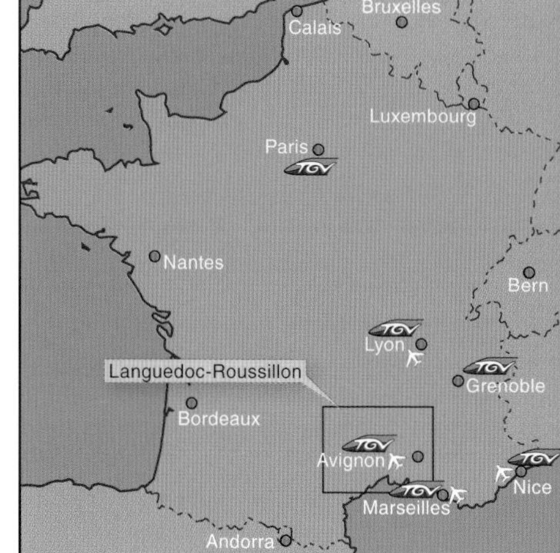

Das dritte Buch der Rockfax Serie Frankreich deckt den großräumigen und ergiebigen Bereich westlich des vorhergehenden Kletterführers vom Autor zur Haute Provence ab.
Die beschriebenen Gebiete befassen sich im Wesentlichen mit dem Bereich um den Nationalpark von Cévennes. Ebenfalls enthalten sind aber auch Felsen in der näheren Umgebung der Städte Nimes und Avignon.
Das Buch beginnt mit dem familienfreundlichen Urlaubsziel von Ardèche, das nächste Kapitel befaßt sich mit dem Gorge du Tarn sowie den Mehrseillängenabenteuern von Jonte und den verschiedenen hochqualitativen Angeboten von Le Boffi. Während wir uns südwärts bewegen, berichten wir über Thaurac, anschließend machen wir eine Pause für ein paar nette Abenteuer der "alten Schule" in Hortus. Wir bewegen uns schließlich wieder ostwärts und wenden uns den modernen Sportkletterrrouten von Claret, Russan sowie Seynes zu, alle mit ihren individuellen Stilen, atemberaubenden Qualitäten und einer auf Lebenszeit ausreichenden Routenanzahl. Wir beenden unsere Tour schließlich an den gut erschlossenen Felsen rings um Avignon, eingeschlossen das legendäre Gebiet von Orgon.

Zugang

Für die meisten Routen in diesem Buch gibt es keine Zugangsbeschränkungen und sie können jederzeit beklettert werden. Häufig wurde dies durch Verhandlungen zwischen den Kletterern und Landbesitzern bzw. Anliegern erreicht. Bitte folgt daher genau den beschriebenen Zustiegen in den Gebietsbeschreibungen. Beachtet bitte außerdem jegliche Schilder in Gebietsnähe, die neue Informationen beinhalten könnten.

Der Kletterführer

Dieses Buch enthält sämtliche Informationen, die Du benötigst, um die besten Felsen des Gebietes zu finden und einzuschätzen - auch wenn Englisch nicht Deine Muttersprache ist. Topos und Symbole veranschaulichen die Art der Routen in diesem Buch.

Ausrüstung

Die meisten Routen in diesem Kletterführer sind voll eingerichtete Sportkletterrouten, für die lediglich ein Satz Expreßschlingen und ein langes Seil benötigt wird. Ein 70 Meter Seil ist angebracht, um sicher abseilen zu können. Wenn Du beabsichtigst, Mehrseillängenrouten zu klettern, sind 9mm Doppelseile mit 50 Metern Länge zum Abseilen nötig.

Internet

Alle beschriebenen Aufstiege dieses Kletterführers sind in der Routendatenbank von Rockfax auf der Internetseite - www.rockfax.com - enthalten. Hier findest Du auch mehr Informationen über die einzelnen Routen, sowie Votings zu Schwierigkeitseinstufungen und Kommentare anderer Kletterer. Wenn Du Routen kletterst und nicht mit diesem Kletterführer übereinstimmst, dann besuche unsere Datenbank, um uns Deine Meinung mitzuteilen.

Rockfax

Rockfax veröffentlicht seit 1990 Kletterführer, darunter 30 Bücher zu Gebieten in Europa und vier Bücher zu Gebieten in den USA. Darüber hinaus sind auf der Rockfax-Website mehr als 50 Miniguides im PDF-Format verfügbar. In letzter Zeit haben wir eine Serie von Büchern zum Thema Training veröffentlicht. Weitere Informationen findest Du auf unserer Internetseite - **www.rockfax.com**

Symbole

{1} Lohnende Kletterei.

{2} Sehr lohnende Kletterei, eine der besten Routen an diesem Felsen.

{3} Brilliante Kletterei, eine der besten Routen im Gebiet.

Technisch anspruchsvolle Kletterei, die eine gute Balance und Technik erfordert oder komplexe und trickreiche Züge beinhaltet.

Anstrengende, kraftvolle Kletterei; Dächer, überhängender Fels oder maximalkräftige Züge.

Durchweg anstrengende Kletterei; entweder mit vielen harten Zügen oder überhängendem Fels, der zu dicken Armen führt.

Kleingriffige Kletterei.

Potentiell weite Stürze bzw. weite Hakenabstände.

Weite Züge, morpho.

Eine Route, die nicht vollständig mit Bohrhaken ausgerüstet ist - Absicherung durch Klemmkeile und Friends notwendig.

Möglicherweise lockerer Fels im Routenverlauf.

Felssymbole

5 min — Steilheit des Zugangsweges mit ungefährer Zeitangabe.

Afternoon — Ungefähre Zeit, zu der der Felsen in der Sonne liegt (wenn sie scheint!).

Dry in the rain — Überhängende Wände, die trockenen Fels bei Regen bieten.

Slabby — Klettern an geneigtem Fels, plattig.

Vertical — Klettern an senkrechtem Fels.

Steep — Klettern an stark überhängendem Fels.

Menschenleer - Zur Zeit wenig besucht und meistens ruhig. Langer Anmarsch und / oder weniger lohnende Routen.

Ruhig - Weniger beliebte Sektoren an Hauptfelsen, oder gute Felsen mit langem Zugangsweg.

Belebt - Plätze, an denen Du selten allein sein wirst, besonders an Wochenenden. Lohnende Routen und leichter Zugang.

Zum Brechen voll - Die populärsten Felspartien, an denen ständig Hochbetrieb herrscht.

Farbig markierte Routennummern

Die Seillängen sind farblich nach Schwierigkeit geordnet:

- ❶ Grad V+ und darunter
- ❷ Grad VI- bis VII-
- ❸ Grad VII bis VIII
- ❹ Grad VIII+ und darüber

Before crediting those whose efforts have been directed at making this book, credit must go to those who created the routes we describe. Creating a sport route is a lot of work, some of which is skilled, some of which is just sheer effort, and placing bolts on overhanging rock is particularly difficult. It is interesting how the experience of having developed new routes makes one far more understanding of the difficulties of the job - and more forgiving of minor misjudgments that lead to bolts not being exactly where one may wish they were. And so to all those who have toiled, sweated, bled, cursed, wondered why they were doing it, vowed never to do it again, and created such wonderful climbs: thank you.

Though there is only one name on the cover, this book is the result of the efforts of a great many more people. There are many whose names I have forgotten to add to this list, and to each of them go both my thanks and my apologies.

Many thanks to...

Alan Rubin, John Eales, Andy Morris, Ali Baylay, Eivind Flobak, Jonathan Ayrton, Pete Bridgwood, Neil Ronketti, Sol, Tim Howell, John Venier, Alexandre Buisse, Jenny Barber, Harry Crank, Jamie Veitch, Tim Parkinson, Kenny Watson, Nikki Holbrook, Andrew Gibb, Laurent Moseley, Sam Harvie, Tom Kendall, Olivier Obin, Simon Rawlinson, Liz Collyer, Matt Heason, Sophie Heason, Juan Varela, Jo Varela, Miles Gibson, Ollie Ryall, Steve McClure, Andy Benson and Pete Benson.

An extra big thank you to photographer Piers Cunliffe (**www.pierscunliffephotography.co.uk**) for coming out on both the 'google-doc' research trips, being so helpful at both ends of the camera, and generally being a star. Thanks Piers.

For help in checking the text and sharing their wisdom, thanks to Chris Craggs, Jack Geldard, Cedric Larcher, Sherri Davy, Stephen Horne and Karsten Kurz.

Finally, a very big thank you indeed to my partner Audrey, who has tolerated both my absences and my presences. Any correct translations from French to English are her doing, incorrect ones are mine.

Adrian Berry, October 2011

Languedoc-Roussillon Logistics

Crags lining the Ardèche gorge - these have probably never been climbed on.

Train

Eurostar operates a direct service from London to Avignon during the summer months. At other times of year, an indirect service is possible on the TGV. Luggage restrictions are far more generous than those imposed by budget airlines, and the journey only takes around 8 hours station to station.

Flying

There are a number of airports in the South of France served by budget airlines. Montpellier, Marseilles and Avignon are the closest, but Grenoble, Nîmes, Lyon and Nice are also options. Expect to pay more at popular times like weekends, the summer months and school holidays.

Driving

The French autoroutes are fast, and usually uncrowded. If you've got a long drive, it makes sense to break the journey, sleeping in rest areas is acceptable, but if you're looking for a bed without spending too much, find a Formula 1 (**www.hotelformule1.com**) or, a bit nicer, an Ibis (**www.ibishotel.com**) or Etap (**www.etaphotel.com**).

Getting Around Without a Car

Some of areas covered in this guide can be accessed by public transport, and if you are visiting at the right time of year, you will doubtless find other climbers with cars who you can share rides with. The obvious choice of destination if you won't be driving is Orgon, where you can turn up by train or bus and never feel you need to use a car. La Gorge de la Jonte is another convenient destination for car-free climbing, once you've got to Le Rozier.

Travel Insurance

UK citizens have reciprocal health care rights in France under the EHIC. Despite this, it is strongly recommended that personal travel insurance is taken out to cover rescue, medical and repatriation in the event of an accident (see inside back cover).

BMC Travel Insurance - **www.thebmc.co.uk**

Satellite Navigation

GPS 44.39626 P 4.19651 All the parking spots are indicated with a precise GPS location. This is in the form of two decimal numbers as in the box to the left. Different GPS devices accept these numbers in alternative formats; some devices are happy with two comma-separated numbers, others require a **N**orth and **E**ast value to be entered separately.

Bear in mind that SatNavs often get it horribly wrong and will delight in taking you through an endless chain of tiny villages when you could have been cruising along on the autoroute. Also note that there are many places in France with the same name - key-in 'Les Vignes', and you could find yourself taking the scenic route to completely the wrong place. The best policy is to use your SatNav in conjunction with a map, use the GPS co-ordinates in this book, and check and review the route as you approach the crag. The map on the facing page gives rough locations. Each chapter has a closer map which should home you in to your chosen crag but a detailed local map will also be found useful.

Where to Stay

A comprehensive listing of all the places to stay in the South of France would require every page of this book to cover. Camping in the South of France is very well provided for. Driving around, you will notice that there are signs for campsites everywhere although many aren't open in the winter months. The best campsites are listed in the introductions to the areas covered in this book. Apartments and gîtes are best found using the Internet: search the web for 'gites France' and you will access a number of listing sites that allow you to book online. Tourist information offices are found in most towns, and are happy to find you somewhere to stay, as well as something to keep you busy on a rest day.

Climbapedia - **www.climbapedia.com**
Online trip planner with accommodation tips and advice for the whole of France.

A constant reminder! Photo: Piers Cunliffe.

Chaulet
Mazet
Actinidias
Cirque Gens
Les Branches
Gorge du Tarn
La Jonte
Le Boffi
Cantobre
Thaurac
Hortus
Claret
Seynes
Russan
Gaussier
Mouriès
Orgon

Chaulet
Mazet
Actinidias
Cirque Gens
Les Branches
Gorge du Tarn
La Jonte
Le Boffi
Cantobre
Thaurac
Hortus
Claret
Seynes
Russan
Gaussier
Mouriès
Orgon

Climbing in the sun on a winter's day in France is always delightful, during the research trips for this book, many days were spent walking-in on snowy or frosty ground to find a sunny crag that allowed us to climb in T-shirts. If you want to climb on the south-facing crags like Seynes or Cantobre, winter is definitely a good time for it. Spring and autumn are the best times for most of the crags when you can choose between optimum cool climbing conditions in the shade or relish the warmth of the sun. Summer is the time to visit the north-facing venues, or choose your venue and time of day so that you chase the shade - alternatively choose somewhere close to a river (like the crags in the Ardèche) where you can jump in the water to cool off. The sheer number and variety of crags in France means there's always somewhere to climb, no matter what time of year you choose to visit.

Average Temp °C	Jan	Feb	Mar	Apr	May	Jun	Jul	Aug	Sep	Oct	Nov	Dec
Millau (maximum)	7	9	12	14	19	23	26	26	21	16	10	7
Millau (minimum)	1	1	3	5	9	12	14	14	11	8	3	1
Nîmes (maximum)	12	13	17	19	24	28	31	31	26	21	15	11
Nîmes (minimum)	3	3	6	8	12	16	19	19	15	11	6	3
Avignon (maximum)	11	13	17	19	24	28	31	31	25	20	14	10
Avignon (minimum)	2	2	5	8	12	15	18	18	14	10	6	2

The average rainfall for the areas covered by in book is relatively low. The high figures in September to November tend to result from storms rather than full days of rain. This may mean that there is a bit of seepage on some routes but you are very unlikely to lose too much climbing time.

Rainfall cm / month	Jan	Feb	Mar	Apr	May	Jun	Jul	Aug	Sep	Oct	Nov	Dec
Millau (average)	5.4	4.1	3.4	6.4	7.1	6.8	3.4	5.3	7.1	8.0	6.9	5.4
Nîmes (average)	7.0	3.3	2.9	5.9	5.3	4.3	2.9	3.3	10.4	9.2	8.0	5.5
Avignon (average)	5.1	3.0	3.3	6.4	5.8	4.0	2.8	3.9	11.2	8.4	8.2	5.2

John Eales breaks trail at Russan during an unexpected cold-snap in March 2010.

John Eales on *Le bloc de Damocles* (5+) - *page 210* - Thaurac.

John Eales starting up *Tamponnoir brisé* (6b) - *page 281* - at Russan.

Languedoc-Roussillon Climbing

Grades

The routes in this book are graded using the usual sport grade system, or 'French Grade' as it is often known. This gives an overall impression of the difficulty of the route. Some of the crags in this book, like Hortus, Thaurac and La Jonte, were developed years ago. Initially they were for trad climbing only and, as is often the case with older climbing areas, this means that they later acquire a reputation for stiff grading, certainly in the lower and mid grades. The best advice at these venues is to drop your expectations a bit and try something a bit below your normal standard just to ease yourself in to the style of climbing.

Belays and Extensions

Routes are bolted so that an ascent ends when you have clipped the belay, grabbing belays is not the custom. Multi-pitch routes are graded assuming you are taking each belay. Single pitches often have additional sections added to them to offer a longer and more difficult route, these are known as extensions. Most extensions are given extra grades in the route description, and often have different names. Extensions are not second pitches, and the grade of an extension assumes you have not rested on the belay - which would make it easier than graded.

Colour-coding

The routes and pitches are colour-coded corresponding to a grade band. The idea is to give a rough comparison between trad routes and sport routes. For example, if you are happy on orange grades on trad, then you should consider routes given orange spot sport grades.

Green Spots

Everything up to 4+

Good for beginners and those wanting an easy life.

Orange Spots

5 to 6a+ inclusive

General ticking routes for those with more experience.

Red Spots

6b to 7a inclusive

Routes for the very experienced and keen climber.

Black Spots

7a+ and above

The hard stuff!

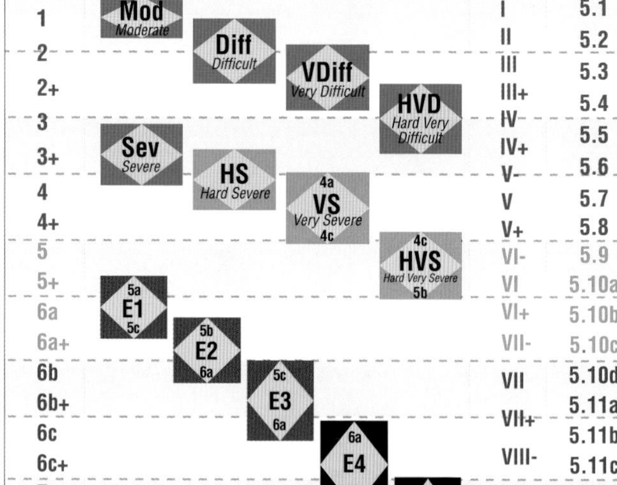

Sport	British Trad Grade (for well-protected routes only)	UIAA	USA
1	Mod Moderate	I	5.1
2	Diff Difficult	II	5.2
		III	5.3
2+	VDiff Very Difficult	III+	5.4
3	HVD Hard Very Difficult	IV	5.5
3+	Sev Severe	IV+	5.6
	HS Hard Severe	V-	
4	4a VS Very Severe 4c	V	5.7
4+		V+	5.8
5	4c HVS Hard Very Severe 5b	VI-	5.9
5+		VI	5.10a
6a	5a E1 5c	VI+	5.10b
6a+	5b E2 6a	VII-	5.10c
6b		VII	5.10d
6b+	5c E3 6a	VII+	5.11a
6c			5.11b
6c+	6a E4 6b	VIII-	5.11c
7a		VIII	5.11d
7a+	6a E5 6c	VIII+	5.12a
7b			5.12b
7b+		IX-	5.12c
7c	6b E6 6c	IX	5.12d
7c+		IX+	5.13a
8a	6c E7 7a	X-	5.13b
8a+			5.13c
8b	6c E8 7a	X	5.13d
8b+		X+	5.14a
8c	7a E9 7b	XI-	5.14b
8c+		XI	5.14c
9a	7a E10 7b		5.14d
9a+		XI+	5.15a

Andy Morris climbing *Séñoritas* (6a)- *page 264* - at Sector Concerto, Seynes.

Rhoslyn Frugtniet on *Abus dangereux* (6c+) - *page 103* - Gorge du Tarn. Photo: Simon Rawlinson

Ropes, Route Lengths and Lowering Off

The most crucial item of gear is your rope. At the very least, you need a 60m rope, but if you're buying a new rope for a trip to France, we strongly recommend getting a 70m rope or longer. Single ropes are now available in thicknesses previously associated with half-ropes. The thinner your rope, the lighter it is to hike up to the crag and the easier it is to pull up to clip. Thicker ropes last longer and are better for working projects. For multi-pitch routes requiring an abseil descent, you may find that using a pair of half-ropes is preferable or a triple-rated rope which can be used both single and double. Alternatively, if you have a 100m single rope, you can make all the abseils and have the convenience of leading on a single rope.

The photo-topos have approximate heights, indicated next to some lower-offs. These are guideline heights only, and it is important to remember that crag bases are not always level, and people stand in different places when belaying. Also, many climbers don't even know exactly how long their rope is, having chopped worn sections off the ends in the past. The golden rule is always tie a knot in the end of the rope to prevent dropping a climber when lowering off.

Other Gear

Only a few routes in this guidebook require more than a single rope and a set of quickdraws - 14 quickdraws is plenty for all but the longest of pitches. For the belays on multi-pitch routes, a couple of screwgate carabiners and a sling each is a good idea. The few routes which need gear are denoted with the symbol.

Make sure your belay device is suitable for your rope: too grabbing and you'll be cursing it each time you pay out rope, too slick and you may struggle to hold your partner. A belay device that you are happy to abseil on is also a good idea.

Beyond these essentials, you may find tape useful for bandaging your fingers if the prickly rock starts to take its toll. For multi-pitch routes a small sack with a water bladder, a long-sleeve shirt and a sun hat are good ideas. A good pair of approach shoes is also worth packing, as some of the crags are a bit of a walk from the parking spots.

Chaulet | Mazet | Actinidias | Cirque Gens | Les Branches | Gorge du Tarn | La Jonte | Le Boffi | Cantobre | Thaurac | Hortus | Claret | Seynes | Russan | Gaussier | Mouriès | Orgon

Other Rockfax Publications

Rockfax produce guidebooks to areas all over Europe. All the books are available from specialist outdoor retailers or direct from **www.rockfax.com**

France: Haute Provence (December 2009)
France: Haute Provence presents many of the finest sport climbing destinations in the world together in one clear and colourful book. Covering all the best areas from the magnificent walls of Céüse in the north to the impeccable climbing playground of Buoux to the south, this book has a lifetime's worth of climbing waiting on its pages.

France: Côte d'Azur (December 2010)
The cliffs of the South of France rocketed to popularity back in the 1980s when it was realised what great climbing was available and how good the weather was down there. Since then other areas have attracted the attention of travelling climbers. France : Côte d'Azur reassesses these famous cliffs and also includes some of the great venues around Toulon, the sunniest city in France. Plus there is the popular winter venue of Châteauvert, the less well known Esterel and Châteaudouble areas, as well as the world famous Verdon Gorge. Add in Saint Jeannet and a selection of cliffs in the Nice area and this is an essential volume for any climber.

France : Ariège
The fourth book in the series will cover the Ariège area in the Pyrenees and is due for publication is 2012/13.

Sport Climbing+ (2006, 2nd Edition 2011)
Sport Climbing+, by Adrian Berry and Steve McClure, makes great companion to this book and it should enable you to get even more out of your trip. The book takes a practical approach to sport climbing, focusing on the improvements that climbers can make immediately, without embarking on a lengthy training program.

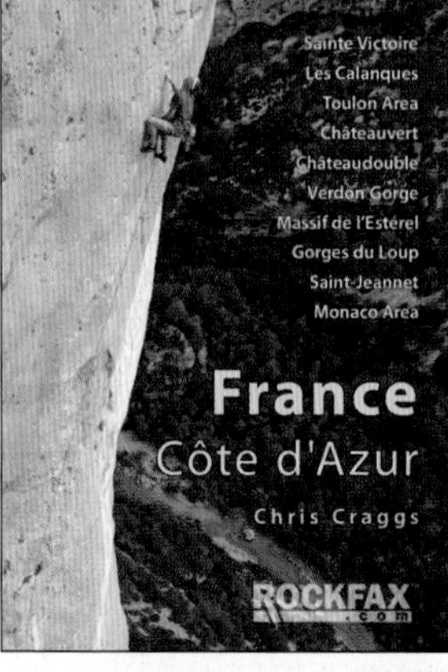

Adrian Berry on *Le tube neural* (6c+) - *page 261* - at Seynes.

Area	Destination	Routes	up to 4+	5 to 6a+	6b to 7a	7a+ and up
The Ardeche	Chaulet Plage	*169*	5	56	58	50
The Ardeche	Mazet Plage	*114*	14	29	49	22
The Ardeche	Actinidias	*61*	3	11	11	36
The Ardeche	Le Cirque des Gens	*313*	12	57	149	95
The Ardeche	Les Branches	*45*	-	-	11	34
The Tarn Area	Gorge du Tarn	*286*	-	26	83	177
The Tarn Area	Gorge de la Jonte	*266*	9	75	91	91
The Tarn Area	Le Boffi	*179*	3	22	47	107
The Tarn Area	Cantobre	*57*	-	1	4	52
Thuarac Area	Thaurac	*158*	12	70	50	26
Thuarac Area	Hortus	*75*	1	19	37	18
Thuarac Area	Claret	*173*	-	15	71	87
The Gard	Seynes	*324*	36	106	92	90
The Gard	Russan	*236*	3	70	78	85
Massif des Alpilles	Mont Gaussier	*120*	-	29	49	42
Massif des Alpilles	Mouriès	*120*	5	36	46	33
Massif des Alpilles	Orgon	*334*	25	157	80	72

Approach	Sun	Multi-pitch	When wet	When hot	When cold	Summary	Page	Crag
15 to 19 min	Lots of sun		✘	✗	✔	A sunny spot with a great variety of grades, and a river to cool off in. It gets some shade in the morning and the campsite is just the other side of the river.	32	Chaulet
2 to 10 min	Afternoon		✘	✗	✔	Show up in the morning if you're looking for some shade, or the afternoon if chasing the sun - there is a river right by the crag for cooling off.	46	Mazet
2 to 5 min	Morning		✓	✓	✘	A pretty hard-core venue, get there in the morning if you want the sun. The Camping sector is a bit different, with much easier routes - almost inside the campsite.	60	Actinidias
10 to 20 min	Sun and shade		✓	✓	✔	An extensive crag that allows you to follow the shade or the sun throughout the day. It can be baking hot at one end, and nice and cool at the other.	70	Cirque Gens
30 min	Not much sun		✔	✔	✘	A hard crag that can be sheltered from rain - but will seep eventually. Hardly any sun, so come here in the summer, paddle across the river, and enjoy the shade.	90	Branches
Roadside 0 to 15 min	Sun and shade		✔	✔	✗	An extensive area where you can find sun and shade if you look for it. Unfortunately the all-weather crag is now closed, but there should be something steep enough to stay dry in rain.	100	Gorge du Tarn
10 to 20 min	Sun and shade	Multi-pitch	✗	✓	✓	An adventurous and exposed crag. It gets a lot of sun, but there are pockets of shade - and when you are high on a route you will probably catch a breeze.	134	La Jonte
30 to 40 min	Sun and shade		✓	✔	✓	Offers sun and shade in equal measures, so pick when and where you're heading carefully. If the weather is desperate, there is a small cave that is always dry, and some of the steeper routes may be OK in rain.	170	Le Boffi
30 to 35 min	Lots of sun		✓	✘	✔	A real furnace, with lots of sun. Good in the winter, but stay well-clear of it when it's hot. Some very steep ground around here so likely to be something dry in rain.	190	Cantobre
4 to 20 min	Sun and shade	Multi-pitch	✘	✓	✓	Many cliffs, facing different directions, but nothing very steep. You should be able to find something to climb here most times of the year.	200	Thaurac
30 to 35 min	Sun and shade	Multi-pitch	✘	✓	✗	A big, adventurous crag that gets lots of sun, but is high and exposed, so not so bad once you're up. Not somewhere you want to be in any extreme of weather; it's adventurous enough already.	218	Hortus
5 to 11 min	Lots of sun		✓	✘	✔	Plenty of sun and technical climbing make this a poor choice for summer, but it can be good in the winter. Some steep ground may provide sport during wet weather.	230	Claret
6 to 12 min	Lots of sun		✓	✘	✔	A reflector oven of a crag - avoid it in the summer. During the winter, you can climb here in shorts - even thought there's snow on the ground. Probably steep enough for some rain shelter.	246	Seynes
20 to 25 min	Sun and shade		✓	✗	✔	You should be able to find shade or sun here, and there are some very steep routes that will offer some protection against the rain. A good winter venue, like Seynes.	272	Russan
Roadside 0 to 22 min	Sun and shade		✓	✓	✓	Generally shady in the morning, but in an exposed position, so you can time your visit to get the sun or shade, there is probably something to do here in the rain if you find a steep project.	294	Gaussier
5 to 20 min	Not much sun		✘	✔	✘	A good choice for avoiding the sun, and very family friendly, you should expect to have to share the crag with others on a sunny weekend. Not steep enough to shelter from rain.	310	Mouriès
Roadside 0 to 20 min	Sun and shade		✔	✔	✔	A very extensive set of crags that surely offers something for everyone, whatever the weather. Head down to Canal if it's raining - you can probably find something to do.	328	Orgon

✔ - Definitely worth a look ✓ - Could be lucky ✗ - Probably not worth the effort ✘ - Forget it!

The Ardèche

What follows is a small selection of crags within an extensive climbing area. The crags of the Ardèche are found lining the banks of the spectacular rivers of the Ardèche and Chassezac. It is during the summer that the region really comes to life, the plentiful campsites fill up and the rivers play host to a steady stream of fair-weather canoeists. Though worthwhile as a climbing destination to anyone at any time of year, it is as a summer family holiday destination with a bit of rock and a bit of river that it truly excels.

Getting There and Getting Around

The nearest TGV stations are in Valence, Montélimar and Avignon. Logical places to fly to are: Nimes, Montpellier, and Marseilles. The areas of the Ardèche described here are around 40km west of the Autoroute du Soleil (A7), you will need a car to get around locally, but the roads are good.

Where to Stay

The area has a staggering array of campsites, far too many to mention here. Campsites are not open after October and before April, so if you're thinking of visiting during the winter, early spring, or late autumn (when conditions for climbing are likely to be at their best) you will need to find yourself a gîte. Winter rates are often very good and if you're sharing it may well work out only a little more than camping would have been. Campsites that are near to the crags are named in their relevant sections, and all have a web presence.

Local Guidebooks

L'escalade en Ardèche covers sport climbing, bouldering, and the numerous multi-pitch routes to be found in the area.

Web Links

www.ardeche.com - has an extensive list of campsites and other accommodation.

www.ardeche-tourisme.com - has plenty of useful information on how to get there on public transport and is available in English.

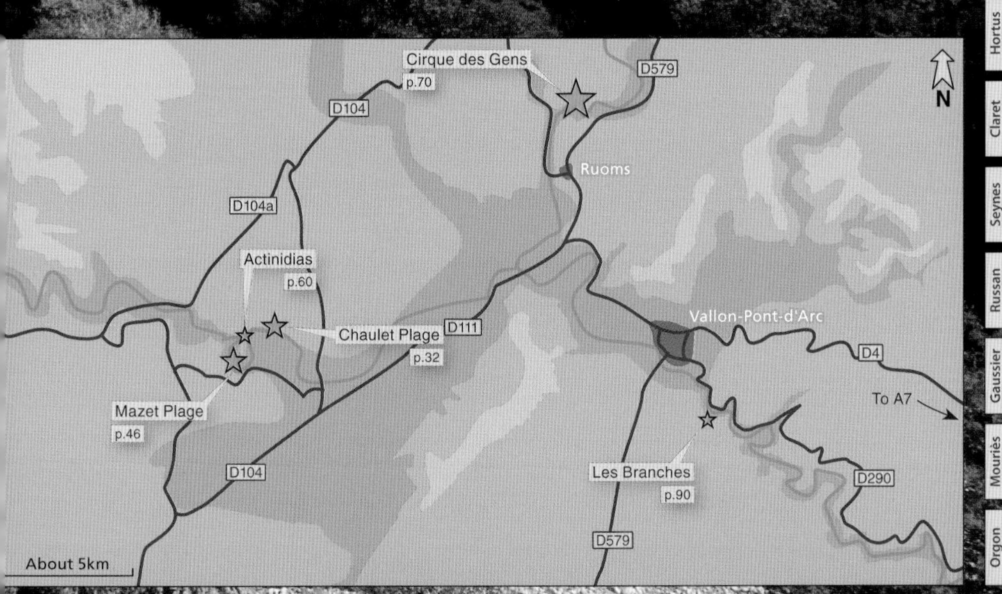

Renouveau
p.35
Mini-doux

Chaulet Plage

Chaulet Plage

	No star	1	2	3
Up to 4+	-	2	2	1
5 to 6a+	2	33	18	3
6b to 7a	3	27	23	5
7a+ and up	5	23	17	5

Chaulet is everything you might expect of an Ardèche crag; sunny limestone, great routes across a wide range of difficulties, camping within a stone's throw and a river that is sure to cool you off in the middle of a summer's day. The central section of crag has a lovely rock-beach that slopes down into the river - perfect for lazy picnics and serious sun-bathing.

The climbing is also top notch; excellent-quality rock and some beautiful, well-bolted routes. The idyllic beach does mean that the crag is quite popular and some of the routes are showing signs of age and polish, especially at the right-hand end of the crag.

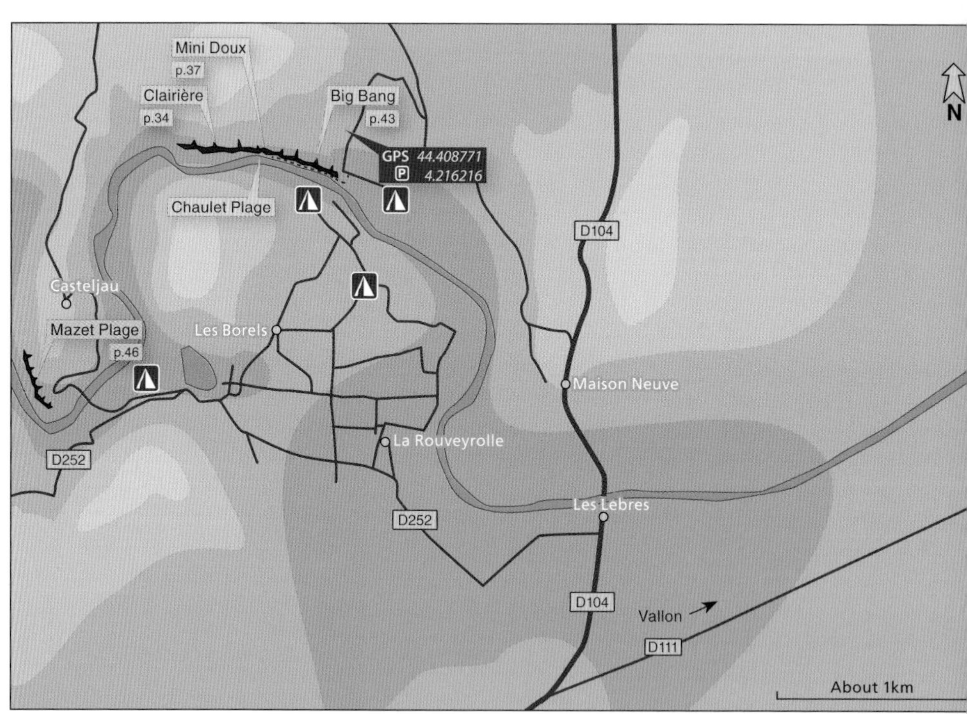

Approach

Also see map on page 29

From the parking area (signed Site d'Escalade), continue on foot down the road, ignoring a marked trail leading off to the right. Turn the bend in the road and take the steep path down on the right. Scramble down and turn right at the bottom, the crag soon appears on your righ
Alternatively, you can approach from the campsite across the river by wading or paddling - this is not an option in the winter, especially if the river is swollen.

Conditions

The crag faces south, and the only shade to be found is amongst the trees at the left-hand sid
During the winter, it's a great sun-trap, but in the summer be prepared to get hot.

Chaulet
Mazet
Actinidias
Cirque Gens
Les Branches
Gorge du Tarn
La Jonte
Le Boffi
Cantobre
Thaurac
Hortus
Claret
Seynes
Russan
Gaussier
Mouriès
Orgon

Jan Hadfield on *L'orange* (4+) - *page 39*

Chaulet
Mazet
Actinidias
Cirque Gens
Les Branches
Gorge du Tarn
La Jonte
Le Boffi
Cantobre
Thaurac
Hortus
Claret
Seynes
Russan
Gaussier
Mouriès
Orgon

No.	Route	Stars	Grade
1	Romuluc	1	6a+
2	Mosa-hic	1	5
3	La collante	1	5+
4	Sta-minette	1	5
5	Casse trop	1	5+
6	Bis trop	1	4+
7	Herbe us	2	4+
8	Bon pied bon deil	2	5+
9	Drine in 1) 5+, 2) 5+	2	5+
10	Sous dures 1) 6a, 2) 6a	2	6a
11	Chaussee glissante 1) 5+, 2) 5+	1	5+
12	Silence on ouvre 1) 5+, 2) 5+	1	5+
13	Un beret basque	1	6b
14	Gavroche 1) 3+, 2) 6a	1	6a
15	Trompe l'oeil	1	4+
16	Entre 2 tournées	1	6a
17	Les esperides 1) 5, 2) 4	1	5
18	Lucane	1	5+
19	A toi	1	5+
20	A moi	1	5+
21	C'est pas le pied 1) 6a, 2) 5+	1	6a
22	Impasse 1) 5+, 2) 5+	1	5+
23	Premiere emotion 1) 5, 2) 5	2	5
24	En guise de dessert	1	6a
25	As.be.lou.tims. 1) 6c, 2) 6a	1	6c

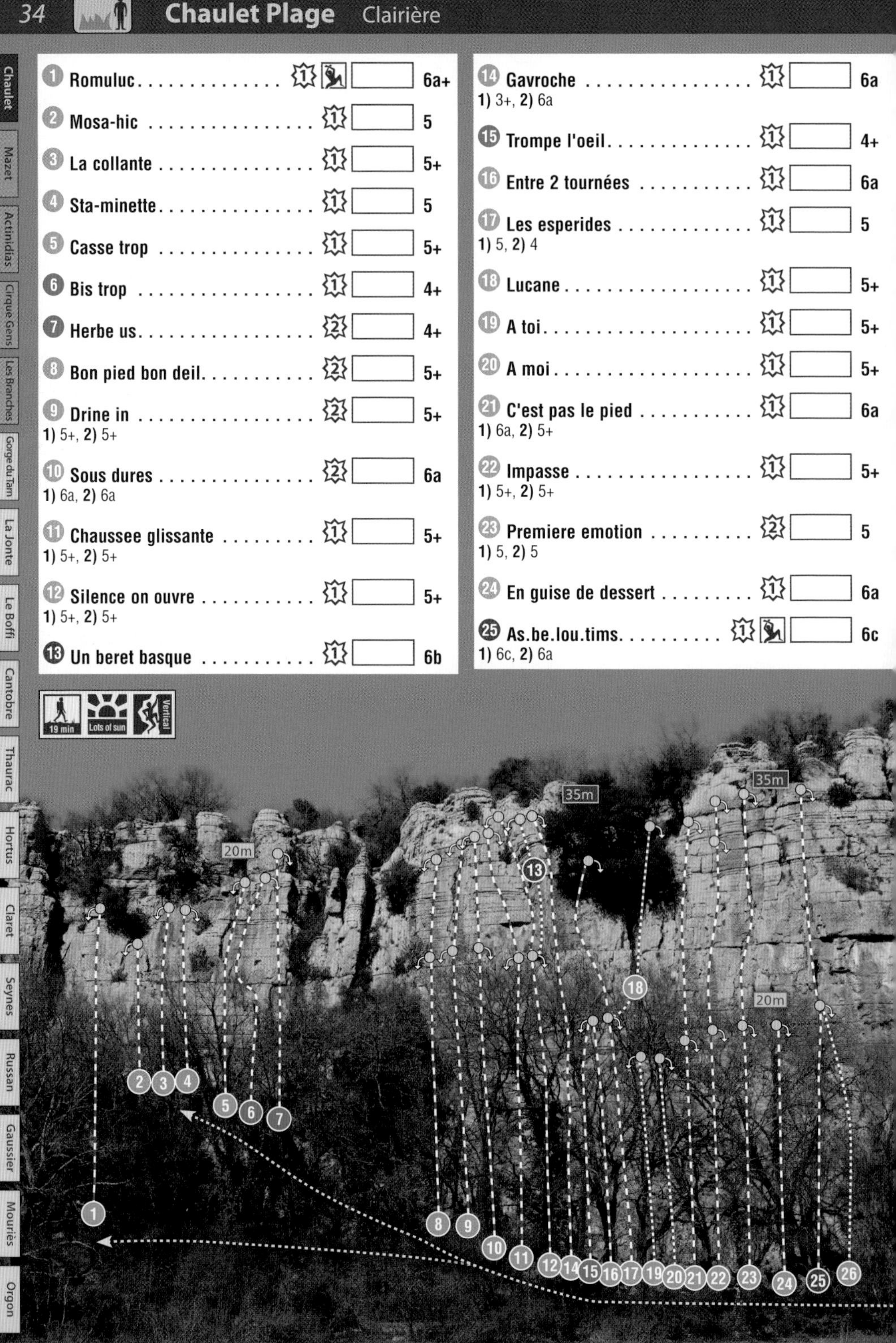

26 **Pain d'épices** .... 2 6a+

27 **Magique** 1 6c
1) 6c, **2)** 5+. May need some gardening.

28 **Adadalle** .... 2 7a+

29 **Con fiance** 2 6a

30 **La conque** 3 6b
1) 6b, **2)** 6a

31 **L'astragale** 1 6a
1) 6a, **2)** 6a

32 **Toto le topo** 2 7a

33 **Cocotte** 2 7b

34 **Passt-dies?** 2 7a

35 **Contre toute apparence** 1 6c
Can be extended into one of the following two routes.

36 **Le joueur deploque** 1 7c

37 **Cheminot** 2 6b

38 **Bychotrope** .... 2 6b+

39 **L'andouille** .... 1 5+

40 **Chez cailliou** 1 7a

41 **D.Day** .... 3 6a+

42 **La didi** 2 6c

43 **Clara** 7b

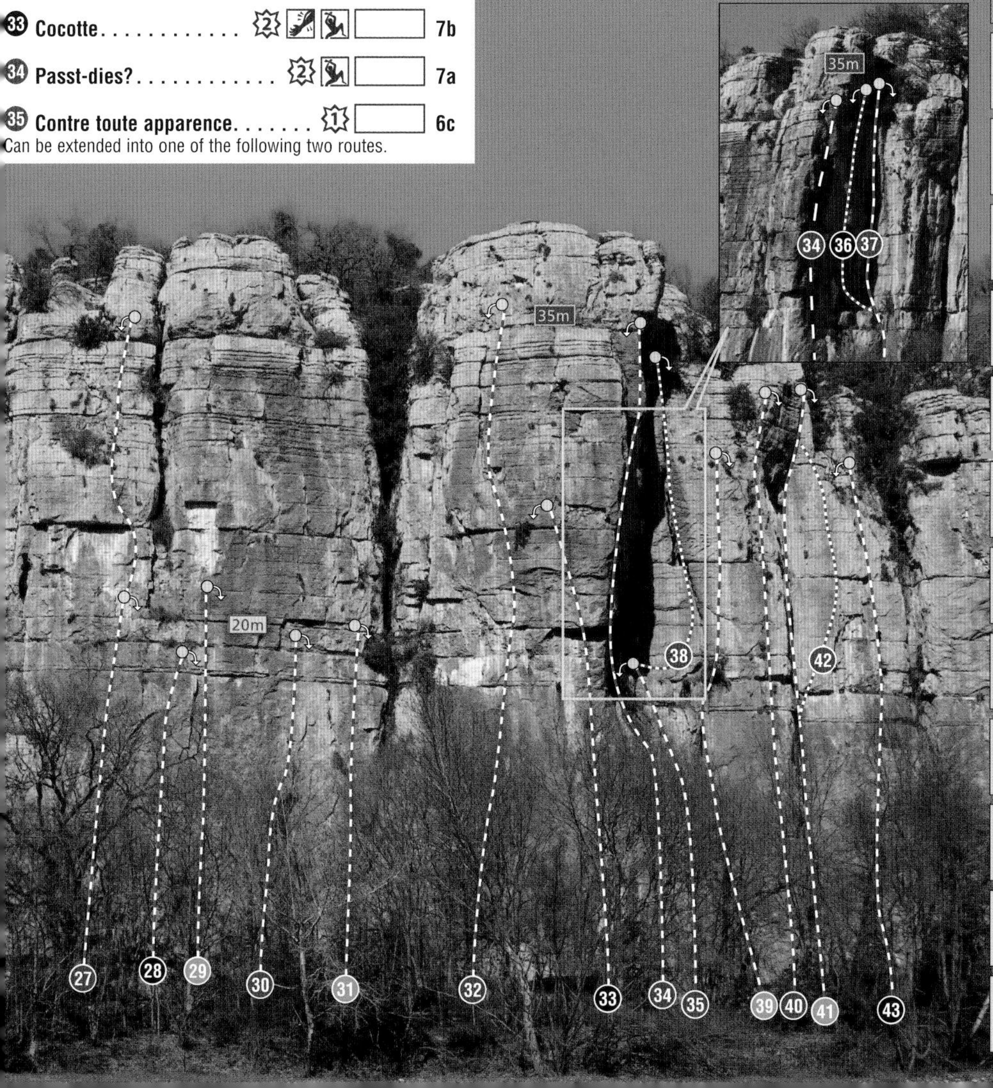

35m

20m

35m

27 28 29 30 31 32 33 34 35 39 40 41 43

34 36 37

38 42

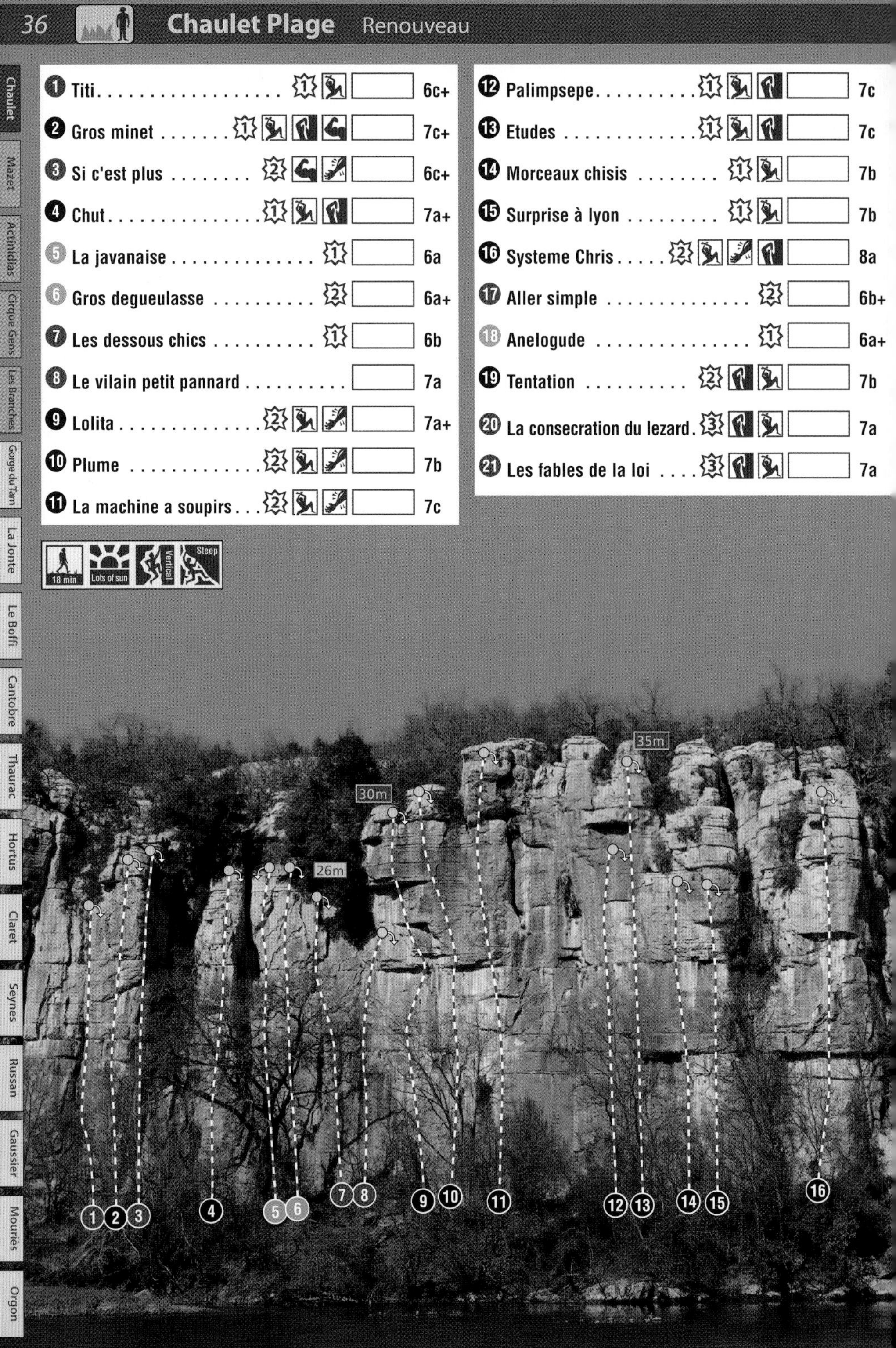

1 Titi 6c+
2 Gros minet 7c+
3 Si c'est plus 6c+
4 Chut 7a+
5 La javanaise 6a
6 Gros degueulasse 6a+
7 Les dessous chics 6b
8 Le vilain petit pannard 7a
9 Lolita 7a+
10 Plume 7b
11 La machine a soupirs 7c
12 Palimpsepe 7c
13 Etudes 7c
14 Morceaux chisis 7b
15 Surprise à lyon 7b
16 Systeme Chris 8a
17 Aller simple 6b+
18 Anelogude 6a+
19 Tentation 7b
20 La consecration du lezard 7a
21 Les fables de la loi 7a
18 min
Lots of sun
Vertical
Steep
35m
30m
26m
1 2 3 4 5 6 7 8 9 10 11 12 13 14 15 16
Chaulet
Mazet
Actinidias
Cirque Gens
Les Branches
Gorge du Tarn
La Jonte
Le Boffi
Cantobre
Thaurac
Hortus
Claret
Seynes
Russan
Gaussier
Mouriès
Orgon

	Route		Grade
22	Penitence	1	7a+
23	Sacrifice	1	7a+
24	Preferences		6b
25	Rn 86	2	5
26	Qu'ouyge	2	6b+
27	Les pieds dans les nuages	3	6b
28	Les morsures de l'aube		6a+
29	Le soleil n'est pas pour nous		6a+
30	Anastasia	1	6a+
31	Ivanhoe	2	6c
32	Les portes du dessert	1	6c

Mini-doux

Along with Les Mots Croisés, this is probably the best section of the crag, with classic routes of all levels of difficulty, and well-placed for a quick swim to the campsite on the opposite side of the river.

	Route		Grade
33	La honte du Chassezac	1	6c+
34	Talon aiguille	1	7b+
35	Coeur croise **1)** 6b, **2)** 6c+	1	6c+
36	Sachez croiser **1)** 5+, **2)** 5	1	5+
37	Les oreilles rouge **1)** 5+, **2)** 6a	2	6a
38	Prix femina	1	7a+
39	Hans a sa place	2	5+
40	Tricosteril	2	6a

Route	Stars	Tick	Grade
1 **Strapal** 1) 5+, 2) 5+	2		5+
2 **L'ebat de nylon** 1) 5+, 2) 5+. The first bolt is a bit high.	2		5+
3 **La prehension** Another high first bolt.	2		6b
4 **Chaulet marron**	1		7a+
5 **Maxi dur**	1		7a
6 **Mini-doux**	2		7a
7 **Solexine**	1		6c
8 **Solioque**	2		6c
9 **Corner**	2		6a
10 **Os court**	3		6b
11 **Tqb**			?

Miles Gibson on *Bombine* 7b+ - *opposite*.

Les Mots Croisés

A popular wall with some great routes on immaculate rock. Don't be tempted to go swing too early in the day otherwise you may find it difficult to get back to the climbing.

12 Le joute en fleur ..... 2 — **7a+**

13 Bombine .... 3 — **7b+**
Photo opposite.

14 Le fils prodigue .... 2 — **6b**

15 Culotte courte .... 3 — **5**
1) 5, **2)** 5

16 Les mots croisés ...... 2 — **6c**

17 Blues en bloc .... 2 — **7c**

18 Audimat .... 1 — **7a+**

19 Bouse en stock .... 1 — **7c**

20 Le grand bleu .... 2 — **7a+**
1) 7a+, **2)** 7a+

21 Un morceau d'histoire .... 1 — **6b**

22 Pourquoi tant de hargne ... 1 — **6c**
1) 6c, **2)** 6b

23 Silex sort .... 2 — **6b**

24 Siesta............... 2 — **6a**

25 L'orange .... 3 — **4+**
1) 4+, **2)** 4+. A great line which can be climbed in one big pitch.
Photo on page 33.

26 Allez au diable .... 3 — **6a+**

27 Gaffe aux formes .... 1 — **7a**

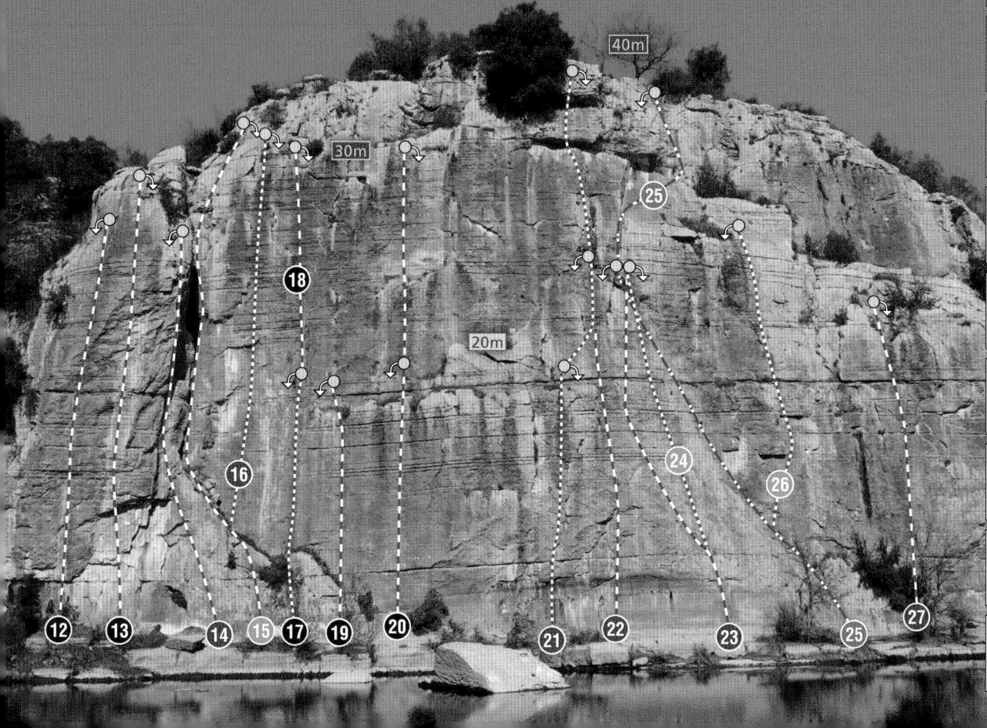

Chaulet
Mazet
Actinidias
Cirque Gens
Les Branches
Gorge du Tarn
La Jonte
Le Boffi
Cantobre
Thaurac
Hortus
Claret
Seynes
Russan
Gaussier
Mouriès
Orgon

No.	Route	Stars	Grade
1	La velo d'yves	2	6b
2	Sans pitié	2	6c
3	Presse bouc	2	7b
4	Devoir de vacances	1	7a+
5	Enigme	2	6a
6	Le ramoneur	2	4+
7	Surprise de taille	1	6c+
8	Alfond	2	5
9	Pince oreille	1	6b+
10	Aaricia	1	6a
11	Alinoé	1	5+
12	Tanatloc	1	5+
13	A loi du talon	1	7a
14	Snake	1	6c
15	L'oubli	1	6b
16	A la bélina	1	6b
17	Primadonna	1	5
18	Primavéra	1	5+
19	Avalon	1	6a
20	Aupres de mon arbre	1	5
21	Hold-up	1	5+

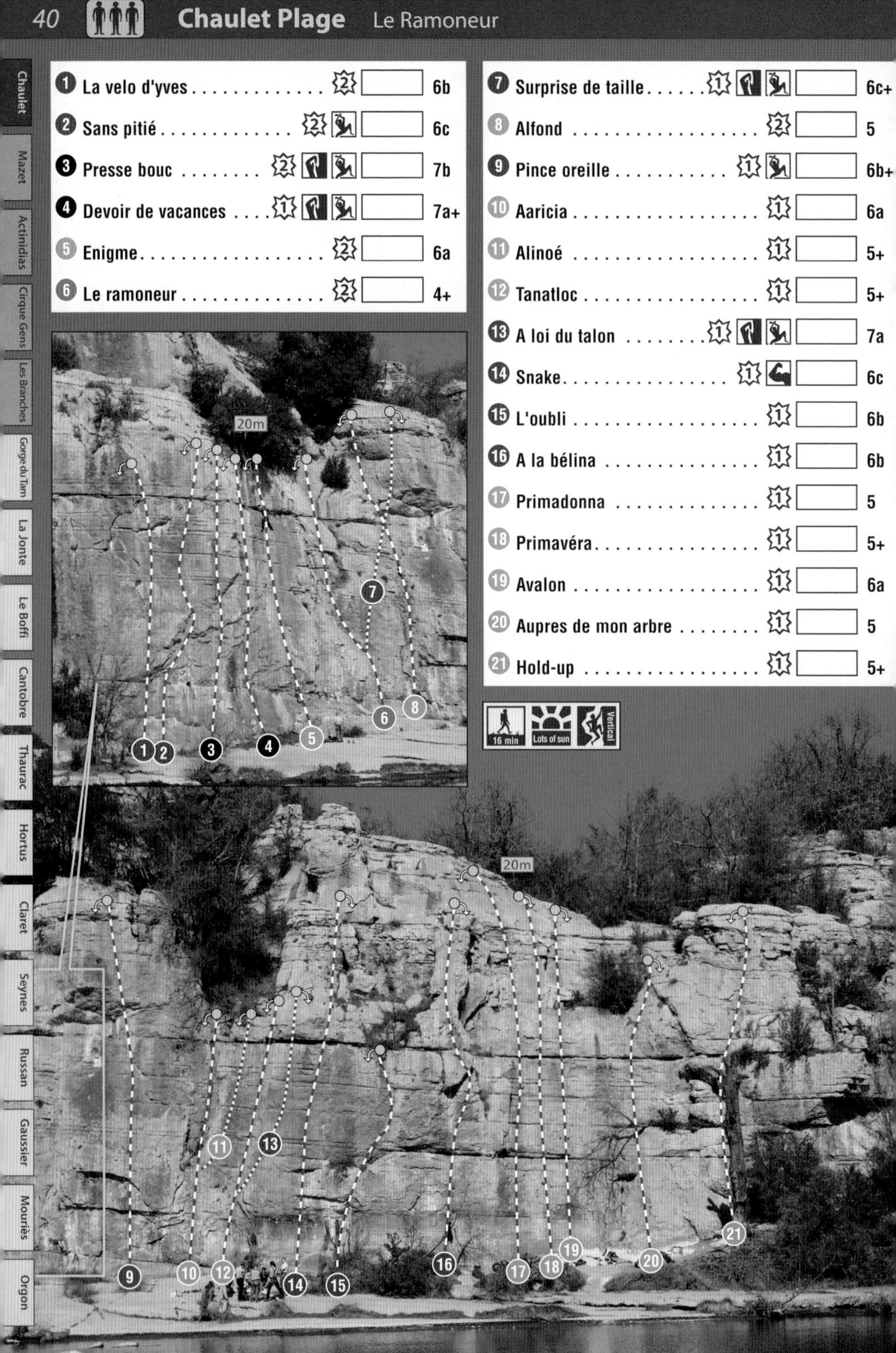

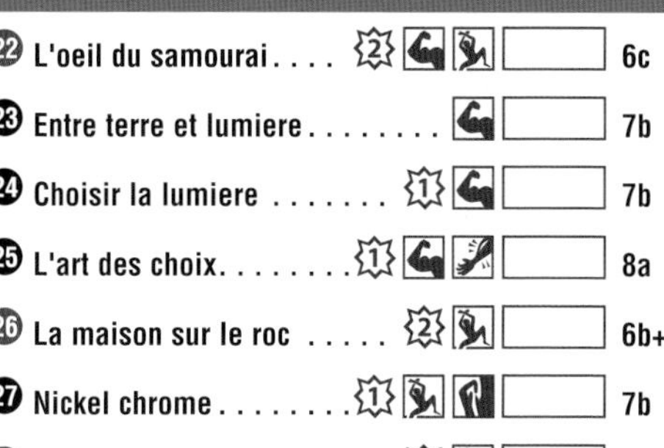

No.	Route	Stars	Grade
22	L'oeil du samourai	2	6c
23	Entre terre et lumiere		7b
24	Choisir la lumiere	1	7b
25	L'art des choix	1	8a
26	La maison sur le roc	2	6b+
27	Nickel chrome	1	7b
28	La vie éternelle	2	6c
29	Ichtis	1	6b
30	Anak raja	1	7b

Chaulet Mazet Actinidias Cirque Gens Les Branches Gorge du Tarn La Jonte Le Boffi Cantobre Thaurac Hortus Claret Seynes Russan Gaussier Mouriès Orgon

No.	Route	Stars	Grade
1	Only by Grace	1	7b
2	Grosse fatigue	2	7a+
3	L'arome antique	2	8a
4	Au seuil du mystere	2	8a+
5	Fortune carée	1	8a+
6	Eva luna	3	7c+
7	Vie d'artiste	3	7c+
8	Halte a la Gariboi	3	7b+
9	Garidroite	2	6c
10	Vibration	3	7c+
11	Ying-yang	2	7c+
12	Jeux de main jeu de villain	2	7c
13	Y'en a qu'une, c'est la tune	1	8a
14	Le repos du guerrier	2	7a+

Jo Varela on *Born Again* (6c) - *opposite*

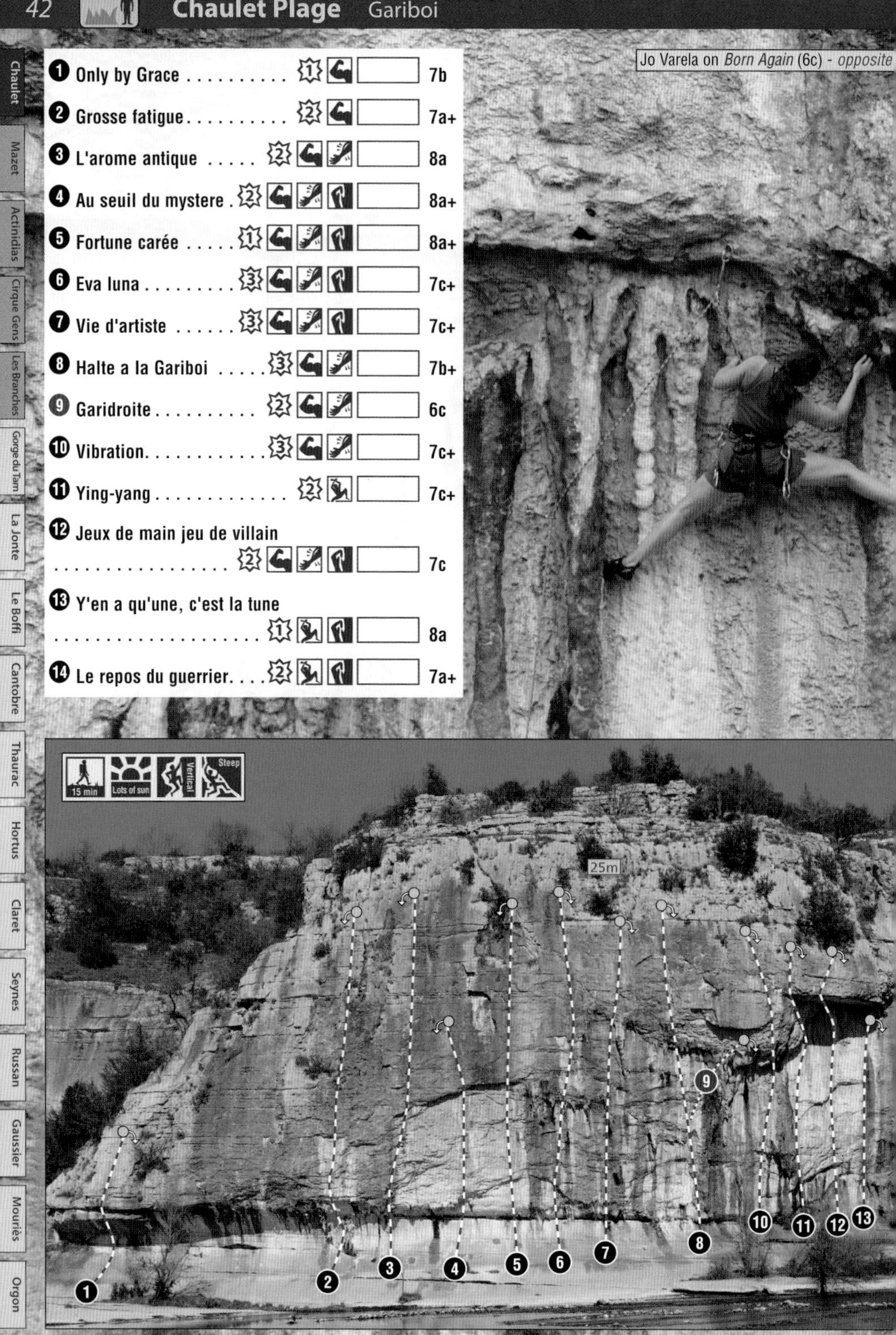

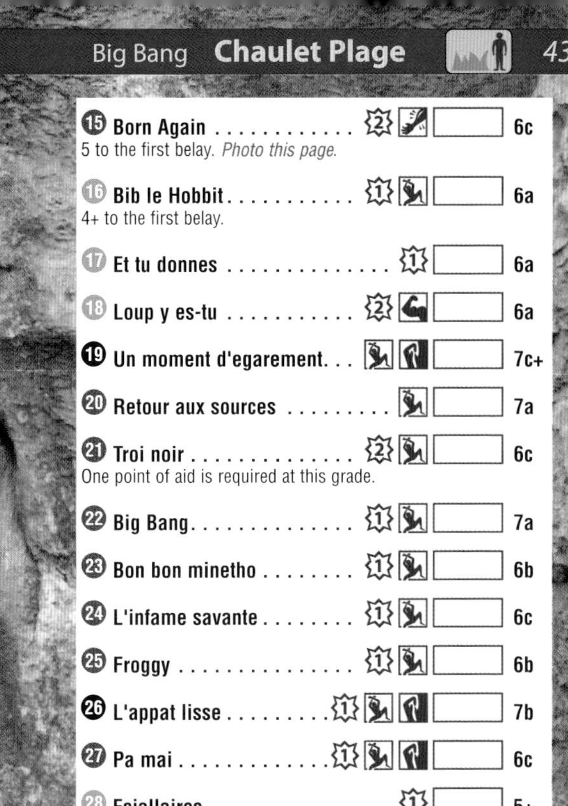

15 Born Again .... 2 stars, 6c
5 to the first belay. *Photo this page.*

16 Bib le Hobbit .... 1 star, 6a
4+ to the first belay.

17 Et tu donnes .... 1 star, 6a

18 Loup y es-tu .... 2 stars, 6a

19 Un moment d'egarement ... 7c+

20 Retour aux sources 7a

21 Troi noir .... 2 stars, 6c
One point of aid is required at this grade.

22 Big Bang .... 1 star, 7a

23 Bon bon minetho .... 1 star, 6b

24 L'infame savante .... 1 star, 6c

25 Froggy .... 1 star, 6b

26 L'appat lisse .... 1 star, 7b

27 Pa mai .... 1 star, 6c

28 Esjallaires .... 1 star, 5+

La Plage
p.48

La Familiale
Chez Les Grands
Pilier Gris
Les Strates
p.54
p.52
p.51
p.53

Mazet Plage

Mazet Plage

	No star	1	2	3
Up to 4+	-	10	4	-
5 to 6a+	7	12	8	2
6b to 7a	9	12	21	7
7a+ and up	11	4	6	1

With a very short approach, a range of excellent routes across the grades, a campsite a short walk away, and a river at its base, there's little wonder that Mazet is a popular spot. Due to its popularity, Mazet does have a fair amount of polish on its classic routes, which does add a grade or so of difficulty to the most severely affected routes. That being said, it is still an enchanting spot, very family friendly and well worth a visit.

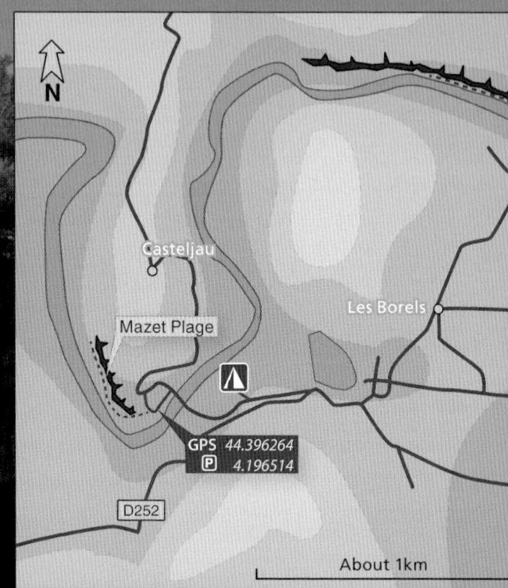

Approach Also see maps on pages 29 and 32

Leave the D252 and follow the road (avoiding the driving into the campsite) across the bridge, and follow the sign into the car park. From here simply follow the river around to the right (looking out) and the crag starts in under a minute.

Conditions

Facing southwest, Mazet gets morning shade and afternoon sun. The river gorge provides some shade in the late afternoon as the shadow slowly works its way up the wall.

Sam Harvie on the superb *Aerostrates* (6c+) - worth a couple of grades more in the heat of the sun - *page 53*.

La Plage
At the far left end of the crag there stands a three-legged tree, which may have something to do with some of the route names hereabouts.
1 Arwen 2 6a+
2 2 chevaur fiaseus 1 6c+
3 Bombadil 1 6c+
4 Gai dol 1 6b
5 Gandalf 3 5
6 Change des vues 2 6c
7 Escargots Show 2 6b
8 Voleur de sang 2 6a
9 Ombre 2 6c
10 Eile doit exister la plage 1 7a
1) 7a, 2) 6c
11 Mystique 2 7a
12 L'odyssee barbare 1 7a
13 Greu du coeur 1 6b
14 La bombe anatomique 1 6b
15 Dégivrage 1 6b+
Morning
10 min
Vertical
50m
30m
30m

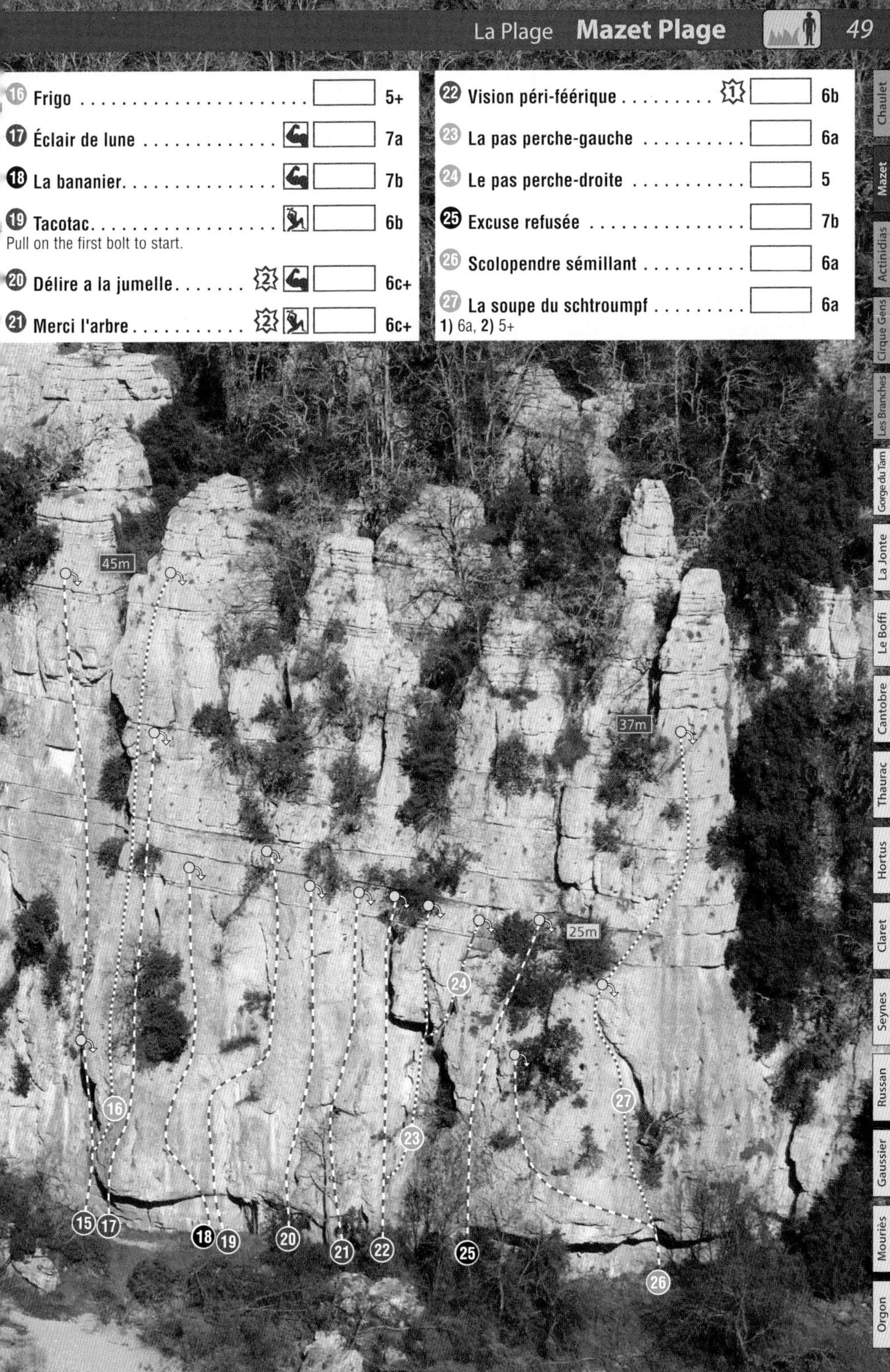

16 **Frigo** .... 5+

17 **Éclair de lune** 7a

18 **La bananier** 7b

19 **Tacotac** 6b
Pull on the first bolt to start.

20 **Délire a la jumelle** .... 2 6c+

21 **Merci l'arbre** .... 2 6c+

22 **Vision péri-féérique** 1 6b

23 **La pas perche-gauche** 6a

24 **Le pas perche-droite** 5

25 **Excuse refusée** 7b

26 **Scolopendre sémillant** 6a

27 **La soupe du schtroumpf** 6a
1) 6a, **2)** 5+

Chaulet
Mazet
Actinidias
Cirque Gens
Les Branches
Gorge du Tarn
La Jonte
Le Boffi
Cantobre
Thaurac
Hortus
Claret
Seynes
Russan
Gaussier
Mouriès
Orgon

Doigt de Fée and Pilier Gris

Doigt de Fée hosts a collection of mostly easier routes that are popular with groups, so expect some polish on the easy ones. A little to the right, Pilier Gris is another popular spot with a wide range of grades on offer.

	Route	Stars		Grade
1	2 cotes plus loin	1		4
2	Nez en l'air	1		4
3	Ballerine fusion	1		4
4	Mains chaudes	1		4+
5	Pied de nez	2		6b
6	Doigt de fée	2		6a
7	De bouche à l'oreille	2		5
8	Diedre a l'oeil	2		4+
9	Genou eclair	1		4
10	Premiere manche	1		3+

The following two routes are to be found on the pillar a little way to the right.

	Route		Grade
11	Pile		5
12	Face		5

No.	Route	Stars	Grade
13	T'as boule (1) 4+, 2) 4+)	2	4+
14	Quelques pattes (1) 5, 2) 5)	2	5
15	Pois chiche (1) 6a+, 2) 6a+)	1	6a+
16	Rio-laid (1) 5, 2) 5)	2	5
17	Tapis au cas (1) 4+, 2) 4+)	2	4+
18	Fenetre sur cour	1	4+
19	Frenzi	1	5
20	Poe	1	7a
21	Les trente-neuf marches	1	5
22	L'ombre d'un doubte	1	4+
23	Pilier gris	2	6b+
24	Les diaboliques	1	4+
25	Magie noire	2	6c
26	Vertigo	1	5
27	La mort aux trousses (1) 5+, 2) 5)	2	5+
28	Complot de famille (1) 6b, 2) 5+)	3	6b
29	Magie blanche	2	7b
30	Reve d'une planete	2	6b
31	La fissure	1	5+

Afternoon · 5 min · Slabby · Vertical

40m

20m

31 in the trees

Chaulet
Mazet
Actinidias
Cirque Gens
Les Branches
Gorge du Tarn
La Jonte
Le Boffi
Cantobre
Thaurac
Hortus
Claret
Seynes
Russan
Gaussier
Mouriès
Orgon

La Familiale and Les Strates

The most popular part of the crag with a good range of excellent routes. Expect some polish on the most popular routes. If you are using a rope shorter than 80m, you will need to stop at a belay either on the way up or the way down to get to the top of the routes at La Familiale.

1. **Touchée manquée** . . . . 1 star ☐ 6a
2. **Les loups entreux** . . . . 1 star ☐ 6a
3. **Je t'aime moi non plus** . . . . 1 star ☐ 5
4. **Rando** . . . . 2 star ☐ 4+
   1) 4+, 2) 4+
5. **Variante** . . . . 1 star ☐ 5
6. **Mauvais limonade** . . . . . 2 star ☐ 6c
   1) 6a+, 2) 6c
7. **Le toit emoi** . . . . 3 star ☐ 6a
   1) 5, 2) Either continue to a belay below the roof (5) or better, climb further right and pull through the roof on jugs (6a).
8. **Le toit du moi** . . . . 2 star ☐ 6b
   1) 5, 2) 6b
9. **La familiale** . . . . 1 star ☐ 4
   1) 4, 2) 4, 3) 4. An interesting link-up taking in the easiest sections to the top - abseil off.
10. **La gellie** . . . . 1 star ☐ 5
11. **La voie du van** . . . . 2 star ☐ 6c
12. **Semoule en transmutation** . ☐ 7a

Eivind Flobak on *Les Strates* (6b) - *this page.*

13 Les uns and les autres . 2 6c

14 Aerostrates . . . . 3 6c+

Photo on page 47.

15 Les strates 3 6b

A classic of the crag is excellent but now polished way above its original 6a grade - a soft 6b, but not *that* soft. The extension to the top of the crag is 6a. *Photo this page.*

16 Pinky . . . . 3 6b+

17 Zab . . . . 1 7a+

Chaulet
Mazet
Actinidias
Cirque Gens
Les Branches
Gorge du Tarn
La Jonte
Le Boffi
Cantobre
Thaurac
Hortus
Claret
Seynes
Russan
Gaussier
Mouriès
Orgon

1 **Ardéchoice quality** . . . . . 2★ 7a

2 **Les matins qui chantent** . 2★ 6c

3 **La roro** . . . . 2★ 6c

4 **La bis-bis** . . . . 3★ 6c

5 **Biscotte** 6c

6 **Rose bis** . . . . 2★ 7b
The left of two prominent tufas.

7 **Prisonnier** . . . . 2★ 7c
The right tufa.

8 **Blablacher** . . . . 2★ 7a
The pale rock to start.

9 **L'isoutenable légèreté de l'être** . . . . 2★ 7b+

10 **Courpatas** 7a

Afternoon 3 min Vertical Steep

Chez Les Grands

At the right-hand side of Mazet is this superb wall featuring a mix of technical wall climbing, and some impressive tufas. These routes will all feel a lot harder in the heat, so get here in the morning if you're not here in the winter.

30m
35m
25m

⓫ **Unknown**			☐	?
⓬ **Colonne pas nette**	2		☐	7a
⓭ **Unknown**	1		☐	?
⓮ **Tu peux gueuler**	2		☐	7b
⓯ **Pince sans rire**			☐	6c
⓰ **Unknown**			☐	?

⓱ **Grand Panda**	3		☐	6c+
⓲ **Unknown**			☐	?
⓳ **Bouboulina**	2		☐	7b
⓴ **Sikamou**	3		☐	7b

Brilliant climbing leads to a depressingly technical finish.

㉑ **Kasidur**	3		☐	7a
㉒ **Sader**	2		☐	6c

No.	Route	Grade
1	Le chachou	7b
2	Affreux pastis	7b+
3	Super bébé	7a
4	Unknown	?
5	Unknown	7a+
6	Unknown	7c
7	Petit break	7a+
8	Les temps des pirates	7b
9	Eau de valse	7b
10	Aloha Aloha	7a
11	Les filles de l'air	5
12	Raison du plus sobre	5
13	Mazette!	6b
14	Yol	5
15	Starting bloc	6b
16	Anthologie mania	6b
17	Zorro	6b

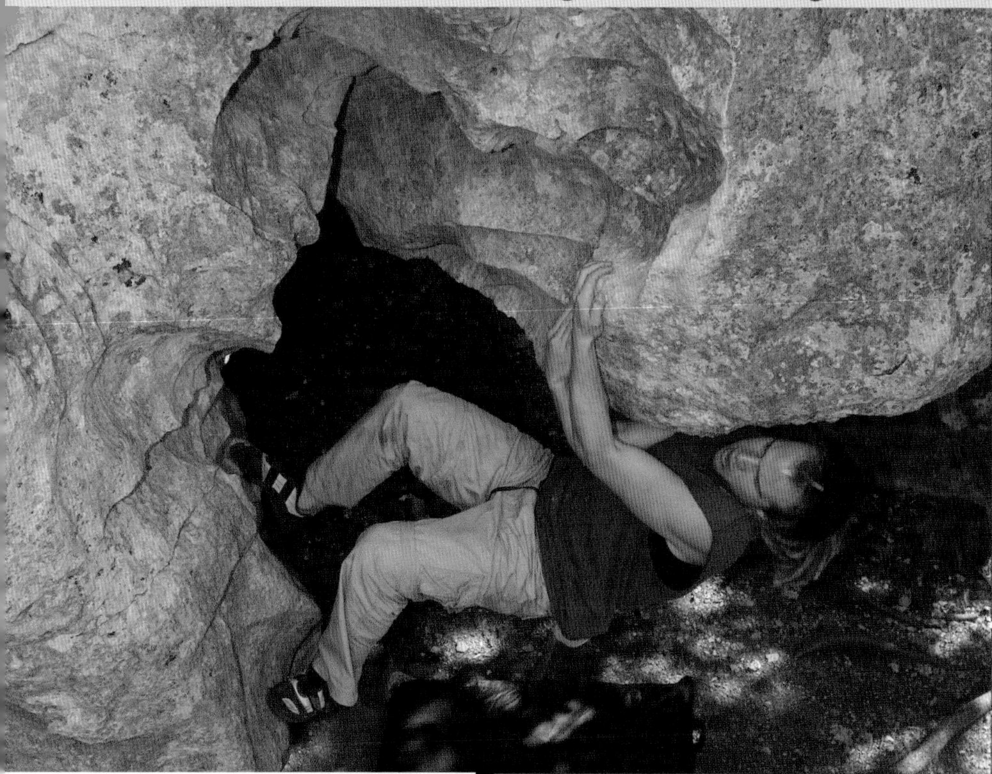

Daniel Hüttel enjoying one of the best problems on the blue circuit.

A short distance from Mazet and Actinidias is this superb little bouldering area. It has a similar feel to Fontainebleau. It offers plenty of high-quality problems with everything from powerful highballs through to children's circuits. This would be a great place to get used to the rock at the start of a trip, and there's plenty here for a day or two. Circuits are arranged by colour. It's well worth bringing a bouldering pad though since some of the problems are quite high.

Approach Also see maps on pages 29 and 32

From Mazet, continue up the hill along the D452, passing a sign to Actinidias campsite. Continue for a short distance and turn right at the T junction. Continue along the road until you reach a parking area on the left, signed l'Agachou. Walk back up the road for a couple of hundred metres, and you should see the boulders through the trees. The area on the left side of the road is mostly easier, and the area on the right is more serious. It should be noted that the area on the right is bordered by a very high cliff and so worth watching out for young ones.

Conditions

There is plenty of shade, so a good place to head if it's a bit too sunny. The rock dries quickly after rain.

Chaulet
Mazet
Actinidias
Cirque Gens
Les Branches
Gorge du Tarn
La Jonte
Le Boffi
Cantobre
Thaurac
Hortus
Claret
Seynes
Russan
Gaussier
Mouriès
Orgon

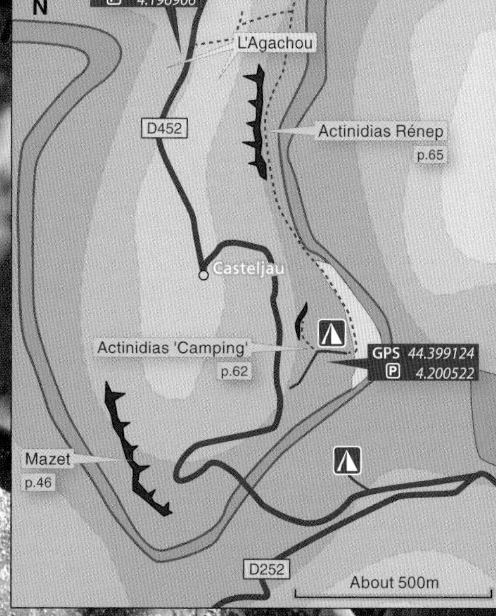

Actinidias

Actinidias

	No star	1	2	3
Up to 4+	2	-	1	-
5 to 6a+	2	7	2	-
6b to 7a	-	3	6	2
7a+ and up	6	14	16	-

A small but significant pair of crags. Sector Le camping is a friendly spot just above the campsite. In contrast, the main crag has a concentration of very accessible hard routes up a jaw-dropping leaning wall. Next to the campsite is a charming beach, with potential for some serious deep-water soloing and even greater potential for some serious sun-lounging.

Approach

Also see maps on pages 29 and 32

To approach the left side of the crag, approach as for Mazet along the D453 (page 46) but continue driving up the hill for a couple of hundred metres until you see a sign to the right for Camping Actinidias, turn down here and park opposite the entrance to the car park. During off season this car park is closed, but there is enough space at the entrance for a few cars. Access the Camping sector by walking back up the road about fifty metres, and following a trail to the right - just above the campsite. To access the main crag - Actinidias Renep - walk down the river-side and follow a path, heading down-river, around the perimeter of the campsite. Do not enter the campsite - unless of course you are staying there.

The alternative approach is quicker for accessing the right-hand side of the crag, and there are a lot more spaces to park. Continue along the D452 past a T-junction until you reach a layby on the left and an extensive parking area in the trees on the right. There are some large trail-maps at the side of the road. Park here and pick up a path that is marked with yellow dashes (it goes left at the first spilt and right at the second). This leads downhill until you reach another path that follows the river. Turn right and you will shortly appear at the right-hand side of the crag.

Conditions

Both walls are east-facing, and get plenty of shade in the afternoon, making this a good venue for lazy starts in the summer months. Expect it to get a bit chilly at other times of the year as the trees provide a lot of shade in the mornings.

Pete Benson exploring the deep-water soloing posibilities at Actinidias. Photo by Andy Benson.

Sam Harvie on *Rataplan* (7a) - *next page*.

Le Camping

Situated above the campsite, this small area has a number of worthwhile routes that have heavy tree cover. Expect to encounter some polish.

1 **Maraboum** . . . . (2 stars) 5+

2 **Patchamama** . . . . (1 star) 6b+

3 **Vol sur un nid de frelons** . . . . . . (1 star) 6a
The start is desperate - use aid at this grade.

4 **Tilt** . . . . (1 star) 6a+
Start at right at this grade - the direct is more like 6b+.

5 **Le retour du lisse** 6a
Climb on the right at this grade - 6c if taken direct.

6 **Castapiane** . . . . (2 stars) 6b+
A tough start leads to much easier

7 **Vol du marcassin** . . . . (3 stars) 6c

8 **Les pantouflards** . . . . (1 star) 5

The next routes are about 15m to the right.

9 **To Mine or not to Mine** . . . . (1 star) 5
The left side of the wall finishing up the hanging slab.

10 **La fee** . . . . (1 star) 5
The shorter line, to the right finishing with a crack.

11 **Du chewing-gum plein les bottles** (2 stars) 4
The slabby wall and groove with a mid-way belay.

12 **Unknown** 4

13 **Suisse Again** 5
The wall just left of a prominent flake.

14 **Aqui lou marie lou** . . . . 4+
A very short pitch ending just left of a big bush.

15 **Vertige** . . . . (2 stars) 5+
Finish up the prominent corner crack.

The last route isn't shown on the topo.

16 **Rataplan** . . . . (2 stars) 7a
The last route is clearly harder than the rest. Start right of the previous route, it shares the mid-section of the previous route. *Photo on previous page.*

Morning
2 min
Slabby
Vertical
Steep
20m
30m
9
10
11
12
13
14
15
16
16
Chaulet
Mazet
Actinidias
Cirque Gens
Les Branches
Gorge du Tam
La Jonte
Le Boffi
Cantobre
Thaurac
Hortus
Claret
Seynes
Russan
Gaussier
Mouriès
Orgon

Tim Parkinson on the crux of *La voie du vévé* (7b) - *page 67*.

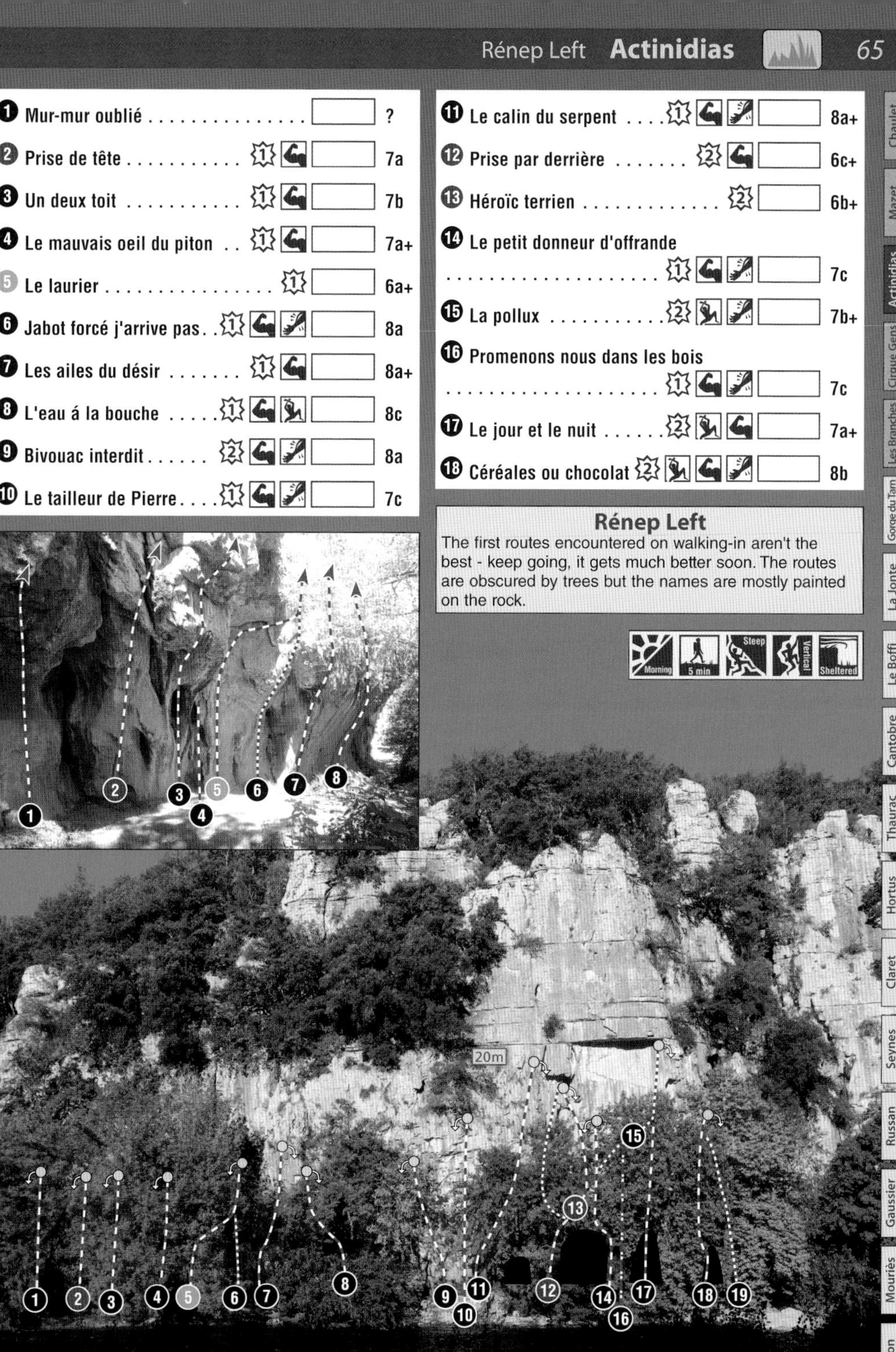

No.	Route	Stars	Grade
1	Mur-mur oublié		?
2	Prise de tête	1	7a
3	Un deux toit	1	7b
4	Le mauvais oeil du piton	1	7a+
5	Le laurier	1	6a+
6	Jabot forcé j'arrive pas	1	8a
7	Les ailes du désir	1	8a+
8	L'eau á la bouche	1	8c
9	Bivouac interdit	2	8a
10	Le tailleur de Pierre	1	7c
11	Le calin du serpent	1	8a+
12	Prise par derrière	2	6c+
13	Héroïc terrien	2	6b+
14	Le petit donneur d'offrande	1	7c
15	La pollux	2	7b+
16	Promenons nous dans les bois	1	7c
17	Le jour et le nuit	2	7a+
18	Céréales ou chocolat	2	8b

Rénep Left

The first routes encountered on walking-in aren't the best - keep going, it gets much better soon. The routes are obscured by trees but the names are mostly painted on the rock.

Chaulet Mazet Actinidias Cirque Gens Les Branches Gorge du Tarn La Jonte Le Boffi Cantobre Thaurac Hortus Claret Seynes Russan Gaussier Mouriès Orgon

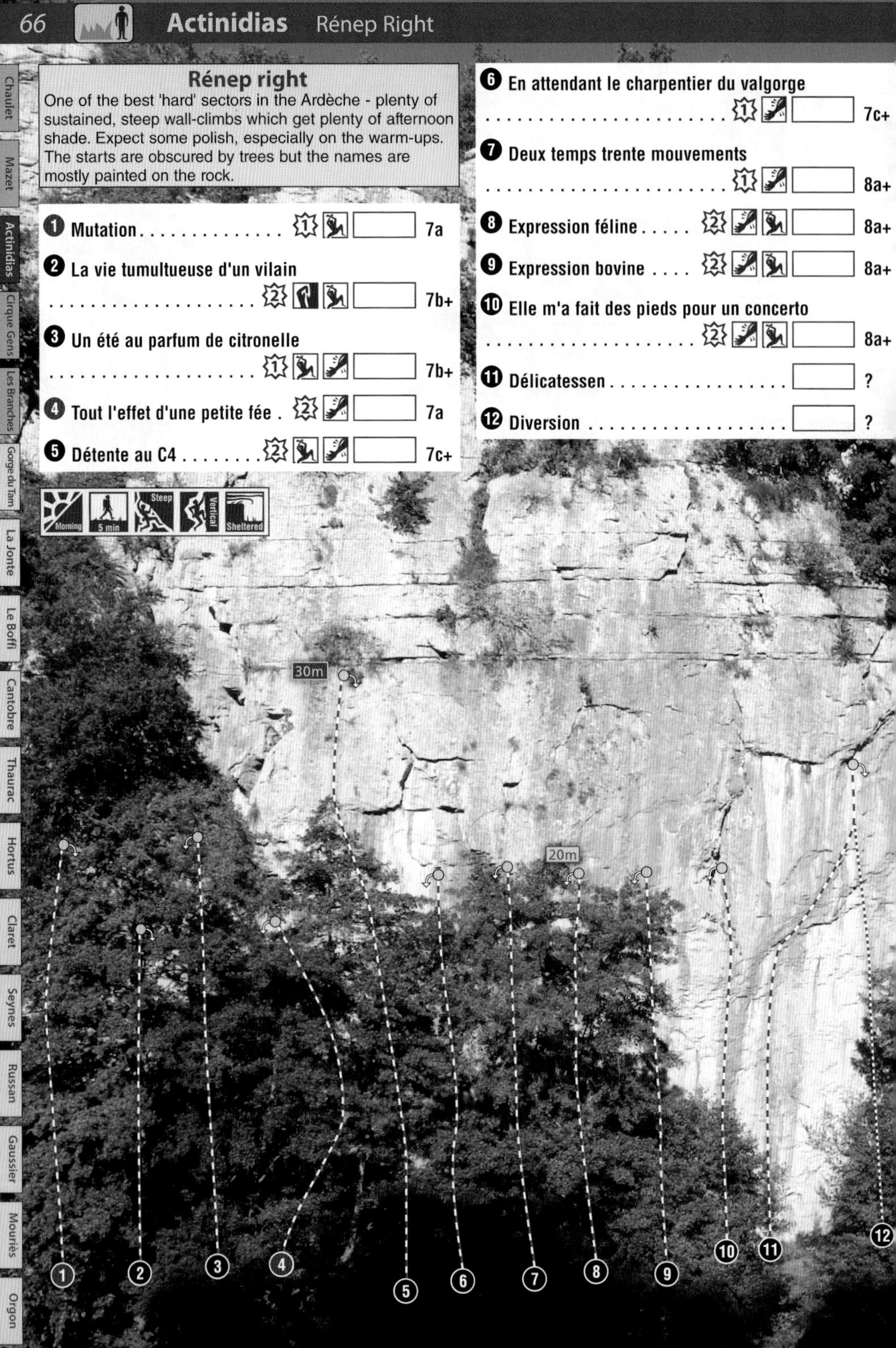

Rénep right

One of the best 'hard' sectors in the Ardèche - plenty of sustained, steep wall-climbs which get plenty of afternoon shade. Expect some polish, especially on the warm-ups. The starts are obscured by trees but the names are mostly painted on the rock.

1. Mutation . . . . 1 star 7a
2. La vie tumultueuse d'un vilain . . . . 2 stars 7b+
3. Un été au parfum de citronelle . . . . 1 star 7b+
4. Tout l'effet d'une petite fée . 2 stars 7a
5. Détente au C4 . . . . 2 stars 7c+
6. En attendant le charpentier du valgorge . . . . 1 star 7c+
7. Deux temps trente mouvements . . . . 1 star 8a+
8. Expression féline . . . . . 2 stars 8a+
9. Expression bovine . . . . 2 stars 8a+
10. Elle m'a fait des pieds pour un concerto . . . . 2 stars 8a+
11. Délicatessen . . . . ?
12. Diversion . . . . ?

13 L'oeil du cyclope . . . . . (2 stars) 8a

14 Le cauchemar de nos rêves . . . . ?

15 Ethique en toc . . . . (2 stars) 7c

16 La voie du vévé . . . . . . (2 stars) 7b
The finger crack. There is a lengthy section with no bolts but it's grade 5 at the most. *Photo on page 64.*

17 Les dentelles de daphnée . . (3 stars) 6c
It helps to be able to hand jam on this one.

18 La voie royale . . . . . (2 stars) 8c

19 ? . . . . ?

20 États d'âmes . . . . . . (2 stars) 8a

21 La carotte atomique . . . (2 stars) 6c
Another test of crack-climbing skills. A hard start makes this less of a warm-up than you might have hoped.

22 Zenzibar . . . . (2 stars) 8a

23 Pince moi je rêve . . . . ?

24 Le grand combat . . . . (2 stars) 8a

Below this route is a collection of boulders with a number of problems established on them. They are marked with blue or black arrows and some are much better than others.

25 Poumapi barabo . . . . (1 star) 7b+

26 Les cryptos du plein-air . . . (1 star) 7b

27 Bretelles d'accès . . . . (1 star) 5+

30m
15m
13
14
15
16
17
18
19
20
21
22
23
24
25
26
27

Chaulet
Mazet
Actinidias
Cirque Gens
Les Branches
Gorge du Tarn
La Jonte
Le Boffi
Cantobre
Thaurac
Hortus
Claret
Seynes
Russan
Gaussier
Mouriès
Orgon

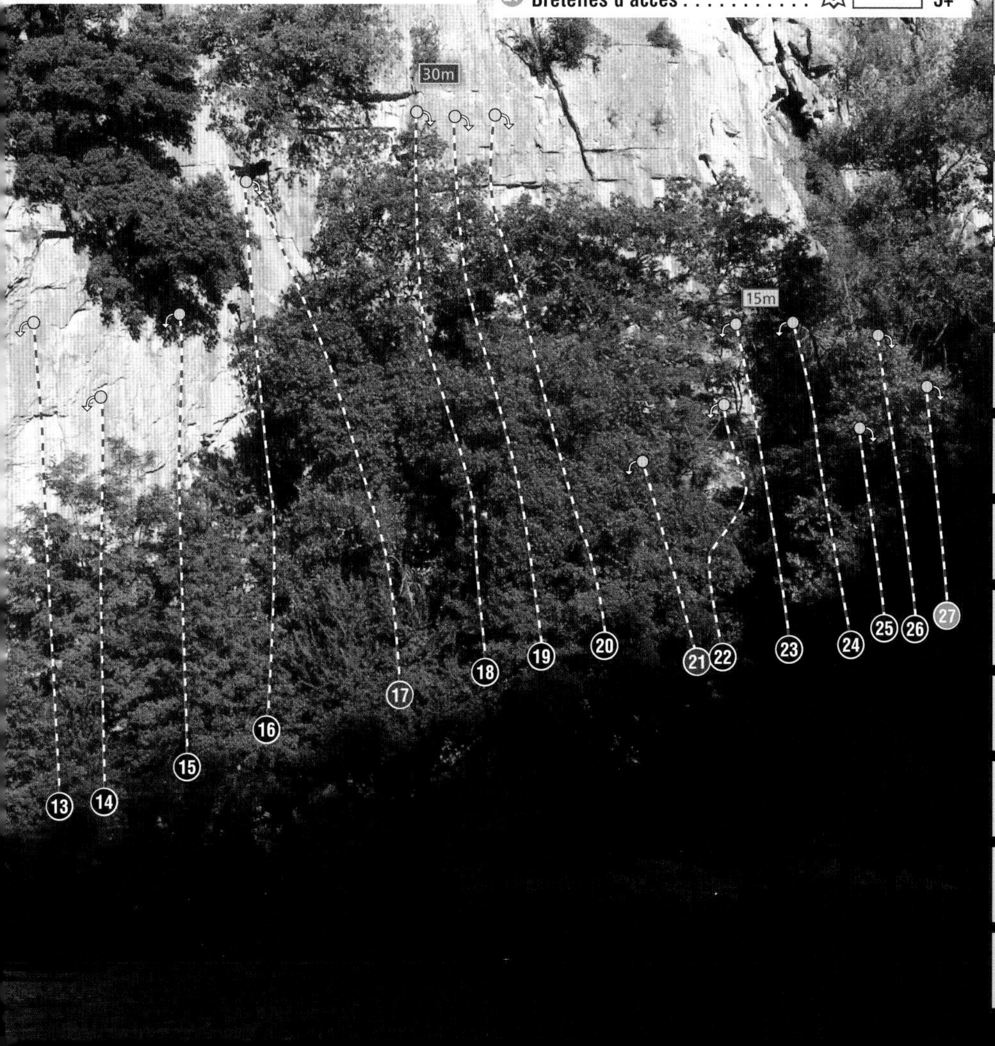

Compét
p.78

Le Cirque des Gens

Chaulet | Mazet | Actinidias | Cirque Gens | Les Branches | Gorge du Tarn | La Jonte | Le Boffi | Cantobre | Thaurac | Hortus | Claret | Seynes | Russan | Gaussier | Mouriès | Orgon

Le Cirque des Gens

	No star	1★	2★	3★
Up to 4+	2	8	1	1
5 to 6a+	5	28	17	7
6b to 7a	14	68	53	14
7a+ and up	6	32	42	15

This giant of a crag is well worth a look just to take in the vastness of the place. Shaped by the river into a perfect semi-circle, the Cirque des Gens offers plenty of sun and plenty of shade often at the same time. There is so much climbing here, that there simply has to be something for everyone.

Approach Also see map on page 29

After exiting the D579 continue along the road for 500m or until the road gets too rough for your vehicle. Eventually you will reach a metal barrier across the road. Continue past some boulders that block the road. From here there are two options: 1) follow the large track left an down past a series of steps until a trail leads off right to the base of the crag. 2) follow a trail across a meadow and into the trees, soon reaching the edge of the crag, from here descend a gulley to the base of the crag.

Conditions

The crag faces every direction except north. The shade tracks along the crag from left to righ through the day. If you are seeking shade, walk all the way to the far end of the crag where you get the shade around mid-morning (depending on the time of year). If you're looking for sun, make your way to the west-most part of the crag that you intend to climb on, and work your way back - this way you should get sun all day.

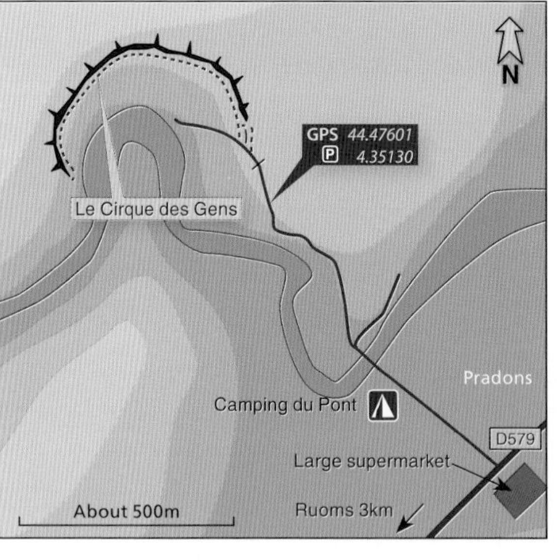

Eivind Flobak on *Consolation* (7a) - *page 82*.

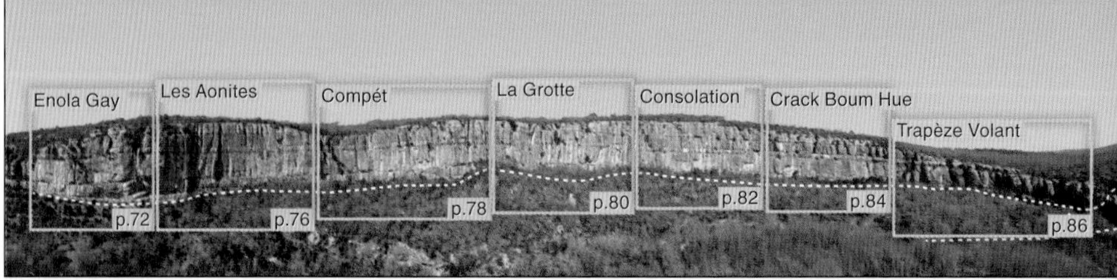

Jamie Veitch on *Totoche* (6c) - *page 79.*

Enola Gay

The furthest section of the crag is probably the most impressive of all, and well-worth the walk. If you're looking for good routes in the mid 7s, come straight here, though be prepared for some spaced bolting.

No.	Route	Stars	Grade
1	Enola Gay		7a
2	La chose	1	7b
3	A léa	2	7a+
4	Patate	2	7c
5	Chocolat	2	7b+
6	Coco	2	7c
7	Turlupitude	1	7b
8	Derriere musical	1	7b
9	Félicie	2	7b
10	Mon chéri	2	7b
11	Facteur cheval	2	6c
12	La mouillette	1	7a
13	Clairette	2	7b
14	Baston	2	7a
15	Le petit kiki	2	6c
16	La modeste	1	7a
17	Le pere ubu		6c
18	Niquez l'ange		6c
19	La midupan		6c+

20 min · Lots of sun · Vertical · Steep

35m

No.	Route	Stars	Grade
20	Risette		6c
21	Grigri d'amour		7b
22	Le papi pechu		7a
23	Viabra		6c
24	Le mamouth		7a
25	Cromignon		7a

The next routes are approached by climbing one of the routes below and walking along the ledge.

No.	Route	Stars	Grade
26	Casse dalle	1	7a+
27	Super phénix	2	6a
28	Nabot minable	2	7a
29	Stretching	2	7a
30	1-2-3 soleil	3	7a
31	Fusion froide	2	7a
32	Premiere émotion	2	6b
33	Brocolis en fleurette	2	7a
34	Poireaux coupés	2	7a
35	La musique du diable	2	7a+
36	Zizi fou	2	7b+
37	Autopsie d'un petit singe	2	7a+
38	Ni vu ni connu	2	7a+

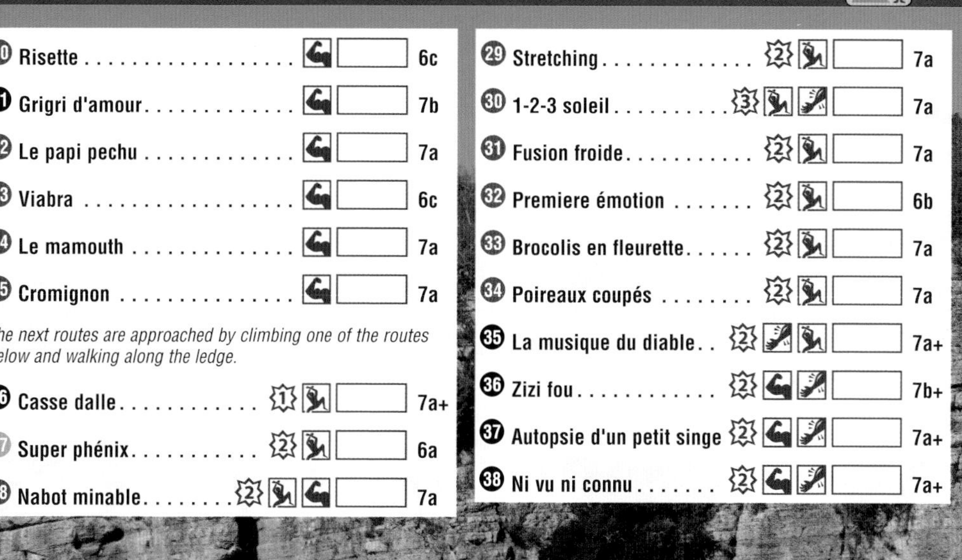

No.	Route	Stars	Grade
1	La grand férule	3	7c
2	Hystérésis	3	7c+
3	Némésis	2	7c
4	Kanabis	3	7c
5	Amuse gueule	3	7b+
6	Casting	1	7a
7	Puce	2	6c
8	Zig	1	6c
9	Le marchand de sable	2	7a
10	Pimprenelle	2	6c
11	Nicholas	3	6a
12	Nounours	1	6c
13	Retaxes	1	6b
14	Flore	1	5+
15	Pom	2	7a
16	Alexandre	1	6a+
17	Cornélius	1	6a
18	Celeste	1	6a
19	Réginald	1	7a
20	Zéphir	2	7a
21	Pocahontas	1	7a
22	Nouveaux nez	1	7b

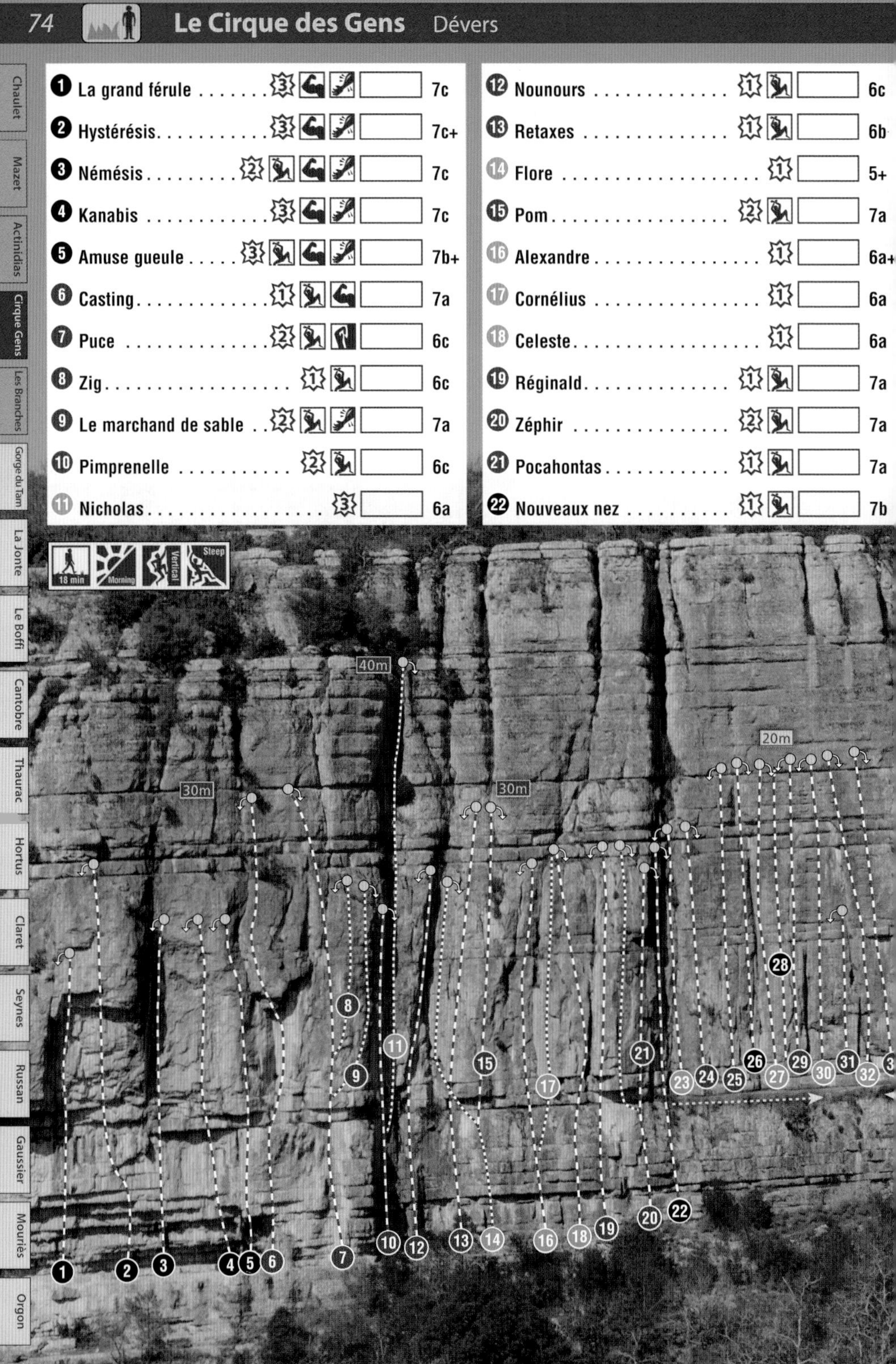

The following routes are accessed by scrambling (see following pages for the approach) then walking along a the ledge.

No.	Route	Stars		Grade
23	Cracotte	3		6a
24	Cracra	1		6b
25	Tarte aux poes	1		7a
26	Big jim	2		7a+
27	Pam pam	2		6a+
28	L'alibis	2		7b
29	Chabania	1		6b+
30	Areilladou	3		6a+
31	Tom pouce	1		6b+
32	Tchin-tchin	2		6a+
33	Les gueules cassées	2		6c

Peet Bridgewood on *Sexto motrice* (6a) on Trapèze Volant - *page 86*.

Les Aonites

A sector above a raised lower wall. Reach the starts by scrambling up below the route *Mi joue*.

No.	Route	Stars	Grade
1	Tant qu'il y aura des si	2	6c
2	La division	1	6a
3	Sous les pavés la plage	1	6b+
4	Joujou	1	6a
5	Bijou	1	5
6	Bar a quoi	1	6b
7	Pour 1 pot de petit musclé	1	5+
8	Allo la terre	1	6a+
9	Mi joue	1	6b+
10	La derniere séance	1	6c
11	Jusqu'au bout **1)** 6a+, **2)** 6a+	1	6a+
12	L'inspiration **1)** 6a+, **2)** 6c	1	6c
13	A bout de souffle	2	6b
14	Le plege	1	6a
15	Les oiseaux	1	6a
16	Glou glou **1)** 6a, **2)** 7a	2	7a
17	Quelle conque	2	6b+
18	La tourista	1	6a
19	Betty Bop	1	6a
20	La rateau	1	6a
21	Bobo	1	6a

35m
20m
18 min
Morning
Vertical
Stee

Tim Parkinson on the impressive tufa of *Tufs en stock* (7a) - *next page.*

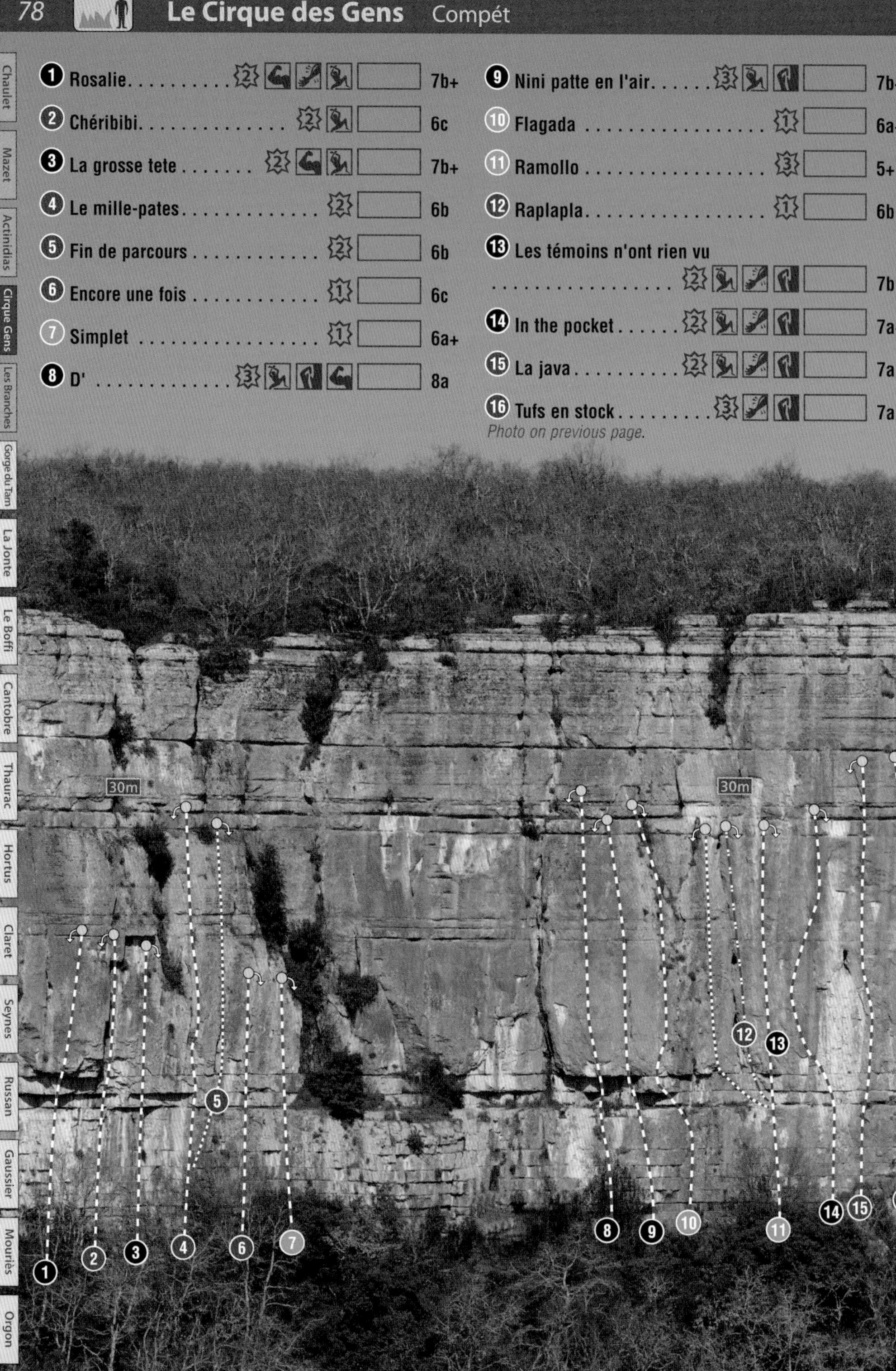
1 Rosalie 2 7b+
2 Chéribibi 2 6c
3 La grosse tete 2 7b+
4 Le mille-pates 2 6b
5 Fin de parcours 2 6b
6 Encore une fois 1 6c
7 Simplet 1 6a+
8 D' 3 8a
9 Nini patte en l'air 3 7b+
10 Flagada 1 6a+
11 Ramollo 3 5+
12 Raplapla 1 6b
13 Les témoins n'ont rien vu 2 7b
14 In the pocket 2 7a+
15 La java 2 7a
16 Tufs en stock 3 7a
Photo on previous page.
30m
30m
Chaulet
Mazet
Actinidias
Cirque Gens
Les Branches
Gorge du Tarn
La Jonte
Le Boffi
Cantobre
Thaurac
Hortus
Claret
Seynes
Russan
Gaussier
Mouriès
Orgon

17 Can I Plus . . . . 3 ☐ 7c

18 Totoche . . . . 3 ☐ 6c

Photo on page 71.

19 Pastis 51 . . . . 2 ☐ 6b

20 Cabernet sauvignon . . . . . . 1 ☐ 7b

21 Mr bricolage . . . . 2 ☐ 7a+

22 Géométrie variable . . . . . . 1 ☐ 7a+

23 Pépito . . . . 1 ☐ 7a

24 Magic banjo . . . . 1 ☐ 7a

25 La tete dans le sac. . . . . 1 ☐ 6b+

26 La voisine. . . . . 1 ☐ 6c

27 Babar . . . . 1 ☐ 6c

28 Le troufignon. . . . . 1 ☐ 6b

29 Chupa chups . . . . 1 ☐ 7a

30 Bénénuts . . . . 1 ☐ 6c+

31 Mimie jolie . . . . 1 ☐ 6b

32 Rondin picotin. . . . . 3 ☐ 7a+

33 Cocagne . . . . 3 ☐ 6b+

34 Grise mine . . . . 3 ☐ 6c

35 Ucova. . . . . 3 ☐ 7a

36 Les abeilles . . . . 1 ☐ 6b

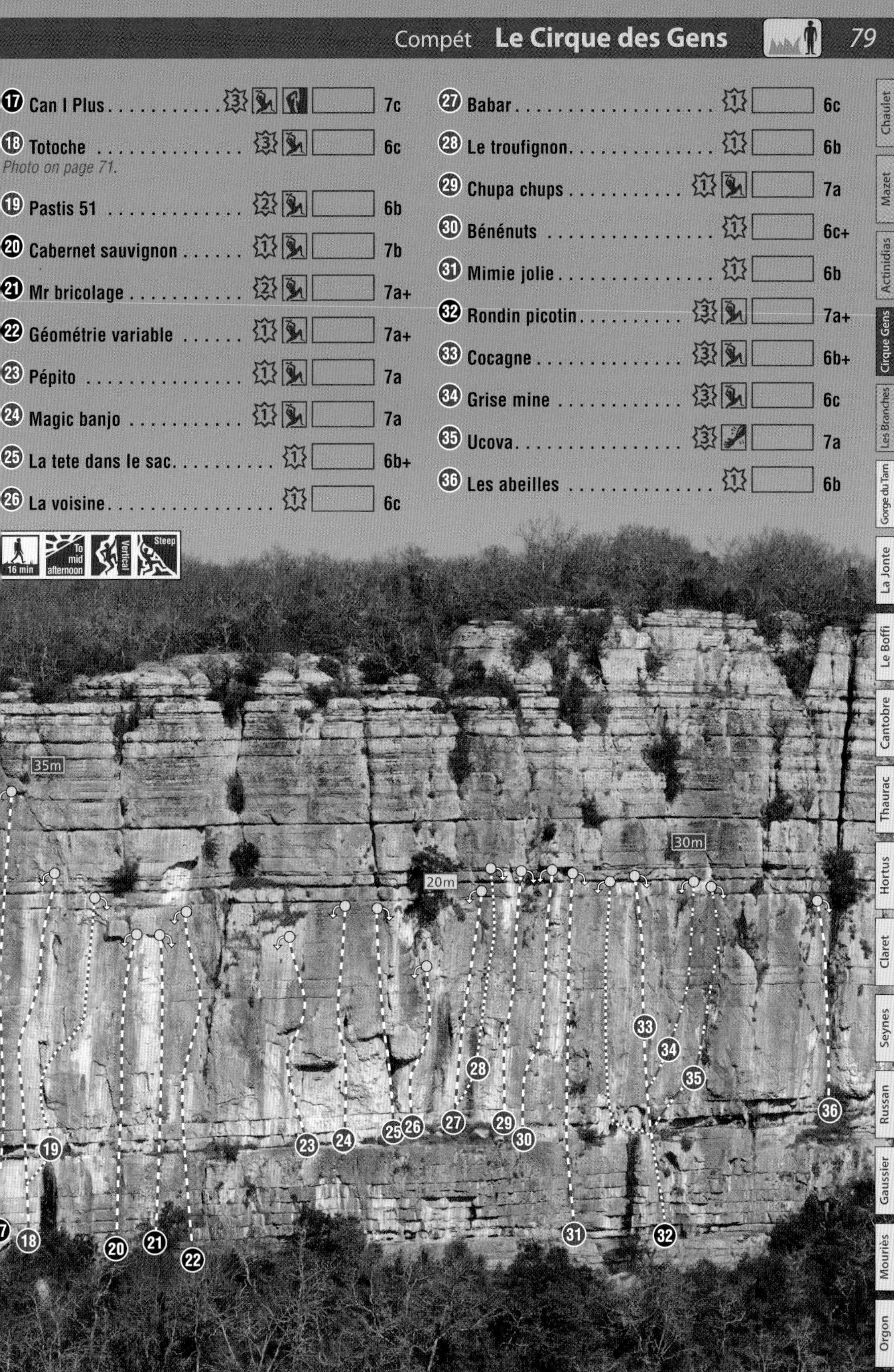

La Grotte

A good mixture of sustained 'old school' wall-climbs with a fine cluster of more modern, steep pump-fests. Approaches in this area frequently involve scrambling up to, and down from, ledges and walking along to the start of the routes. The easiest approaches are indicated on the photo-topo.

14 min | Lots of sun | Vertical | Steep

1. Sculpteur de pierre ... 2 stars ... 7a
2. Cracos ... 2 stars ... 6b
3. Voyageurs de glace ... 6a+
4. Brosseur de poussiere ... 1 star ... 6a+
5. Katiouchka ... 2 stars ... 6b+
6. Top Adventure ... 2 stars ... 6c
7. Les triplés en vadrouille ... 2 stars ... 6c
8. Grimpatorzore prograé ... 2 stars ... 6b+
9. La dégoulinasse ... 2 stars ... 6b+
10. Nouvelles sensations ... 2 stars ... 6b+
11. Altitude Sport ... 1 star ... 7b
    1) 6b, **2)** 7b
12. Derniere valise ... 3 stars ... 7c
    The right-hand variation is 7b+.
13. Minnie ... 1 star ... 7a
14. La belle et ... 1 star ... 7a
15. Le clochard ... 1 star ... 6a
16. Peter Pan ... 1 star ... 6c
17. Daisy ... 2 stars ... 6c
18. Géo ... 1 star ... 7a
19. Trouvetou ... 3 stars ... 7a
20. Picsou ... 1 star ... 7a+
21. Riri ... 3 stars ... 7b
22. Donald ... 3 stars ... 7b+
23. Fifi ... 3 stars ... 7b

No.	Route	Stars	Grade
24	Loulou	2	6c
25	Léo	1	7b
26	Léa	1	7a+
27	Corso	2	7c
28	L'écho des savanes	2	7b
29	Tomato Ketchup	3	7b+
30	Tam tam	3	8a+
31	Belladone	2	7c+
32	Le gong	3	7c
33	Ettcheque	2	7c
34	Et mat	3	7a
35	Troquet	2	7b+
36	Bidule	1	7a+
37	Exo 6	3	6c
38	La chouette	2	7b
39	Lio	2	7a
40	Jour de fete	3	6a+
41	La raignée	1	6b
42	La tarentelle	2	6a
43	Clara	2	7b+
44	Local héros	3	6c+

1) 6c+, **2)** 6b

Chaulet
Mazet
Actinidias
Cirque Gens
Les Branches
Gorge du Tam
La Jonte
Le Boffi
Cantobre
Thaurac
Hortus
Claret
Seynes
Russan
Gaussier
Mouriès
Orgon

Chaulet | Mazet | Actinidias | Cirque Gens | Les Branches | Gorge du Tarn | La Jonte | Le Boffi | Cantobre | Thaurac | Hortus | Claret | Seynes | Russan | Gaussier | Mouriès | Orgon

No.	Route	Stars	Grade
1	Uranus		7c+
2	Madame foldingue		6c
3	H20		6a
4	Dudule	1	7a
5	Le tourmentin		6b+
6	Pioupiou		6a
7	Castafiore	2	6b+
8	Wolf	2	6b+
9	Tournesol	2	5+
10	Mille sabords	1	7b
11	Ad hoc	1	7b
12	Tintin	2	7a
13	Milou	2	6a+
14	Baby hop	1	7b
15	Docteur popol	3	6a
16	Roudoudou	2	7a+
17	Toto	2	6b+
18	Dupont	2	7a
19	Calinette	1	7c
20	Consolation	3	7a
21	Mobil	1	6b
22	Eclipse	1	7a

Route 3 (H20): Pull on a bolt at the start.

Route 20 (Consolation): *Photo on page 70.*

35m

45m

20m

Local héros - previous page

	Route	Stars	Grade
23	A cul et a toi	2	7a+
24	Dallas	2	7c+
25	Derniere balise	2	7b+
26	C'est beau mais ça fatigue	2	7b
27	Gros coeur	2	7b
28	Boui-boui	1	8a
29	Concerto pour détraqués **1)** 7b, **2)** 7c, **2a)** 7b	1	7c
30	Plaisirs d'amour **1)** 7a+, **2)** 6c+	1	7a+
31	La rose pourpre	2	7b+
32	Turbulence	2	7b+
33	Quasimollo	2	7a
34	Train-train	1	6b
35	Victor h	1	7a
36	Hot Chocolate	1	6b
37	Point chaud	2	6a+
38	Couleur locale	1	7b+
39	Totomatic	2	7c
40	Mygale	2	8a
41	Les survoltés du bounty	2	7b
42	Titine	1	7a+
43	Le marché aux oiseaux	2	7b+
44	Mickey l'ange	1	7c
45	Le pause de minnie	1	7b
46	Vol 4807	3	6c

14 min From mid morning Vertical

45m 25m 20m

28 29 30 31 32 33 34 35 36 37 38 39 40 41 42 43 44 45 46

No.	Route	Stars	Grade
1	Magnésite	1	7b+
	1) 7a, 2) 7b+		
2	Grouchodevant	1	6c
3	Jeanticipe	1	6a+
4	Pente religieuse	1	6b
5	Roberjerie	2	6a
6	Total gaz		7c
7	Mousee a bras	2	8a
8	Nez rouge	2	7c+
9	Carnival	1	7b+
10	Crack boum hue	3	6a+
11	Licken de paques	1	6b+
12	Mousse a cas		7a
13	Stalag miteux	1	7a
14	L'enverdure	2	7b
15	Calcul pental	2	7a
	Pull on the first bolt at this grade, though it does go free.		
16	Bise en question	1	7a
17	L'antibaise	2	6c
18	Glas double	1	6c
19	Jeudi noir	2	7a
20	L'envers de gris		7c

12 min | Afternoon | Vertical

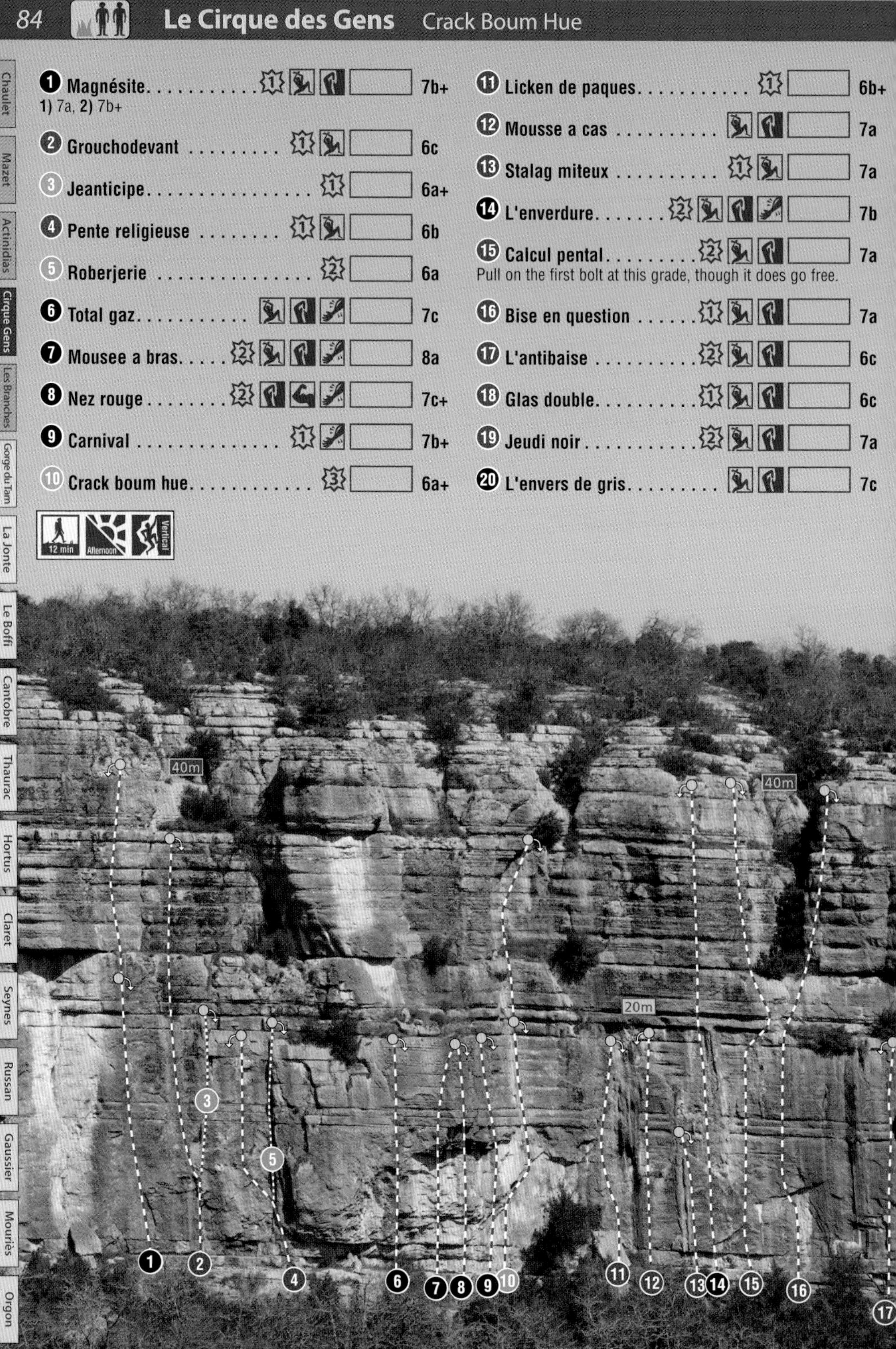

No.	Route	Grade
21	Gravisceptique	7a+
22	Décriptograe	7c+
23	Cool coulée	6a
24	Sweet gnome	6b+
25	Chargé a blanc	7b
26	Pitagoresse	7a+
27	Hard-déche	7a
28	Passipolis	6b
29	Savate bardée	6c+
30	Agens tourix	4
31	Lagoinable	6b+
32	Récalcitron	6b
33	Crochette surprise	4+
34	Chauzon bis	4
35	Epigne épogne	5+
36	Métropolitain	4+
37	Délirance	7a
38	Barda bardée	6a+
39	Radieux radius	6b
40	Baba lourd	6c+
41	Gros beau dard	6a+
42	Béta molle	6a+

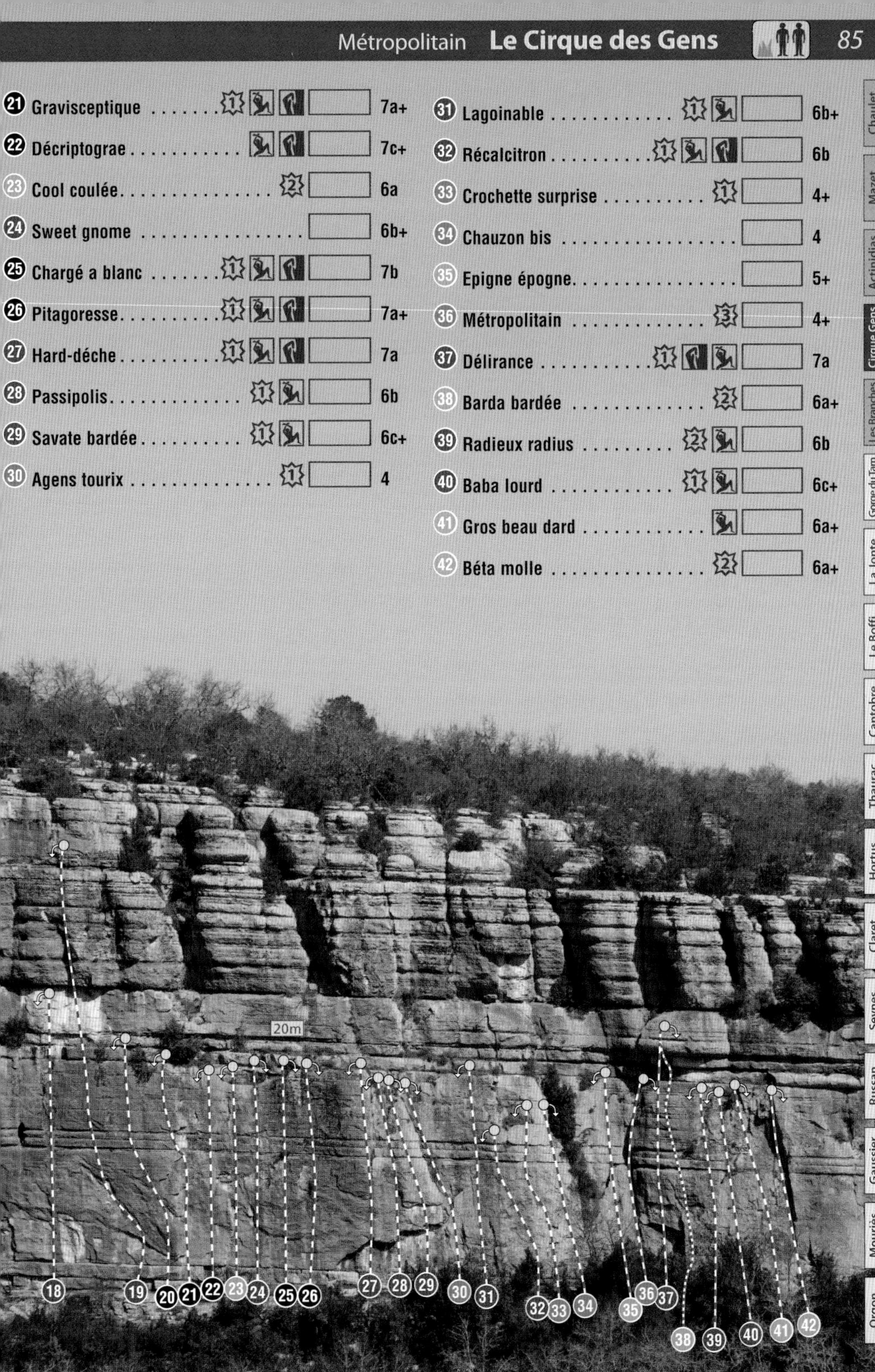

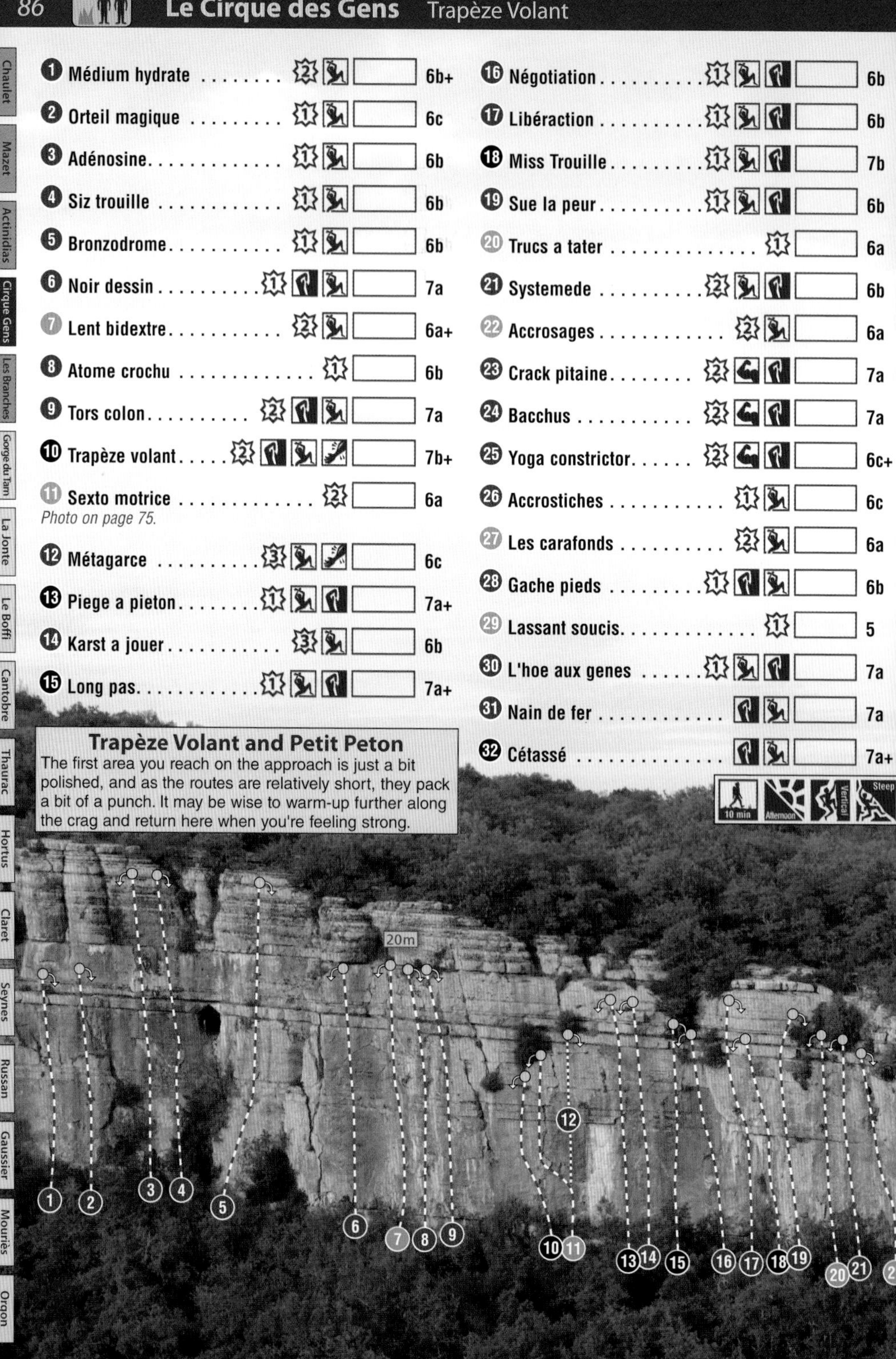

1. Médium hydrate .... 2 stars 6b+
2. Orteil magique .... 1 star 6c
3. Adénosine .... 1 star 6b
4. Siz trouille .... 1 star 6b
5. Bronzodrome .... 1 star 6b
6. Noir dessin .... 1 star 7a
7. Lent bidextre .... 2 stars 6a+
8. Atome crochu .... 1 star 6b
9. Tors colon .... 2 stars 7a
10. Trapèze volant ..... 2 stars 7b+
11. Sexto motrice .... 2 stars 6a

Photo on page 75.

12. Métagarce .... 3 stars 6c
13. Piege a pieton .... 1 star 7a+
14. Karst a jouer .... 3 stars 6b
15. Long pas .... 1 star 7a+
16. Négotiation .... 1 star 6b
17. Libéraction .... 1 star 6b
18. Miss Trouille .... 1 star 7b
19. Sue la peur .... 1 star 6b
20. Trucs a tater .... 1 star 6a
21. Systemede .... 2 stars 6b
22. Accrosages .... 2 stars 6a
23. Crack pitaine .... 2 stars 7a
24. Bacchus .... 2 stars 7a
25. Yoga constrictor ...... 2 stars 6c+
26. Accrostiches .... 1 star 6c
27. Les carafonds .... 2 stars 6a
28. Gache pieds .... 1 star 6b
29. Lassant soucis .... 1 star 5
30. L'hoe aux genes ...... 1 star 7a
31. Nain de fer 7a
32. Cétassé .... 7a+

Trapèze Volant and Petit Peton

The first area you reach on the approach is just a bit polished, and as the routes are relatively short, they pack a bit of a punch. It may be wise to warm-up further along the crag and return here when you're feeling strong.

No.	Route	Stars	Grade
33	Cafard breton		4
34	L'inversatile	1	7a
35	Sinciput	2	6a
36	Petit peton	1	5
37	Accrochoco	1	4+
38	La chauzonaise	1	4
39	Jeux interdits	1	6a+
40	La danse des clowns	1	6c
41	Oulla	2	4
42	Doucement les basses	1	4
43	Jeu de crack	1	4+
44	Partir et revenir	1	5
45	Nervi	1	6b
46	Coup de nerf	1	7c
47	Alligator 427	2	6b+
48	Passage forcé	1	4
49	Dérepage inversé	1	5+
50	Patte de chat	1	5+
51	La barre du rire	1	4+
52	Les derniers grimpatozores	2	6c
53	Manfred nan	2	5+

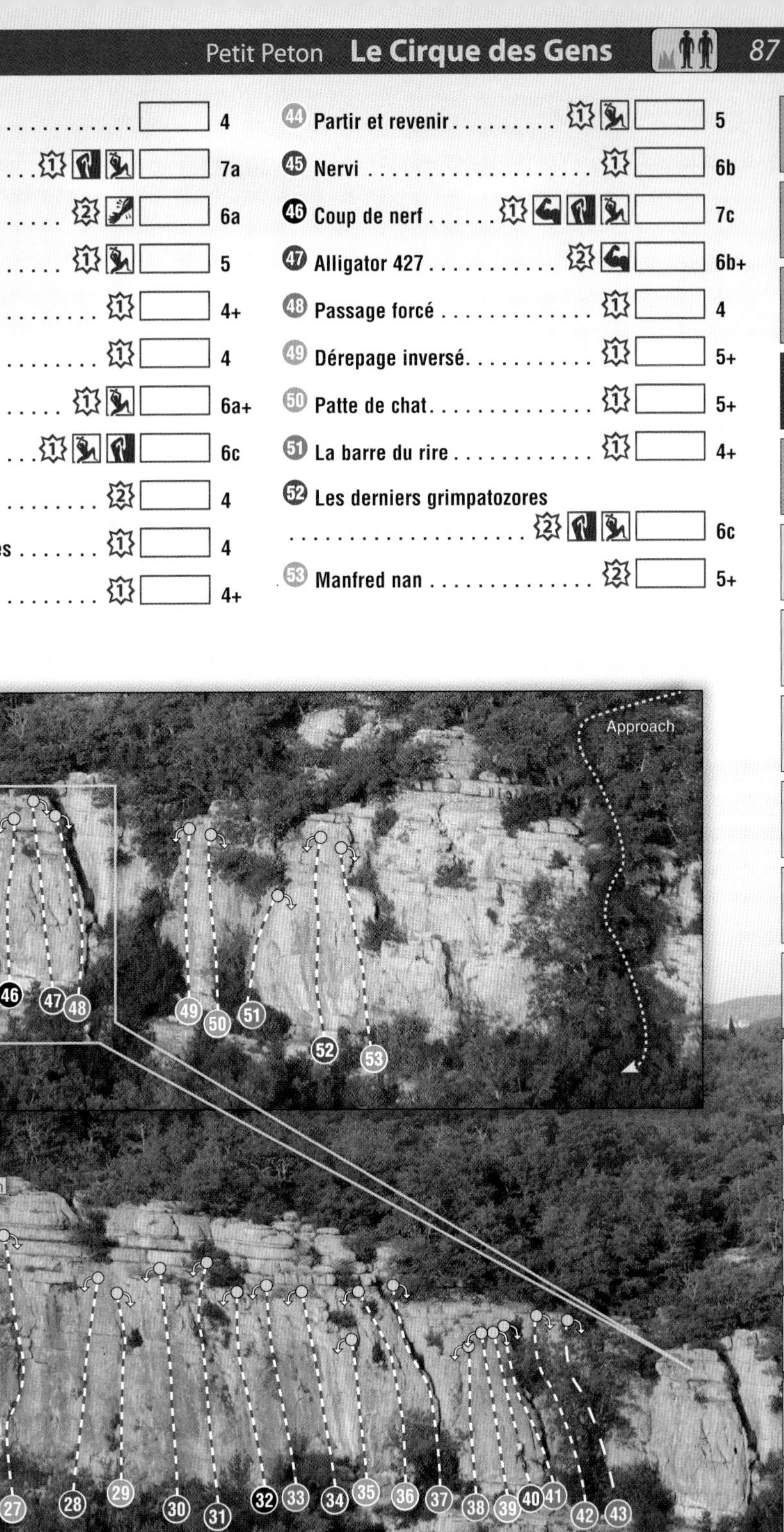

Les Branches

Chaulet
Mazet
Actinidias
Cirque Gens
Les Branches
Gorge du Tarn
La Jonte
Le Boffi
Cantobre
Thaurac
Hortus
Claret
Seynes
Russan
Gaussier
Mouriès
Orgon

Les Branches

	No star	1	2	3
Up to 4+	-	-	-	-
5 to 6a+	-	-	-	-
6b to 7a	2	5	4	-
7a+ and up	5	9	12	8

A tough crag with a mixture of steep tufa climbs and long technical wall climbs. A great place to escape the heat.

Approach

Also see map on page 29

The following approach can be used from September to May (when the campsite is closed). From Vallon, follow the D579 towards Salavas and Barjac. On leaving Salavas, take a road on the left named Route des Chassel, the turning is marked by a plethora of signs, including a sign for Les Blanches Camping. Continue along this road until a cliff on the right with space to park below, a couple of hundred metres before Les Blanches.

Continue on foot past a couple of gates respecting the fact that this is private land, when you reach a very large building on the right (the one made from stone, wood, and metal) drop down and pass a small playground on your right. Continue close to the river, the road crosses a small stream and ends. Just before it ends, head up on another road to another camping area. Take the first turning on your left and follow the road until it ends at a wide area. From here things get a bit Indiana Jones. Follow a trail next to the river, crossing a small stream (very slippery - the stream can be bypassed on the right if it's really flowing). After a short while you come to a crag, the second half of which is traversed using a fixed rope. Continue along the trail for about 250m to reach the right-hand end of the crag.

From September to May you must cross the river from the Pont d'Arc. From Vallon pick up the D290 and follow it for 4km until you see an extensive car park on your left next to a restaurant. Park here, cross the road and walk back in the direction of Vallon for no more than 50m, and you will reach a smaller parking area on the left side of the road. From here a track leads down to a pleasant beach west of the Pont d'Arc. Cross the river however you choose and continue in a westerly direction (up-river) until you reach the crag on your left.

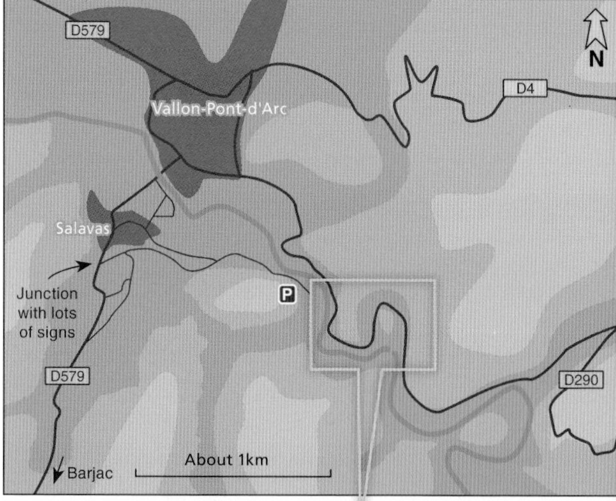

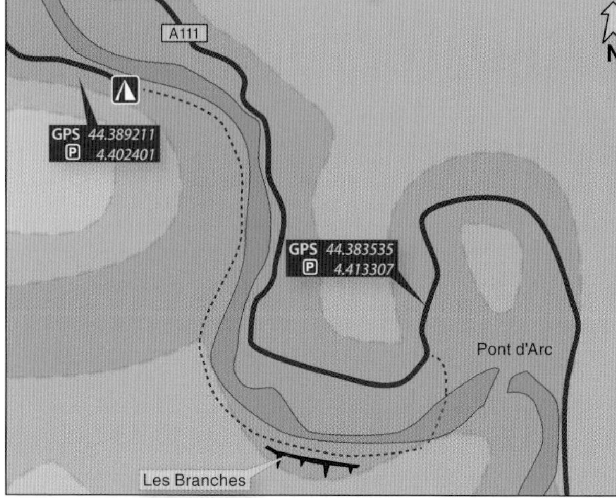

Conditions

Facing north, the crag gets almost no sun, so is a fine place to head to avoid the heat. During the winter and spring you should expect to find some or all of the tufas dripping wet, but there are plenty of routes on the vertical walls further left.

Tim Parkinson on *Le roi de l'olympe* (7a) - *next page.*

Les Branches - Left

Very much in contrast to La Grotte further right, the left-hand side of Les Branches consists mainly of long technical face climbs, often with extensions that take them all the way to the top of the cliff. The routes are better than they look, will always be in the shade, but not much of a warm-up for the Grotte routes.

1 ? . . . . ?
Unknown line right of the big cave.

2 Le scalp 6c

3 Cague braille s'abstenir . . . . ?
Looks about 7a - 60m long.

4 Le roi de l'olympe . . . . . 2 stars 7a
The extension is 8a+. *Photo on previous page.*

5 La puta madre . . . . 1 star 6c
The extension is 8a+

6 Le mât de cocagne . . . . . 1 star 7a+
The left-hand extension is 8a, the right-hand extension is 7c+.

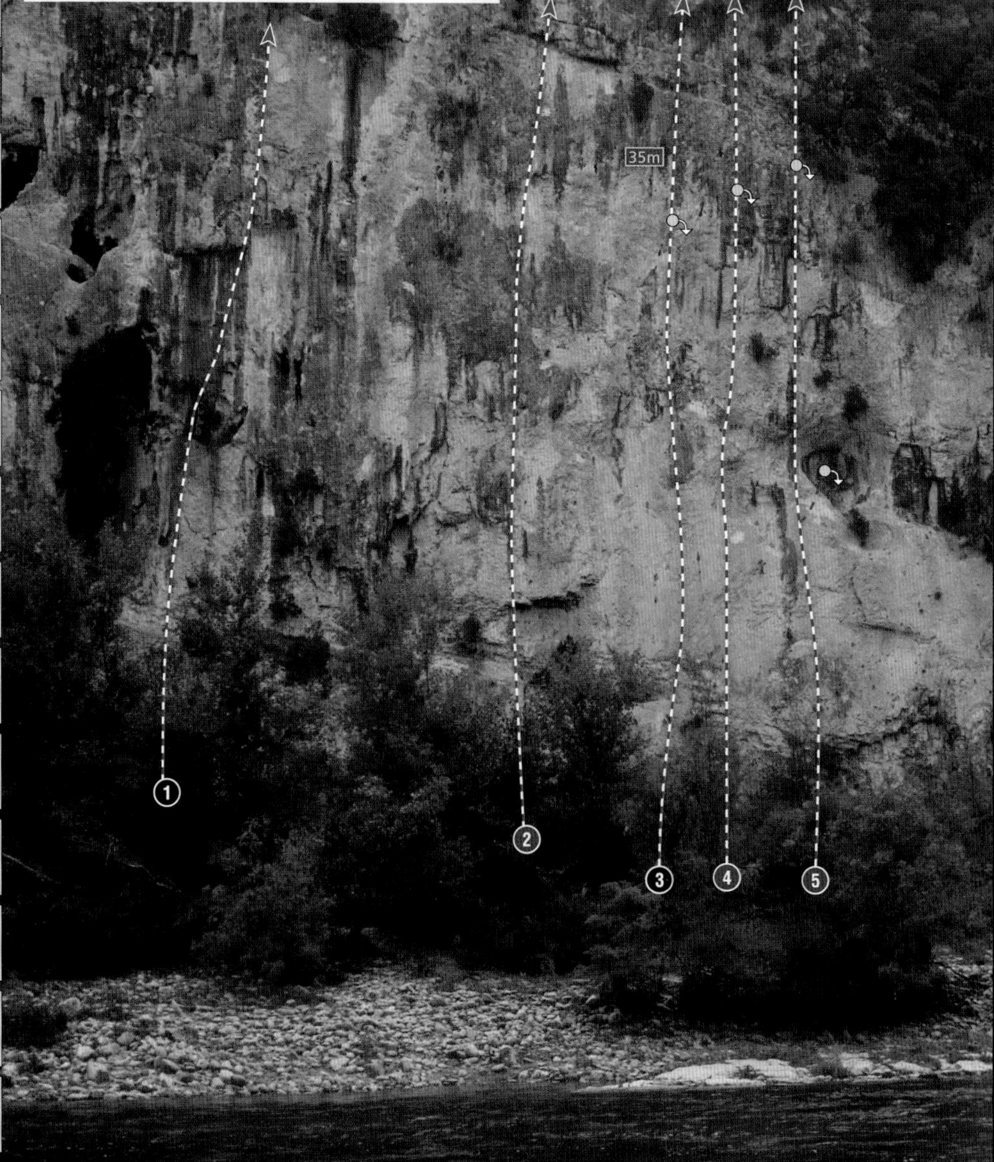

35m

7 **Les 400 coups de Pépé and Roger** . . . . 6c+
he extension is 7b.

8 **Chaouchinadeaux tunnels** 7a
he extension is 7b+.

9 **Poupouille la lionne**. . . . 7a+
he left-hand extension is 8a, the right-hand extension is 7b.

10 **?** . . . . ?

11 **Du gazon sur la plage**. . . . . 6b+
he extensions are both 7a+.

12 **Katia ou un soleil venu du froid** 7a
he extension is 7c.

13 **La petite croisière** . . . . . 7b+

14 **El cochongliero fiero** . . . 8a
he extension is 8a+

15 **Le corps a la parole** 7b
The extension is 7c+.

16 **Premiers baisers** . . . . . . 7c+

17 **Viva kenza** 8a

18 **Les devoirs de vacances** 7b+
The extension is 7c.

19 **Godivaux merguez** 8a

20 **La saison des merguez** . . 7c+

21 **Secret défonce** 7a
The extension is 8a.

22 **Réunion tupperware**. . . . . . 7a+

23 **Quand vibre l'âme, la semelle colle** . . . . 6c+
The extension is 8a.

24 **Orbital** . . . . 8a+

Not much sun | 30 min | Vertical | Steep

35m

6 7 8 9 10 11 12 13 14 15 16 17 18 19 20 21 22 23 24

La Grotte

A very impressive piece of rock with some neck-achingly steep routes forcing their way to the top. Expect the stalactites and tufas to be dripping during the winter and after heavy rain.

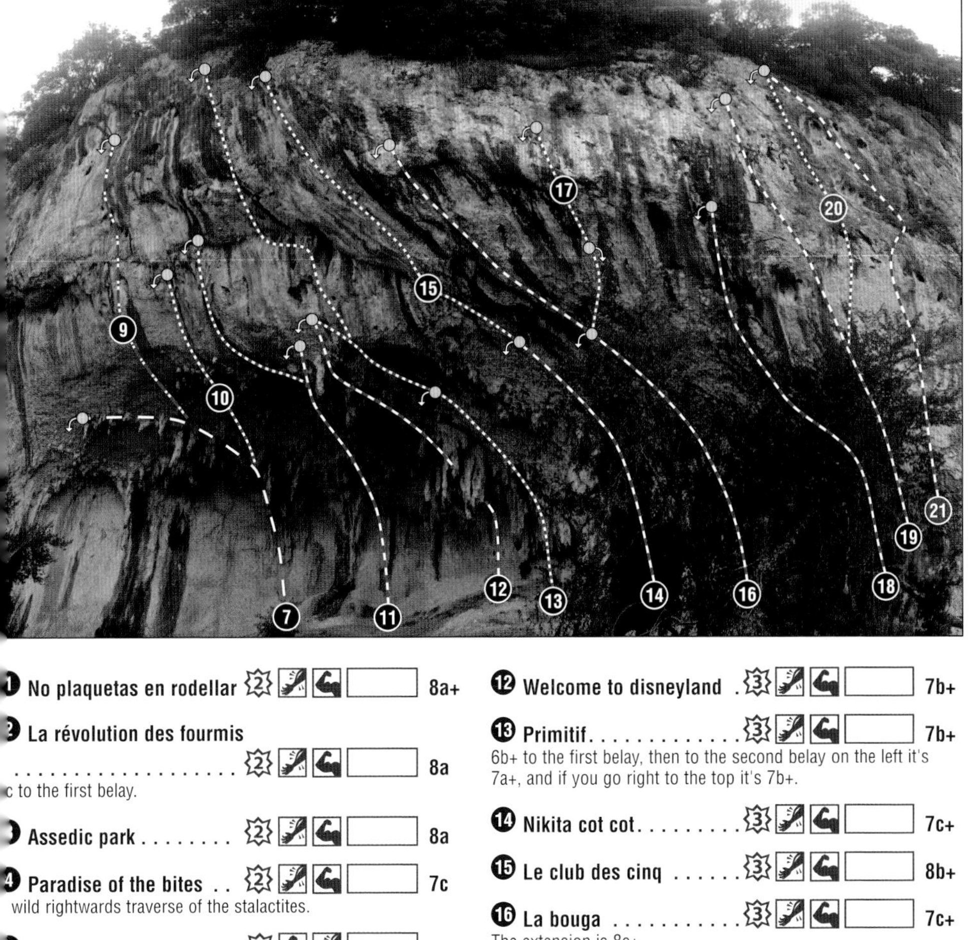

1 No plaquetas en rodellar 2 ☐ 8a+

2 La révolution des fourmis
. . . . 2 ☐ 8a
c to the first belay.

3 Assedic park . . . . 2 ☐ 8a

4 Paradise of the bites . . 2 ☐ 7c
wild rightwards traverse of the stalactites.

5 OGM . . . . 3 ☐ 8b
ranch off leftwards before the top of *La mauvaise graine*, join *ssedic park* and just keep going.

6 La mauvaise graine . . . 2 ☐ 8a+

7 Bite of paradise . . . . . . 2 ☐ 7b+
wild leftwards traverse of the stalactites.

8 Transgénèse . . . . 2 ☐ 8c
tart as for *Bite of paradise*, and carry on to the top of *OGM*.

9 Unknown . . . . ☐ ?

10 Amour et compassion . . 2 ☐ 8b+

11 Chronopost . . . . 3 ☐ 8c
topping at the first belay is worth 8a.

12 Welcome to disneyland . 3 ☐ 7b+

13 Primitif . . . . 3 ☐ 7b+
6b+ to the first belay, then to the second belay on the left it's 7a+, and if you go right to the top it's 7b+.

14 Nikita cot cot . . . . 3 ☐ 7c+

15 Le club des cinq . . . . . . 3 ☐ 8b+

16 La bouga . . . . 3 ☐ 7c+
The extension is 8c+.

17 Unknown . . . . ☐ ?

18 Le complexe de la fourmi
. . . . 3 ☐ 8b

To the right, the angles eases considerably.

19 Couci . . . . 1 ☐ 7b+

20 Un été d'enfer . . . . ☐ 6c

21 Pour doudou . . . . 1 ☐ 6b

Chaulet
Mazet
Actinidias
Cirque Gens
Les Branches
Gorge du Tarn
La Jonte
Le Boffi
Cantobre
Thaurac
Hortus
Claret
Seynes
Russan
Gaussier
Mouriès
Orgon

A truly spectacular area with everything from short, friendly, low-grade crags, to long exposed trad routes. The crags around the river Tarn are not just visually impressive, but offer climbing of the very highest quality. Generally, the routes tend to be quite long, with the emphasis on endurance. Having been developed, largely, since the late 1990s, the Gorge du Tarn, Le Boffi and Cantobre tend to be well bolted, though it is worth noting that belays are often spaced so as to require an 80m rope. La Jonte is an older crag with older gear and grades to match.

Getting There and Getting Around

The areas covered are a short distance from the A75 autoroute (and the famed Millau Viaduct which it crosses). Millau is the closest large town, and has a train station (not TGV). Rodez is a little further from the action, but has a train station that is served by an overnight service from Paris. The nearest airports are Rodez and Montpellier. La Jonte is close enough to the climbing to allow a completely car-free trip (though with a bit more walking, naturally). A 35 minute bus journey connects Millau to Le Rozier/Peyreleau. Search online for times.

Where to Stay

This is a popular holiday-destination in the summer, and there are plenty of campsites to choose from. The only problem is that the campsites are only open (at most) from April to October. If you do find yourself here when the campsites are shut, you should be able to find yourself a splendid gîte at a bargain rate. Wild car-camping is common but does not help the delicate access situation, so please stay well out of sight if you do so.

Web Links

www.le-rozier.com - local tourist information
www.keolis-aveyron.com - operate a bus service from Millau to Le Rozier.

Local Guidebooks

There are three stylish local guidebooks covering this area in greater depth **La Dourbie** (Le Boffi), **La Jonte**, and **Le Tarn**. These are available, at the time of writing, in Le Rozier and Les Vignes.

Ali Baylay, linking into the second pitch of *Retour aux sources* (5+) - *page 183* - Le Boffi.

Fœtus
p.102

Gorge du Tarn

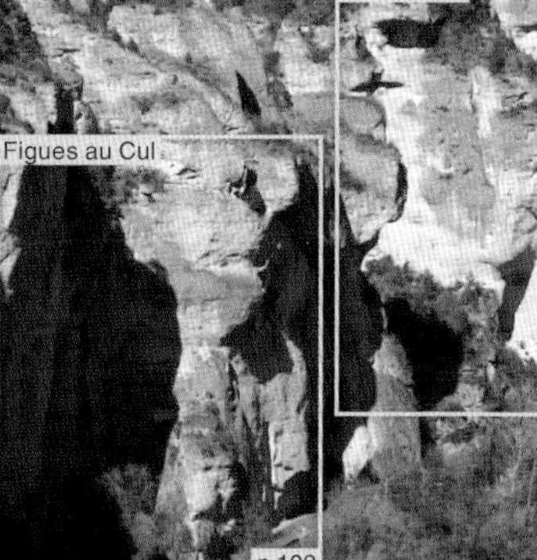

	No star	1 star	2 star	3 star
Up to 4+	-	-	-	-
5 to 6a+	3	9	10	4
6b to 7a	6	24	34	18
7a+ and up	26	23	86	40

Of the three areas in this section, the Gorge du Tarn is the most widely recognised. With both superb quality rock and a mostly road-side approach, it is a justifiably popular venue. The climbing has only been developed since the late 1990s, and new-route activity is on-going. There is no doubt that the Tarn is of more interest to climbers operating in the 7s and 8s than it is to those looking for 5s and 6s, though there is plenty enough for a short trip if you can stretch to mid 6s. The routes are largely characterised as stamina tests, and pitches up to 50m are not uncommon, the usual method for doing the very long pitches is to use two ropes - switching from one to the other (and dropping the unneeded one) along the way to reduce rope-drag.

Approach Also see map on page 97

The climbing is found on the north bank of the river Tarn, two kilometres north of the village of Les Vignes. There are a number of parking areas on the side of the road. From the road, paths lead up to the crags.

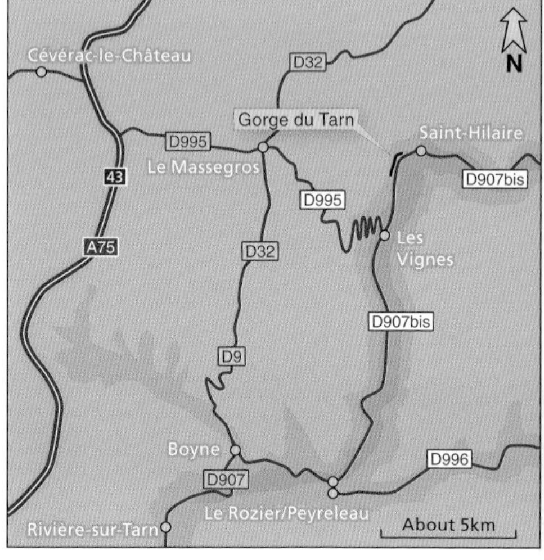

Access

During 2011 the failure of an expansion bolt at the left side of the Tennessee sector highlighted a problem with the use of expansion bolts in soft limestone. In reaction to this, all routes where bolts were suspected of being liable to failure were partially de-bolted in order to close the route and prevent further injury. This has affected much of the climbing in the Tarn. To make matters worse, much of the climbing in the Tarn takes place on private land, and on learning of the risk of bolt failure, and the possibility of being held liable, landowners were understandably fearful. This has lead to one landowner removing all access rights to a number of crags (see map opposite) including the magnificent 'all-weather' Grand Toit.

There is a plan to re-bolt many of the de-bolted routes over the winter (2011/12). Under a deal with the Mayor, the local authority will meet 90% of the cost of re-bolting and the local climbing organisation will find the rest from sales of the local topo. In total €100,000 will be raised, and used to re-bolt 200 routes and fund toilets and other access requirements. The situation is fluid, and there is no definitive list of which routes are open and which are closed, however the intention is to get the re-bolting completed by spring 2012.

If you plan to visit the Tarn, please respect the wishes of landowners and do not climb at closed crags. Be aware that the route you wish to climb may not have been re-bolted, and will be unclimbable. Please use the described approaches, and observe any signs placed at crags with regard to paths, parking and access in general. On the positive side, there will probably be enough climbing for several weeks, and there are other areas (Boffi, Jonte) close by if you start running out of routes to do.

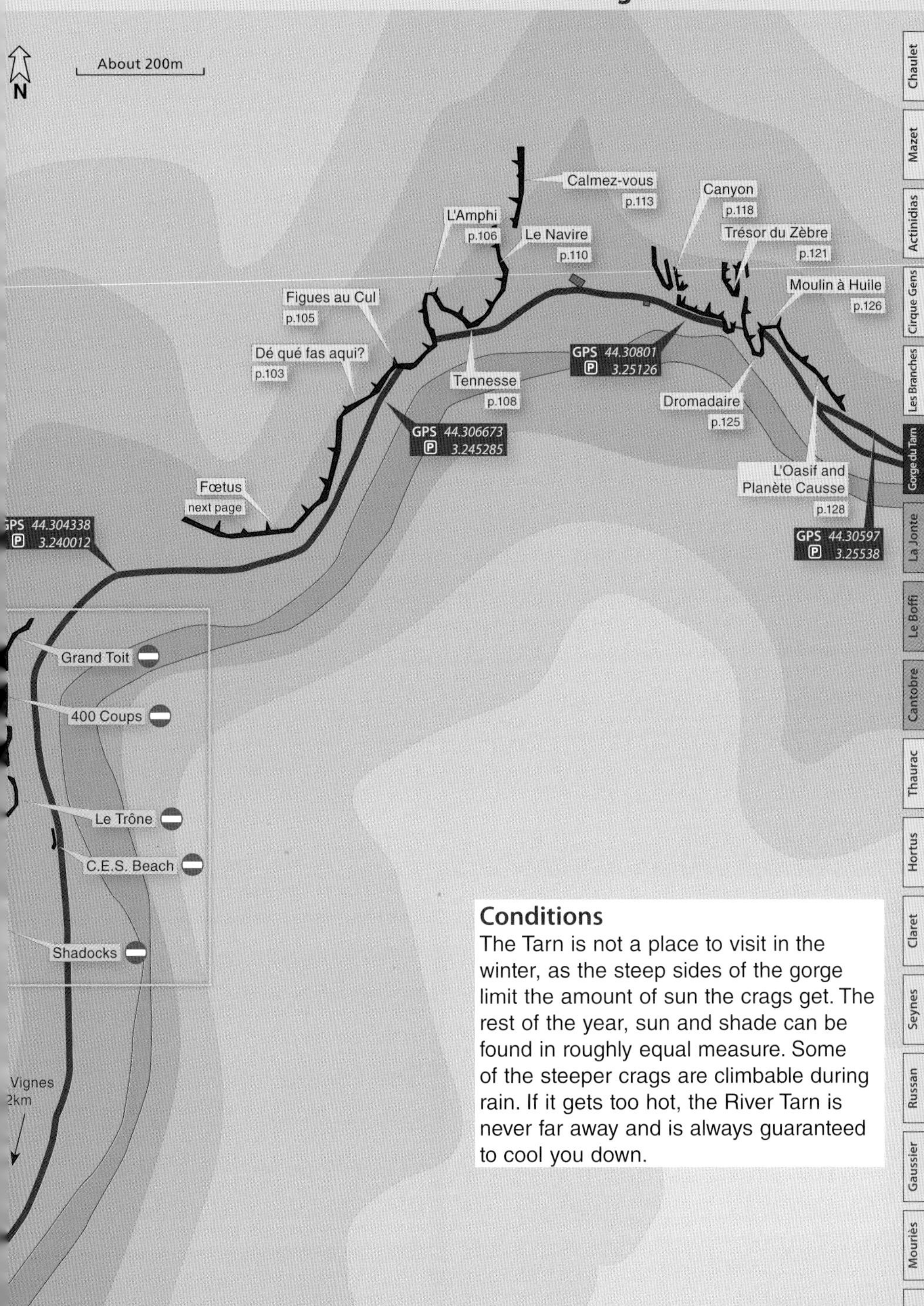

Conditions

The Tarn is not a place to visit in the winter, as the steep sides of the gorge limit the amount of sun the crags get. The rest of the year, sun and shade can be found in roughly equal measure. Some of the steeper crags are climbable during rain. If it gets too hot, the River Tarn is never far away and is always guaranteed to cool you down.

Fœtus

A two-tier crag that has much potential for future development.

Approach - Driving up the gorge, past the impressive Grand Toit, a very generous layby is reached on the left. Park here and follow a path (signed to 'Le Point Sublime') that leads to the left-hand side of both tiers.

5 min | Afternoon | Steep

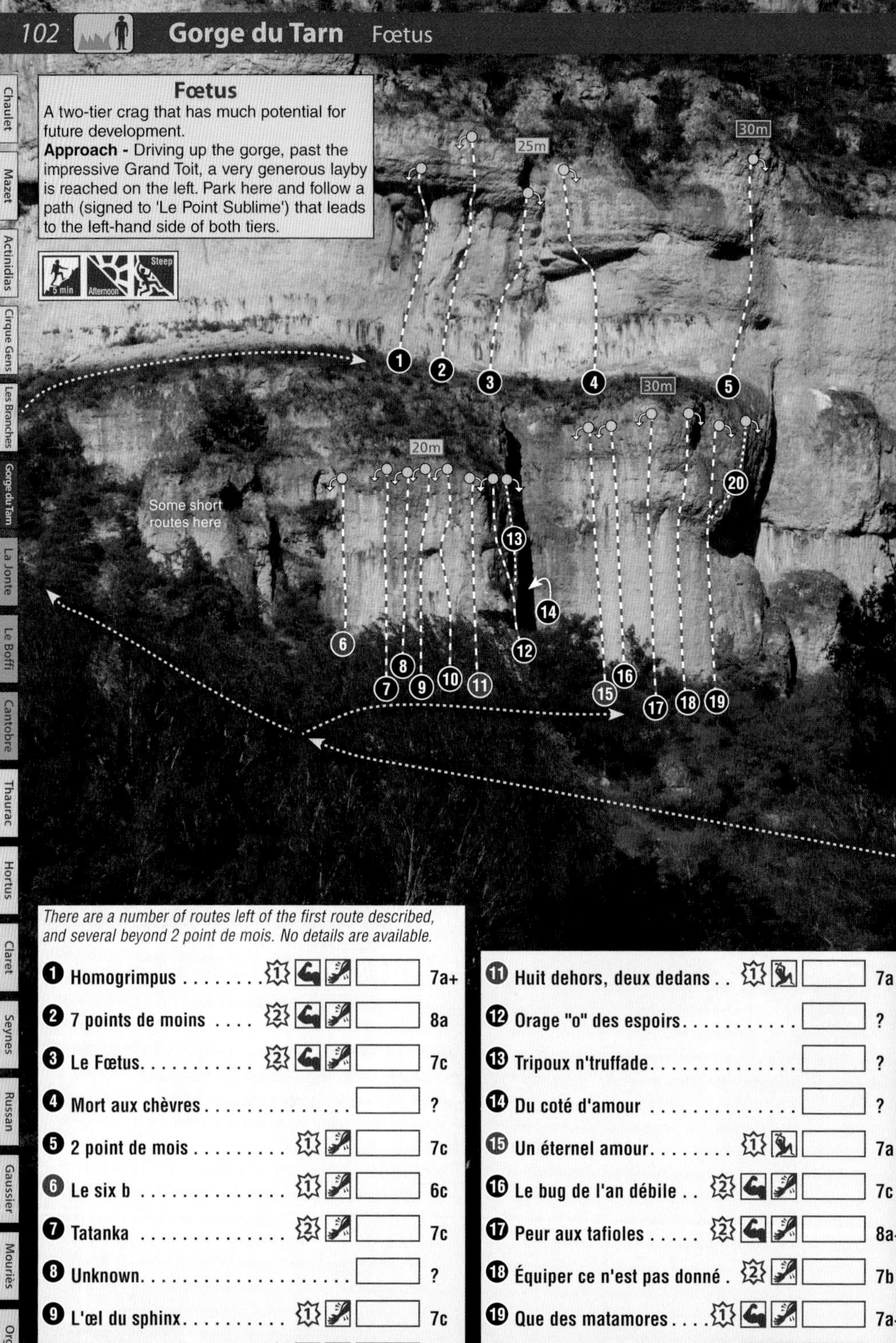

There are a number of routes left of the first route described, and several beyond 2 point de mois. No details are available.

No.	Route	Stars	Grade
1	Homogrimpus	1	7a+
2	7 points de moins	2	8a
3	Le Fœtus	2	7c
4	Mort aux chèvres		?
5	2 point de mois	1	7c
6	Le six b	1	6c
7	Tatanka	2	7c
8	Unknown		?
9	L'œl du sphinx	1	7c
10	Poussière d'or	1	7b
11	Huit dehors, deux dedans	1	7a
12	Orage "o" des espoirs		?
13	Tripoux n'truffade		?
14	Du coté d'amour		?
15	Un éternel amour	1	7a
16	Le bug de l'an débile	2	7c
17	Peur aux tafioles	2	8a
18	Équiper ce n'est pas donné	2	7b
19	Que des matamores	1	7a
20	Des pieds et mains	2	7b

1 La camera de la vitesse . . . . ?

2 L'australopithique du samedi . . . . . ?

3 La femme gri gri . . . . ?

4 Caforobe. . . . . 1 7a+

5 Dé qué fas aqui? 1 7a

6 Yaqui . . . . 6c+

7 Samedi ouvre . . . . ?

8 Dimanche vagabond. . . . . 6b+

9 Lundi chome . . . . ?

0 Nulle par ailleurs. 2 6a

1 Unknown. . . . . 3 6b+

2 Unknown. ?

3 Unknown. ?

4 Abus dangereux. . . . . 3 6c+

6c+, **2)** 6b+, **3)** 6b+. *Photo on page 22.*

5 Unknown. ?

6 Écaille volante non identifiée 2 7c+

adside | Lots of sun | Vertical | Steep

Dé qué fas aqui?

A good selection of both single- and multi-pitch routes to go at here. There has been a fair bit of development fairly recently, so expect to find routes not listed here.

Approach - The parking area is found on the right, just before you reach the first tunnel (when coming from Les Vignes). Walk up the wide track (**do not block this track**), taking a path off to the right after about 50m, this leads you the left-side of the base of the crag.

80m

50m

35m

25m

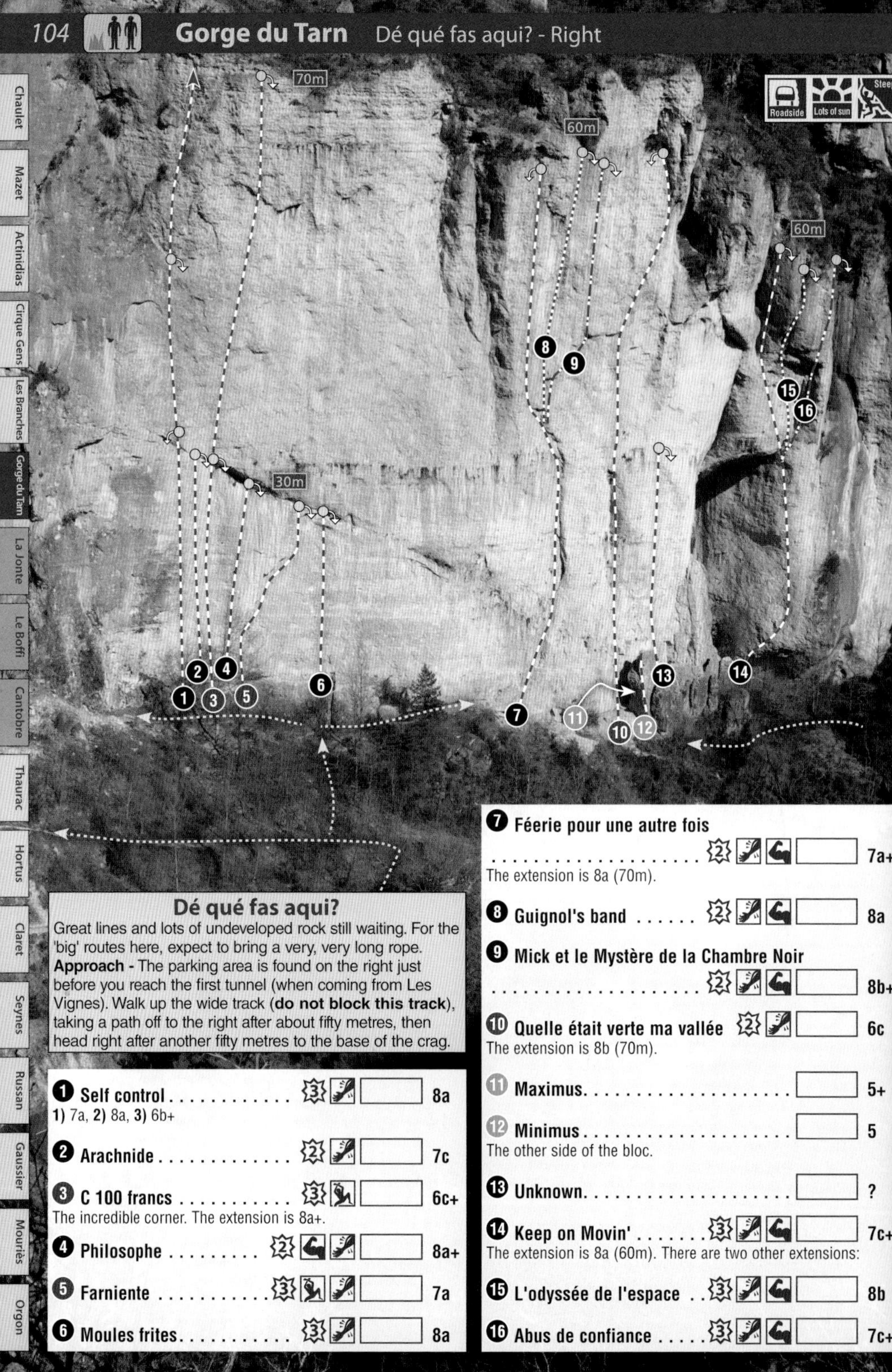

Dé qué fas aqui?

Great lines and lots of undeveloped rock still waiting. For the 'big' routes here, expect to bring a very, very long rope.

Approach - The parking area is found on the right just before you reach the first tunnel (when coming from Les Vignes). Walk up the wide track (**do not block this track**), taking a path off to the right after about fifty metres, then head right after another fifty metres to the base of the crag.

1 Self control ... 3 ... 8a
1) 7a, **2)** 8a, **3)** 6b+

2 Arachnide ... 2 ... 7c

3 C 100 francs ... 3 ... 6c+
The incredible corner. The extension is 8a+.

4 Philosophe ... 2 ... 8a+

5 Farniente ... 3 ... 7a

6 Moules frites ... 3 ... 8a

7 Féerie pour une autre fois ... 2 ... 7a+
The extension is 8a (70m).

8 Guignol's band ... 2 ... 8a

9 Mick et le Mystère de la Chambre Noir ... 2 ... 8b+

10 Quelle était verte ma vallée 2 ... 6c
The extension is 8b (70m).

11 Maximus ... 5+

12 Minimus ... 5
The other side of the bloc.

13 Unknown ... ?

14 Keep on Movin' ... 3 ... 7c+
The extension is 8a (60m). There are two other extensions:

15 L'odyssée de l'espace ... 3 ... 8b

16 Abus de confiance ... 3 ... 7c+

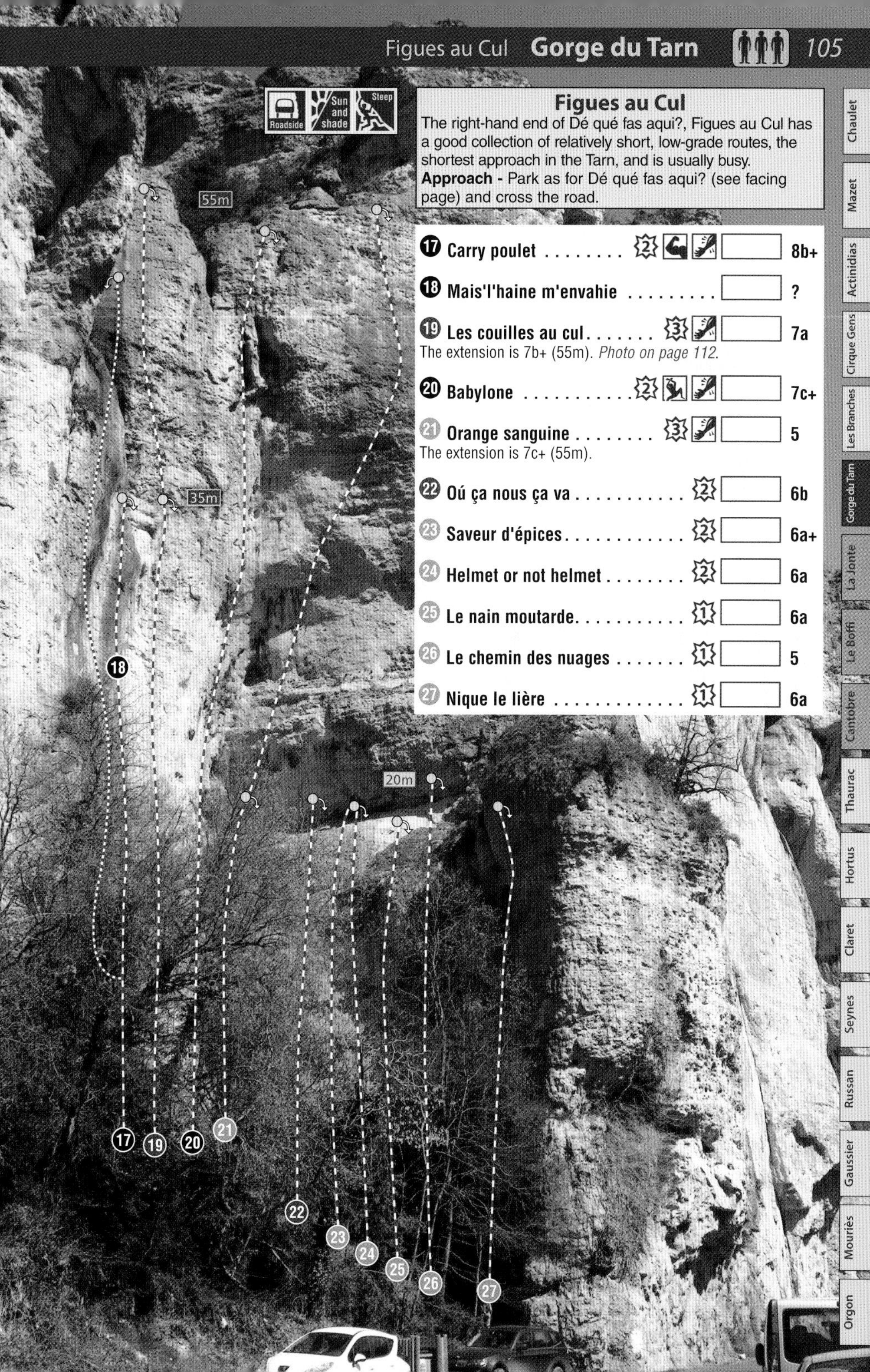

Figues au Cul

The right-hand end of Dé qué fas aqui?, Figues au Cul has a good collection of relatively short, low-grade routes, the shortest approach in the Tarn, and is usually busy.

Approach - Park as for Dé qué fas aqui? (see facing page) and cross the road.

No.	Route	Stars	Grade
17	**Carry poulet**	2	8b+
18	**Mais'l'haine m'envahie**		?
19	**Les couilles au cul**	3	7a
	The extension is 7b+ (55m). *Photo on page 112.*		
20	**Babylone**	2	7c+
21	**Orange sanguine**	3	5
	The extension is 7c+ (55m).		
22	**Oú ça nous ça va**	2	6b
23	**Saveur d'épices**	2	6a+
24	**Helmet or not helmet**	2	6a
25	**Le nain moutarde**	1	6a
26	**Le chemin des nuages**	1	5
27	**Nique le lière**	1	6a

1	Frit confi	7a
2	L'homme pressé	7c
3	Coup de foudre	7c
4	Jour de perf	8a
5	La napouse	7c+
6	Living Colour	7c

L'Amphi

Approach - Park on the Les Vignes side of the first tunnel - just after Dé qué fas aqui? Walk through the tunnel and take a path on the left just before you get to a large meadow, also on the left. Follow this path for about 50m, until you reach a yellow sign. Take the left-hand trail and follow it until about 20m from a stone chapel, a path leads down to the left. Take this path and follow it around the base of Tennessee. L'Amphi is up and left of Tennessee, and is reached by ascending a short section of via ferrata, then following a trail up into the amphitheatre.

No.	Route	Stars	Grade
7	**Planète groove**	2	8a
8	**La bohème**	2	7c
9	**Tatopani**	2	7b+
10	**Salvador Dali**	2	7c
11	**Gynécotraverse**	1	7c+
12	**La tarte aux poils**	1	8a+
13	**La veuve noire**	2	7b
14	**Jour de doye**	2	7a

he extension is 7a+ (40m).

No.	Route	Stars	Grade
15	**Le stress de la vielle pute**	2	7b
16	**Salut les copines**	3	6b
17	**Mélancolie rasta**	2	6c+
18	**Gr15**	3	6c+
19	**Objecteur consciencieux**	2	7c+
20	**La tarte chauve**		?

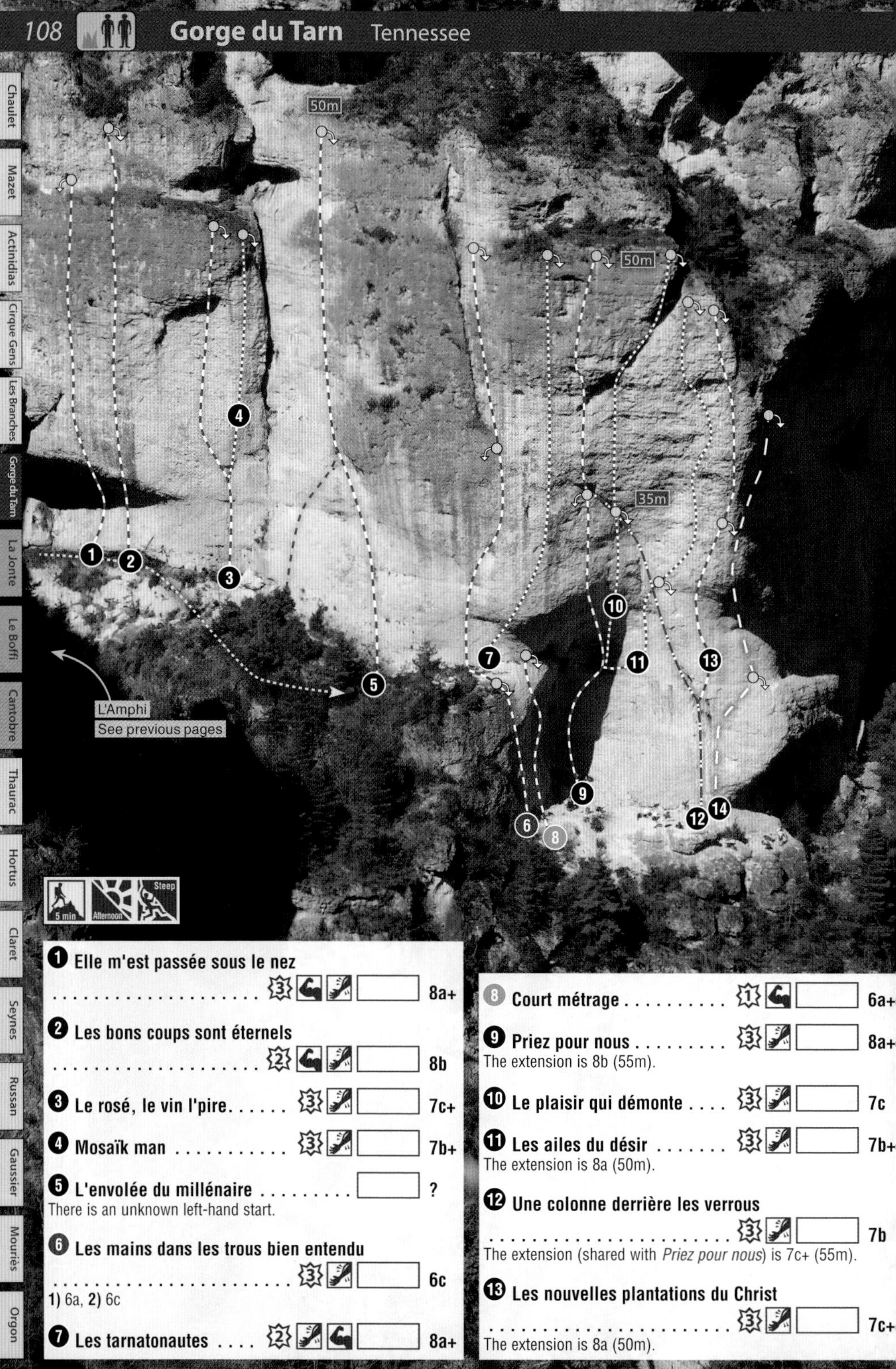

1 Elle m'est passée sous le nez . . . . [3] 8a+

2 Les bons coups sont éternels . . . . [2] 8b

3 Le rosé, le vin l'pire . . . . . . [3] 7c+

4 Mosaïk man . . . . [3] 7b+

5 L'envolée du millénaire . . . . ?
There is an unknown left-hand start.

6 Les mains dans les trous bien entendu . . . . [3] 6c
1) 6a, **2)** 6c

7 Les tarnatonautes . . . . [2] 8a+

8 Court métrage . . . . [1] 6a+

9 Priez pour nous . . . . [3] 8a+
The extension is 8b (55m).

10 Le plaisir qui démonte . . . . [3] 7c

11 Les ailes du désir . . . . [3] 7b+
The extension is 8a (50m).

12 Une colonne derrière les verrous . . . . [3] 7b
The extension (shared with *Priez pour nous*) is 7c+ (55m).

13 Les nouvelles plantations du Christ . . . . [3] 7c+
The extension is 8a (50m).

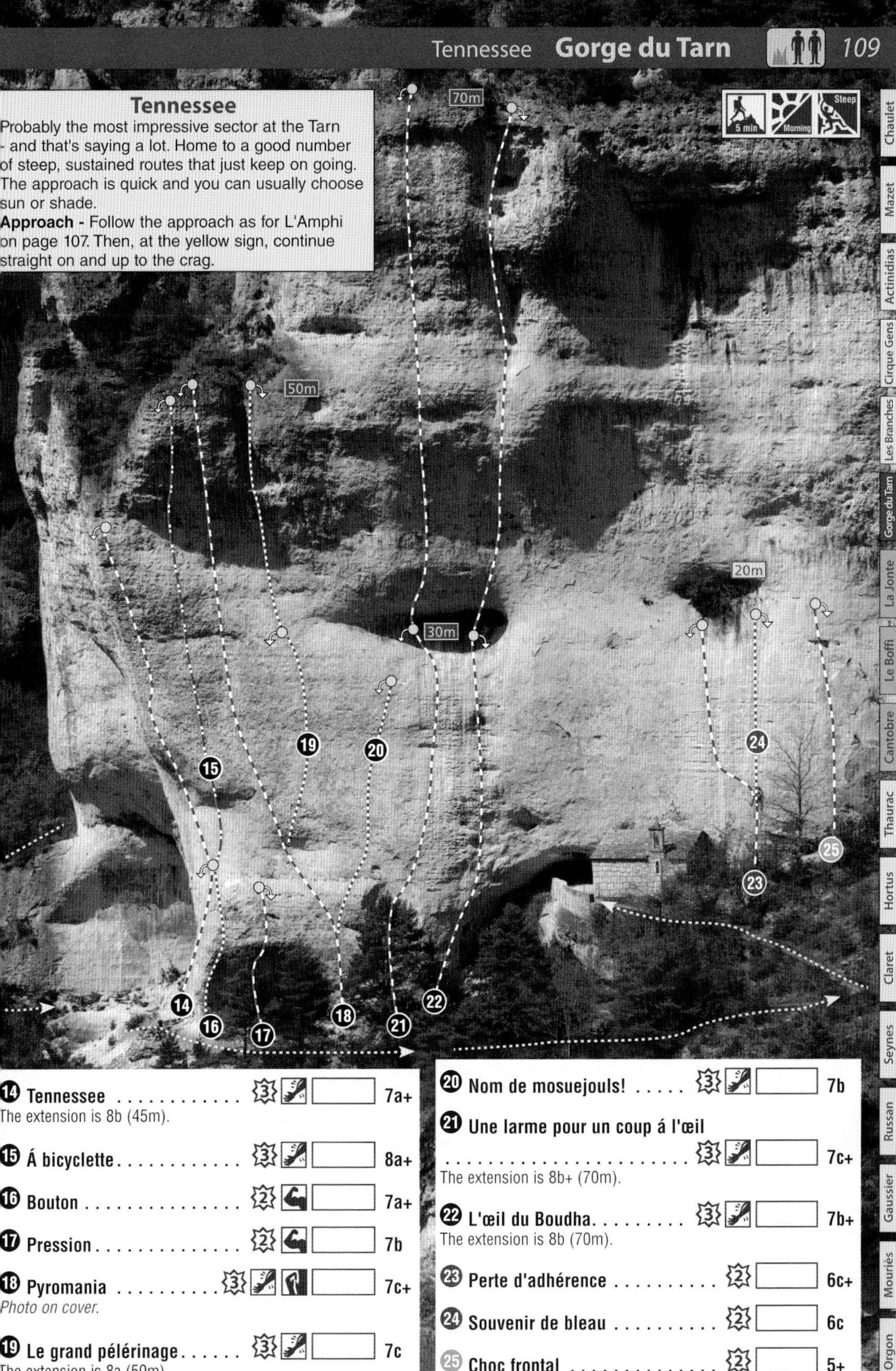

Tennessee

Probably the most impressive sector at the Tarn - and that's saying a lot. Home to a good number of steep, sustained routes that just keep on going. The approach is quick and you can usually choose sun or shade.

Approach - Follow the approach as for L'Amphi on page 107. Then, at the yellow sign, continue straight on and up to the crag.

14 Tennessee .... 3 ☐ 7a+
The extension is 8b (45m).

15 Á bicyclette .... 3 ☐ 8a+

16 Bouton .... 2 ☐ 7a+

17 Pression .... 2 ☐ 7b

18 Pyromania .... 3 ☐ 7c+
Photo on cover.

19 Le grand pélérinage ...... 3 ☐ 7c
The extension is 8a (50m).

20 Nom de mosuejouls! ..... 3 ☐ 7b

21 Une larme pour un coup á l'œil .... 3 ☐ 7c+
The extension is 8b+ (70m).

22 L'œil du Boudha .... 3 ☐ 7b+
The extension is 8b (70m).

23 Perte d'adhérence .... 2 ☐ 6c+

24 Souvenir de bleau .... 2 ☐ 6c

25 Choc frontal .... 2 ☐ 5+

Chaulet
Mazet
Actinidias
Cirque Gens
Les Branches
Gorge du Tarn
La Jonte
Le Boffi
Cantobre
Thaurac
Hortus
Claret
Seynes
Russan
Gaussier
Mouriès
Orgon

10 min · Morning · Steep

Le Navire

A fine wall with a good range of routes to go at, and well-placed as a warm-up for its neighbours. Le Navire is a good option for avoiding the sun - just turn up after midday.
Approach - Park on the Les Vignes side of the first tunnel - just after Dé qué fas aqui? Walk through the tunnel and take a path on the left just before you get to a large meadow, also on the left. Follow this path for about 50m, continuing straight on when you get to the yellow sign. Continue steeply up and right to get to the base of the routes.

35m
20m
6

No.	Route	Stars	Grade
1	69 avant Jésus Christ	2	7b
2	Les équipeurs du dimanche	2	6a+
3	Les trois payots	1	6b+
4	Caco3	1	7b
5	Ces no more		6c+
6	Bas les brosses		6c+
7	Le perf volant	2	6b+
8	Anton et le za	2	6b
9	Grandeur nature	2	7b
10	Les poules aux yeux d'or	3	7c
11	Retourné, volée	2	7b+
12	Un poil sur la langue	2	7c
13	El diablo perverso	2	7b
14	La case du petit chef	2	7a+
15	Ten years after	2	7b
16	L'équipeur désagrégé	2	7a+
17	Nationalistes, mon cul!	1	6c
18	Le petit massoro	1	6b+
19	Les sœurs pétard	1	6a

30m
30m
20m
5
6
7
8
9
10
11
12
13
14
15
16
17
18
19
Chaulet
Mazet
Actinidias
Cirque Gens
Les Branches
Gorge du Tarn
La Jonte
Le Boffi
Cantobre
Thaurac
Hortus
Claret
Seynes
Russan
Gaussier
Mouriès
Orgon

Sylvain Berger on the brilliant *Les couilles au cul* (7a) - *page 105.*

Calmez-vous

Together with Arc-en-ciel, this area is collectively also known as Cirque des Baumes and gives a pleasant collection of short walls that enjoy the afternoon shade and a position away from the road.

Approach - Follow the approach as for L'Amphi on page 107. Then, at the yellow sign, take the right fork at the sign and follow the path up. From the start of *Calmez-vous*, a path leads under the base of the cliffs.

1. **Petit ruisseau** .... 2 7b+
2. **T'as pas un nom?** .... 2 7a+
3. **Prise de carre** 2 7b
4. **Arnasquecom** .... 2 7c+
5. **Super Vixens** .... ?

Chaulet
Mazet
Actinidias
Cirque Gens
Les Branches
Gorge du Tarn
La Jonte
Le Boffi
Cantobre
Thaurac
Hortus
Claret
Seynes
Russan
Gaussier
Mouriès
Orgon

No.	Route	Stars	Grade
1	Démarrages à froid 1	2	6c
2	Démarrages à froid 2	2	6b+
3	Démarrages à froid 3	2	6c
4	Porc et camion	2	6b+
5	Parfum d'infâme	2	6c
6	Les odieux du stade	2	7a+
7	Corps des canines	2	7a
8	Prise de bec	2	7b
9	Main basse sur le cochonnet	2	7a+
10	L'esthète en l'air	3	6c+

	Route		Grade
11	Calmez-vous, ça va passer!	3	7a+
12	Idées fausses sur la défonce	2	7c
13	L'arrache clou	2	7a
14	Coq en stock	2	7a+
15	Moustifolies	2	7a
16	Massacre à la tronçonneuse		7b
17	Le plaisir qui monte		6c+
18	Patinage artistique	1	7b+

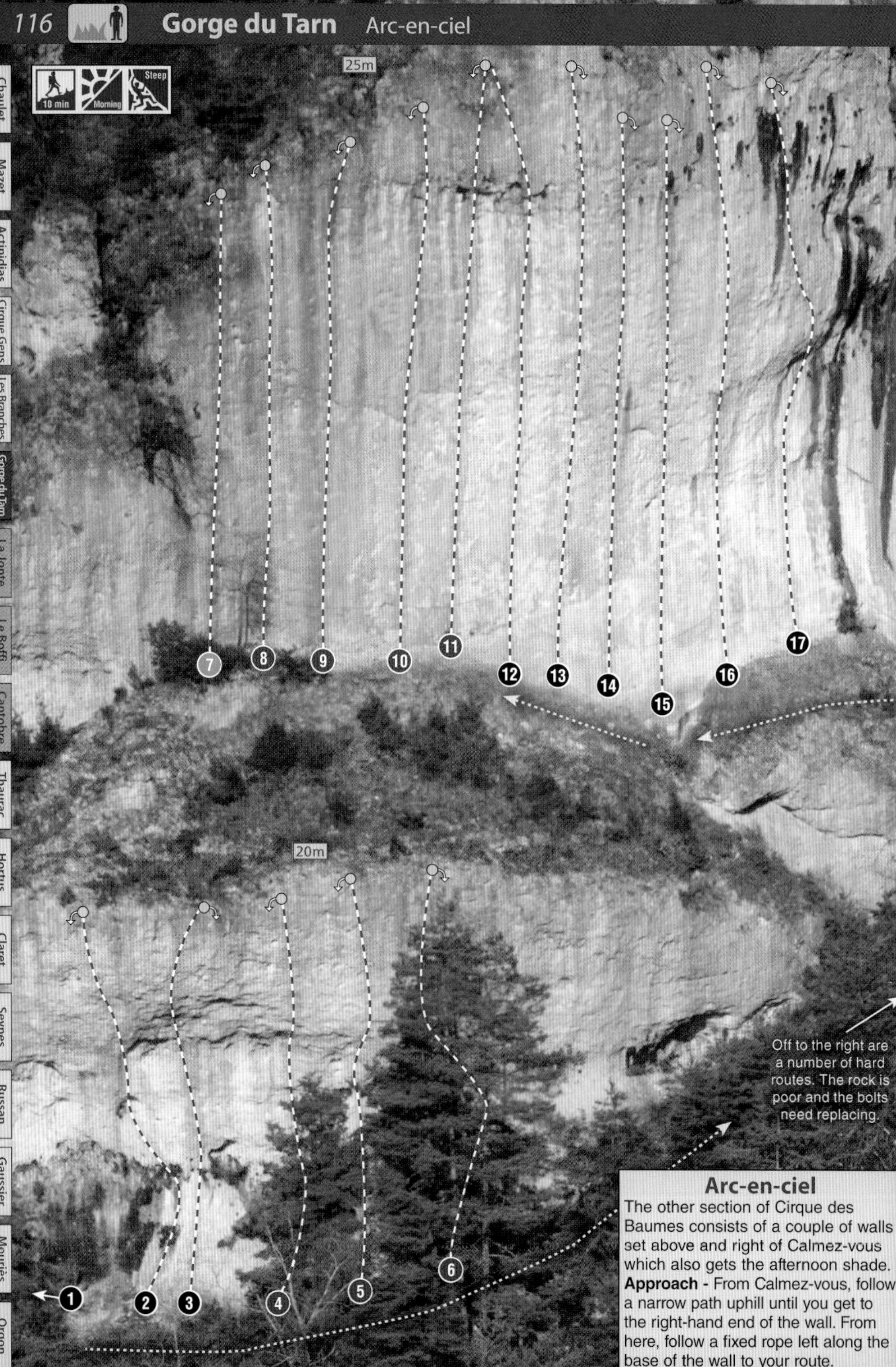

Arc-en-ciel

The other section of Cirque des Baumes consists of a couple of walls set above and right of Calmez-vous which also gets the afternoon shade.

Approach - From Calmez-vous, follow a narrow path uphill until you get to the right-hand end of the wall. From here, follow a fixed rope left along the base of the wall to your route.

	Route	Stars	Grade
1	Coma idyllique	2	7a+
2	Simone garnier sent-elle des pieds?	2	7b
3	Les enfants du paradis	2	7b
4	Tartine	2	7a
5	L'éloge de la fruite	2	6c
6	Valstar-choucroute	1	6c
7	Parole donneur	1	5+
8	Welcome to paradise	2	6b+
9	Arc-en-ciel	2	7a
10	La folie des couleurs	2	6c+
11	Rose d'argent	3	7a
12	Little Bob Story Possibly 7b.	3	7a+
13	Complicaction Possibly 8a.	2	7c+
14	Degré de force	2	7b+
15	Le cru qui pue	2	7b+
16	Rage dedans	2	8a
17	Le petit prince	1	8a

Climber on *Tarn is business* (6c), Trésor du Zèbre - *page 121*.

Canyon

Probably the trickiest crag in the Tarn to approach, so make the effort if you want some solitude.

Approach - Follow the approach described opposite to the left-hand end of Trésor du Zèbre. Just before this path becomes bounded on the left by a small crag (a handful of new routes) follow a small path left and upwards, but mostly leftwards. This leads to another small crag (and another small collection of short routes) but before you reach it, turn off left and continue through vegetation up to the top of the wall opposite Trésor du Zèbre. You should soon see the routes at the top of Canyon. To reach the rest of the routes, descend through a narrow, dark Canyon.

Initial approach - The five sectors shown above all share the same initial approach. Park just before the second tunnel. Walk through the tunnel to between the second and third tunnels. A path leads off up to the left just before the third tunnel. The first crag you see is Gullich up on the left. Continue on the path and you reach Trésor du Zèbre. If you follow Trésor around to the right, you can follow the path up to reach Club House and Hollandaise.

1 **Le cri du margouillat** . . . . . 2 7a+
Possibly 7b.

2 **Tôt ou tarn** 2 7b

3 **Canjon Trekking** . . . . 1 6c+

4 **Va savoir** . . . . 2 6c+

5 **Toutes les brunes** 1 6a

6 **Les girafes c'est grand** 1 6b

7 **Tant qu'on aura des spits** 1 6a

8 **Les poneys ça pue** . . . . 1 6b+

9 **Le houblon c'est bon** . . . . . 1 6b+

10 **Je hais les caniches** . . . . 1 6a+

11 **Bison futé voit rouge** 1 6c

12 **Laurel** 2 7b

13 **Hardy** . . . . 2 8a+

14 **Le maître des lieux** 1 6c

15 **Le cubi** . . . . 1 6c+

16 **Souvenir de la gare** 1 7a

Chaulet
Mazet
Actinidias
Cirque Gens
Les Branches
Gorge du Tarn
La Jonte
Le Boffi
Cantobre
Thaurac
Hortus
Claret
Seynes
Russan
Gaussier
Mouriès
Orgon

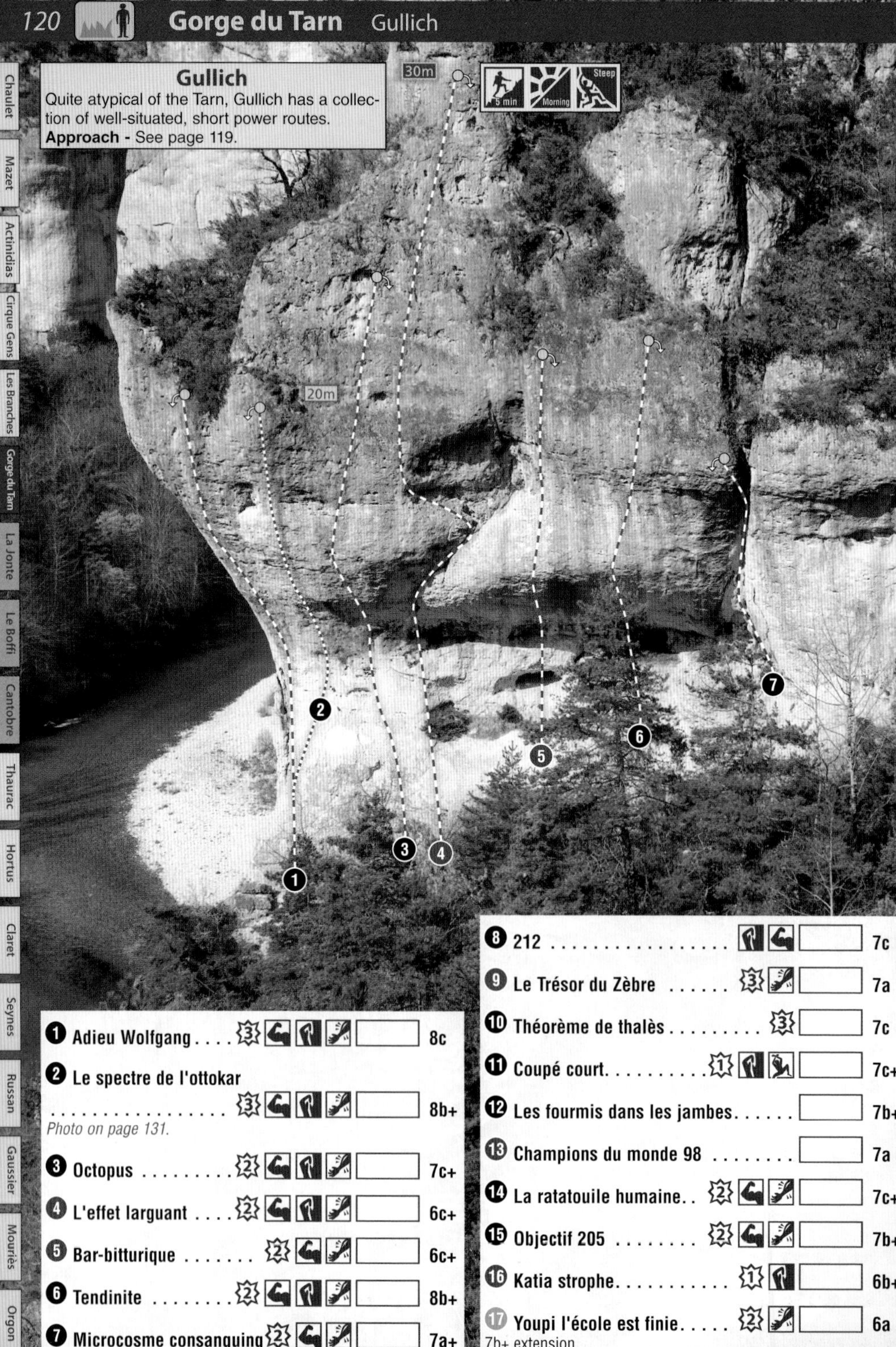

Gullich

Quite atypical of the Tarn, Gullich has a collection of well-situated, short power routes.

Approach - See page 119.

1. Adieu Wolfgang . . . . 3 stars — 8c
2. Le spectre de l'ottokar . . . . 3 stars — 8b+
   Photo on page 131.
3. Octopus . . . . 2 stars — 7c+
4. L'effet larguant . . . . 2 stars — 6c+
5. Bar-bitturique . . . . 2 stars — 6c+
6. Tendinite . . . . 2 stars — 8b+
7. Microcosme consanguing 2 stars — 7a+
8. 212 . . . . — 7c
9. Le Trésor du Zèbre . . . . 3 stars — 7a
10. Théorème de thalès . . . . 3 stars — 7c
11. Coupé court. . . . 1 star — 7c+
12. Les fourmis dans les jambes. . . . — 7b+
13. Champions du monde 98 . . . . — 7a
14. La ratatouile humaine. . 2 stars — 7c+
15. Objectif 205 . . . . 2 stars — 7b+
16. Katia strophe. . . . 1 star — 6b+
17. Youpi l'école est finie. . . . 2 stars — 6a
    7b+ extension.

Trésor du Zèbre

A deservedly popular spot with great routes from 6a upwards.
Approach - see page 119.

18 **Time is Money** . . . . 3 stars 6c

19 **Tarn is Business** . . . . 3 stars 6c
Photo on page 117.

20 **Jeux de plage** . . . . 3 stars 6a

21 **Serpent cyclope** . . . . 1 star 6b

22 **Branli branlo branlette** . . . . 1 star 6b+

23 **Unknown** . . . . ?

24 **Mécontence mammouthale** . . . . 1 star 6c

25 **Zorg est méchant** . . . . . . 2 stars 7a+

26 **Unknown** . . . . ?

Club House

Just around the corner from Trésor du Zèbre, Club House has a few more lower-grade routes to go at although they are short, so expect them to be tough.

Approach - See page 119.

	Route	Stars		Grade
1	Luna rossa	2		6a+
2	Oh Lands!	2		5+
3	Trix	3		6b
4	Stairway to Heaven	3		6a+
5	Caldéron	3		6a+
6	Glispstick	2		6b

Hollandais

Located above Club House, the routes are short and powerful.
Approach - See page 119.

On the wall opposite Hollandais are two more routes:

7 **La cave où le rock est fort** . . 2 ☐ 6a+

8 **Convoqués pour le bac** . . . . 2 ☐ 6a

...and the Hollandais wall is home to six harder routes.

9 **Inimini** . . . . 2 ☐ 6c

10 **Jiskefet** . . . . 2 ☐ 6b+

11 **Claus' trofiel** . . . . 2 ☐ 6c+

12 **Les yeux de vert** . . . . . 2 ☐ 7a+

13 **La fille rouge** . . . . 2 ☐ 7b+

14 **0031** . . . . 2 ☐ 7a

Chaulet
Mazet
Actinidias
Cirque Gens
Les Branches
Gorge du Tarn
La Jonte
Le Boffi
Cantobre
Thaurac
Hortus
Claret
Seynes
Russan
Gaussier
Mouriès
Orgon

Moulin à Huile, Dromadaire, L'Oasif and Planète Causse

Approaches - These four sectors are accessed from parking at the extensive parking area at the furthest end (from Les Vignes) of the climbing area. Walking back down the gorge, the first area you find on your right is Planète Causse, the next is L'Oasif then Moulin à Huile - these are right next to the road. To get to Dromadaire, take a path that leads off leftwards just before you reach the tunnel, and follow it down towards the river.

1. **Le bonheur est dans le pré** . 1 7a
2. **C'est mortel!** . . . . 1 7c+
3. **Il n'y a d'horreur que dans le nom** . . . . 2 7b+
4. **Ya qua!** 2 7c
5. **La bomba** . . . . 3 8a+
6. **Aligot** 2 8a
7. **Géométrie dans l'espace** 1 7c

Dromadaire
he only crag on the river side of the road,
romadaire has a few good hard routes
d easy access to the river for a swim.
min
Lots of sun
Steep
30m
25m
1
2
3
4
5
6
7
Chaulet
Mazet
Actinidias
Cirque Gens
Les Branches
Gorge du Tarn
La Jonte
Le Boffi
Cantobre
Thaurac
Hortus
Claret
Seynes
Russan
Gaussier
Mouriès
Orgon

Moulin à Huile

Two sections of wall with just a few routes between them. The roof is wild but bring some long quickdraws to kee drag to a minimum and a very long rop if you want to get down in one go.
Approach - see page 124.

	Route	Stars	Grade
1	Unknown		?
2	Roco ci frédo	3	7b+
3	Suprème dimension	3	6c+
4	Bras de fer	3	7b

	Route	Stars	Grade
5	Relatopms humaines	3	7b
6	Kikibelli	1	6c
7	Auver gniaque	2	7c

Kikibelli: A line of bolts now continues direct up the crack, but this route moves right.

Néfaste food . . . . 1 7c+
ssibly 8a.

Clin d'œil ou vision . . . . 1 7c+

Ma queue Donald. . . . . . 1 7b+

11 La pierre philosophale 2 7a

12 Le cinquième élément 1 6c

13 Mets de l'huile 1 6b

14 Unknown. . . . . 6a+

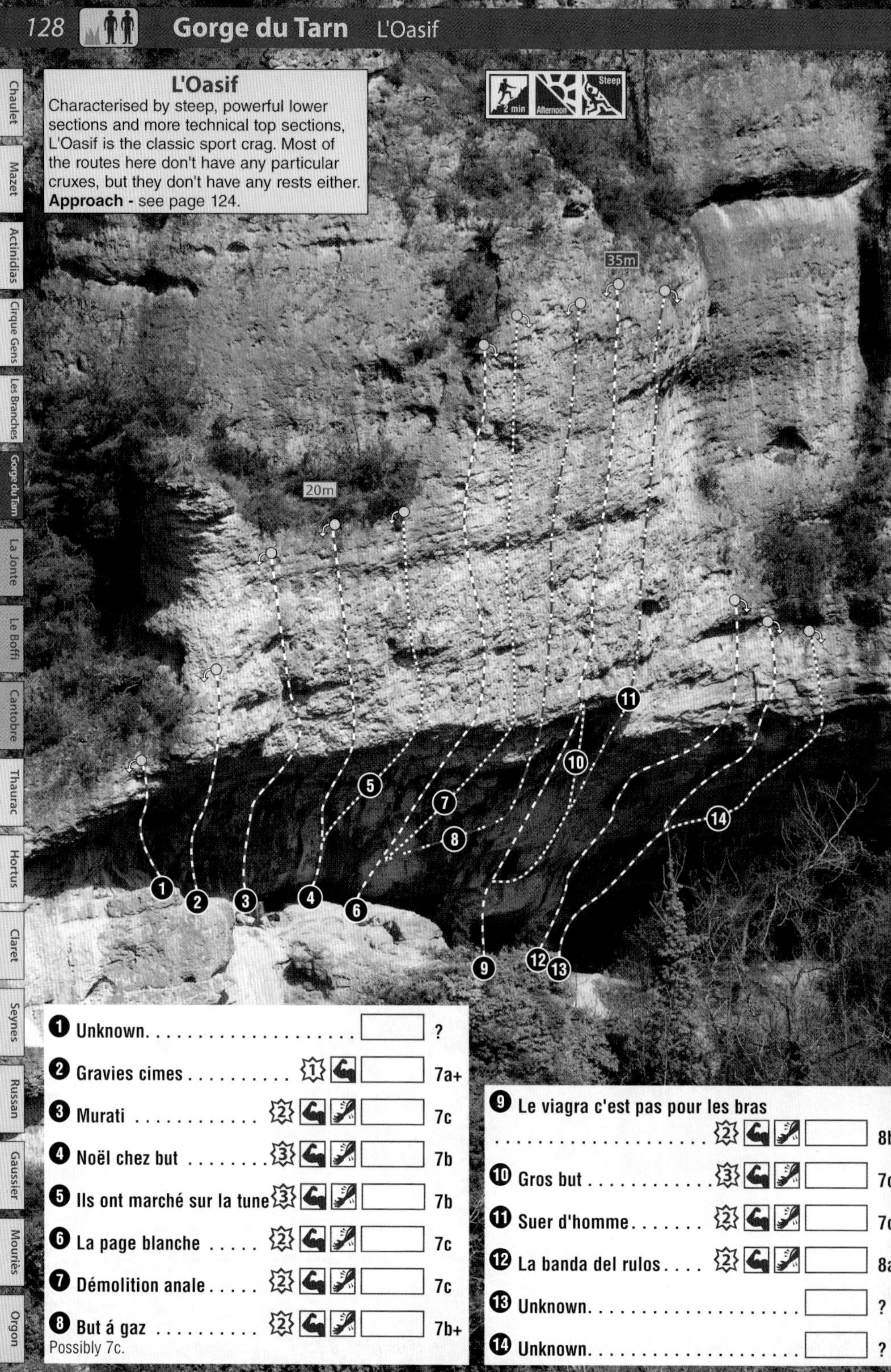

L'Oasif

Characterised by steep, powerful lower sections and more technical top sections, L'Oasif is the classic sport crag. Most of the routes here don't have any particular cruxes, but they don't have any rests either.
Approach - see page 124.

No.	Route	Stars	Grade
1	Unknown		?
2	Gravies cimes	1	7a+
3	Murati	2	7c
4	Noël chez but	3	7b
5	Ils ont marché sur la tune	3	7b
6	La page blanche	2	7c
7	Démolition anale	2	7c
8	But á gaz Possibly 7c.	2	7b+
9	Le viagra c'est pas pour les bras	2	8b
10	Gros but	3	7c
11	Suer d'homme	2	7c
12	La banda del rulos	2	8a
13	Unknown		?
14	Unknown		?

No.	Route	Stars	Grade
15	Unknown		?
16	Monstre trou	2	7c
17	Rasta vaut rien	3	8b
18	Starting bloc	3	7c
19	Putain de papiers	3	7b+
20	Alambic	3	7a+

There is now an extension - grade unknown.

No.	Route	Stars	Grade
21	Butinage alienique	3	7a
22	Déconnage immédiat	3	7a
23	Flexion	3	7a
24	Extention	2	7a
25	Cosmopolite	2	6c
26	Honky tonche	2	6c+

Planète Causse

A stunning wall with stacks to go at in the mid 7s. Being very close to the biggest parking area in the Tarn, expect to share this wall with others.

Approach - see page 124.

No.	Route	Stars	Grade
1	Mon dide	2	7b
2	Pas d'pognon	2	7b+
3	Omar m'a tuer	2	7b
4	Show Room	2	7b
5	Planète Causse	3	7a+
6	Hoy me voy	2	8a
7	Une vague dans la tête	3	7c+
8	Vague à l'âme	3	7c
9	L'oubliée du temps	2	7c
10	Le grand sot	2	7c
11	Le jus de chaussette de chez Ivan	1	7c+
12	Laisse à moi rêver	1	7c
13	Upercut au mentor	1	7b
14	Soloboy	1	7c
15	Final jeunes cailles	1	7b+

Unknown climber on *Le spectre de l'ottokar* (8b+) - *page 120.*

La Diagonale du Gogol
Le Bitard
Roche Décollée
p.156
p.158
p.159
Le Révérend
La Cathédrale
Les Patates
p.136
p.138
p.147
P
Le Rozier

Air de Temps
p.160
La Fusée
p.162
La Licorne
p.166

Chaulet
Mazet
Actinidias
Cirque Gens
Les Branches
Gorge du Tarn
La Jonte
Le Boffi
Cantobre
Thaurac
Hortus
Claret
Seynes
Russan
Gaussier
Mouriès

Gorge de la Jonte

	No star	1 star	2 star	3 star
Up to 4+	2	6	1	-
5 to 6a+	7	26	24	18
6b to 7a	6	17	43	24
7a+ and up	8	14	42	27

The Jonte is not a particularly well-known area, climbers visiting the Gorge du Tarn just up the road are often entirely unaware of its existence, which is surprising, when you consider it has a much longer climbing history. The Jonte is home to an astounding number of superb routes, following a mixture of strong natural lines and stark faces, reaching about 150m in height. While not exactly big-wall climbs, they provide a great deal of atmosphere and exposure.

Many of the routes in the Jonte were originally climbed before the era of bolting, and many traditionally-protected routes remain, offering something that few French crags can. A word of warning though: its traditional past is very much in evidence in the grades (especially in the 5s and low 6s) which will feel distinctly tough in comparison to those of the nearby Tarn and Boffi, especially when you're three pitches up, so take it easy to begin with.

N
Gorge du Tarn
p.100
D995
Le Massegros
D907bis
D005
Les Vignes
A75
A32
D907bis
La Bourgarie
Gorge de la Jonte
Boyne
D907
D996
D547
Le Rozier/ Peyreleau
D809
Compeyre
About 5km

Approach Also see map on page 97

The crag lies just north of the D996, and is walking distance from Le Rozier/Peyreleau. From the road, a number of paths lead up to the various sectors. Parking on the roadside is limited, and it is important to not obstruct traffic.

Conditions

The crag generally faces south and gets a lot of sun. However, it is worth noting that routes following corners will get sun or shade depending on the time of day. The long routes, which are typical of the crag, are likely to get a cooling breeze when you get towards the top, so it's worth taking a windproof even if it's hot down low.

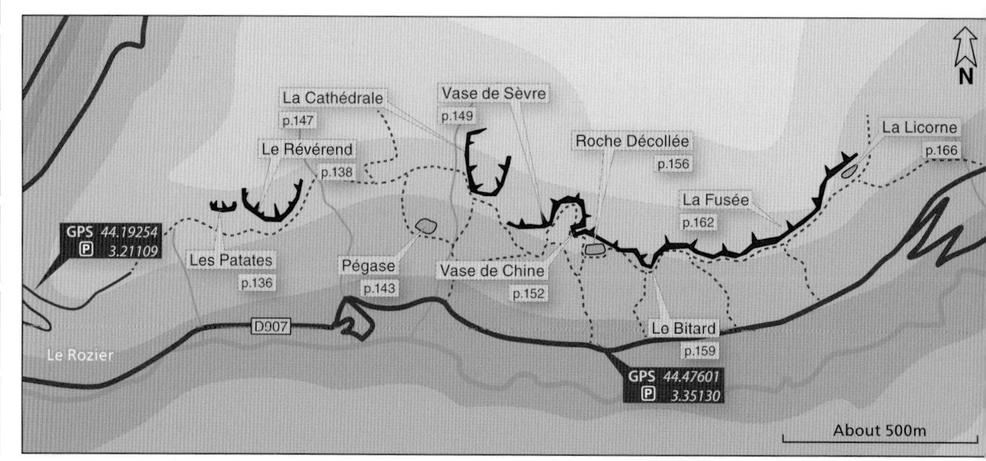

Alexandre Buisse and Neil Ronketti on the second pitch of *Aquo es quicon* (6a) - *page 163.*

Chaulet
Mazet
Actinidias
Cirque Gens
Les Branches
Gorge du Tarn
La Jonte
Le Boffi
Cantobre
Thaurac
Hortus
Claret
Seynes
Russan
Gaussier
Mouriès
Orgon

Les Patates

Within walking distance of Le Rozier, this sector has some low-grade single-pitches, and is right next to Le Révérend, with its much bigger, multi-pitch routes.

Approach - Follow the switchback road above Le Rozier until it turns into a track - it is possible to drive most of the way, though the parking is limited. Follow this to the hilltop settlement, then follow a path towards Le Révérend. Les Patates is reached by turning off to the left, Le Révérend is a little further along the main path.

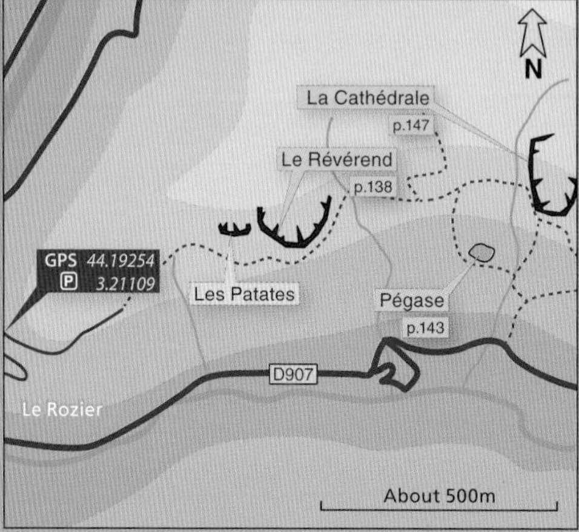

Tim Howell on *La grosse et le vampire* (6a+). Photo by Alexandre Buisse - *opposite.*

Le Révérend
Les Patates
p.138
To Le Rozier

	Route		Grade
1	Le perfo qui dérape	1	6a
2	Rouquintête	1	6b+
3	Taxe obinne	1	6c
4	100% à gauche		6b+
5	Château neuf	1	6c+
6	Ludo cuvée rouge	2	6b
7	La papamobile passe	2	6a
8	La vipère endormie	1	5+
9	Quatre est mon chiffre	1	4+
10	La grosse et le vampire		6a+
11	Elle rit au bi	1	7a
12	Chalaindrôme	1	6b
13	Calumette	2	5+
14	Watch Out		6b

Photo opposite. (10)

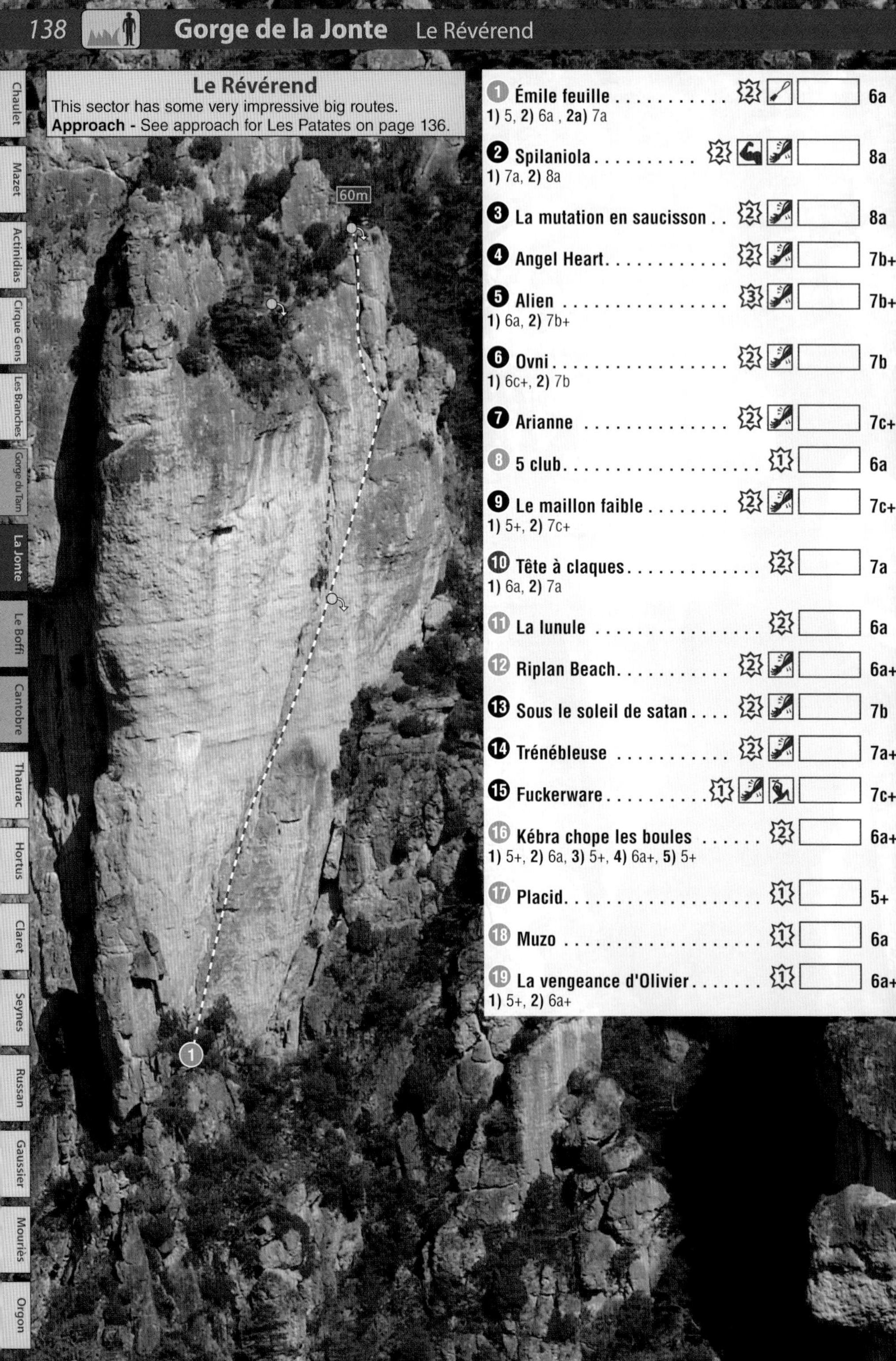

Le Révérend

This sector has some very impressive big routes.
Approach - See approach for Les Patates on page 136.

No.	Route	Stars	Grade
1	**Émile feuille** 1) 5, 2) 6a , 2a) 7a	2	6a
2	**Spilaniola** 1) 7a, 2) 8a	2	8a
3	**La mutation en saucisson**	2	8a
4	**Angel Heart**	2	7b+
5	**Alien** 1) 6a, 2) 7b+	3	7b+
6	**Ovni** 1) 6c+, 2) 7b	2	7b
7	**Arianne**	2	7c+
8	**5 club**	1	6a
9	**Le maillon faible** 1) 5+, 2) 7c+	2	7c+
10	**Tête à claques** 1) 6a, 2) 7a	2	7a
11	**La lunule**	2	6a
12	**Riplan Beach**	2	6a+
13	**Sous le soleil de satan**	2	7b
14	**Trénébleuse**	2	7a+
15	**Fuckerware**	1	7c+
16	**Kébra chope les boules** 1) 5+, 2) 6a, 3) 5+, 4) 6a+, 5) 5+	2	6a+
17	**Placid**	1	5+
18	**Muzo**	1	6a
19	**La vengeance d'Olivier** 1) 5+, 2) 6a+	1	6a+

20 Sale coup pour la fanfare . . . . . ★3 ☐ **6c**
1) 5+, **2)** 6a+, **3)** 6c, **4)** 6a+

21 Unknown. . . . . ☐ **?**

22 Mélo direct . . . . ☐ **7b+**

23 Unknown. . . . . ☐ **?**

24 À flasher. . . . . ★2 ☐ **7a**
Approach by descending from *Sale coup*.

17 min
Lots of sun
Vertical
Chaulet
Mazet
Actinidias
Cirque Gens
Les Branches
Gorge du Tarn
La Jonte
Le Boffi
Cantobre
Thaurac
Hortus
Claret
Seynes
Russan
Gaussier
Mouriès
Orgon
110m
75m
50m
35m
35m
Sale coup... - previous page
Melocoton start - previous page
1
2
3
4
5
6
7
8
9
10
11
12
13
14
15
16
17
18
19
20
21

1 Melocoton 3 stars — 6b+
1) A1/7b+ 2) 5+, 3) 6a, 4) 5+, 5) 6b+. See previous page for start.

2 Essuie glace 1 star — 7b+

3 Entre le doubte et l'espoir. 3 stars — 7c+

4 Unknown. — ?

5 L'abbée traille ses ouailles. 3 stars — 7c

6 Unknown. — ?

7 Génération virtuelle 2 stars — 7a+

8 Unknown. — ?

9 À varier 2 stars — 5

10 Au doigt et à l'œil 2 stars — 7a+

11 Où est passé mon rateau? 2 stars — 7b+

12 Deux perfs c'est mieux 2 stars — 7b

13 Le triomphe des gros 2 stars — 6b+

14 Le Révérend 3 stars — 5+
1) 5, 2) 5, 3) 5+, 4) 5+

15 Calculs raynaud 2 stars — 6b

16 Cayenne 2 stars — 6b
1) 6a, 2) 5+, 3) 5, 4) 6b

17 Les grossiers de l'écran 2 stars — 6b+
1) 6b+, 2) 5

18 Les misérables 2 stars — 6a
1) 5+, 2) 5, 3) 6a

19 Premiers émois 3 stars — 7b

20 Le maître d'école 3 stars — 7b

21 Cérébrotonic 3 stars — 7b
1) 7a, 2) 5+, 3) 7b

22 Ozone 2 stars — 7b
1) 6c+, 2) 7b. The first pitch is 7a+ if taken on the left.

23 Fuck Line! 2 stars — 7c

24 Du plomb dans les ailes. 3 stars — 8a+

25 El monstro del muesli! 3 stars — 8a
Ending at the low belay out right is *Petite variante* (7b).

26 Mick Crack 3 stars — 7b+

27 Plaisir de l'effort 2 stars — 7b+
1) 7a, 2) 7b+

28 Chagrin d'amour 3 stars — 7c+

29 Extra muros 3 stars — 7b

La Cathédrale Area

A mix of good steep single pitch routes and some epic multi-pitch adventures across the grade spectrum.

Approaches - It is possible to approach from Le Révérend, but quicker to approach directly from the road. Park at the first major parking area after leaving Le Rozier, and follow the path (from the orange emergency telephone) avoiding the right turn that would take you to Cirque des Vases. Contine until the path splits, the left fork taking you to Pégase, the right taking you on to La Cathédrale, L'Arête, and Carol Caline.

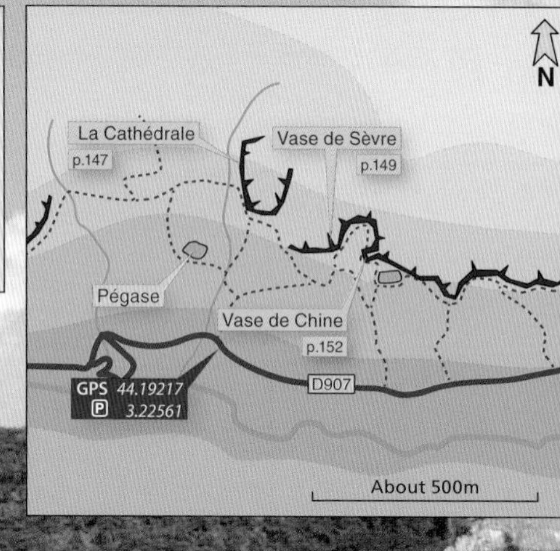

1 **Ça gaze!** 1) 6a, 2) 6b	2		**6b**
2 **Pégase** 1) 5, 2) 5+, 3) 4+	3		**5+**
3 **La rougne**			**4+**
4 **La coupe est pleine** 1) 5+, 2) 6a+	1		**6a+**

No.	Route	Stars	Grade
1	Mister T	2	7c+
2	Le pirate	3	6b
3	Unknown		?
4	Nad bab café	3	6c
5	Protections rapprochées	3	6a+
6	Carole Caline	3	6c+
7	Lou buis del ces	2	6c+

Unknown climber on *Le nez rouge* (7c+) - *next page*.

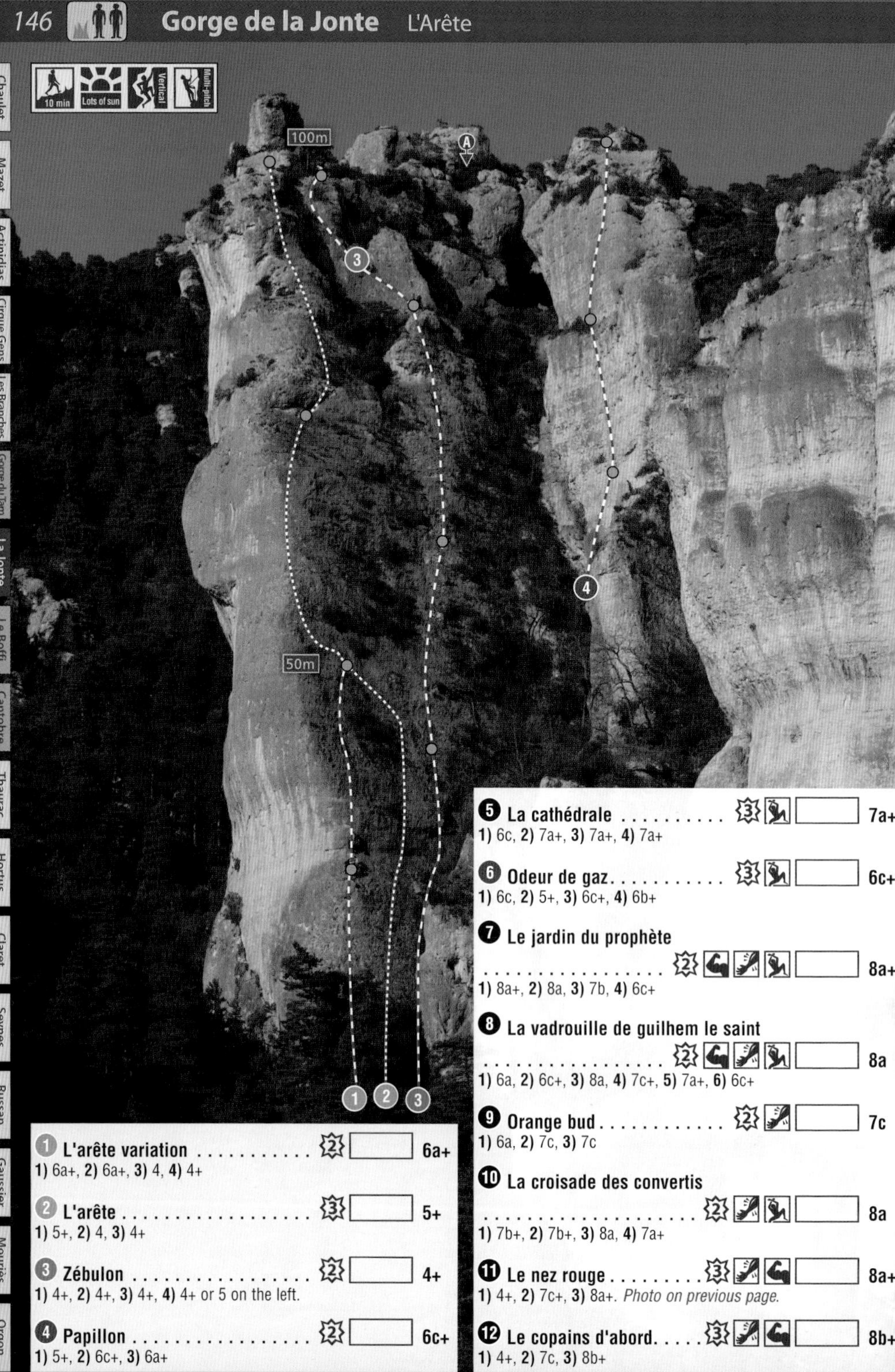

1 **L'arête variation** . . . . 2 6a+
1) 6a+, 2) 6a+, 3) 4, 4) 4+

2 **L'arête** . . . . 3 5+
1) 5+, 2) 4, 3) 4+

3 **Zébulon** . . . . 2 4+
1) 4+, 2) 4+, 3) 4+, 4) 4+ or 5 on the left.

4 **Papillon** . . . . 2 6c+
1) 5+, 2) 6c+, 3) 6a+

5 **La cathédrale** . . . . 3 7a+
1) 6c, 2) 7a+, 3) 7a+, 4) 7a+

6 **Odeur de gaz** . . . . 3 6c+
1) 6c, 2) 5+, 3) 6c+, 4) 6b+

7 **Le jardin du prophète** . . . . 2 8a+
1) 8a+, 2) 8a, 3) 7b, 4) 6c+

8 **La vadrouille de guilhem le saint** 2 8a
1) 6a, 2) 6c+, 3) 8a, 4) 7c+, 5) 7a+, 6) 6c+

9 **Orange bud** 2 7c
1) 6a, 2) 7c, 3) 7c

10 **La croisade des convertis** 2 8a
1) 7b+, 2) 7b+, 3) 8a, 4) 7a+

11 **Le nez rouge** . . . . 3 8a+
1) 4+, 2) 7c+, 3) 8a+. *Photo on previous page.*

12 **Le copains d'abord**. . . . . 3 8b+
1) 4+, 2) 7c, 3) 8b+

10 min | Afternoon | Vertical | Steep | Multi-pitch

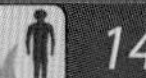

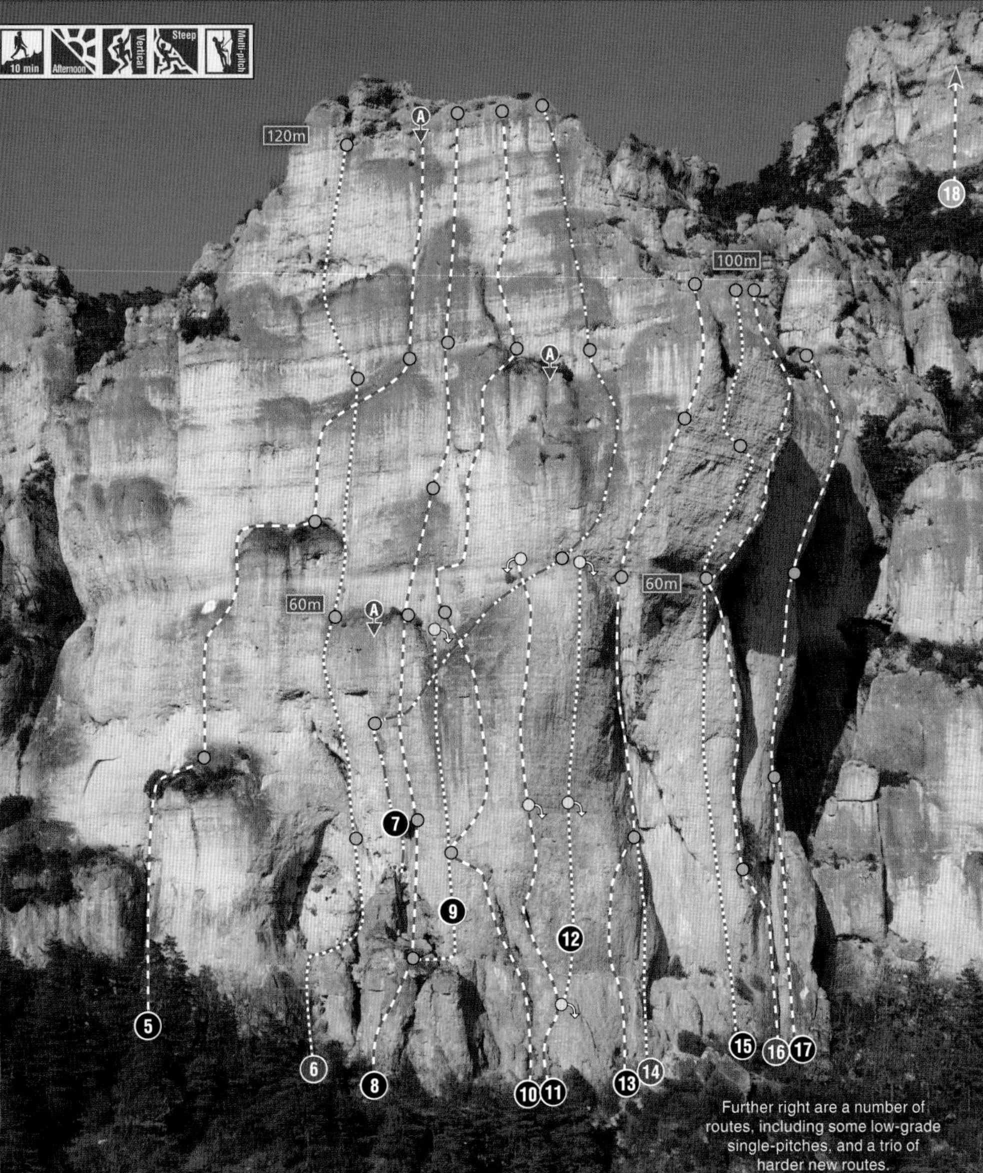

Further right are a number of routes, including some low-grade single-pitches, and a trio of harder new routes.

13 Le muscle et la plume . . {1} 7c+
1) 7b, 2) 7c+, 3) ? 4) ?

14 La belle hélène . . . . {2} 7a

15 Les chemins de Katmandou . . . . {3} 8c
1) 8b, 2) 7c, 3) 8c

16 L'envers dy devoir . . . . {3} 7a
1) 6c+, 2) 7a, 3) 7a

17 Massada . . . . {3} 7c
1) 7b, 2) 7b+, 3) 7c

There are a four short, low-grade routes to the right of Massada. The next route is to be found at the very top of the crag.

18 Libre max . . . . 6a+
1) 6a+, 2) 6a, 3) 5+

Chaulet
Mazet
Actinidias
Cirque Gens
Les Branches
Gorge du Tarn
La Jonte
Le Boffi
Cantobre
Thaurac
Hortus
Claret
Seynes
Russan
Gaussier
Mouriès
Orgon

Cirque des Vases

The area between Le Vase de Sèvre and le Vase de Chine is popular, and understandably so. The curious formations that make the vases are both climbable, offering a novel finish to one of the lower routes.

Approaches - Park at the first major parking area after leaving Le Rozier, and follow the path, turning right at a sign. It is also possible to follow the path that runs along the base of the crag and get to this area from La Cathédrale or Roche Décollée.

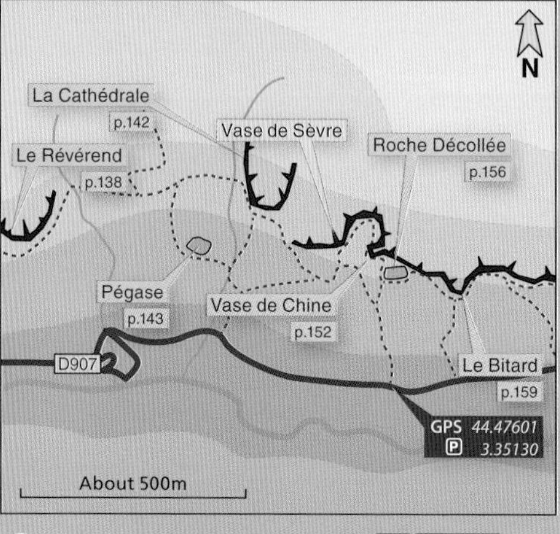

1 Jump . . . . 1 star **7c**
1) 6b+, **2)** 6b, **3)** 7c. The line on the topo is approximate.

2 Biotone . . . . 2 stars **6a+**
1) 5, **2)** 6a+, **3)** 5+, **4)** 5

3 Feu foret . . . . 1 star **5**
1) 5, **2)** 5

4 Spindizzy . . . . 2 stars **6c**

5 Troglobo . . . . 2 stars **6b**

6 Les femmes et les grimpeurs d'abord . . . . 3 stars **5+**
1) 5+, **2)** 5, **3)** 5+

7 Putain, ma corde!? . . . . 2 stars **6b+**
1) 6b, **2)** 6b+, **3)** 6b+

8 Krups idéal . . . . 2 stars **6c**
1) 6b+, **2)** 5, **3)** 6c. The third pitch takes a line parallel to the final pitch of *Ça bastogne*.

9 Bon baiser, bulon . . . . 2 stars **7a**
1) 7a, **2)** 6c, **3)** 7a, **4)** 6a+

10 Démons et mervieilles . . . . 1 star **5**
1) 5, **2)** 5

Pitch 1 of Démons is used to gain a couple of other routes.

11 Ça bastogne . . . . 2 stars **7a**
1) 7a, **2)** 6b

12 Atteinte aux doigts de l'homme . . . . 2 stars **6b+**

13 Crise éléphantine . . . . 1 star **6a**
1) 5, **2)** 6a

Pitch 1 of Crise éléphantine can be used to reach two higher pitches:

14 Varappeur à vapeur . . . . 1 star **6b**

15 Albaricoke . . . . 1 star **6b**

Two more routes are on the 'vase' at the top of the wall.

16 En chine par le tyrol . . . . . . 1 star **7a+**

17 Le vase de Sèvre . . . . 1 star **6c**
It can be climbed at 5+, with plenty of aid.

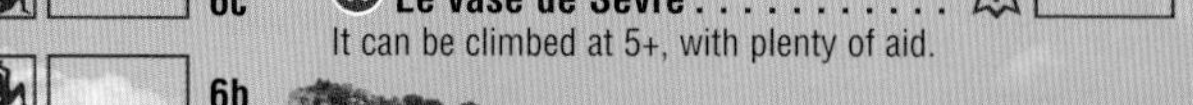

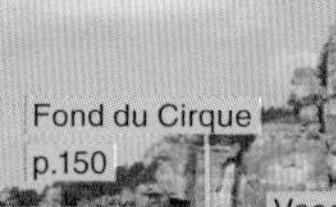

20 min
Lots of sun
Vertical
100m
30m to ledge
60m
40m
Traverse in to routes 4 & 5
25m
25m
Chaulet
Mazet
Actinidias
Cirque Gens
Les Branches
Gorge du Tarn
La Jonte
Le Boffi
Cantobre
Thaurac
Hortus
Claret
Seynes
Russan
Gaussier
Mouriès
Orgon

Chaulet
Mazet
Actinidias
Cirque Gens
Les Branches
Gorge du Tarn
La Jonte
Le Boffi
Cantobre
Thaurac
Hortus
Claret
Seynes
Russan
Gaussier
Mouriès
Orgon

1 Atomyologie .... 1 — 7a
2 Abominaffreuse .... 1 — 6c+
3 Tequila .... 2 — 7a
4 Sergent Peppers ...... 2 — 7a+
5 Voyage au bout de la nuit 2 — 7b
6 Pervers pépère .... 1 — 6a
7 Licence iv.......... 2 — 7c+
8 Lyonnais, on y reste... 2 — 7c+
9 Mort à crédit........ 2 — 7c
10 Promis au boucher............. — ?
11 Nkosi sikelle Africa ... 2 — 7b+
12 Homo aryen connardus.... 2 — 7a+
13 Frontispice .... — 4+
14 Greenpeace........... 2 — 7a
15 Contrisplaction .... — 6b+
16 Des petits brun et des grands roux .... 1 — 6a
17 Génocide masturbatif........ 1 — 6b+
18 Feu follet .... — 6c+
19 Fissure et certaine.......... 1 — 6b
20 Parfums funambules .... 1 — 5
21 Fenêtre sur cours........... 1 — 7b+
1) 6c, 2) 7b+
22 Le dièdre du piton oublié ..... — 5+

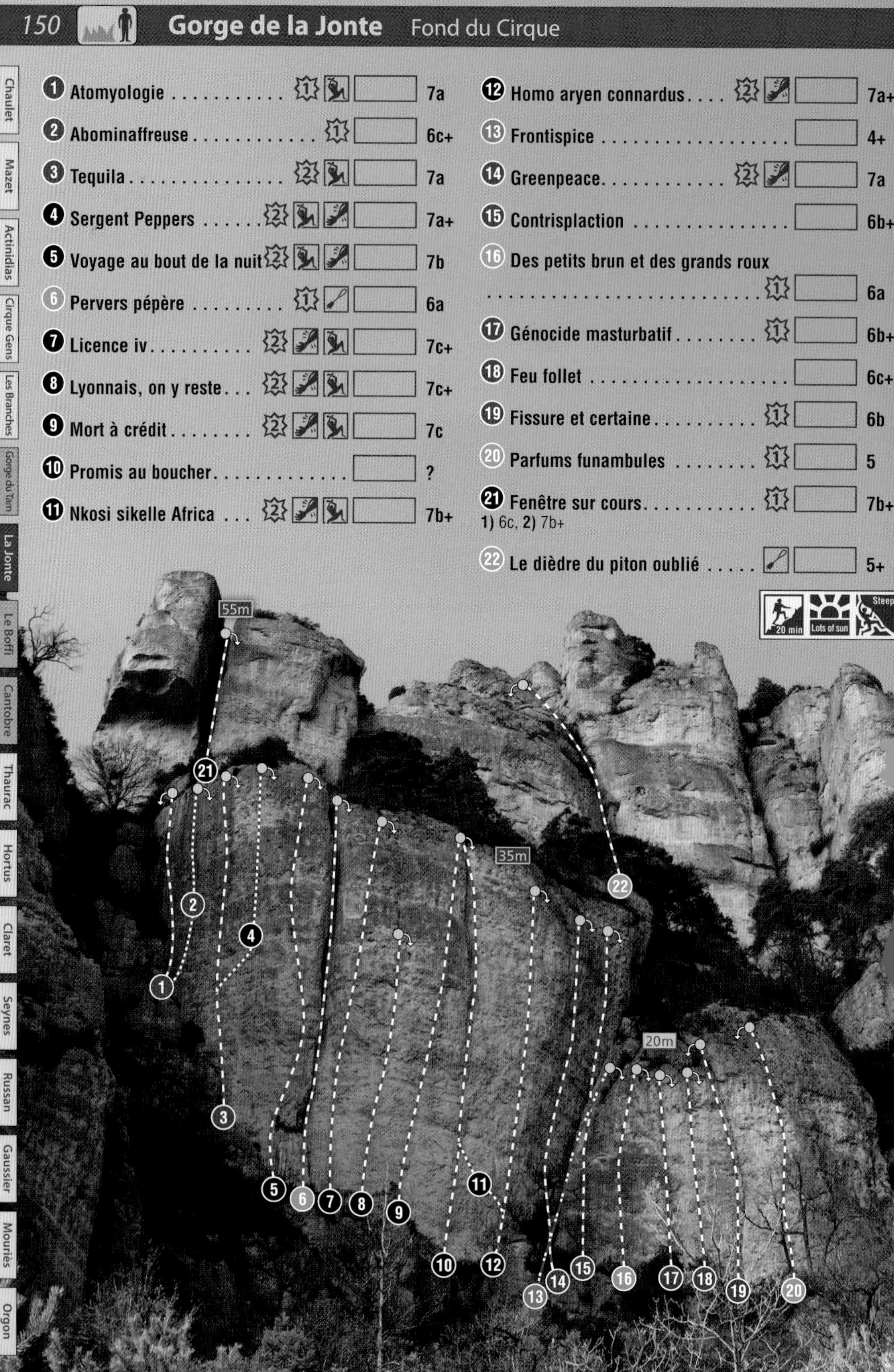

Climbers on *Le Bitard* (5+) - *page 159* - Photo by Alexandre Buisse.

1 Flash 6c
1) 5+, 2) 6c

2 Bad max 1 6a
1) 6a, 2) 5

3 Monstresse 1 6a
1) 6a, 2) 6a

4 Sniffeurs de madnésie . . . . 2 6b+
1) 6a+, 2) 6b+

5 Sem . . . . 5+
1) 5+, 2) 5+

6 Le voyageur ailé 2 6b
1) 6b, 2) 6a+

7 Les pets de damoclès . . . . 2 6a+
1) 5, 2) 6a, 3) 6a+

8 L'envie au bout des doigts . 2 6c

9 Perte d'énergie 2 7a
1) 3+, 2) 5+, 3) 7a, 4) 5

10 Le fond de l'air effraie . . . . 6a+

11 Une belle dans la tête .... 2 stars — 7a
1) 6b+, 2) 7a, 3) 6b

12 Orgues, amours et délices .... 3 stars — 7c+
1) 6a+, 2) 7c+, 3) 7b+

13 Le ramonaïre .... 1 star — 5+
1) 4, 2) 5, 3) 5+, 4) 5+

20 min — Sun and shade — Steep

14 Ça glisse au pays des marveilles .... 3 stars — 7b
1) 6b, 2) 7b

15 Plume .... 3 stars — 6a+
1) 5, 2) 6a+, 3) 6a+

16 Tastejo pas sul clavel .... 2 stars — 6c
1) 6a, 2) 6b, 3) 6c (bolted)

17 L'éthique est toc .... 1 star — 6b
1) 6b, 2) 6b

18 Acidose .... 3 stars — 7b

The 'vase' on this side is tackled from the top of Une belle dans la tête.

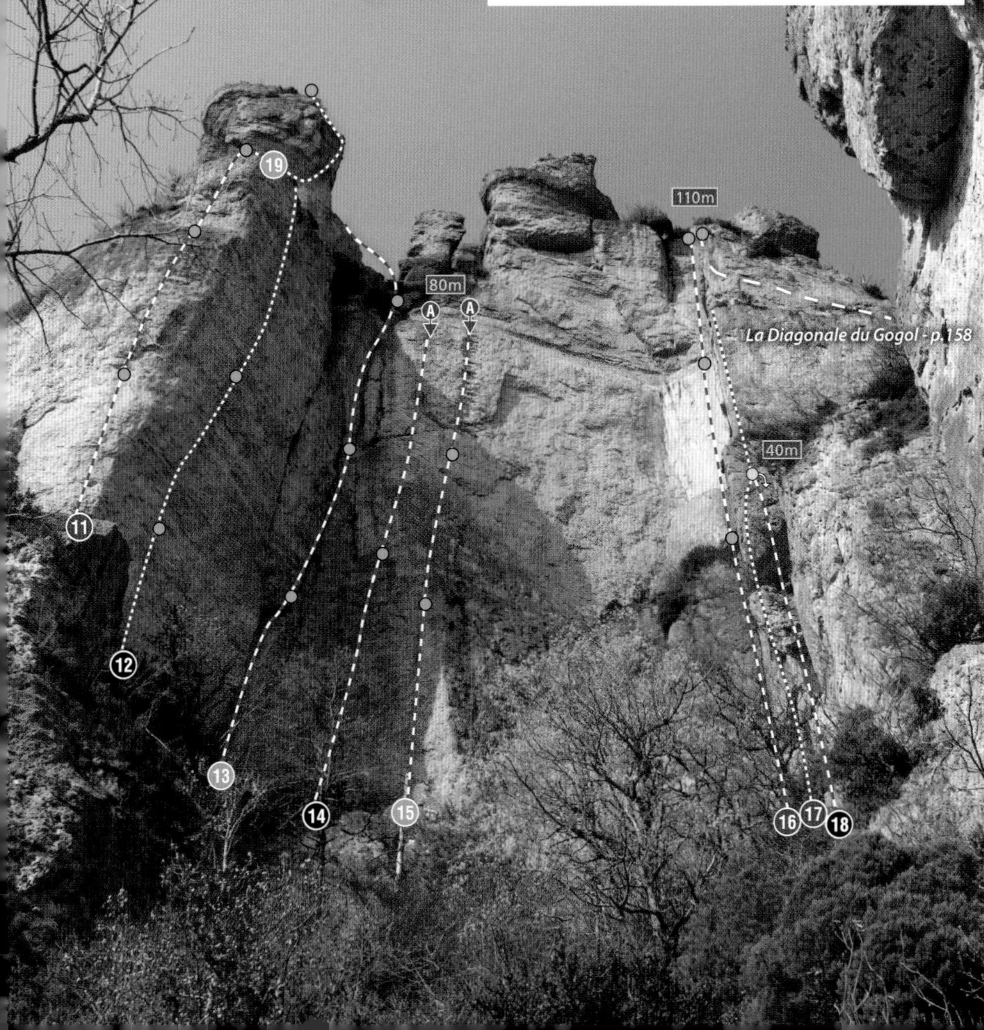

19 Vase de Chine .... 1 star — 5+

110m
80m
40m
La Diagonale du Gogol - p.158
11 12 13 14 15 16 17 18 19

Chaulet
Mazet
Actinidias
Cirque Gens
Les Branches
Gorge du Tarn
La Jonte
Le Boffi
Cantobre
Thaurac
Hortus
Claret
Seynes
Russan
Gaussier
Mcuriès
Orgon

La Roche Décollée to La Fusée

Arguably the main even of La Jonte, this area is packed with classic routes, mostly bolted, but with a fair number of traditionally protected routes too.

Approaches - There are various paths from the road to most of the sectors. Parking is quite limited and your approach may be dictated more by where you park than where you wish to go.

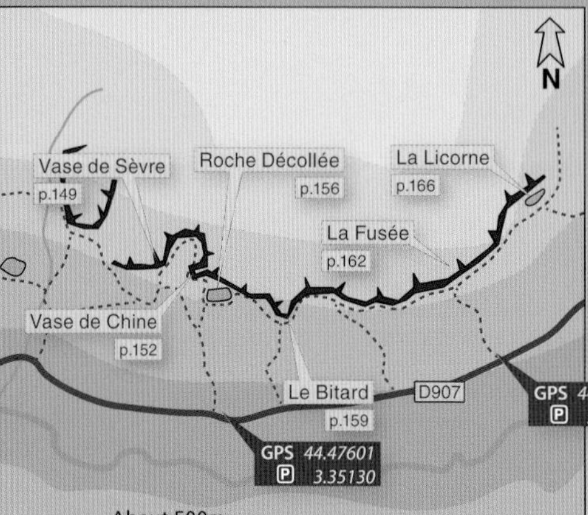

Body Building

Perched next to the road is a large free-standing boulder with a number of short, steep, powerful routes on its pocketed south face. The routes are listed from left to right and do not appear on a topo.

No.	Route	Stars	Grade
1	25° à l'ombre		6c
2	Tétanie	1	7b+
3	Body Building	1	7a+
4	Dévers tonic	1	7c+
5	Turquoise	1	7b+
6	Les vacances du nain de jardin	1	7c+

Climbers on *L'arête ouest* (6a+) - *page 157*.

La Roche Décollée

An irresistible feature that is surprisingly amenable, though be prepared for some airy positions. Use either 100m rope, or a pair of 50s to get down.

Descent - See topo for the line of abseil.

1) At the back of the rock, abseil from a tree to a ledge.

2) Descend the west side of the rock by another abseil.

3) Abseil to just left of the base of the routes on the west face.

1 Effet de style . . . . 1☆ 6c+

2 La colère des anciens . . . . 1☆ 6a+

3 Le bouldras attaque . . . . . . 2☆ 6b+
1) 6b, 2) 6b+, 3) 6b

4 Un bonheur qui dérape . . . . 2☆ 6b
1) 6b, 2) 6a, 3) 5+

5 Mer calme à très agitée . . . 3☆ 7a
1) 6c+, 2) 7a, 3) 7a. See previous pages for start.

6 L'arête ouest . . . . 3 — 6a+
1) 5+, 2) 6a+, 3) 5+. *Photo on page 155.*

7 Pierrot y mondino . . . . 3 — 5+
1) 5, 2) 5+, 3) 5+, 4) 5+. Gear needed for first pitch only.

8 La gueule du look . . . . 1 — 6a
1) 5, 2) 6a, 3) 6a, 4) 5+

9 La 8ème leffe . . . . 3 — 7a+
1) 5, as for *La gueule*, 2) 7a+, 3) 6a+, 4) 6c, 5) 6b+. Pitch 2 can be aided.

10 Histoire deux fous . . 3 — 8a
1) 5), 2) 7a+, 3) 8a, 4) 7b, 5) 7b

La Diagonale du Gogol

A set of easier routes than benefit from the shadow of the Roche Décolée later in the day.

Approach - As for La Roche Décolée and skirt right along the base (see page 154).

No.	Route	Stars	Grade
1	**Vietnam**	1	4+
2	**Pluie de buis**	1	5
3	**Les gros bras ne sont pas invités à la fête du mollet**	2	5
4	**La diagonale du gogol** — **1)** 5, **2)** 5, **3)** 5, **4)** 6a+, **5)** 5+, **6)** 6a. See page 153 for finish.	3	6a+
5	**Terre minologie**	2	5
6	**Berlingots sous roch**	2	5+
7	**L'arsouille a des couilles!**	2	5
8	**Marcel et ginette au pique-nique**	2	5
9	**Lichen chrome**	1	4+
10	**Passage haut niveau**	1	5
11	**Plaisirs de cocagne** — **1)** 5, **2)** 5+, **3)** 5, **4)** 5+	2	5+
12	**Vent arctique** — **1)** 5, **2)** 5+, **3)** 5, **4)** 5+	2	5+

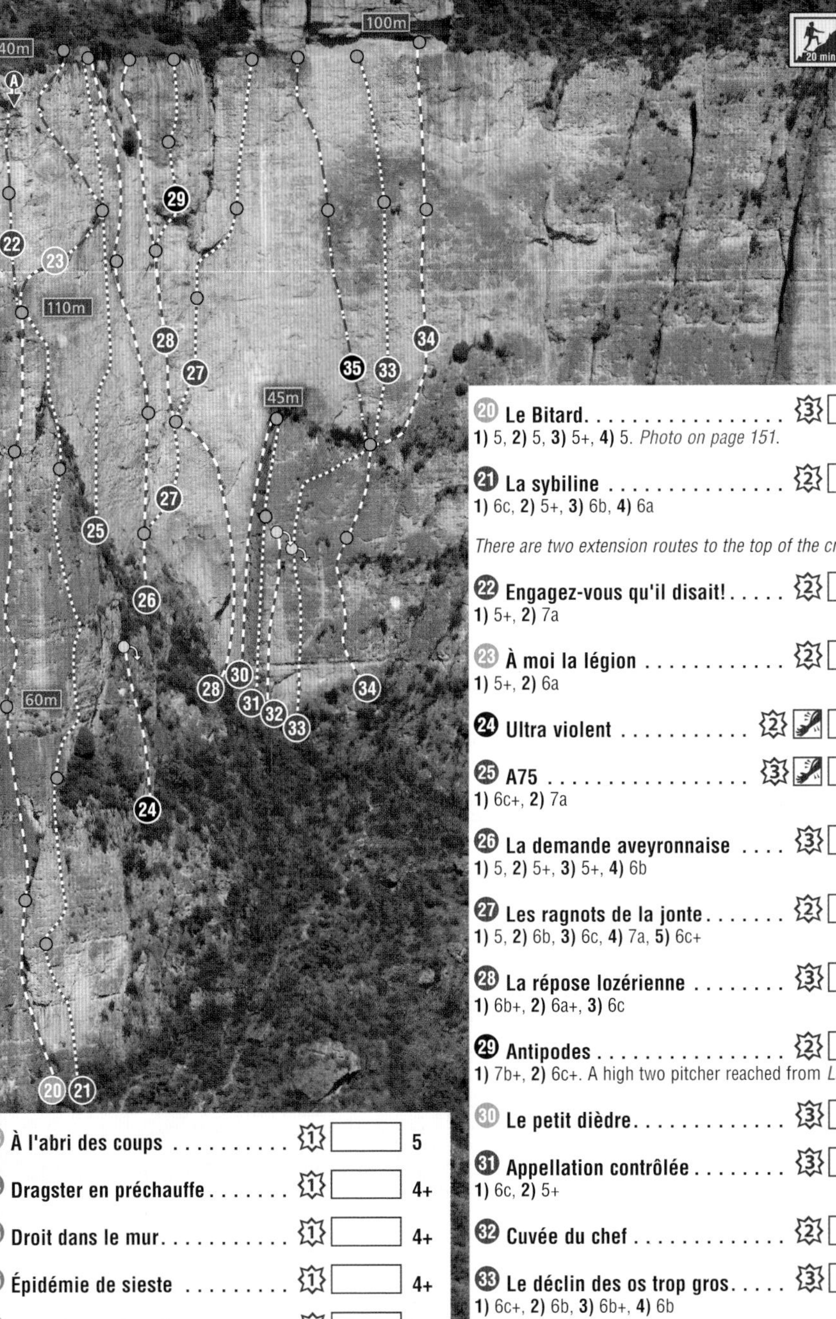

À l'abri des coups .... 1 ☐ 5

Dragster en préchauffe .... 1 ☐ 4+

Droit dans le mur........... 1 ☐ 4+

Épidémie de sieste .... 1 ☐ 4+

Le jardin enchanté.......... 3 ☐ 5+
4+, **2)** 5, **3)** 5+, **4)** 5

Roc in Chair .... 1 ☐ 5+

Andalouse................ 1 ☐ 5+

20 Le Bitard................ 3 ☐ 5+
1) 5, **2)** 5, **3)** 5+, **4)** 5. *Photo on page 151.*

21 La sybiline .... 2 ☐ 6c
1) 6c, **2)** 5+, **3)** 6b, **4)** 6a

There are two extension routes to the top of the crag.

22 Engagez-vous qu'il disait!..... 2 ☐ 7a
1) 5+, **2)** 7a

23 À moi la légion .... 2 ☐ 6a
1) 5+, **2)** 6a

24 Ultra violent .... 2 ☐ 7b+

25 A75 .... 3 ☐ 7a
1) 6c+, **2)** 7a

26 La demande aveyronnaise .... 3 ☐ 6b
1) 5, **2)** 5+, **3)** 5+, **4)** 6b

27 Les ragnots de la jonte....... 2 ☐ 7a
1) 5, **2)** 6b, **3)** 6c, **4)** 7a, **5)** 6c+

28 La répose lozérienne .... 3 ☐ 6c
1) 6b+, **2)** 6a+, **3)** 6c

29 Antipodes .... 2 ☐ 7b+
1) 7b+, **2)** 6c+. A high two pitcher reached from *La répose.*

30 Le petit dièdre............. 3 ☐ 5

31 Appellation contrôlée........ 3 ☐ 6c
1) 6c, **2)** 5+

32 Cuvée du chef .... 2 ☐ 7a

33 Le déclin des os trop gros..... 3 ☐ 6c+
1) 6c+, **2)** 6b, **3)** 6b+, **4)** 6b

34 Jéroboam .... 2 ☐ 6b
1) 5+, **2)** 5+, **3)** 6b, **4)** 6b

35 Salem malekoum........... 2 ☐ 7b
1) 7b, **2)** 7a+. Start from the top of pitch 2 of *Jéroboam.*

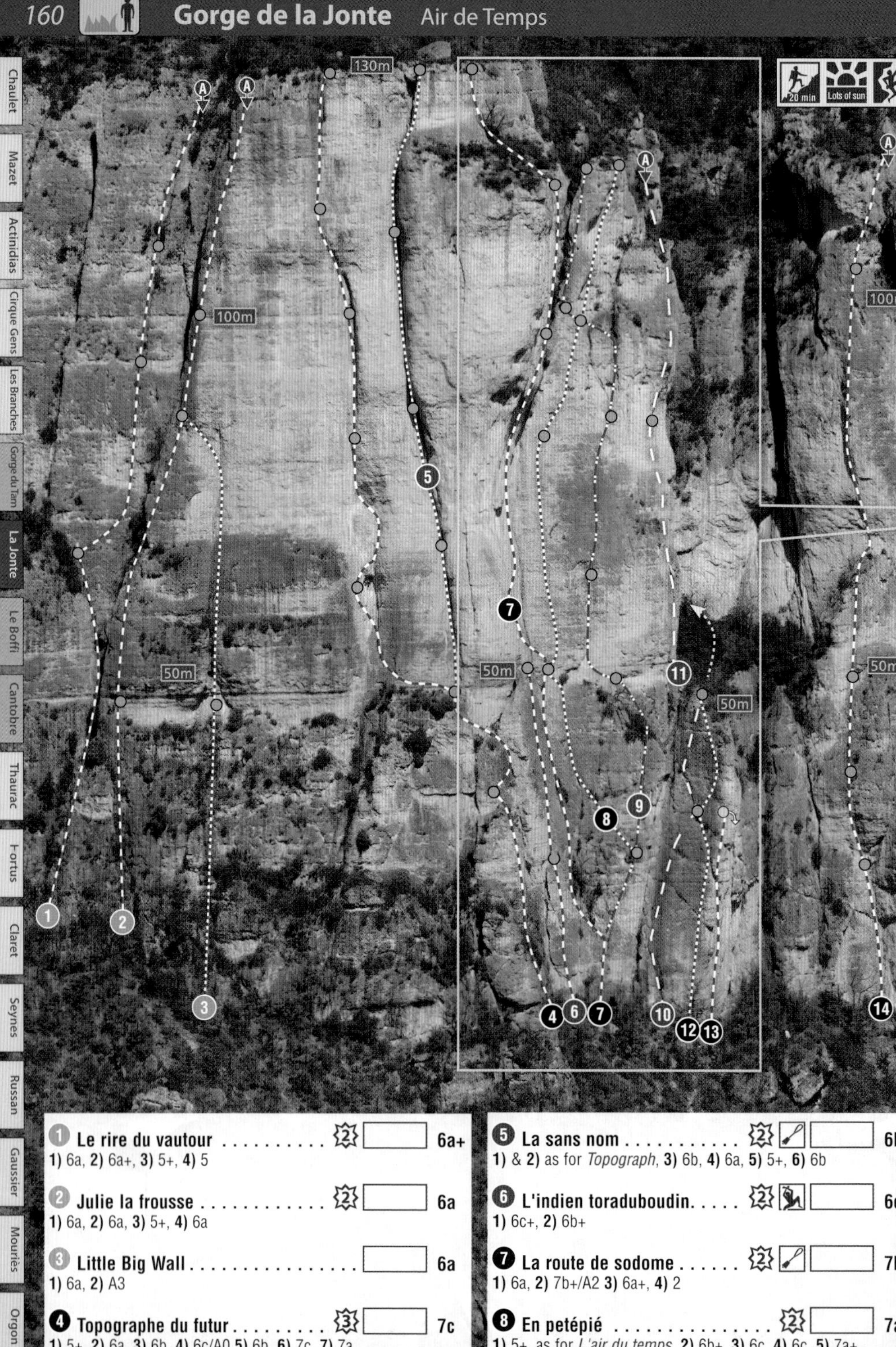

1 Le rire du vautour .... 2 stars ☐ **6a+**
1) 6a, **2)** 6a+, **3)** 5+, **4)** 5

2 Julie la frousse .... 2 stars ☐ **6a**
1) 6a, **2)** 6a, **3)** 5+, **4)** 6a

3 Little Big Wall .... ☐ **6a**
1) 6a, **2)** A3

4 Topographe du futur .... 3 stars ☐ **7c**
1) 5+, **2)** 6a, **3)** 6b, **4)** 6c/A0 **5)** 6b, **6)** 7c, **7)** 7a

5 La sans nom .... 2 stars ☐ **6b**
1) & **2)** as for *Topograph*, **3)** 6b, **4)** 6a, **5)** 5+, **6)** 6b

6 L'indien toraduboudin..... 2 stars ☐ **6c+**
1) 6c+, **2)** 6b+

7 La route de sodome ...... 2 stars ☐ **7b+**
1) 6a, **2)** 7b+/A2 **3)** 6a+, **4)** 2

8 En petépié .... 2 stars ☐ **7a+**
1) 5+, as for *L'air du temps*, **2)** 6b+, **3)** 6c, **4)** 6c, **5)** 7a+

Air de Temps

Some stunning big routes taking striking, exposed lines.
Approach - As for La Fusée and walk around to the left (see page 154).

9 L'air du temps . . . . 3★ **6b**
1) 5+, **2)** 5, **3)** 6a, **4)** 6b, **5)** 5, **6)** 6a

10 Éosine . . . . 2★ **6c**
1) 5+, **2)** 6a, then walk across a ledge system to below a long corner, **3)** 6c, **4)** 5+, **5)** 6b

11 Un dieu est tombé sur la tête . . 3★ **6c**
1) 6a+, **2)** 6c/A0 **3)** 6a. Approach up *Éosine*.

12 L'au-delà . . . . 2★ **7b+**
1) 7b+, **2)** 6c

13 C'est ici . . . . 2★ **7a+**

14 Les canons de la baronne 2★ **7a+**
1) 6a, **2)** 6b+, **3)** 5, **4)** 7a+, **5)** 5+

20 min
Lots of sun
Vertical
Chaulet
Mazet
Actinidias
Cirque Gens
Les Branches
Gorge du Tarn
La Jonte
Le Boffi
Cantobre
Thaurac
Hortus
Claret
Seynes
Russan
Gaussier
Mouriès
Orgon
120m
110m
90m
150m
90m
80m
40m
40m
25m
See opposite for routes 4 and 5

1 Luc à tout heurt . . . . 2 stars 7a+

2 Atenciòn . . . . 2 stars 7b

3 Peril! . . . . 2 stars 7b

4 Gallo loco . . . . 3 stars 6a
1) 5, **2)** 6a, **3)** 6a, **4)** 6a

5 Compte à rebours . . . . 3 stars 6c
1) 5, as for *Gallo loco*, **2)** 6b, **3)** 6c

6 La Fusée . . . . 3 stars 6c
1) 5, **2)** 6a, **3)** 6b, **4)** 6c

7 Jolicône . . . . 3 stars 7b
1) 5, **2)** 7b, **3)** 6a+, **4)** 6c, **5)** 6b+

8 Fais caf c'est dur . . . . 3 stars 6b+
1) 6a+, **2)** 6b+, **3)** 6a+, **4)** 6b

9 Aquo es quicon . . . . 3 stars 6a
1) 5+, **2)** 6a, **3)** 5+, **4)** 5+, **5)** 5+. *Photo on pages 6 and 135.*

10 Caminado de l'autan blanc . 2 stars 6a
1) 5, **2)** 5, **3)** 5+, **4)** 6a

11 Les balcons de Josephine . . 3 stars 6c
1) 5, on *Caminado*, **2)** 6c, **3)** 5+, on *Caminado*, **4)** 6a+, **5)** 6b+

12 Keep cool Raol . . . . 3 stars 6c+
1) 6c, **2)** 6b, **3)** 6c+, **4)** 6c, **5)** 6b+, **6)** 2. *Photo on page 5.*

13 Ne pleure pas Marinette . . . . . . 3 stars 7a+
1) 7a/A0 **2)** 6a+, **3)** 7a+/A0 **4)** 6b, **5)** 5+, **6)** 6a+

14 La grande Jacqueline . . . . 2 stars 7a+
1) 7a+/A0 **2)** 6b, **3)** 6c, **4)** 6a, **5)** 6c+, **6)** 7a

15 L'inachevée . . . . 3 stars 7a+
1) 6c+, **2)** 7a, **3)** 7a, **4)** 7a+

La Fusée

La Fusée itself is an awesome feature that just begs to be climbed, either side of it are more brilliant routes.
Approach - A paths lead from the road directly to La Fusée (see page 154).

Joyeux Merdier and La Licorne

The final sectors have a good selection of fine single- and multi-pitch routes to go at. The pinnacle of La Licorne is a stunning feature which is hard to pass by.

Approaches - It is possible to walk along the base from La Fusée (about 20mins). The direct approach is to park at the final parking area (as shown below in the photo) and follow a trail that leads to another trail that runs along the base of the crag. From here, less distinct paths lead up to the routes.

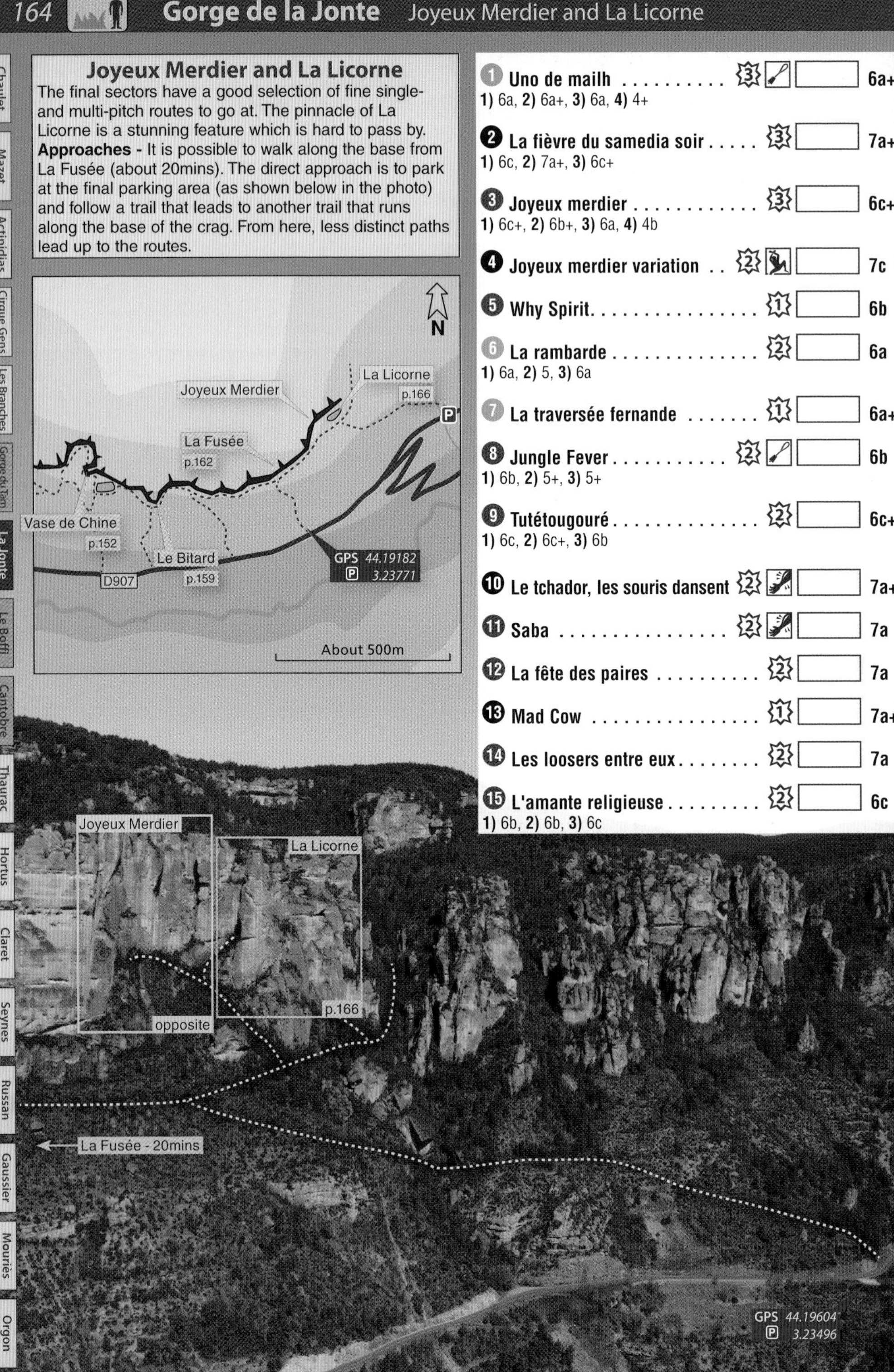

No.	Route	Stars	Grade
1	**Uno de mailh**	3	6a+
	1) 6a, **2)** 6a+, **3)** 6a, **4)** 4+		
2	**La fièvre du samedia soir**	3	7a+
	1) 6c, **2)** 7a+, **3)** 6c+		
3	**Joyeux merdier**	3	6c+
	1) 6c+, **2)** 6b+, **3)** 6a, **4)** 4b		
4	**Joyeux merdier variation**	2	7c
5	**Why Spirit**	1	6b
6	**La rambarde**	2	6a
	1) 6a, **2)** 5, **3)** 6a		
7	**La traversée fernande**	1	6a+
8	**Jungle Fever**	2	6b
	1) 6b, **2)** 5+, **3)** 5+		
9	**Tutétougouré**	2	6c+
	1) 6c, **2)** 6c+, **3)** 6b		
10	**Le tchador, les souris dansent**	2	7a+
11	**Saba**	2	7a
12	**La fête des paires**	2	7a
13	**Mad Cow**	1	7a+
14	**Les loosers entre eux**	2	7a
15	**L'amante religieuse**	2	6c
	1) 6b, **2)** 6b, **3)** 6c		

10 min
Morning
Vertical
130m
90m
70m
60m
100m
30m
60m
A
1
2
3
4
5
6
7
8
9
10
11
12
13
14
15
Chaulet
Mazet
Actinidias
Cirque Gens
Les Branches
Gorge du Tarn
La Jonte
Le Boffi
Cantobre
Thaurac
Hortus
Claret
Seynes
Russan
Gaussier
Mouriès
Orgon

15 min
Morning
Vertical
Chaulet
Mazet
Actinidias
Cirque Gens
Les Branches
Gorge du Tarn
La Jonte
Le Boffi
Cantobre
Thaurac
Hortus
Claret
Seynes
Russan
Gaussier
Mouriès
Orgon
100m
100m
A
30m
35m
1
2
3
4
5
6
7
8
9
9
14

Le temps des cerises . . . 8a
more central line is 8a+.

La cage aux folles 7a
6a+, **2)** 6b, **3)** 7a, **4)** 7a

Sérvices compris . . . . 6b+

Alysée 6a

Adieu carlos 6a
5+, **2)** 6a

Un jardin en plus 7b
6b+, **2)** 7b, **3)** 5+

Totem 7a
7a, **2)** 6c+, **3)** 6c+

La licorne . . . . 5+
3, **2)** 5+, **3)** 5, **4)** 4

9 La douceur des choses . . . . 5+
1) 3, **2)** 5+, **3)** 5, **4)** 5+

10 Départ avorté . . . . 5+

11 Dévers trop court . . . . . . 7c+
1) 7c+, **2)** 6a+

12 Oecuménique, c'est le printemps
. . . . 6b+

13 Silence dans l'errant 6b

14 La rampe . . . . 5+

15 Le calvaire du cri 7b

16 Fissure du ravin 6c

Chaulet
Mazet
Actinid as
Cirque Gens
Les Branches
Gorge du Tarn
La Jonte
Le Boffi
Cantobre
Thaurac
Hortus
Claret
Seynes
Russan
Gaussier
Mouriès
Orgon

Le Boffi

Chaulet
Mazet
Actinidias
Cirque Gens
Les Branches
Gorge du Tarn
La Jonte
Le Boffi
Cantobre
Thaurac
Hortus
Claret
Seynes
Russan
Gaussier
Mouriès
Orgon

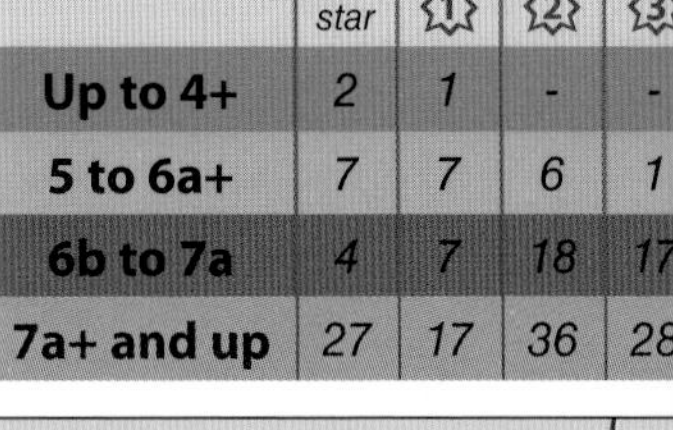

	No star	1 star	2 star	3 star
Up to 4+	2	1	-	-
5 to 6a+	7	7	6	1
6b to 7a	4	7	18	17
7a+ and up	27	17	36	28

When you consider how much quality rock there is next to the road in the nearby Gorge du Tarn, to be worth the thirty minute approach walk, the quality of climbing at Le Boffi would have to be nothing short of fantastic - fortunately, it is! Catering mostly for climbers operating in the mid 6s upwards, there is a huge amount to go at, and a visit is highly recommended even if you're not a big fan of walking. It is worth noting that there are some very long pitches at Le Boffi, and your experience of climbing here will be enhanced by bringing an 80m rope.

Approach Also see map on page 97

The crag can be accessed from Le Rozier/Peyreleau by following the D29 then the D110 to the Hamlet of Longiers. Go past Longiers for 300m, and turn left on a dirt track (there is a sign to the climbing). The D110 can also be accessed from Millau, in this direction you will find the dirt track leading off to the right 300m before you reach Longiers (keep an eye out for the sign). Drive down the dirt track for 800m until you reach a barrier and a parking area.

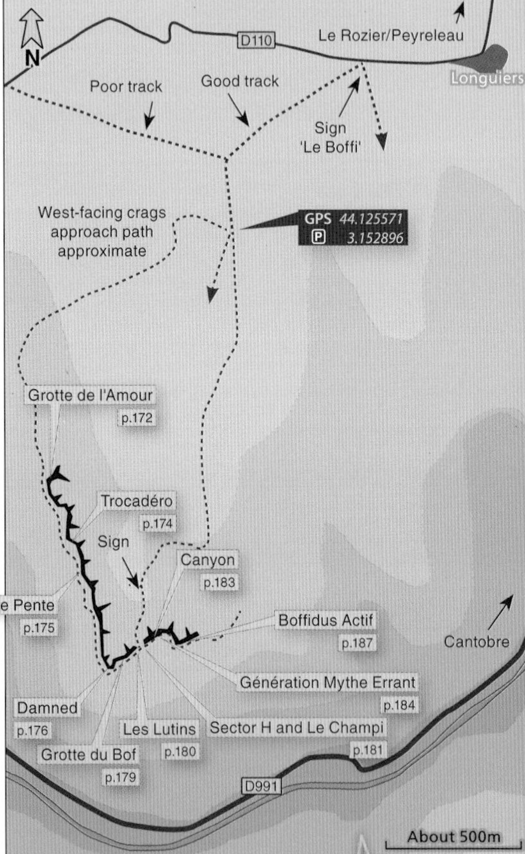

To reach Grotte de l'Amour, Trocadéro and Mauvais Pente, follow the track behind the right-hand barrier until you reach a large cairn. From here, follow a narrow track on the left which leads down into the woods and onto the path at the base.

To reach the sectors from The Damned to Boffidus Actif, pass the barrier and continue along the track in the same direction as you were driving. After 1.6km you will reach a sign regarding the Via Ferrata - take the left fork in the path and continue along then down a steep gully to the crag. The first crag you come to is Les Lutins, continue down to the base.

Conditions

The area is exposed, but gets sun and shade in roughly equal measures. The Damned and all the crags to the right soak up the sun up to mid afternoon, sectors left of The Damned get sun from mid afternoon. You can chase sun or shade to allow comfortable climbing and pretty much any time of year, though in the winter you will be wanting the sun to be out.

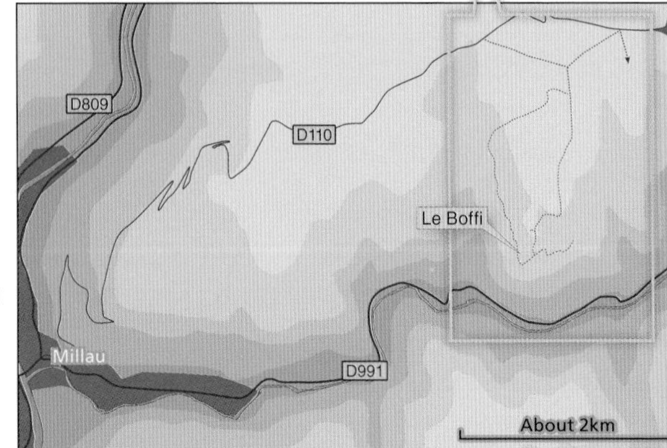

Nick Doyle on *Mac du mal* (7a+) - *page 178.* Photo: Simon Rawlinson

Grotte de l'Amour

A good selection of both steep technical wall climbs, with a couple of very steep cave routes to go at.
Approach - See page 170.

The precise location of the first three routes isn't known.

No.	Route	Grade
1	Gris souris	6c
2	Sister Morphine	6a
3	Summertime	6b+
4	Jontesque	7c
5	l'homme descend du singe	7b+
6	Cerveau lent	7a+
7	En céphale	7b+
8	La fortier	6b
9	Le bianchi	7b
10	La durand	7a
11	Mattet ma tique	6b
12	La mere Denis	6c
13	Les vieux chaussons	6c-
14	Bébicotage alienlque	7a
15	Orgasme	7a
16	Se fait plaisir avant tout	7a

17 Fois gras de tripoux		?
18 Joe's Garage Act I	1	7b+
19 Joe's Garage Act II	1	7b
20 Joe's Garage Act III	1	7a+
21 Popotin	2	7a
22 Allez paulette	2	6b+
23 Magret de canard	2	7a
24 Rust Never Sleeps 1) 6b, 2) 7a	3	7a
25 Brother Loste 1) 6b, 2) 7c	3	7c
26 Le contes de pets rots	2	7a+
27 Corsica du bas	1	7a+
28 Viva zapatta	2	7b
29 Grotte de l'Amour	2	8a
30 Vanessa au paradis	2	8a+
31 Petit Nico	1	6a+
32 Résistance	2	8a

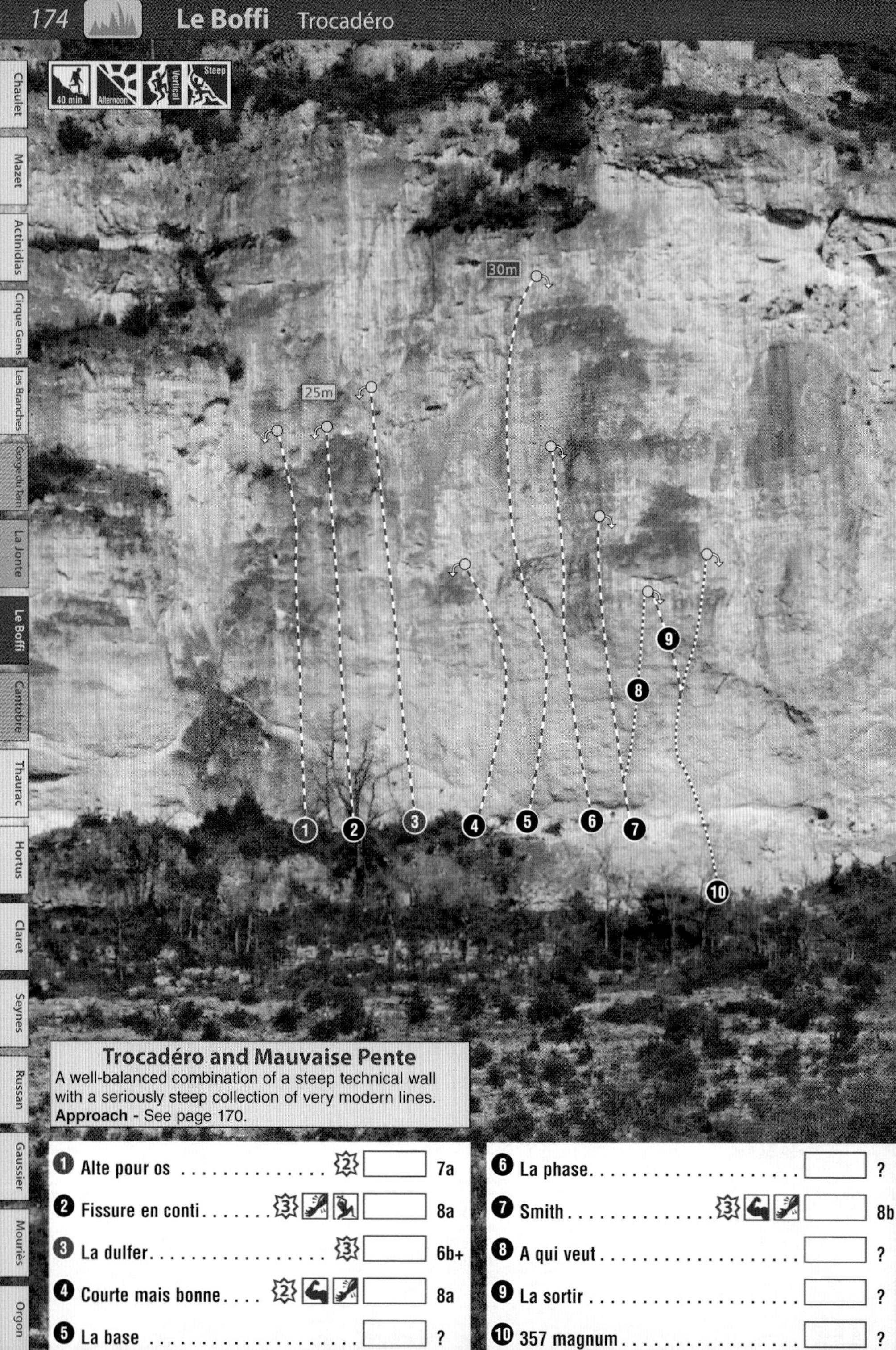

Trocadéro and Mauvaise Pente

A well-balanced combination of a steep technical wall with a seriously steep collection of very modern lines.
Approach - See page 170.

1. Alte pour os . . . . 2 . . . 7a
2. Fissure en conti. . . . . 3 . . . 8a
3. La dulfer. . . . . 3 . . . 6b+
4. Courte mais bonne. . . . 2 . . . 8a
5. La base . . . . ?
6. La phase. . . . . ?
7. Smith. . . . . 3 . . . 8b
8. A qui veut . . . . ?
9. La sortir . . . . ?
10. 357 magnum . . . . ?

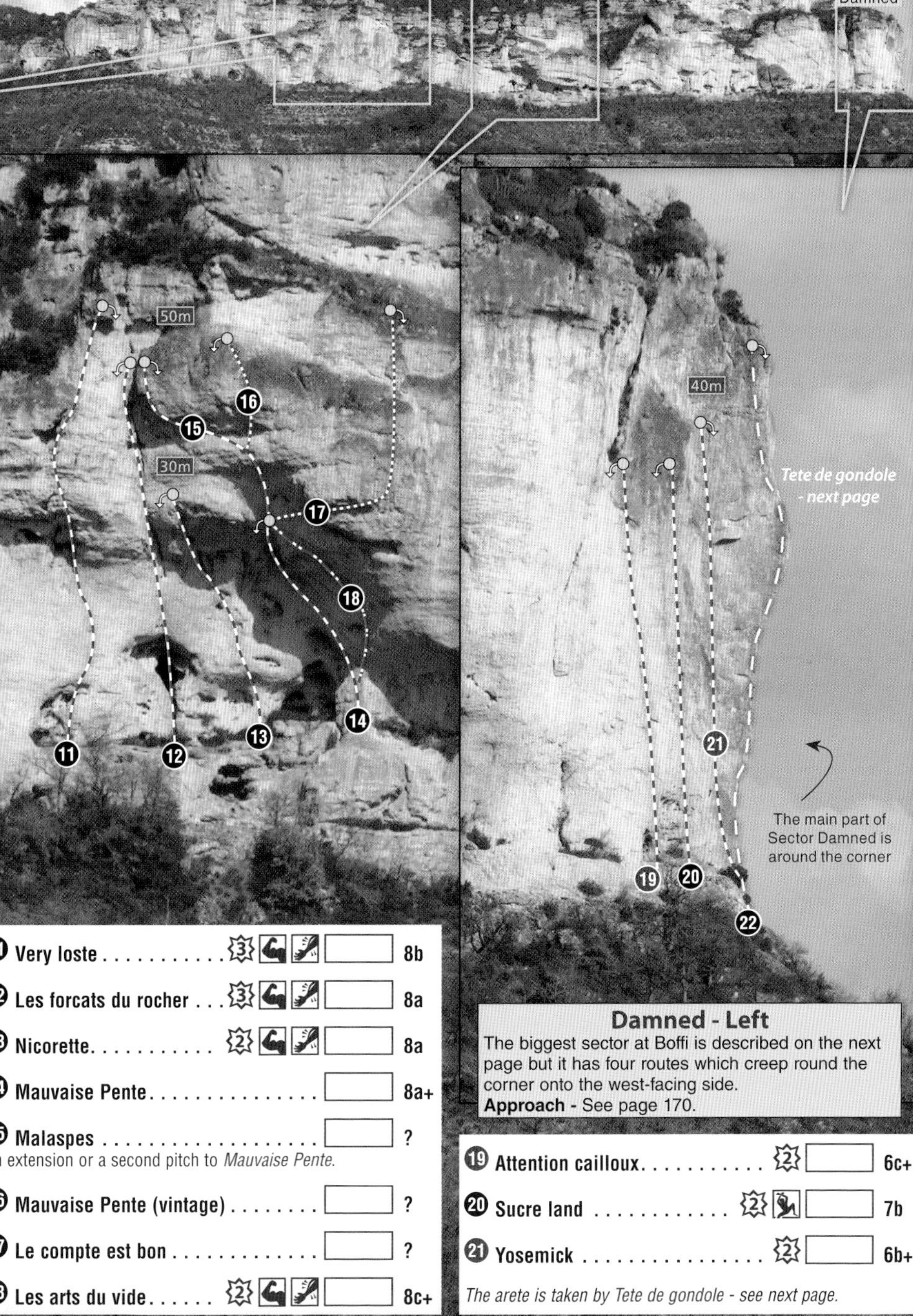

11 **Very loste** . . . . 3 stars ☐ **8b**

12 **Les forcats du rocher** . . . 3 stars ☐ **8a**

13 **Nicorette** . . . . 2 stars ☐ **8a**

14 **Mauvaise Pente** . . . . ☐ **8a+**

15 **Malaspes** . . . . ☐ **?**
An extension or a second pitch to *Mauvaise Pente*.

16 **Mauvaise Pente (vintage)** . . . . ☐ **?**

17 **Le compte est bon** . . . . ☐ **?**

18 **Les arts du vide** . . . . . . 2 stars ☐ **8c+**

Damned - Left

The biggest sector at Boffi is described on the next page but it has four routes which creep round the corner onto the west-facing side.
Approach - See page 170.

19 **Attention cailloux** . . . . 2 stars ☐ **6c+**

20 **Sucre land** . . . . 2 stars ☐ **7b**

21 **Yosemick** . . . . 2 stars ☐ **6b+**

The arete is taken by Tete de gondole - see next page.

Damned

A brilliant sector with the best range of routes in the area, and understandably popular.
Approach - See page 170.

No.	Route	Stars	Grade
1	Tete de gondole		8b+
2	Face de péniche		8a
3	Long parcours obscur		8a

Around the arete is a long wall with a good set of mid-grade routes - see topo opposite.

No.	Route	Stars	Grade
4	La luxure de l'épaule	2	7a+
5	Fracture de fatigue	2	5+
6	Duriff fifi	2	6c+
7	Vivement dimanche	2	6c
8	Club des ex 1) 6c, 2) 6c, 3) 6c	3	6c
9	Tête de mule	2	6c
10	Le blues du guide	2	6b+
11	Top model	2	6a+
12	Beveil-matin	2	6a+
13	Gardons l'ésprit tintin	1	5+
14	Rando+	1	5
15	Rando-	1	5

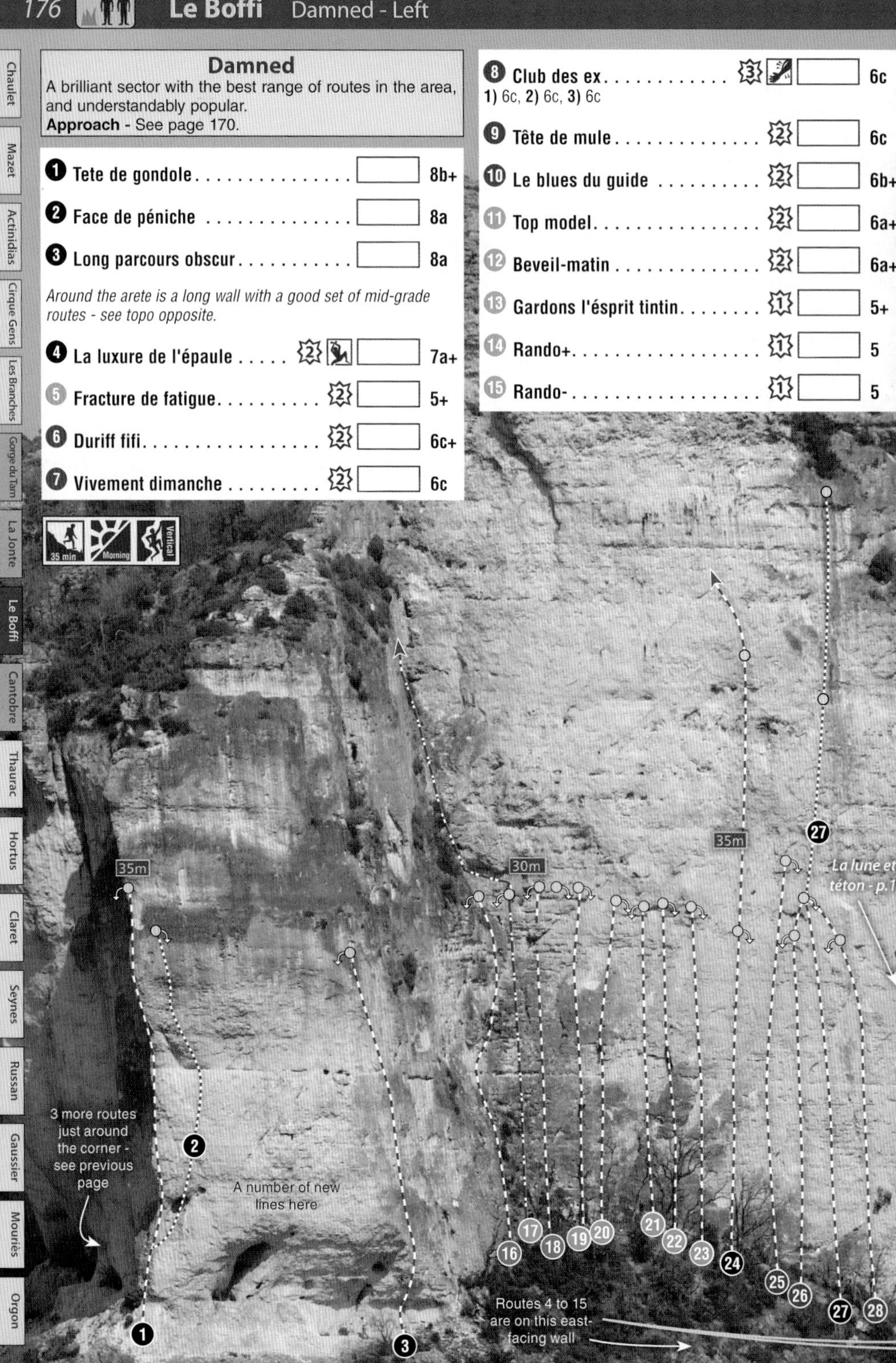

16 **Récré kid** 4

17 **Bac pour tous** . . . . 5+
1) 4+, **2)** 4+, **3)** 5+

18 **Pierre st marc** . . . . 4+

19 **Total recall** 5

20 **Mal bouffe** . . . . 6a+

21 **Tous sur orbite** . . . . 2 . . 5+

22 **Docteur globule** . . . . 5+

23 **Fripouille gratouille** 6a

24 **Prise direct** 7b
1) 6b, **2)** 7b

25 **Les régles de l'art** . . . . 3 . . 6c

26 **Les dessins c'est plus sain** . 3 . . 6c

27 **Damned** . . . . 3 . . 7b
1) 6c, **2)** 7b, **3)** 7a+

28 **Chair de poule** . . . . 3 . . 6c
Photo on page 182.

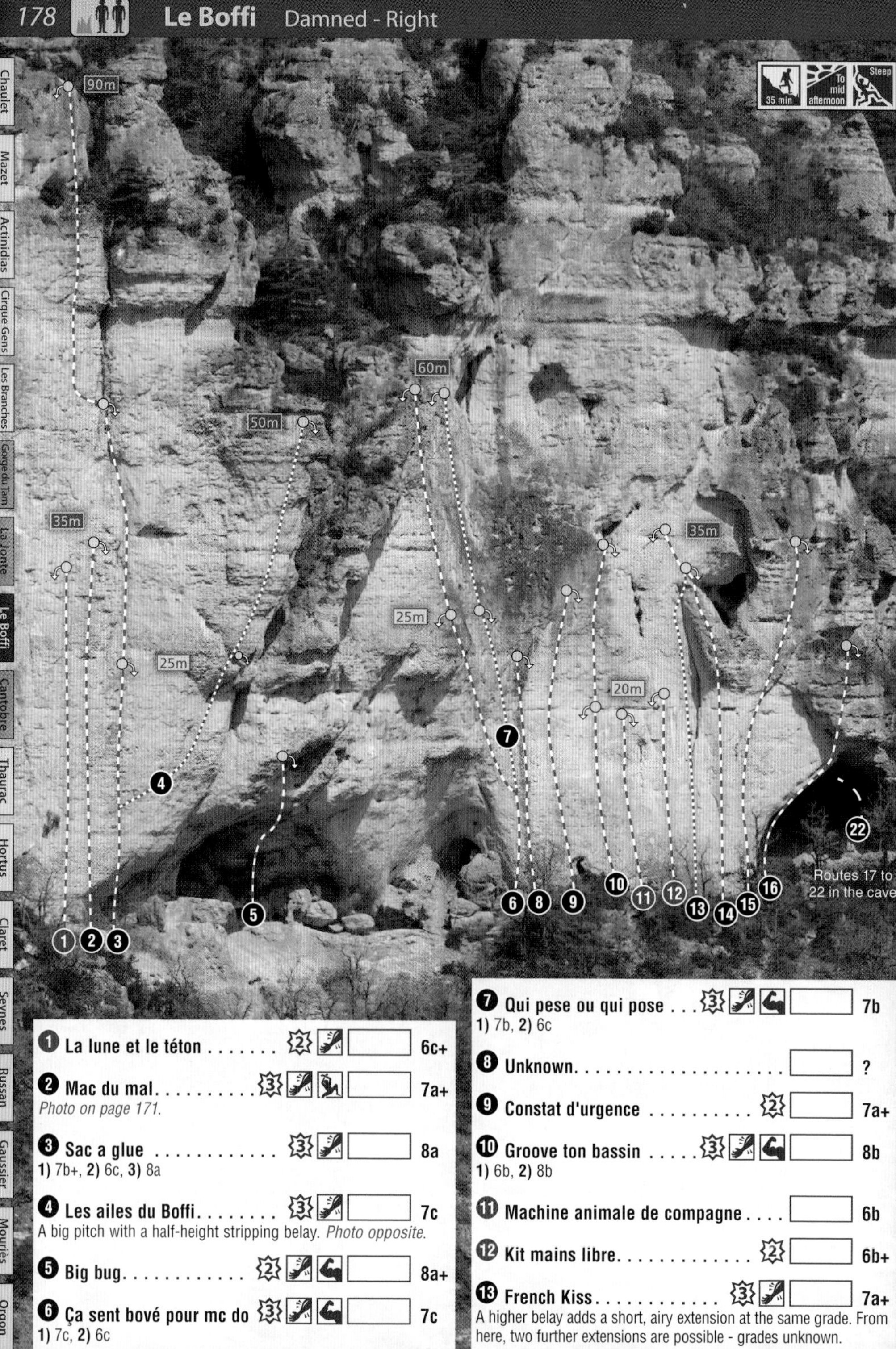

❶ **La lune et le téton** . . . . 2 stars 6c+

❷ **Mac du mal**. . . . . 3 stars 7a+
Photo on page 171.

❸ **Sac a glue** . . . . 3 stars 8a
1) 7b+, **2)** 6c, **3)** 8a

❹ **Les ailes du Boffi**. . . . . 3 stars 7c
A big pitch with a half-height stripping belay. *Photo opposite.*

❺ **Big bug**. . . . . 2 stars 8a+

❻ **Ça sent bové pour mc do** 3 stars 7c
1) 7c, **2)** 6c

❼ **Qui pese ou qui pose** . . . 3 stars 7b
1) 7b, **2)** 6c

❽ **Unknown**. ?

❾ **Constat d'urgence** . . . . 2 stars 7a+

❿ **Groove ton bassin** . . . . . 3 stars 8b
1) 6b, **2)** 8b

⓫ **Machine animale de compagne** 6b

⓬ **Kit mains libre**. . . . . 2 stars 6b+

⓭ **French Kiss**. . . . . 3 stars 7a+
A higher belay adds a short, airy extension at the same grade. From here, two further extensions are possible - grades unknown.

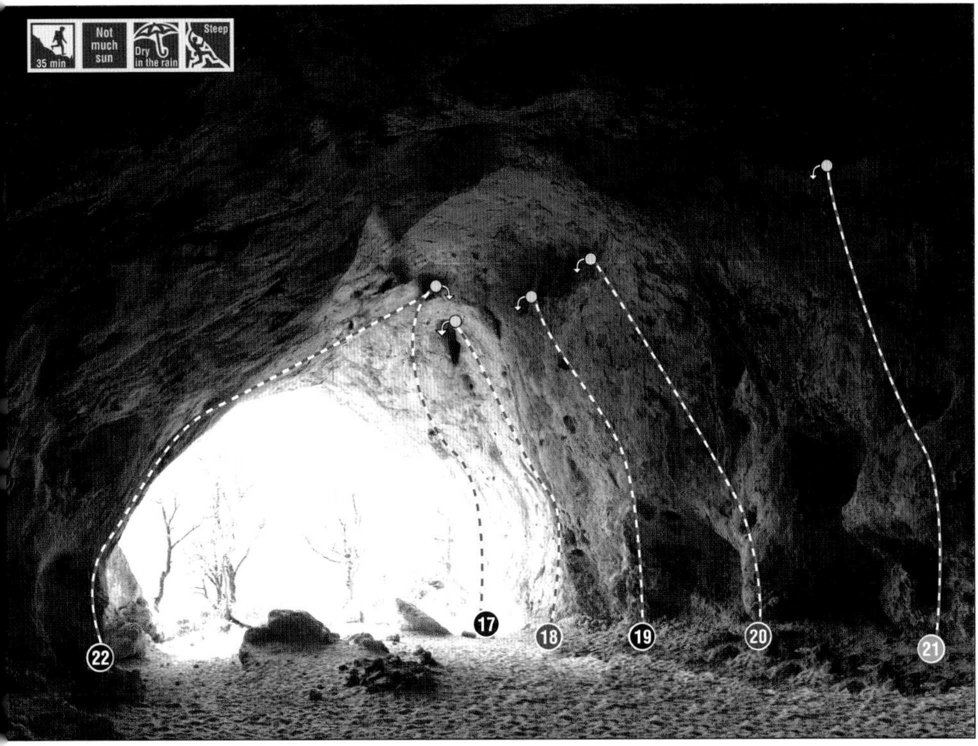

35 min
Not much sun
Dry in the rain
Steep
17
18
19
20
21
22

Grotte du Bof

The grotte itself is a bit...grotty, but the routes around it are well-worth seeking if you're looking for something hard to sink your teeth into.

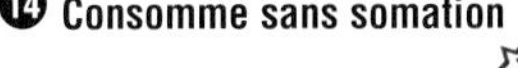

14 Consomme sans somation 3 7b

15 La politique s'occupera de vous .... 2 7a+

16 La voie lactée 3 8a

The next routes are inside the cave.

17 Les perres a feu .... ?

18 Conflit d'équilibre 1 7a

19 Biceps enfumé 7b

20 Juridic parc 6b

21 La bouse 5

22 Riz - thon - mayo 2 8a

7c+ to the first belay.

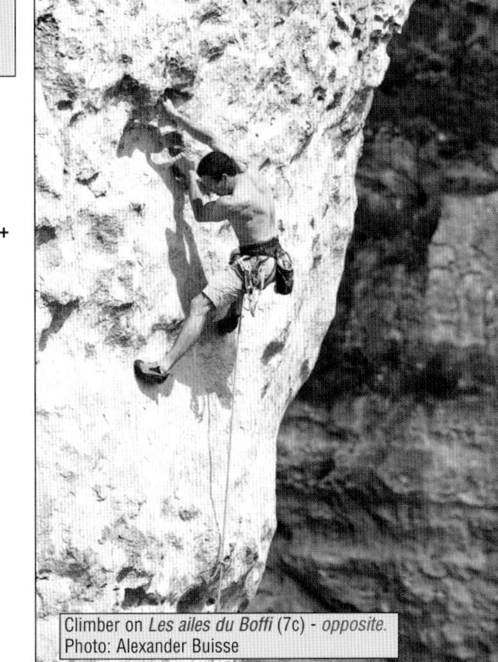

Climber on *Les ailes du Boffi* (7c) - *opposite.*
Photo: Alexander Buisse

Chaulet
Mazet
Actinidias
Cirque Gens
Les Branches
Gorge du Tarn
La Jonte
Le Boffi
Cantobre
Thaurac
Hortus
Claret
Seynes
Russan
Gaussier
Mouriès
Orgon

Damned
Les Lutins
Canyon
Génération Mythe Errant
Boffidus Actif
Grotte du Bof
previous page
p.176
Sector H and Le Champi
p.183
p.184
p.187

On the right of the approach gully is Sector Les Lutins.

1 **Blanche neige** . . . . 1 star 6c

2 **Rage de dent**. . . . . 1 star 6a

3 **Les 7 mains** . . . . 1 star 7b+
1) 5, **2)** 7b+

4 **Les Lutins en surnombre** . . 2 star 8a+

5 **Les pirates du son** . . . . 2 star 7b
1) 6b, **2)** 7b

6 **Signal blancheur** . . . . . 2 star 7b

7 **Pj** . . . . 2 star 7b

30 min | Morning | Steep

Les Lutins, Sector H and Le Champi

These are the first areas you reach on the descent to the east-facing sectors. Les Lutins will be found on your right, then Sector H is on your left, and finally Le Champin is on the left further down when you reach the path that runs along the base. Sector H has several more walls, though the quality is not as high as the remainder of Le Boffi, and the routes are not included here.

Approach - See page 170.

On the left of the approach gully is Sector H.

8 **Roc truc** . . . . 1 star 4+

9 **Les nains c'est bourrin** . . . . 2 star 7a+

10 **Les doigts dans le nez** . 2 star 7b+

11 **Le jardin des nains** . . . 2 star 7a

15m
20m

	Route	Stars		Grade
12	**Pas glop**	1		6b+
13	**Lee scratch bouillie**	1		5+
14	**L'instinct perdu**	2		7a+
15	**La route elle connait le chemin**	1		6b

There are three isolated routes on Sector Le Champi.

	Route	Stars		Grade
16	**Tagueul je grimpe**	2		7b
17	**Mr pec**	2		7b
18	**Sifilice**	2		7a+

Liz Collyer on *Chair de poule* (6c+) - *page 177.*

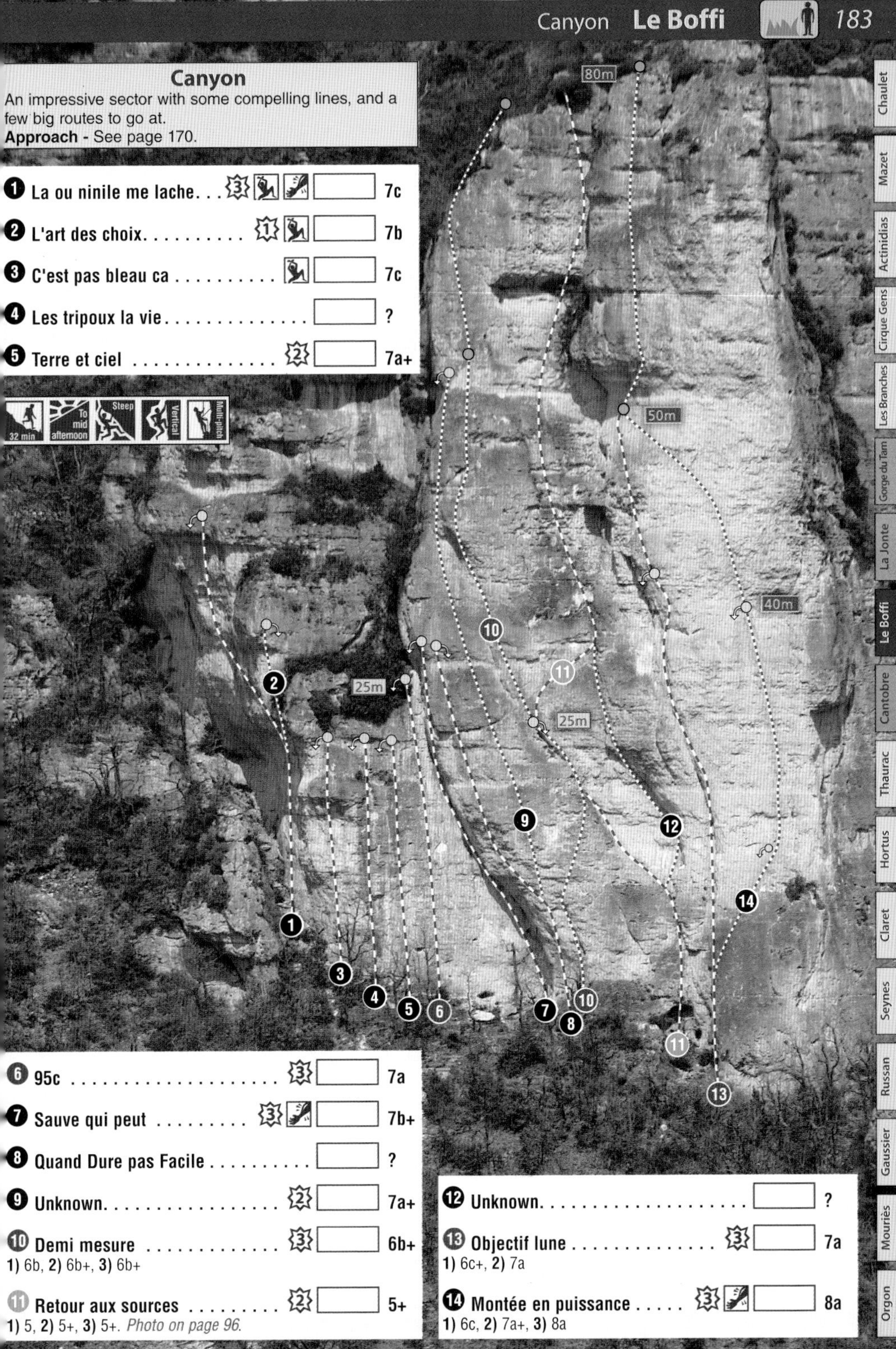

Canyon

An impressive sector with some compelling lines, and a few big routes to go at.

Approach - See page 170.

1 La ou ninile me lache. . . 3-star ☐ 7c

2 L'art des choix. . . . . 1-star ☐ 7b

3 C'est pas bleau ca . . . . ☐ 7c

4 Les tripoux la vie. . . . . ☐ ?

5 Terre et ciel . . . . 2-star ☐ 7a+

6 95c . . . . 3-star ☐ 7a

7 Sauve qui peut . . . . 3-star ☐ 7b+

8 Quand Dure pas Facile . . . . ☐ ?

9 Unknown. . . . . 2-star ☐ 7a+

10 Demi mesure . . . . 3-star ☐ 6b+
1) 6b, **2)** 6b+, **3)** 6b+

11 Retour aux sources . . . . 2-star ☐ 5+
1) 5, **2)** 5+, **3)** 5+. *Photo on page 96.*

12 Unknown. ☐ ?

13 Objectif lune . . . . 3-star ☐ 7a
1) 6c+, **2)** 7a

14 Montée en puissance . . . . . 3-star ☐ 8a
1) 6c, **2)** 7a+, **3)** 8a

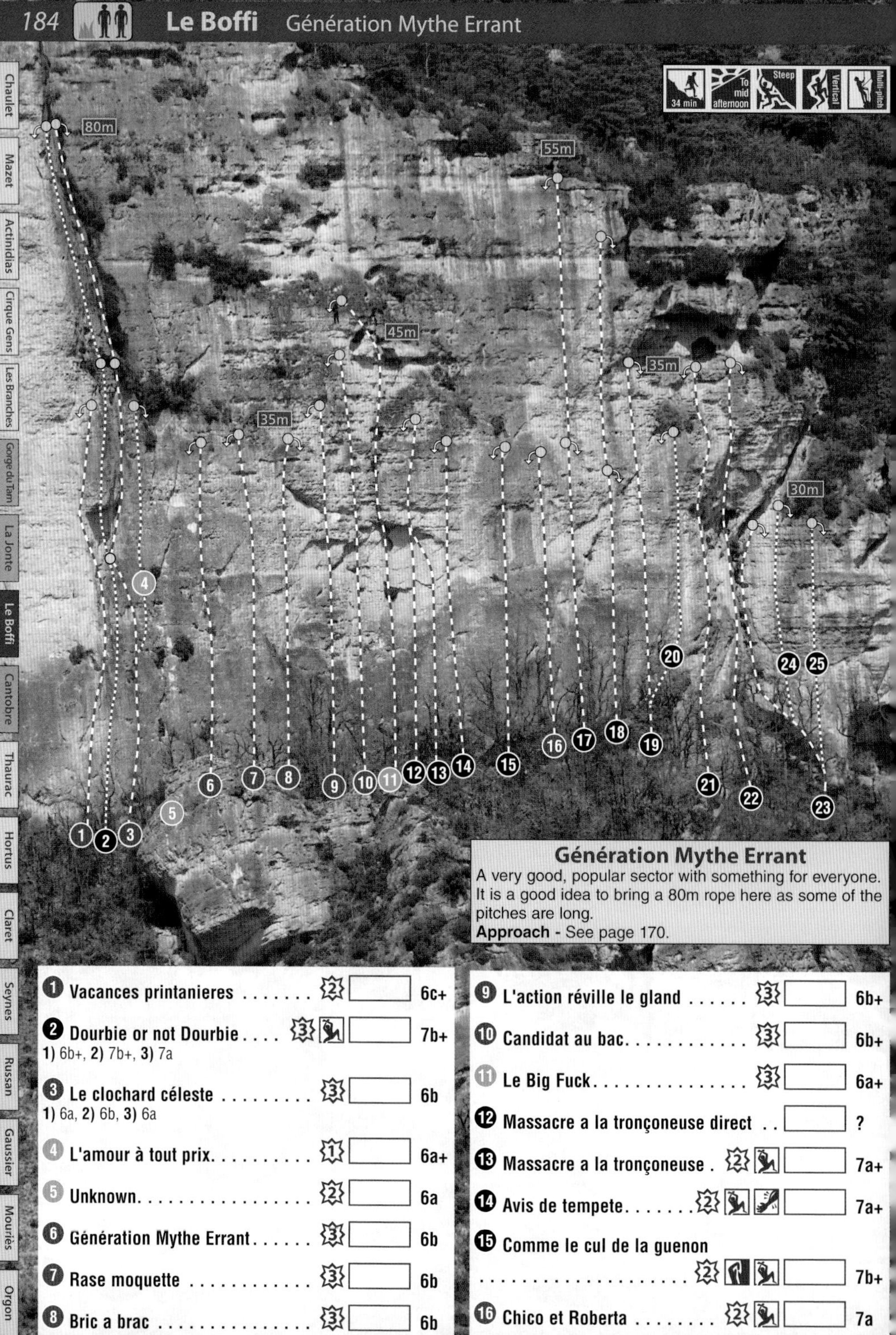

Chaulet
Mazet
Actinidias
Cirque Gens
Les Branches
Gorge du Tarn
La Jonte
Le Boffi
Cantobre
Thaurac
Hortus
Claret
Seynes
Russan
Gaussier
Mouriès
Orgon

Génération Mythe Errant

A very good, popular sector with something for everyone. It is a good idea to bring a 80m rope here as some of the pitches are long.

Approach - See page 170.

1. **Vacances printanieres** .... (2 stars) 6c+
2. **Dourbie or not Dourbie** .... (3 stars) 7b+
   1) 6b+, **2)** 7b+, **3)** 7a
3. **Le clochard céleste** .... (3 stars) 6b
   1) 6a, **2)** 6b, **3)** 6a
4. **L'amour à tout prix**.......... (1 star) 6a+
5. **Unknown**................. (2 stars) 6a
6. **Génération Mythe Errant**...... (3 stars) 6b
7. **Rase moquette** .... (3 stars) 6b
8. **Bric a brac** .... (3 stars) 6b
9. **L'action réville le gland** ...... (3 stars) 6b+
10. **Candidat au bac**............ (3 stars) 6b+
11. **Le Big Fuck**............... (3 stars) 6a+
12. **Massacre a la tronçoneuse direct** .. ?
13. **Massacre a la tronçoneuse** . (2 stars) 7a+
14. **Avis de tempete**....... (2 stars) 7a+
15. **Comme le cul de la guenon** .... (2 stars) 7b+
16. **Chico et Roberta** .... (2 stars) 7a

⑰ **Un horizon bouché** .... 7a+
1) 7a, **2)** 7a+

⑱ **Faut que ça saute** 7b
1) 6c+, **2)** 7b

⑲ **Tart à la crême** .... 7b+

⑳ **Indigestion** .... 7b+

㉑ **No la guerra** .... 7a+

㉒ **L'as de trefle qui pique ton coeur** 7b
1) 6a+, **2)** 7b

㉓ **L'age des casernes** ... 7b+

㉔ **Guilhem n'aimait pas la chasse** .... 8a+

㉕ **Rage against the chasseurs** 8a

Rhoslyn Frugtniet on *Escrologiste* (6c+) - Photo by Simon Rawlinson - *page 186.*

1 **A mon boffis directe** .... ?

2 **A mon boffis** 3 7c

3 **El deseo escondido** .... 3 8a+

4 **Qui t'as fait roi?** .... 3 8a+

5 **Hominisation** 3 7b
1) 7a, **2)** 7b

6 **Bert rend quand il a peur** 2 7a

7 **Escrologiste** .... 3 6c+
Photo on page 185.

8 **Les ames de construction massive**
.... 1 7c+

9 **Disney contre rené** .... 1 7a+

10 **Le jardin des sens** 3 6c

11 **Chico cosmos** .... 3 7a+

12 **Hight tone** .... 2 7b+
1) 6b+, **2)** 7b+

Boffidus Actif

The final wall listed has three very big pitches.

Approach - See page 170.

13 **Flamenco Chill Out** . . . . 1 ☐ 7a+

14 **La revancha del mono** . . 1 ☐ 8a

15 **Intimidanté intimité de dame Boffi** . . . . 2 ☐ 6b

1) 6a, **2)** 6b, **3)** 6a

16 **Bofidus actif** . . . . 3 ☐ 8b+

17 **Voie ultime** . . . . 3 ☐ 9a

18 **Project** . . . . ☐ ?

Turbulence
p.192

Cantobre

Cantobre

	No star	1	2	3
Up to 4+	-	-	-	-
5 to 6a+	-	-	-	1
6b to 7a	-	-	3	2
7a+ and up	4	12	31	5

A beautiful crag in a splendid setting, though it is mostly hard climbing. There are a number of wildly-steep overhangs nearby, which make even Turbulence look like a soft touch - these are described in the local topo - though are clearly still in development.
While you are here it is well worth a quick walk around the village - there is plenty of parking available by the side of the road after the village.

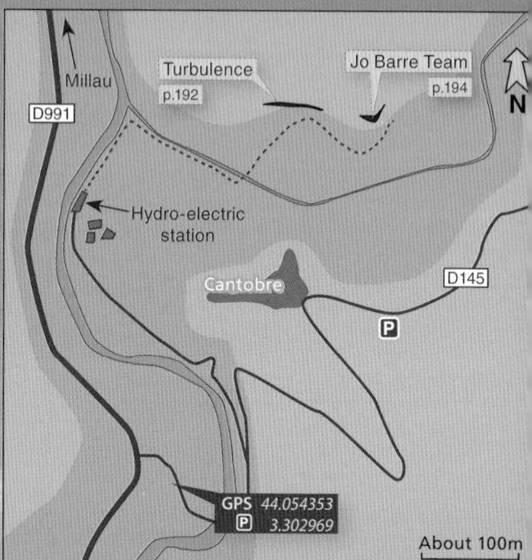

Approach Also see map on page 97

Cantobre lies just off the D991 that links Millau to Nant. About 28km from Millau, turn off the D991 in the direction of Cantobre. The official advice is to park on the right before you reach the bridge and walk - though most drive all the way along the narrow road to the hydro-electric station, where there is very limited parking. From the official parking spot, follow the road towards the village, and take the first left. Continue for 500m and you will reach a small hydro-electric station. Continue on a trail along the edge of the field, to a stream. Walk upstream for a short while until it is possible to cross on some stepping-stones. The path continues up to Turbulence, and then over to Jo Barre Team.

Conditions

Facing south, these crags get a lot of sun, and you should factor that in when deciding to pay a visit. Unless you're going for a quick tan, aim to come in winter or on a cloudy day. Turbulence is steep, so naturally prone to seepage if it has been raining heavily. Jo Barre Team also faces south, but does at least allow some shade for belaying.

Adrian Berry on *Gazoline* (7c+) - *page 193*. Photo by Andy Gibb

Chaulet | Mazet | Actinidias | Cirque Gens | Les Branches | Gorge du Tarn | La Jonte | Le Boffi | Cantobre | Thaurac | Hortus | Claret | Seynes | Russan | Gaussier | Mouriès | Orgon

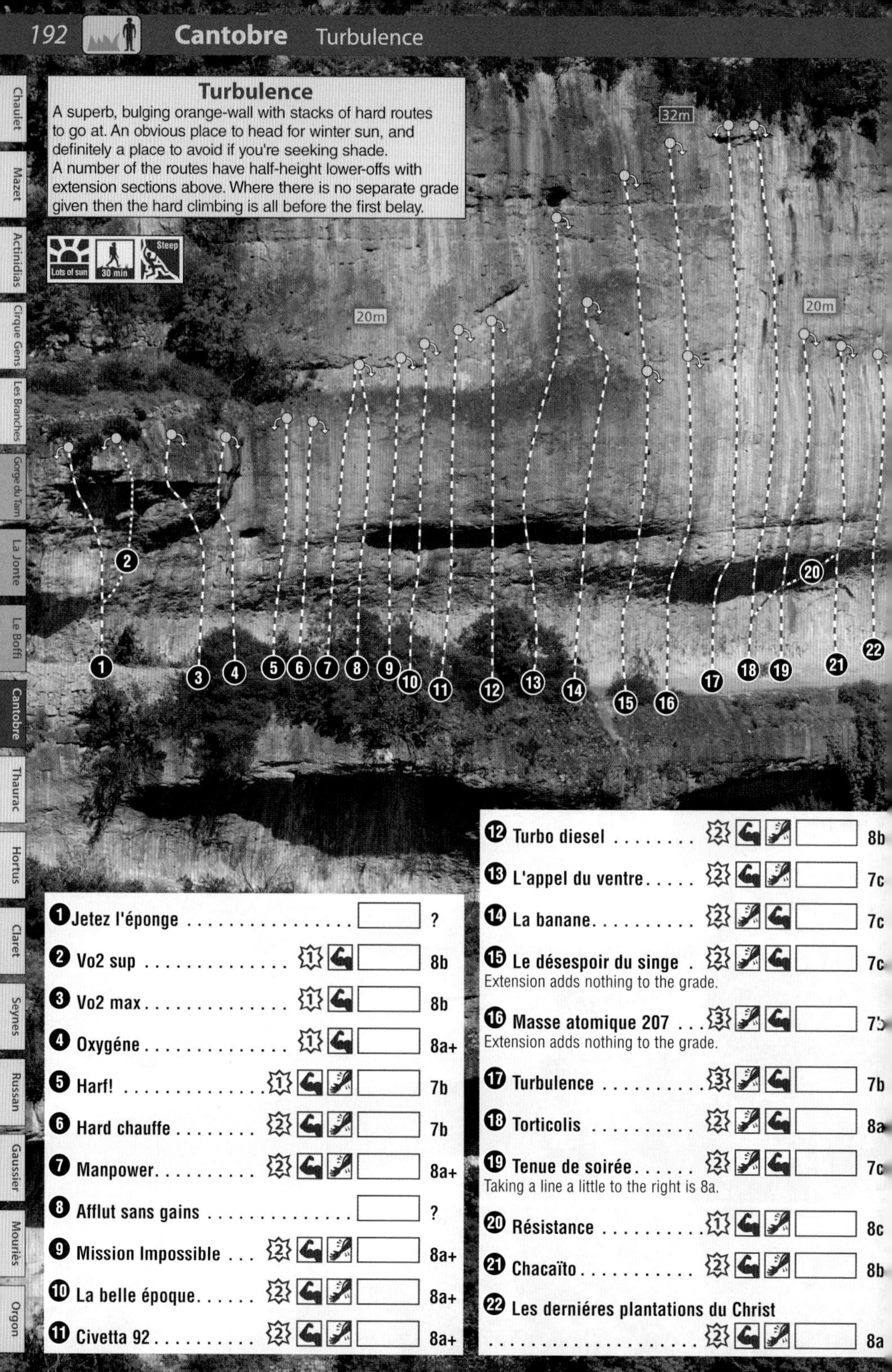

Turbulence

A superb, bulging orange-wall with stacks of hard routes to go at. An obvious place to head for winter sun, and definitely a place to avoid if you're seeking shade.
A number of the routes have half-height lower-offs with extension sections above. Where there is no separate grade given then the hard climbing is all before the first belay.

No.	Route	Stars	Grade
1	Jetez l'éponge		?
2	Vo2 sup	1	8b
3	Vo2 max	1	8b
4	Oxygéne	1	8a+
5	Harf!	1	7b
6	Hard chauffe	2	7b
7	Manpower	2	8a+
8	Afflut sans gains		?
9	Mission Impossible	2	8a+
10	La belle époque	2	8a+
11	Civetta 92	2	8a+
12	Turbo diesel	2	8b
13	L'appel du ventre	2	7c
14	La banane	2	7c
15	Le désespoir du singe — Extension adds nothing to the grade.	2	7c
16	Masse atomique 207 — Extension adds nothing to the grade.	3	7b
17	Turbulence	3	7b
18	Torticolis	2	8a
19	Tenue de soirée — Taking a line a little to the right is 8a.	2	7c
20	Résistance	1	8c
21	Chacaïto	2	8b
22	Les derniéres plantations du Christ	2	8a

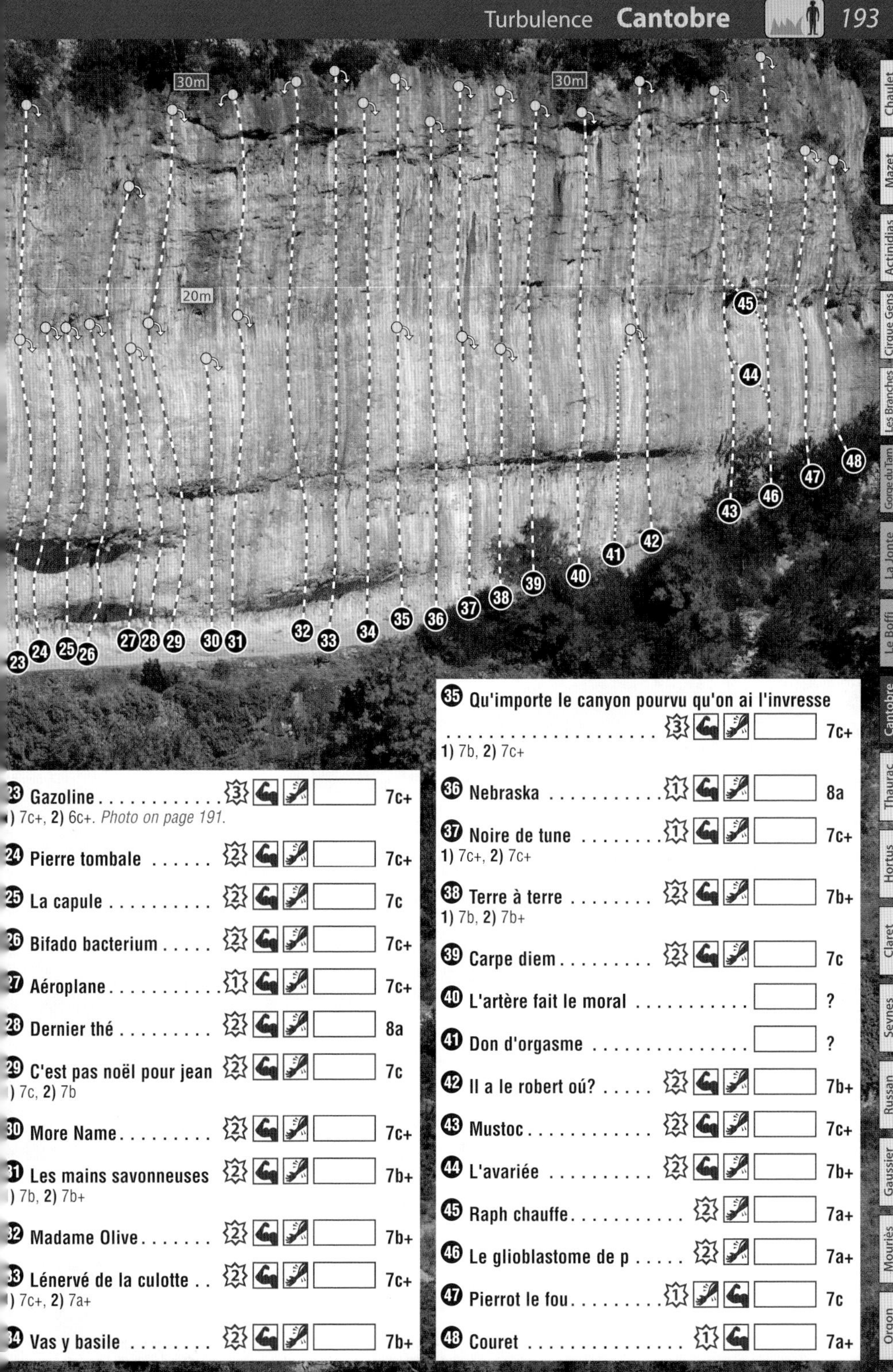

No.	Route	Stars	Grade
23	Gazoline	3	7c+
	1) 7c+, 2) 6c+. *Photo on page 191.*		
24	Pierre tombale	2	7c+
25	La capule	2	7c
26	Bifado bacterium	2	7c+
27	Aéroplane	1	7c+
28	Dernier thé	2	8a
29	C'est pas noël pour jean	2	7c
	1) 7c, 2) 7b		
30	More Name	2	7c+
31	Les mains savonneuses	2	7b+
	1) 7b, 2) 7b+		
32	Madame Olive	2	7b+
33	Lénervé de la culotte	2	7c+
	1) 7c+, 2) 7a+		
34	Vas y basile	2	7b+
35	Qu'importe le canyon pourvu qu'on ai l'invresse	3	7c+
	1) 7b, 2) 7c+		
36	Nebraska	1	8a
37	Noire de tune	1	7c+
	1) 7c+, 2) 7c+		
38	Terre à terre	2	7b+
	1) 7b, 2) 7b+		
39	Carpe diem	2	7c
40	L'artère fait le moral		?
41	Don d'orgasme		?
42	Il a le robert oú?	2	7b+
43	Mustoc	2	7c+
44	L'avariée	2	7b+
45	Raph chauffe	2	7a+
46	Le glioblastome de p	2	7a+
47	Pierrot le fou	1	7c
48	Couret	1	7a+

Jo Barre Team

In total contrast to Turbulence, this sector has a number of vertical or slabby routes in the mid grades.

1 Casse croûte . . . . 2 ☐ **7b**
The mid-height lower-off is for stripping the route.

2 Casse croûte left-hand . . . . 3 ☐ **8b**

3 Jo Barre Team . . . . 3 ☐ **6c**

4 Soirée mousse . . . . 2 ☐ **6b+**
1) 5+, **2)** 6b+

5 Tati repésente . . . . 3 ☐ **6a+**
Photo opposite.

6 L'ascenceur au fond du précipice
. . . . 2 ☐ **6b+**

7 Coup de mayet . . . . 3 ☐ **6c**

8 Changement de décors . . . . 2 ☐ **7a**

9 La théorie de la pratique 1 ☐ **8a**

10 Il était une voie dans l'ouest
. . . . 1 ☐ **7b**

Andy Gibb on *Tati repésente* (6a+) - *opposite*.

The Thaurac area contains the most esoteric crags in this guidebook and it is likely that many climbers visiting this region will never have heard of Thaurac and Hortus. Slightly odd when you consider well-known crags like the Gorge du Tarn only really started development in the late 1990s, whereas climbs at Hortus date back to the 1940s. We have chosen to include Hortus and La Grand Face at Thaurac not in spite of the fact that they are unpopular, uncool and unheard of, but because of it. You will find vegetation, loose rock, and pitons but we hope that you will also find these places exciting, interesting, and worth checking out. They are certainly different. If you find them too much to cope with then Claret is included because of it's proximity and is very much a sport crag of the modern world.

Getting There and Getting Around

Ganges is 45km north of Montpellier, and 62km north-west of Nîmes, and about 50km from the A75 autoroute that links fairly directly to Paris. You will need a car to explore this area.

Where to Stay

If you want to sample all three areas, the Herault Gorge south of Ganges caters well for visitors, though it is thirty minutes by car to Claret. Check out Camping Val d'Herault near Brissac (**www.camping-levaldherault.com**) and the municipal campsite in Laroque (Le Tivoli - 04 67 73 97 28).

Hortus rising high above the vineyards

Local Guidebooks

If you want the complete picture of climbing in these areas, we suggest getting the local guide-books. At time of writing, the **Thaurac** and **Hortus** guides are available in a small bookshop in Laroque (it's on a street parallel to the main road). The **Claret** guide is best obtained from large climbing shops.

Web Link

www.topo-thaurac.com - has updated information on new routes and re-equipping for Thaurac, Hortus, and other nearby climbing areas.

Petit Prince
p.209
Romane
p.210
Sycophantes
p.211

Chaulet
Mazet
Actinidias
Cirque Gens
Les Branches
Gorge du Tarn
La Jonte
Le Boffi
Cantobre
Thaurac
Hortus
Claret
Seynes
Russan
Gaussier
Mouriès
Orgon

Climbing Prohibited

Thaurac

Thaurac

	No star	1	2	3
Up to 4+	2	10	-	-
5 to 6a+	8	32	23	8
6b to 7a	1	16	27	7
7a+ and up	4	13	6	3

Thaurac is an extensive area with many different crags and buttresses - this guidebook covers less than half of what it has to offer. The area has a good range of single- and multi-pitch routes with short approaches. There are plenty of short, low-grade routes for novices, and if you're looking for adventure, a day on La Grande Face should leave you satisfied.

Approach Also see map on page 196

Thaurac lies 45km north of Montpelier, right on the edge of the Parc National des Cévennes. For the crags near the Grotte, you need to approach from St. Bauzille - follow signs from the main road to the Grotte des Demoiselles (there are plenty of signs) and park at the Visitors' Centre. Note that the road is mostly one-way, so you need to drive all the way around each time. To climb at La Grand Face you can park where the one-way road from the Grotte meets the D986 and save driving all the way around.

Conditions

Crags mostly face south or west, so expect to get plenty of sun here. The exception is Arrache-cœur which gets afternoon shade.

Chaulet
Mazet
Actinidias
Cirque Gens
Les Branches
Gorge du Tarn
La Jonte
Le Boffi
Cantobre
Thaurac
Hortus
Claret
Seynes
Russan
Gaussier
Mouriès
Orgon

udrey Seguy on *L'inter-minable* (7a) - *page 207.*

Chaulet
Mazet
Actinidias
Cirque Gens
Les Branches
Gorge du Tarn
La Jonte
Le Boffi
Cantobre
Thaurac
Hortus
Claret
Seynes
Russan
Gaussier
Mouriès
Orgon

Audrey Seguy on the exposed crux-pitch of *Voie du capucin* (6a+) - *page 205*.

La Grande Face

An intimidating wall, which you're either up for, or you're not. The level of bolting varies from very well equipped to rotten old gear and whatever you can place yourself, so it's worth bringing a small rack unless you're climbing well within your limits. Descent is by abseil from indicated points, if you have to retreat down the route, you will need to leave gear behind. A pair of half ropes works best as the routes do weave around a fair bit, but a single 70m rope will do.

Approach - If you've taken the one-way road around past the Grotte, you can park at the last bend before the road goes to meet the main road. There are usually a few cars parked here. Otherwise, it is probably quicker to park at the bottom of the road before it becomes one-way, and walk up to the corner. From the corner, a path leads up to 'L'Ombre d'un Doubt', about 20m before you reach this cliff, follow a trail off to the left. This goes all the way along a narrow ledge at the base of the routes. Some parts of the ledge are quite exposed, but cables and ropes are in place.

① **L'envers du clocher** 1 **5**
1) 5, **2)** 5

② **Voie ferée**. 1 **4**
1) 4, **2)** 4, **3)** 3

③ **Entre gris clair et gris foncé** 2 **6b+**
1) 6b, **2)** 6a+. **3)** 5+, **4)** 6b+

④ **Légitime démence** . . . . 2 **6b+**
1) 6b, as for the prevous route, **2)** 6b+, **3)** 6a+, **4)** 5+, **5)** 6a+

⑤ **Illusion humaniste** . . . . 2 **6b+**
1) 6b, **2)** 6b+, **3)** 6a, **4)** 6b, there is a direct variation at 6c

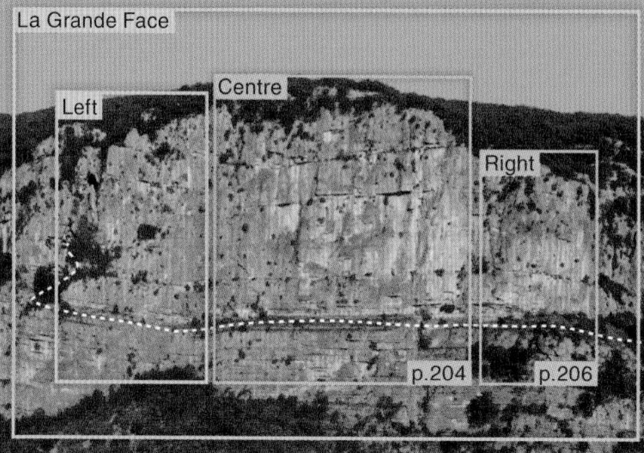

Afternoon
20 min
Vertical
Multi-pitch
35m
A
1
2
3
4
5
Chaulet
Mazet
Actinidias
Cirque Gens
Les Branches
Gorge du Tam
La Jonte
Le Boffi
Cantobre
Thaurac
Hortus
Claret
Seynes
Russan
Gaussier
Mouriès
Orgon

1 Voie guilhem chafiol 1 **6b**
1) 6a+, **2)** 6b, variation is 6c, **3)** 5+, **4)** 5, **5)** 6a

2 Les lianes du temps . . . . 1 **5+**
1) 5+, **2)** 5+, **3)** 5+, **4)** 5+

3 Voie du pot 1 **6a**
1) 5, **2)** 4+, **3)** 6a, **4)** 4+

4 La dalle à chichois . . . . 2 **6a+**
1) 6a, **2)** 6a+, **3)** 6a+, **4)** 6a+, direct is 5+

5 L'été en pente douce . . . . . 2 **6b+**
1) 6a, **2)** 5+, **3)** 6b+, **4)** 6a

6 Voie du susadou 2 **6b**
1) 6b, **2)** 6a, **3)** 6b, **4)** 5

7 Voie de la plaque 1 **6c**
1) 6b, **2)** 6c, **3)** 6b, **4)** 5+

8 La nichée de pinsons 1 6b
1) 6b, **2)** 6a and A0, **3)** 6a, **4)** 5+

9 Voie du capucin . . . . 3 6a+
1) 6a+, **2)** 5+, **3)** 6a. *Photo on page 202.*

10 Voie du capucin direct . . . . 2 6b+
1) and **2)** as for the original, **3)** 5+, **4)** 6b+

11 Giulia au pays des girafes
. . . . 2 7a+
1) 6b, direct start is 7b, **2)** 6b+, **3)** 7a+

12 Mandarine . . . . 2 8b+
1) 7a, **2)** 8b+

13 Sans commentaire . . . . . 3 7a+
1) 7a, **2)** 7a+, **3)** 6a+

1 Chuppa chups saveur inox 1 — 7b+

2 Au bonheur des dames. . . . 2 — 6c
1) 6a+, 2) 6c, 3) 5+

3 Mirage . . . . 1 — 7a+

4 Fantomas . . . . 2 — 7c

5 Paroles et musique . . . . . . 2 — 7a
1) 6a, 2) 7a, 3) 5+. A point of aid is used above the ledge on pitch 1.

6 Les murs de poussière . . . . 1 — 6a

7 Estudio rhum. . . . . 1 — 6b

8 Ishi et l'aigoualus . . . . 1 — 6b+

9 **La douzième affligem** . . . . . 3 stars 7c

10 **L'ombre d'un Doute** . . . . . . 3 stars 7b

11 **A la table des Hallus** . . . 2 stars 7b+

L'Ombre d'un Doute

A very worthwhile sector that has some excellent routes, and a good spread of grades.

Approach - This crag is passed on the way to La Grande Face, see page 202.

Afternoon 12 min Vertical

35m 30m 45m 18m

La Grande Face 200m

Approach to La Grande Face

12 **Génération gallinacés** . . 2 stars 6c+

13 **Jeudi noir** . . . . 2 stars 6a

14 **La diagonale**. . . . . 2 stars 6a

1) 6a, start up *Génération gallinacés*, **2)** 5+

15 **Ne cassez pas les assiettes...c'est du limoges** . . . . 3 stars 6b+

16 **Elsa** . . . . 3 stars 6a

17 **Le doux regard de Coco** . 2 stars 6c

18 **Gode** . . . . 2 stars 6b+

19 **Michet** 6b

20 **Unknown**. . . . . ?

21 **Carmela** . . . . 2 stars 6a

22 **Bouche dorée** . . . . 3 stars 6b

23 **Chatila** . . . . 3 stars 6a+

24 **La 3ème fissure**. . . . . . . 1 star 7b

25 **Dure limite** . . . . 3 stars 6c

26 **L'inter-minable** . . . . 2 stars 7a

Photo on page 201.

27 **La sourate** . . . . 2 stars 6a+

28 **Mauvaise limonade** . . . . . . 3 stars 6b+

The walls around the Grotte des Demoiselles have a lot going for them, plenty of single- and multi-pitch routes in the low-to-mid grades, a very short approach, and a greater sense of solitude than can be found in the Thaurac crags that are closer to the main road. They are generally quite sunny, though heavy tree-cover will give welcome shade when it's warm. The visitor's centre has a café and toilets. The Grotte itself is fantastic and well worth the entrance fee.

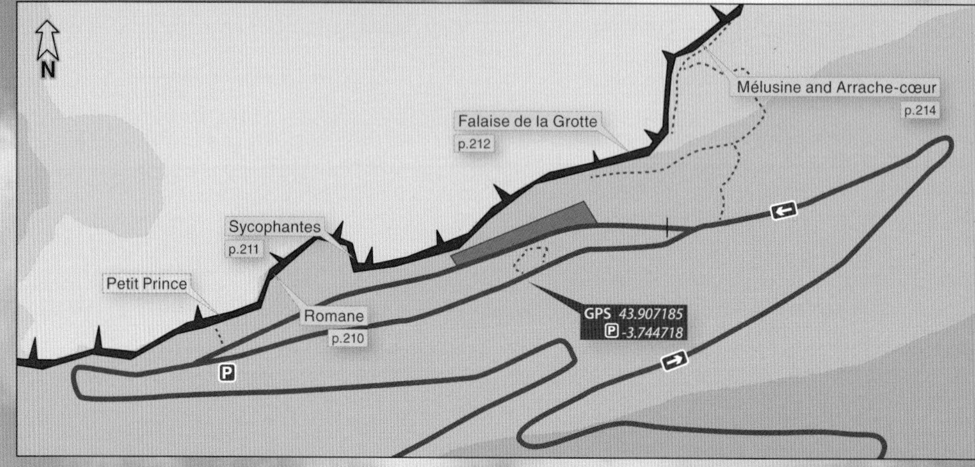

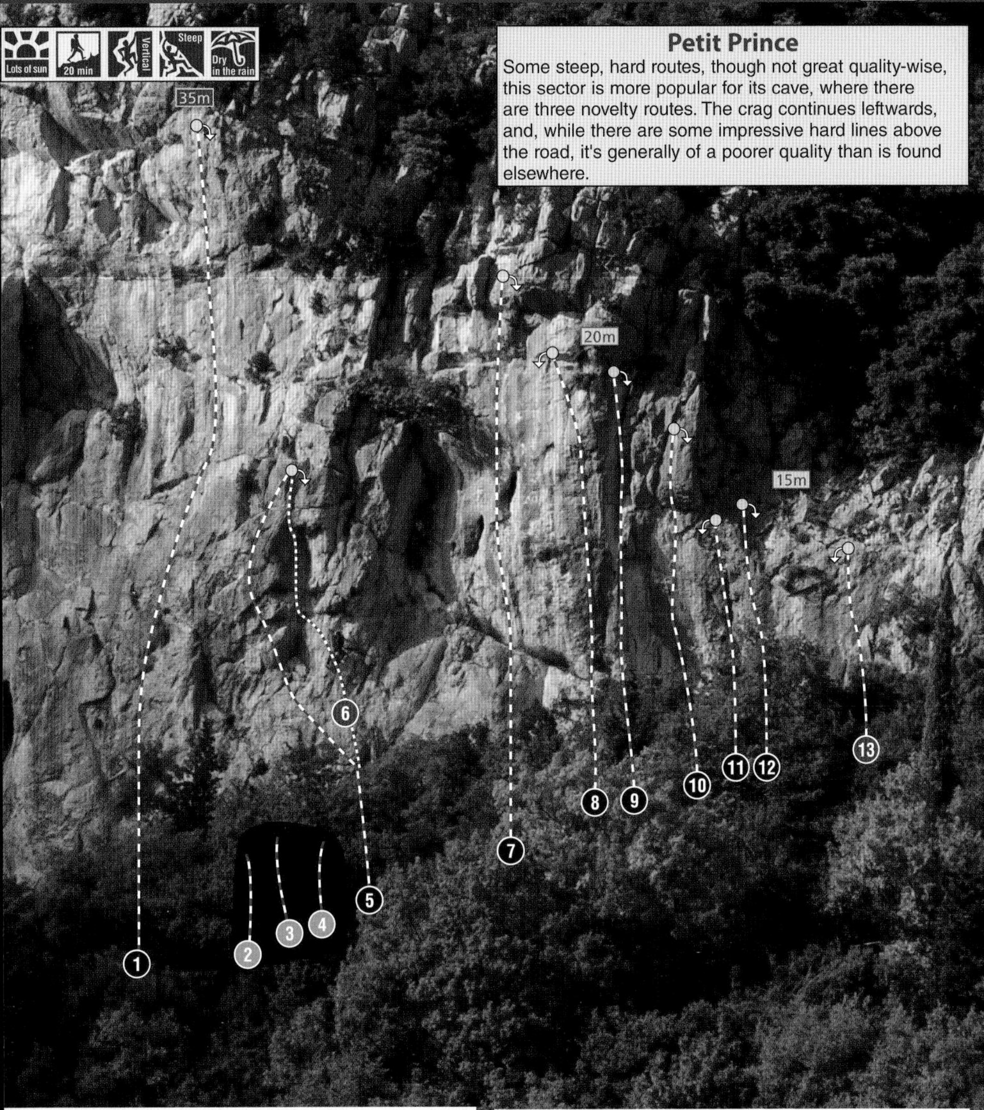

Petit Prince

Some steep, hard routes, though not great quality-wise, this sector is more popular for its cave, where there are three novelty routes. The crag continues leftwards, and, while there are some impressive hard lines above the road, it's generally of a poorer quality than is found elsewhere.

1 **Délit de faciès** . . . . 2 . . . 7c

The next three routes are situated in the cave - which is not visible on the photograph - handy if it rains, but do remember your head-torch.

2 **La fin du mange poire** . . . . 1 . . . 6a

3 **Asphyxie au Ryobi** . . . . 1 . . . 5+

4 **Aquarium** . . . . 1 . . . 5+

5 **Facile service** . . . . 2 . . . 7b+

6 **Abo Service International** . . 2 . . . 7a

7 **Les humanoïdes associés** 1 . . . 7b+

8 **Raymond laffatigue redescend sur terre** 8b

9 **Sibériades** . . . . 7c+

10 **Aquarelle** . . . . 1 . . . 7c+

11 **Pentacarinat** . . . . 1 . . . 7b

12 **Les trois tests d'ésprit** . . . . 1 . . . 7b+

13 **www.equipeh.com** . . . . 1  6c+

Chaulet
Mazet
Actinidias
Cirque Gens
Les Branches
Gorge du Tarn
La Jonte
Le Boffi
Cantobre
Thaurac
Hortus
Claret
Seynes
Russan
Gaussier
Mouriès
Orgon

Romane

A popular spot for families due to the supply of low-grade routes, plus some good stuff in the mid-grades.

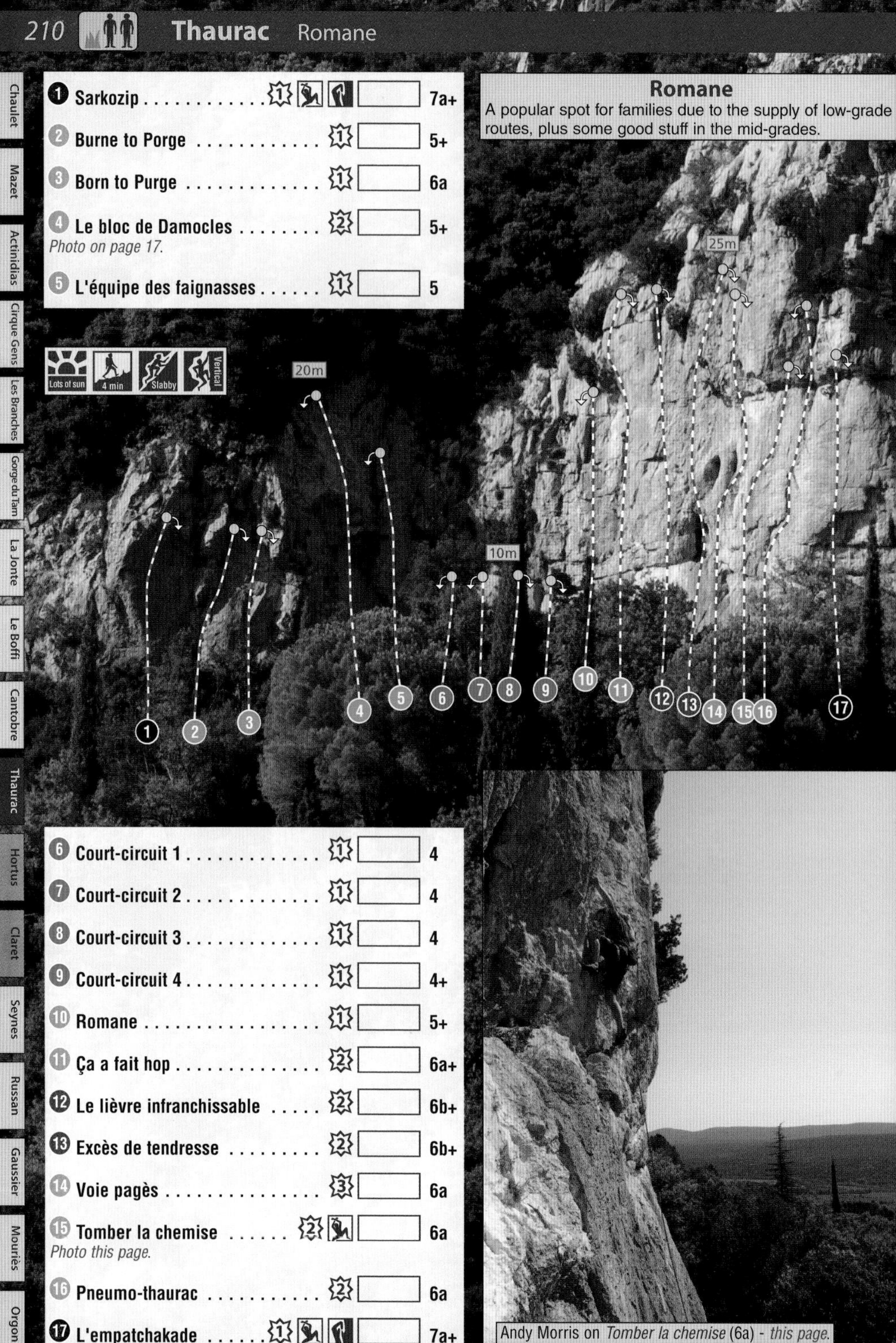

	Route	Stars	Grade
1	Sarkozip	1	7a+
2	Burne to Porge	1	5+
3	Born to Purge	1	6a
4	Le bloc de Damocles *Photo on page 17.*	2	5+
5	L'équipe des faignasses	1	5
6	Court-circuit 1	1	4
7	Court-circuit 2	1	4
8	Court-circuit 3	1	4
9	Court-circuit 4	1	4+
10	Romane	1	5+
11	Ça a fait hop	2	6a+
12	Le lièvre infranchissable	2	6b+
13	Excès de tendresse	2	6b+
14	Voie pagès	3	6a
15	Tomber la chemise *Photo this page.*	2	6a
16	Pneumo-thaurac	2	6a
17	L'empatchakade	1	7a+

Andy Morris on *Tomber la chemise* (6a) - *this page.*

Sycophantes

Probably the best of the sectors left of the Grotte - plenty of highly enjoyable wall climbs that just keep on going. Some of the starts are way harder than anything above - so pick your warm-ups carefully.

No.	Route	Stars	Grade
18	Rouge	1	4+
19	Noire et blanc	1	4+
20	Sang et or	1	4+
21	L'abbé kane coule une bièle	1	5
22	Subtilités calcicoles	2	6c
23	Les jeux sont faits	2	6b
24	Cauchemar psychomoteur	1	6a
25	Voie de la Benje	2	5+
26	Acta fabula est	2	6b

The left-hand variation joins the previous route (same grade).

No.	Route	Stars	Grade
27	Les bras tomberont trois fois	3	6c
28	Les sijaphyantes	2	6a
29	Les sycophantes	3	6a
30	L'airbus de 16 heures	1	5
31	Renard Végétarien	3	6c
32	Super XII	3	6a+
33	Y a pas de doute	2	6c+
34	Sex Beat	2	6c
35	Dérive à droite		5

Chaulet
Mazet
Actinidias
Cirque Gens
Les Branches
Gorge du Tarn
La Jonte
Le Boffi
Cantobre
Thaurac
Hortus
Claret
Seynes
Russan
Gaussier
Mouriès
Orgon

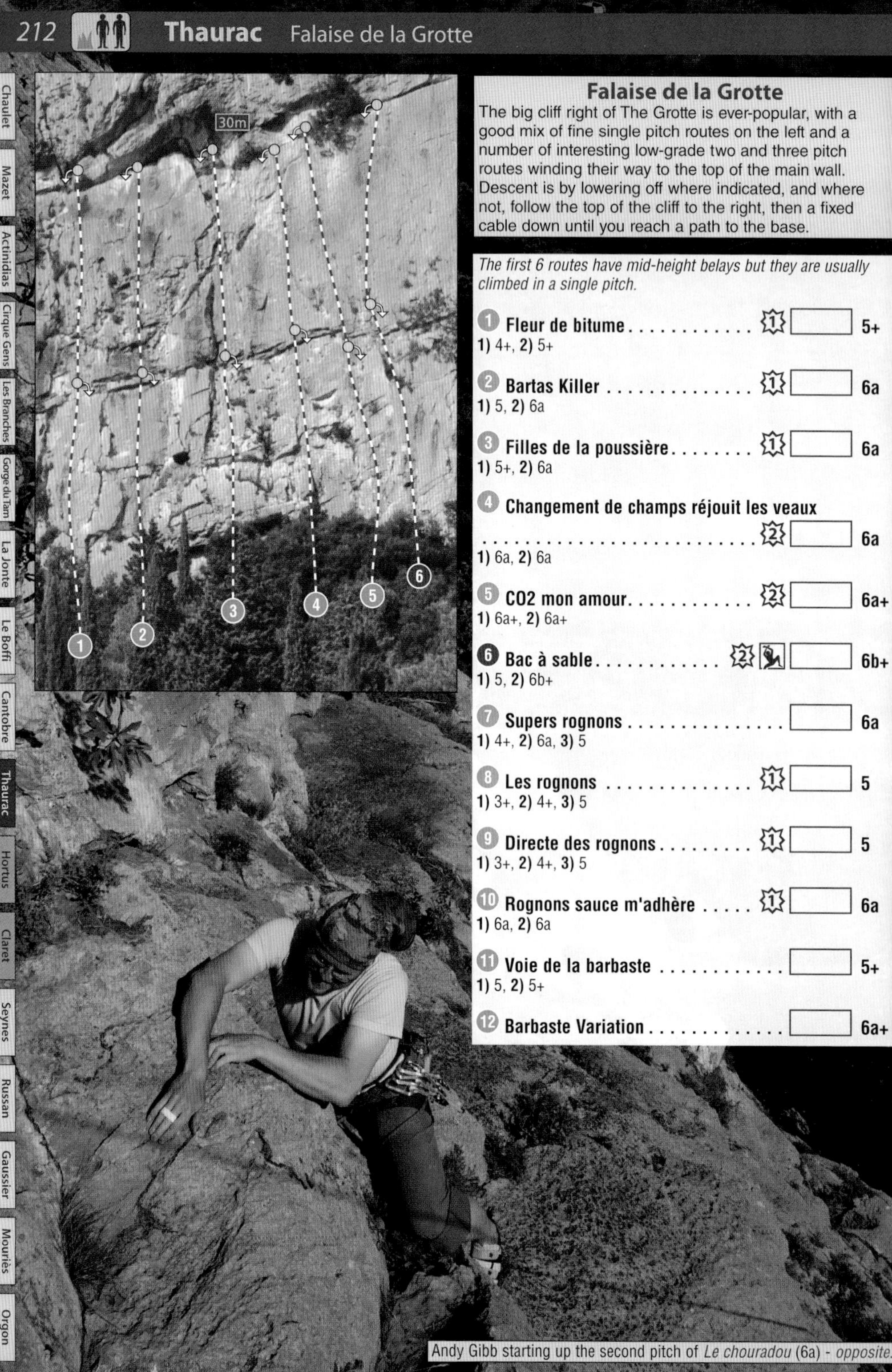

Falaise de la Grotte

The big cliff right of The Grotte is ever-popular, with a good mix of fine single pitch routes on the left and a number of interesting low-grade two and three pitch routes winding their way to the top of the main wall. Descent is by lowering off where indicated, and where not, follow the top of the cliff to the right, then a fixed cable down until you reach a path to the base.

The first 6 routes have mid-height belays but they are usually climbed in a single pitch.

1 **Fleur de bitume** . . . . 1 ☐ 5+
1) 4+, **2)** 5+

2 **Bartas Killer** . . . . 1 ☐ 6a
1) 5, **2)** 6a

3 **Filles de la poussière** . . . . 1 ☐ 6a
1) 5+, **2)** 6a

4 **Changement de champs réjouit les veaux** . . . . 2 ☐ 6a
1) 6a, **2)** 6a

5 **CO2 mon amour** . . . . 2 ☐ 6a+
1) 6a+, **2)** 6a+

6 **Bac à sable** . . . . 2 ☐ 6b+
1) 5, **2)** 6b+

7 **Supers rognons** . . . . ☐ 6a
1) 4+, **2)** 6a, **3)** 5

8 **Les rognons** . . . . 1 ☐ 5
1) 3+, **2)** 4+, **3)** 5

9 **Directe des rognons** . . . . 1 ☐ 5
1) 3+, **2)** 4+, **3)** 5

10 **Rognons sauce m'adhère** . . . . . 1 ☐ 6a
1) 6a, **2)** 6a

11 **Voie de la barbaste** . . . . ☐ 5+
1) 5, **2)** 5+

12 **Barbaste Variation** . . . . ☐ 6a+

Andy Gibb starting up the second pitch of *Le chouradou* (6a) - *opposite*.

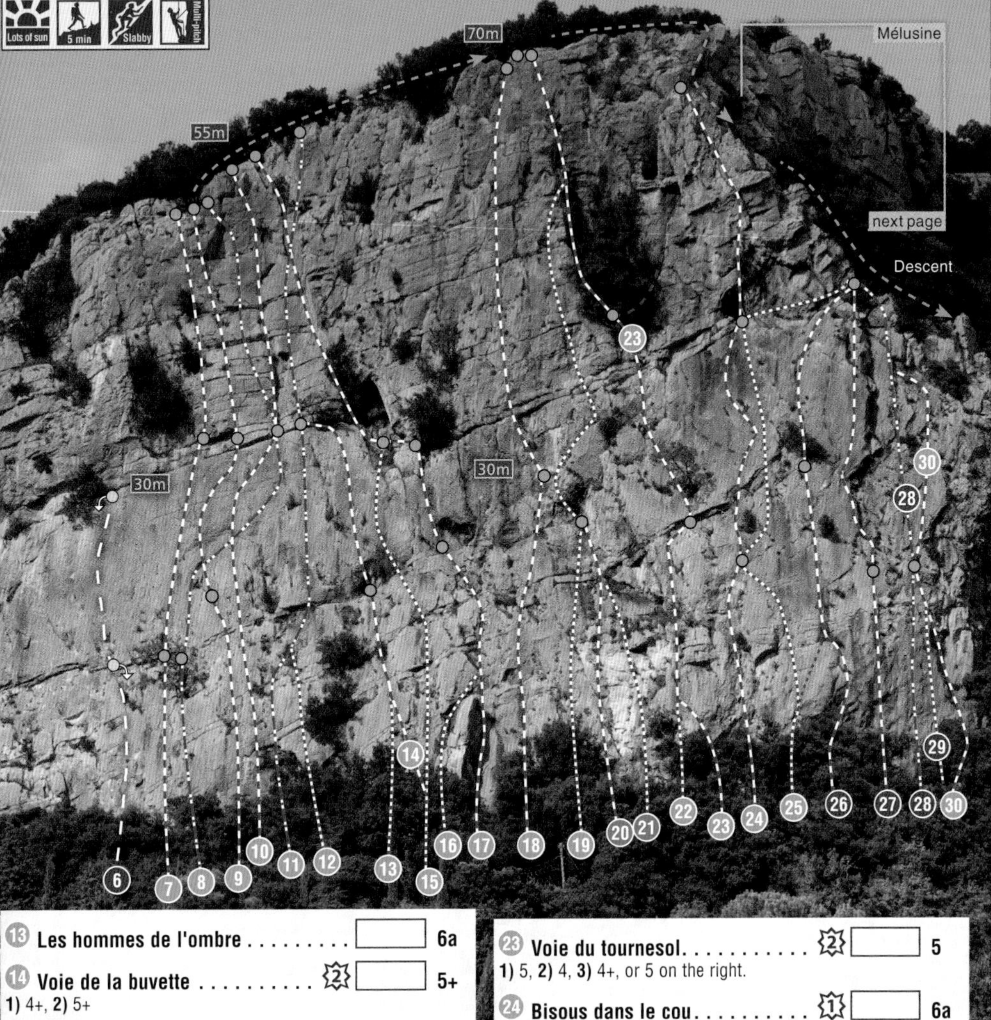

13 **Les hommes de l'ombre** 6a

14 **Voie de la buvette** . . . . (2) 5+
1) 4+, **2)** 5+

15 **Voie des manchots**. . . . . (2) 5+
1) 4+, **2)** 5+, as for *Voie des pigoins.*

16 **Le menhir**. 5

17 **Voie des pingoins** . . . . (2) 5+
1) 5+, **2)** 4+, **3)** 5+

18 **Voie de l'institueur**. . . . . (2) 5+
1) 5, **2)** 5+, the right-hand variation line is 6a

19 **Le chouradou** . . . . (1) 6a
1) 5, **2)** 6a. *Photo opposite.*

20 **Après nous le déluge** . . . . 4+

21 **Poteau rentrant** . . . . 4+

22 **Le filet** 5

23 **Voie du tournesol**. . . . . (2) 5
1) 5, **2)** 4, **3)** 4+, or 5 on the right.

24 **Bisous dans le cou**. . . . . (1) 6a
1) 4+, **2)** 5+, on the left, or 6a more directly, **3)** 6a.

25 **Voie de Mécano**. . . . . (1) 5+
1) 5+, **2)** 5, **3)** An easy traverse right.

26 **La tartane**. . . . . (1) 6c
1) 6c, **2)** 4+. It is possible to start from the previous route and reduce the grade of the first pitch to 6a.

27 **Rhapsodie nègre** . . . . . . (1) 7a
1) 7a, **2)** 7a, left or right is the same grade.

28 **Sage exalté**. . . . . (2) 6b
1) 6b, **2)** 5

29 **Anthracite**. . . . . (1) 6b

30 **Roumegaïre** . . . . (1) 5+
1) 5+, **2)** 5

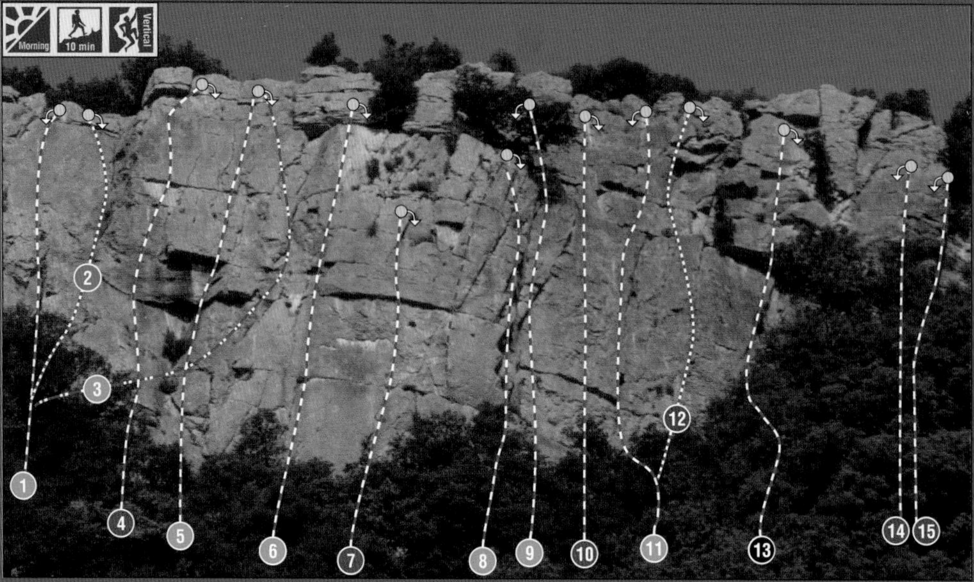

Morning · 10 min · Vertical

1. **Héliotropismee** .... 1 star ☐ **5**
2. **Douceur de vivre** .... 1 star ☐ **4+**
3. **Sous le soleil** .... 1 star ☐ **5**
4. **Vent sud** .... 1 star ☐ **6b**
5. **Viure al païs** .... 1 star ☐ **5+**
6. **La cardabelle** .... 2 stars ☐ **6a**
7. **R.D.V. sur l'asteroïde B 612** .... 2 stars ☐ **6b**
8. **Partir revenir** .... 2 stars ☐ **5**
   The left-hand variation is 6a.
9. **Mélusine** .... 1 star ☐ **5+**
10. **Merlin** .... 1 star ☐ **6b**
11. **Brocéliande** .... 3 stars ☐ **5+**
12. **La belle région** .... 2 stars ☐ **6b**
13. **A nous deux** .... 1 star ☐ **7a+**
14. **Parfum d'asie** .... 1 star ☐ **6c+**
15. **Consensus** .... 1 star ☐ **6b**

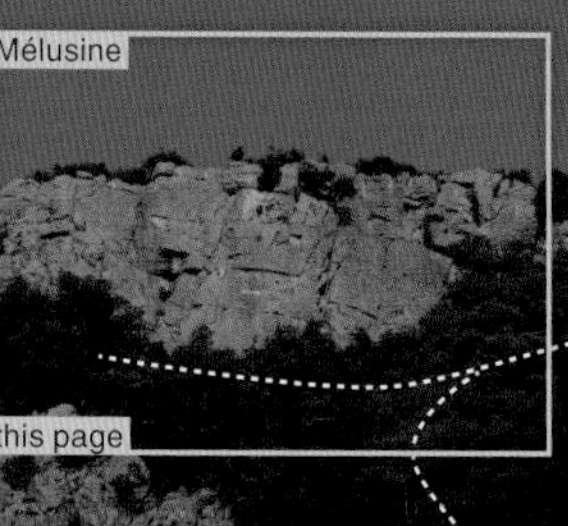

Lots of sun | 10 min | Vertical | Steep

Mélusine and L'arrache-cœur

Two popular little sectors, each with a good range of low- to mid-grade routes and excellent rock. Mélusine has the advantage of afternoon shade, and when it is hot, expect it to be pretty busy. Arrache-cœur has a few hard routes at its right-hand end, and a hermit cave where you can lock up your climbing partner if you tire of them.

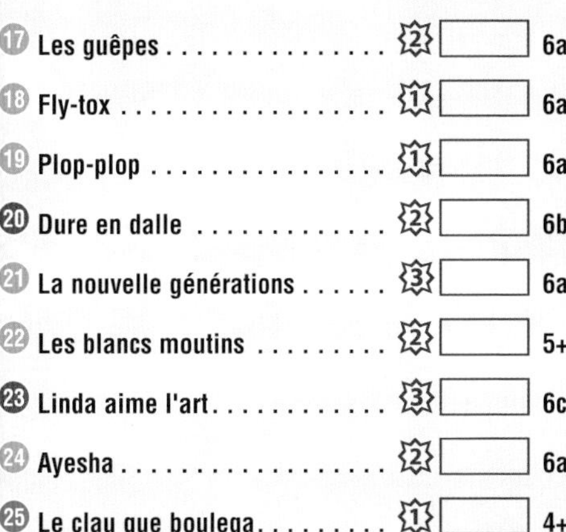

No.	Route	Stars	Grade
16	Moi aimer toit	1	6a
17	Les guêpes	2	6a
18	Fly-tox	1	6a+
19	Plop-plop	1	6a+
20	Dure en dalle	2	6b+
21	La nouvelle générations	3	6a
22	Les blancs moutins	2	5+
23	Linda aime l'art	3	6c
24	Ayesha	2	6a
25	Le clau que boulega	1	4+
26	Le spleen de Paris	1	6a+

No.	Route	Stars	Grade
27	Première soirée	1	6c
28	Les réparties de Nina	1	6c
29	Vent des étoiles	2	6c
30	Abraracoursix	2	6c
31	Cœur de rocker	1	6c+
32	Au pavillon de la boucherie	1	7a+
33	Lola R		8a
34	L'arrache-cœur	1	7c+
35	L'écume des Lourds	1	7c
36	La dérive des sentiments		5+

Chaulet
Mazet
Actinidias
Cirque Gens
Les Branches
Gorge du Tarn
La Jonte
Le Boffi
Cantobre
Thaurac
Hortus
Claret
Seynes
Russan
Gaussier
Mouriès
Orgon

Hortus

Chaulet
Mazet
Actinidias
Cirque Gens
Les Branches
Gorge du Tarn
La Jonte
Le Boffi
Cantobre
Thaurac
Hortus
Claret
Seynes
Russan
Gaussier
Mouriès
Orgon

Hortus

	No star	1	2	3
Up to 4+	-	-	-	-
5 to 6a+	3	11	3	2
6b to 7a	1	15	19	3
7a+ and up	1	8	8	1

Hortus is a crag unlike any other in this guide. Although just down the road from Claret, Hortus is not somewhere you will ever find a crowd. In fact, you are likely to have the crag to yourself. The reason for this is that Hortus is a lot more adventurous than your typical French crag. Although there are bolts, you should not rely on your chosen route being a clip-up, and a small trad rack is worth having even if you are confident you won't need it.

The crag has a number of aid routes - these have mostly been left out, but their existence should be noted when route-finding. Belays are not always the neat two-bolts-and-a-chain affairs found elsewhere - expect to hunt around for pitons and threads and be able to equalise them - and be prepared to leave gear behind if you need to retreat. The designated abseil descents should be used and having a pair of half ropes is preferable to a single rope. Grades will often feel quite stiff here, so it's worth starting off conservatively to get a feel for the place.

If you haven't been put off, Hortus is well-worth your time - the lines are stunning, the positions memorable, and you're sure to have an adventure to remember long after you've forgotten the rest of your trip.

Approach Also see map on page 196

The crag lines north of the D1 section of road linking St. Martin-de-Londres and St. Mathieu-de-Tréviers. Right next to the 28km marker-post on the D1, a large track leads off towards the cliff. Park at the wide parking area at the start of this track, and walk up about 1km towards the crag, until 50m before you reach an old metal gate ('Interdit' sign). From here, take a winding path leading off to the left. A path leads along the base of the crag in both directions. Take care if you find yourself below other climbers, as there is a fair amount of loose rock about.

Conditions

The crag is south-facing and gets a lot of sun. It is also exposed to the wind.

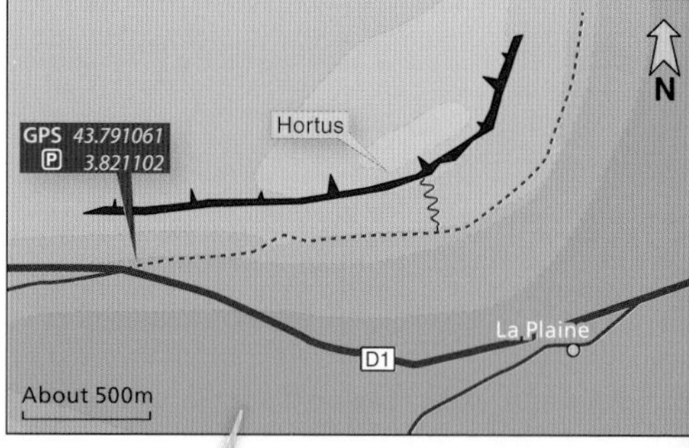

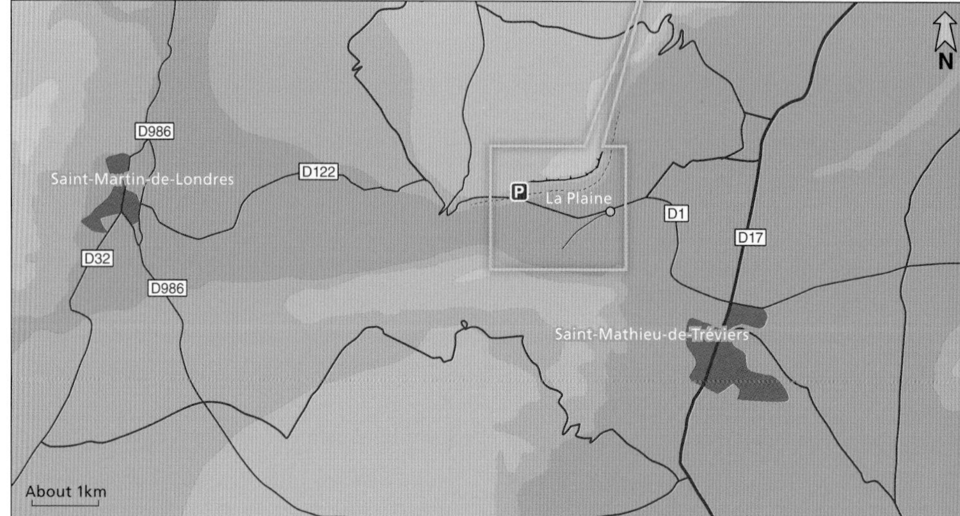

Jenny Barber on the first pitch of the superb *La cagne* (5+) - *page 227*.

Chaulet
Mazet
Actinidias
Cirque Gens
Les Branches
Gorge du Tarn
La Jonte
Le Boffi
Cantobre
Thaurac
Hortus
Claret
Seynes
Russan
Gaussier
Mouriès
Orgon

Secteur des Dalles

Home to a number of big traditional lines, plus a few more-recent, hard single-pitch routes. No climbing is permitted on the walls left of *L'araignée*.

1 L'araignée . . . . 1★ 7a+
1) 5+, **2)** 6a+, **3)** 7a+/A1, **4)** 6b+, **5)** 6c

2 Atlantis . . . . 1★ 8a+

3 Jihad . . . . 2★ 6c+
1) 6c+, **2)** 6c+, **3)** 6a, **4)** 5+, on *L'anathème*.

4 Le choucas aux yeux bleus 1★ 8a

5 La sécottitine . . . . 1★ 8a

6 L'anathème . . . . 2★ 6c
1) 6a, **2)** 5, **3)** 6b, **4)** 5+, **4a)** 6c, **5)** 5+. Pitch **4a** (the more direc one) is better equipped.

7 Les dalles . . . . 2★ 6c+
1) 6a, as for *L'anathème*, **2)** 6a+, **3)** 6c+

8 Les mules c'est leste . . . . . 2★ 7a+
1) 6b+, **2)** 6c, **3)** 7a+, **4)** 6a+

Grenoblois

An impressive wall with some adventurous routes - not the best rock, but certainly engaging. Most of the routes are well equipped, but expect to use the odd bit of trad gear where indicated.

9 La mangani **A2**
1) 6a, **2)** 5, **3)** A0, **4)** A2

10 La tartarouge **6c**
1) & **2)** as for *La mangani*, **3)** A0/6c, **4)** 6c

11 Zénith . . . . **7b+**
1) 6b+, **2)** 7b, **3)** 7b+

12 La roche aux fées **6c**
1) 6a+, **2)** 6c, **3)** 6b&A0, **4)** 6c&A2, **5)** 5+

13 Gloire à Ryobi **7b**
1) 6b, **2)** 7b, **3)** 7a

14 Les grenoblois **7a**
1) 5+, **2)** 6a+, **3)** 6a, **4)** 7a or 6a&A0, **5)** 5+, **6)** 5+

15 Le plaisir naît dans l'attente . . . **7a**
1) 6c, **2)** 6b, **3)** 7a, **4)** 6a+, **5)** 5+, **6)** 4+, as for *Les plombiers.*

16 Au loin la liberté **7b**
1) 7b, **2)** 6c, then finish as for *Les plombiers.*

17 Toute l'afrique est dans l'attente . . . . **6b+**
1) 6b, **2)** 6b, **3)** 6b+, **4)** 6a, then finish as for *Le plaisir .....*

18 Les guerriers du désespoir . . . . **7c+**

19 Liaisons dangereuses . . **7b**

20 L'utopie **7b**
A direct finish over the big roof. 7b or A2&5+.

21 Les plombiers . . . . **6a+**
1) 5+, or 6c just to the left, **2)** 6a+, **3)** 6a ,**4)** 5+ ,**5)** 5+, **6)** 4+
A headtorch may be useful on the interesting caving pitch.

Pendentif

Following the approach path, this is the first sector you reach. It is very impressive. Descend either by abseil, where possible, or walking off to the right to the abseil descent down *La Cheminée Arnal*.

1 La pinacothèque . . . . {2} 6b
1) 5+, **2)** 6a+, **3)** 6b

2 Super Banco . . . . {1} 7a
1) 5+, as for *La pinacothèque*, belay on right, **2)** 6c, **3)** 6c, **4)** 7a

3 Le Pendentif . . . . {3} 6b
1) 5+, as for *La pinacothèque*, belay on right, **2)** 6b, **3)** 6b

4 Étoiles et tempêtes . . . . . . {2} 7b+
1) 6a, **2)** 6c, **3)** 7a+, **4)** 7b+

5 Couche culotte. . . . . {2} 7a+
1) 6b+, **2)** 6c, **3)** 6b+, **4)** 7a+

6 Dédicace . . . . {1} 7b
1) 6c, **2)** 7b, **3)** 6b+ and A0

7 La persévérance . . . . {1} 6c
1) 6c, **2)** 6a, **3)** 6b

8 Dépêche, la mer monte . . . {2} 6c+
1) 6c+, or on the left at 7a, **2)** 6b+, **3)** 6b+, **4)** 6c+

On the upper tier:

9 Pinsut. . . . . {1} 6a+

10 Zoreille . . . . {1} 6a+

11 Mzougou. . . . . {1} 6a+

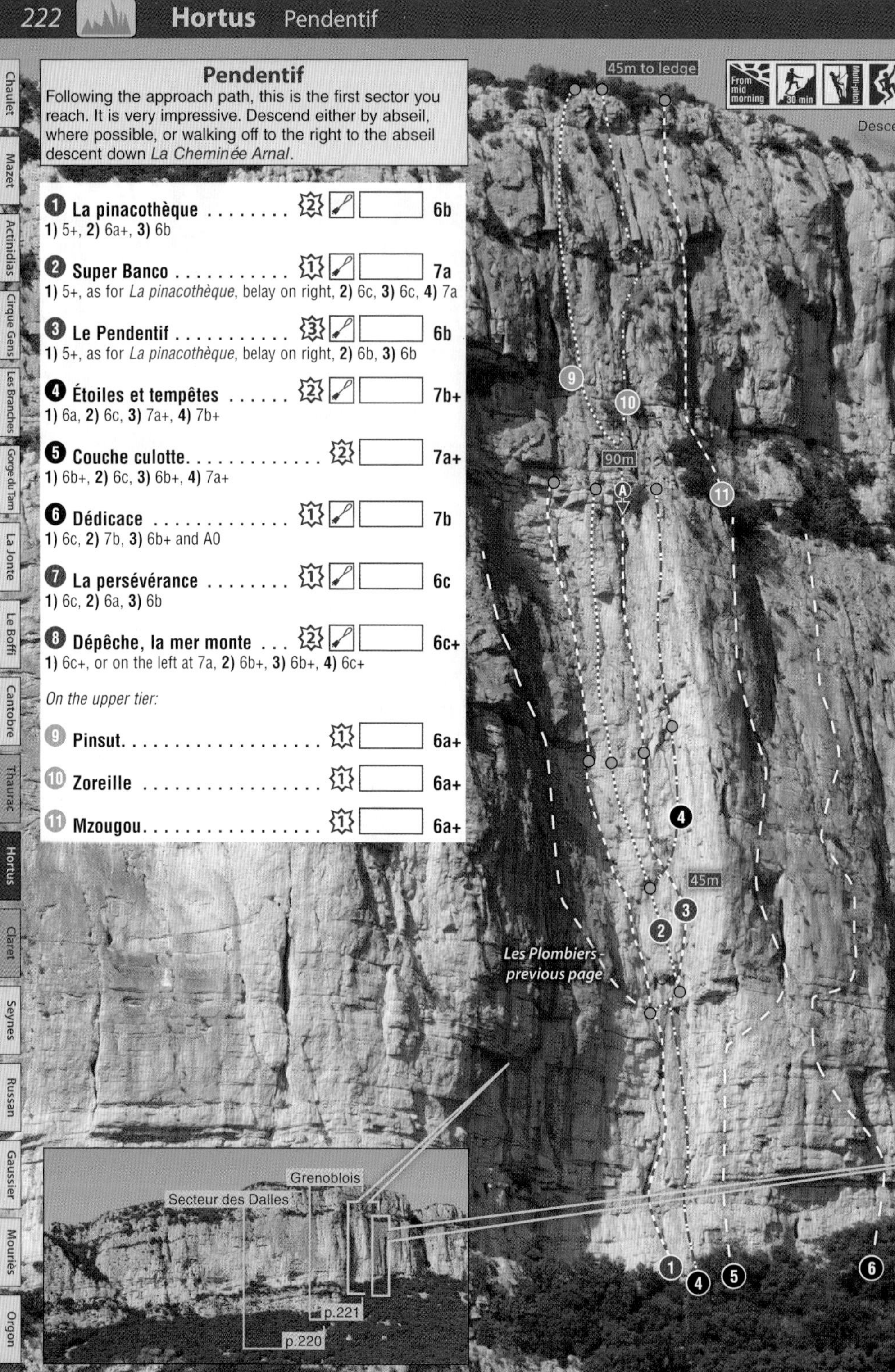

Lots of sun
30 min
Multi-pitch
Vertical
Walk this way to descend La Cheminée Arnal.
80m
50m
4
5
6
7
8
Chaulet
Mazet
Actinidias
Cirque Gens
Les Branches
Gorge du Tarn
La Jonte
Le Boffi
Cantobre
Thaurac
Hortus
Claret
Seynes
Russan
Gaussier
Mouriès
Orgon

Cheminée Arnal

More striking mulit-pitch lines, plus a number of more-recent single-pitch routes from the ledge.
The prominant gully is *La Cheminée Arnal*, and is the main point of descent. The top is marked by cairns, scramble down to the edge and then make one or two abseils to reach the ground. The descent is also a grade 5 route, but best avoided for obvious reasons.

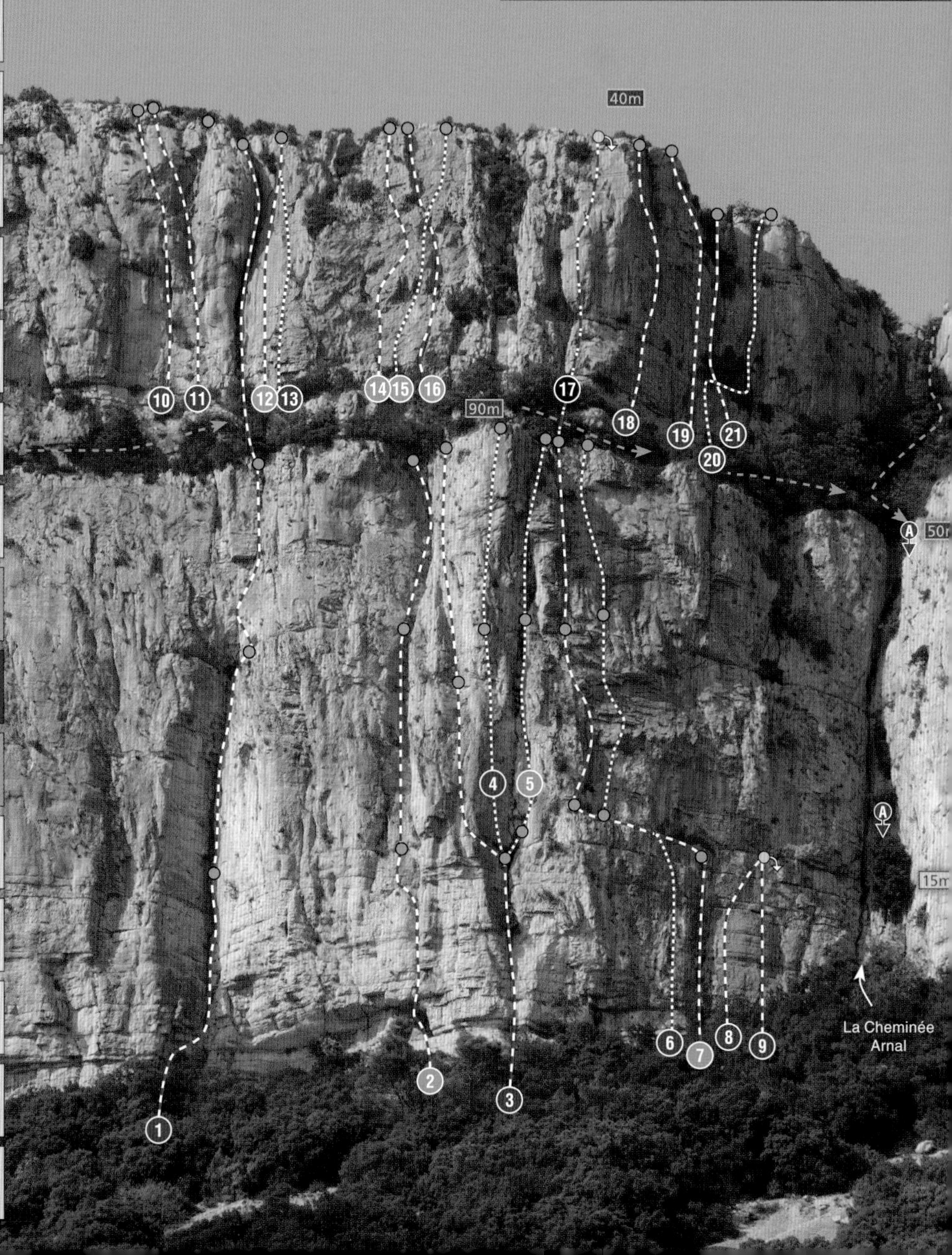

40m
90m
50m
15m
La Cheminée Arnal

Chaulet Mazet Actinidias Cirque Gens Les Branches Gorge du Tarn La Jonte Le Boffi Cantobre Thaurac Hortus Claret Seynes Russan Gaussier Mouriès Orgon

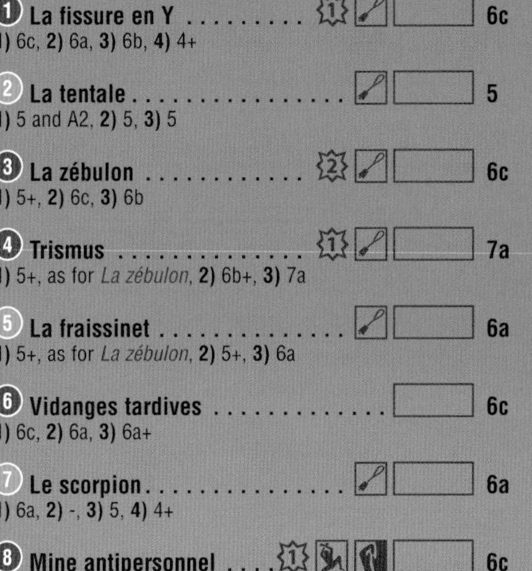

1 La fissure en Y 6c
1) 6c, **2)** 6a, **3)** 6b, **4)** 4+

2 La tentale 5
1) 5 and A2, **2)** 5, **3)** 5

3 La zébulon 6c
1) 5+, **2)** 6c, **3)** 6b

4 Trismus 7a
1) 5+, as for *La zébulon*, **2)** 6b+, **3)** 7a

5 La fraissinet 6a
1) 5+, as for *La zébulon*, **2)** 5+, **3)** 6a

6 Vidanges tardives 6c
1) 6c, **2)** 6a, **3)** 6a+

7 Le scorpion 6a
1) 6a, **2)** -, **3)** 5, **4)** 4+

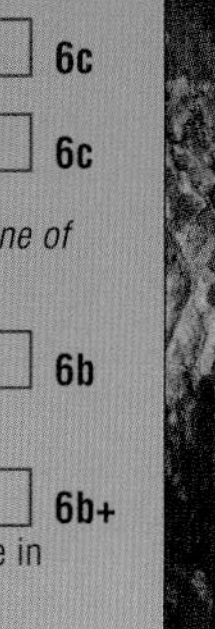

8 Mine antipersonnel 6c

9 Putain de Véronique 6c

The rest of the routes are on the upper tier reached by one of the lines below.

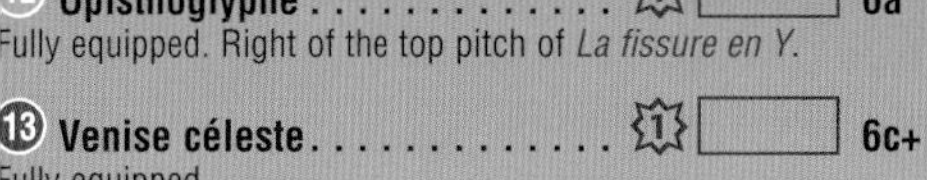

10 Malacologie 6b
Fully equipped.

11 Anamnèse .... 6b+
The right-hand finish is a little easier, but the same grade in total. Fully equipped.

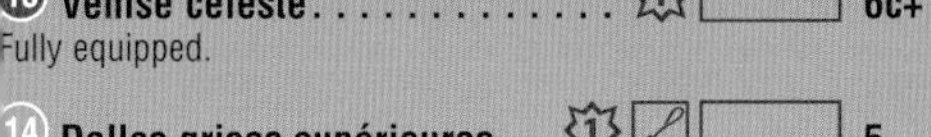

12 Opisthoglyphe 6a
Fully equipped. Right of the top pitch of *La fissure en Y*.

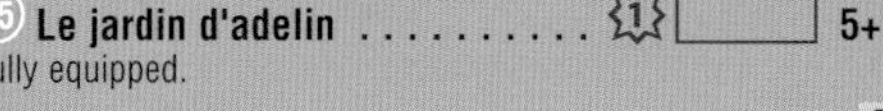

13 Venise céleste .... 6c+
Fully equipped.

14 Dalles grises supérieures .. 5

15 Le jardin d'adelin .... 5+
Fully equipped.

16 Le courédou 5

17 Coléoptère fou .... 7a+
Fully equipped.

18 L'asclépios 6b

19 Marinasse 6b

20 L'envol du polatouche 6b
Fully equipped.

21 L'asclépios 6b

John Eales on the second pitch of *La cagne* (5+) - *page 227*.

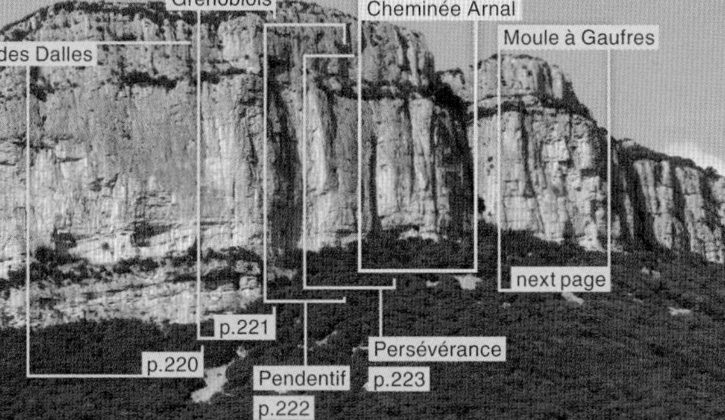

Chaulet
Mazet
Actinidias
Cirque Gens
Les Branches
Gorge du Tarn
La Jonte
Le Boffi
Cantobre
Thaurac
Hortus
Claret
Seynes
Russan
Gaussier
Mouriès
Orgon

Lots of sun
35 min
Multi-pitch
Vertical
Steep
25m to ledge
90m
70m
45m
30m
28m
1
2
3
4
5
6
7
8
9
10
11
12
13
17
18
19
20
21
22

Moule à Gaufres

Striking groove-lines and plenty of big routes to follow them. Descend by abseiling down *Sybarites spartiates* or walk left along the top to descend *La Cheminée Arnal*.

1 Liberté d'expression 7b
1) 7b, **2)** 6c+. Pitch 1 can be done at 6c/A0.

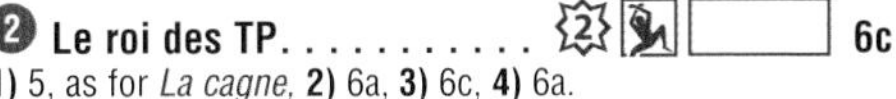

2 Le roi des TP 6c
1) 5, as for *La cagne,* **2)** 6a, **3)** 6c, **4)** 6a.

3 La cagne . . . . 5+
1) 5, **2)** 5+, **3)** 5. Fully equipped, but take a sling for the last pitch. *Photos on page 219 and 225.*

4 Les carnets du virtige . . . . . 6c+
1) 5, as for *La cagne,* **2)** 6c and A0, **3)** 6c+.

5 La super enclume . . . . 6a+
1) 6a, **2)** 6a+, **3)** 6a+

6 L'enclume 6a
1) 5+, **2)** 5, **3)** 5+, **4)** 6a. Start as for *La cagne,* but break right mid-way through the first pitch.

7 L'hyper enclume 6c
1) 5+, as for *La super enclume,* **2)** 5, **3)** 6c, **4)** 6b.

8 L'arche 6c
1) 6b, **2)** 5, **3)** 6c

9 La dyonisos 6b
1) 5+, start as for *La cagne*, **2)** 5, **3)** 5, **4)** 6b and A1

10 Les honneurs, ça m'emmerde . . 7b
1) 6c+, start as for *L'arche* but break right, **2)** 6b, **3)** 7b

11 Le moule à gaufres . . . . 6a+
1) 5+, **2)** 5+, **3)** 6a+

12 J'y crois, j'y crois pas? . 7c

13 Le trypanosome flagellé en colère 6c
1) 5, **2)** 6b+, **3)** 6a+, **4)** 6c

14 La Herbert Stratix 6c
1) 5, **2)** 6c, **3)** 6b+

15 Les sybarites 6c
1) 5, as for *La Herbert Stratix*, **2)** 6c, **3)** 6b

16 Sybarites spartiates 6c
Alternative finish to *Les sybarites.*

There are a number of single pitches on the upper tier.

17 Les peites compresses 6b
Fully Equipped.

18 Sortilège . . . . 5+
Fully Equipped.

19 Redescente climatisée . . . . 6c+
Fully Equipped.

20 Le rivage des syrtes . . . . 5+
Fully Equipped.

21 Escaroucle 6a
Fully Equipped.

22 La goule du diable 5
Fully Equipped.

Claret

	No star	1	2	3
Up to 4+	-	-	-	-
5 to 6a+	3	5	5	2
6b to 7a	2	15	39	15
7a+ and up	4	7	31	45

Perched high above an expanse of vineyards, Claret is a crag that makes you think. The holds always seem to face the wrong way, and those that do face the way you want are almost always flat or sloping, making for some surprisingly pumpy climbing on largely vertical terrain. The grades here often feel a bit stiff, a few changes have been made, but it is worth bearing in mind that Claret is technical, and tough, so don't be too hard on yourself if day one wasn't the scene of personal bests being broken.

Approach Also see map on page 196

From Claret village, follow the D107 for 3.3km, through Les Embruscalles in the direction of the big crag on the hillside. There are a couple of parking bays on the side of the road just past a tower on the right.

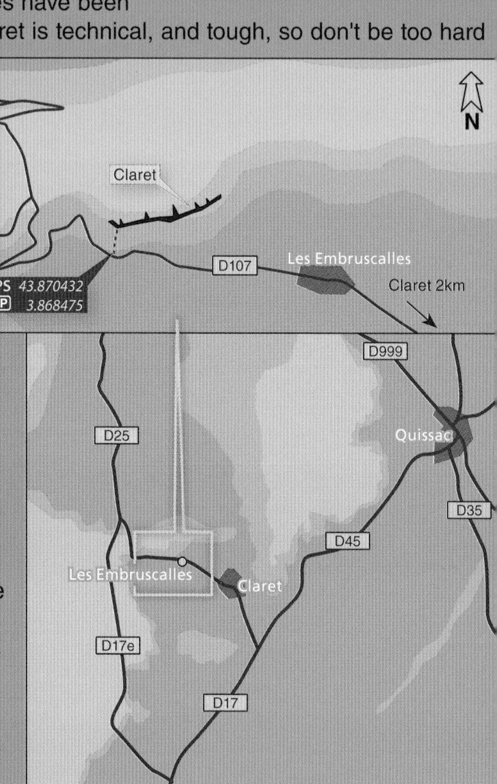

Conditions

The crag faces south and gets plenty of sun. On a sunny winter's day Claret can be a delight. In warm weather the polished, sloping holds do not make for an enjoyable climbing experience, although there is plenty of shade for your belayer. Steeper routes will tend to seep a bit after prolonged rain, but the compact rock dries very quickly making it a good destination if it's been wet and the tufas are dripping.

Piers Culiffe on *Les miracules de Claret* (6c+) - *page 234.*

1 **Miss pascale** .... {1} 5+
Deviate left at the top at this grade.

2 **Miss Helene** .... {1} 6a

3 **The Nose** .... {2} 6b+
Take the overhanging prow directly.

4 **Dirty Old Town** .... {1} 6b

5 **Crapaudrome** .... {2} 6a+
Big flat holds all the way, but quite tiring.

6 **Le peril jaune** .... {3} 6b+
Thin fingers prove useful for the holds in the flake.

7 **L'escaille est** .... {1} 6a

8 **Spleen d'un jour d'ete** .... {1} 6a+

9 **Martin Luther King** .... {3} 6b+
Big flat holds, few rests, and a few tricky bits.

10 **Equip' blues** .... {1} 6b

11 **Offre partie culiere** .... {2} 6b+
A hard start, then pumpy to the top.

12 **Fiesta dies** .... {1} 7a+
Follow the smooth flowstone, relenting higher up.

13 **Columna** .... {2} 6c+
Some aggressive laybacking needed here.

14 **Cabine 13** 6a

15 **Escalator** 5

16 **La berge du ravin** .... 5+

nknown on *Clair-obscur* (6c+) - *page 236*.

Chaulet
Mazet
Actinidias
Cirque Gens
Les Branches
Gorge du Tarn
La Jonte
Le Boffi
Cantobre
Thaurac
Hortus
Claret
Seynes
Russan
Gaussier
Mouriès
Orgon

1 **Miss terre en peril** . . . . 2 — 6c+
Some perplexing moves, and a sense that the bolts aren't entirely following the best holds.

2 **Room 105** . . . . 1 — 6c+

3 **Le pompon** . . . . 1 — 7a

4 **Densite 2,7** . . . . 2 — 6b+

5 **Phlyctene** . . . . 2 — 6c

6 **Margot** . . . . 2 — 6a

7 **Tac tac** . . . . 2 — 6a+

8 **For Lulu** . . . . 2 — 5+

9 **Reve de loup** . . . . 2 — 6b

10 **Cool Fine Nice** . . . . 2 — 6b+

11 **Escalope sur belle salade** . . 2 — 6c

12 **Double emploi** . . . . 2 — 6b+

13 **Hoegaarden** . . . . 2 — 6c

14 **Les miracules de Claret** . . . 3 — 6c+
Photo on page 231.

15 **Je participe assez** . . . . 1 — 5+

16 **Jolie bouse** . . . . 1 — 6b+

17 **Faim: maux de l'histoire** . . . 3 — 7a+

18 **King of Bongo** . . . . 3 — 7a+

19 **L'odyssee noire** . . . . 3 — 7a+

20 **Suzanne** . . . . 2 — 7b+

21 **L'agonie pour les tontons macoutes** . . . . 2 — 7b

22 **La rancon du succes** . . . . . 2 — 7a+
Stick to the groove towards the top at this grade. It is possible to climb further left, but add a grade or two.

23 **Voodoo** . . . . 2 — 7b

24 **Faraboum** . . . . 3 — 7c+

25 **Les cretins en surnombre** 3 — 7c+

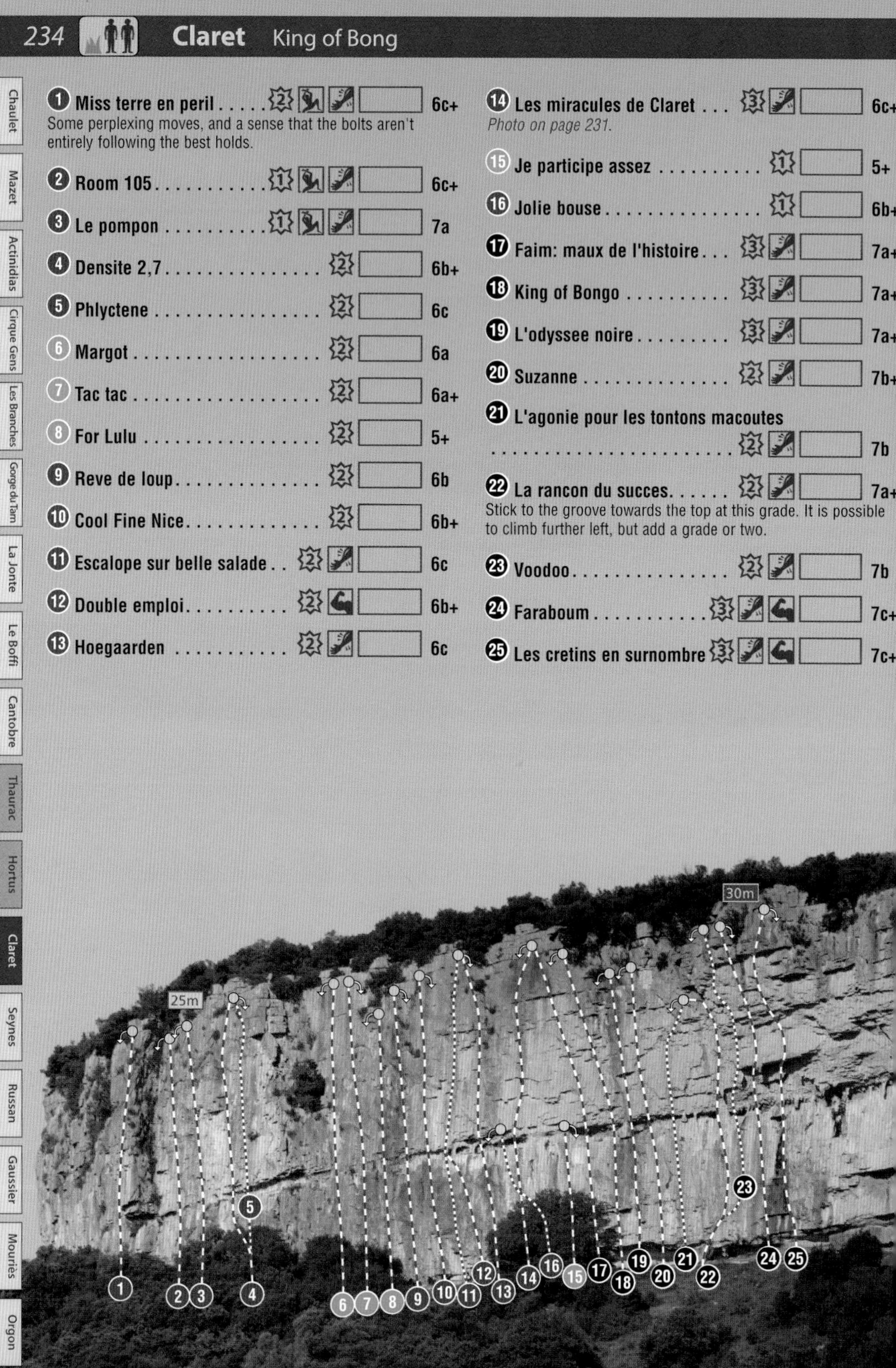

·drian Berry on *Toussaint louvertude* (6c+) *page 238* - Photo: Piers Cunliffe.

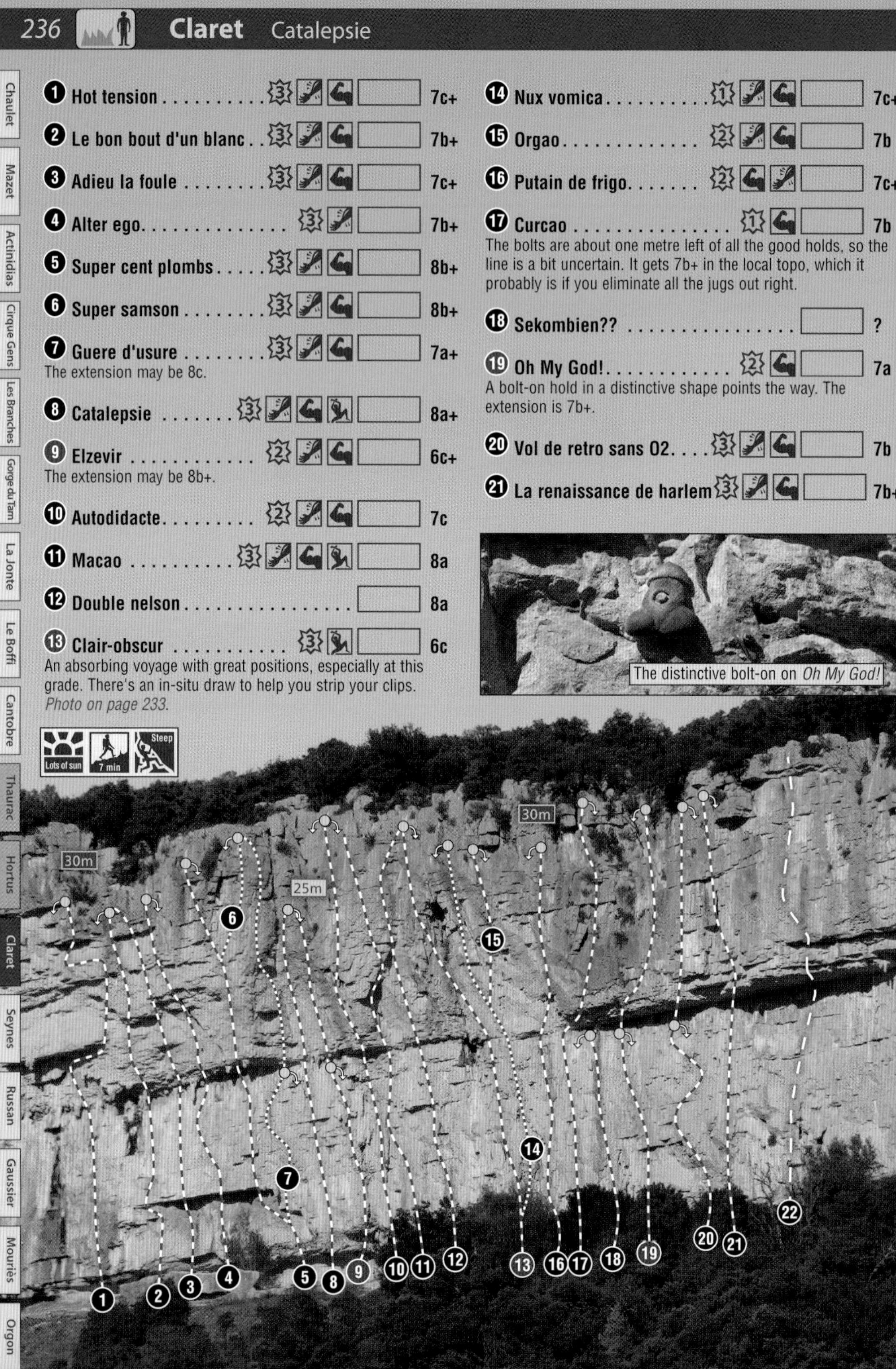

1 **Hot tension** . . . . 3 7c+

2 **Le bon bout d'un blanc** . . 3 7b+

3 **Adieu la foule** . . . . 3 7c+

4 **Alter ego**. . . . . 3 7b+

5 **Super cent plombs** . . . . 3 8b+

6 **Super samson** . . . . 3 8b+

7 **Guere d'usure** . . . . 3 7a+
The extension may be 8c.

8 **Catalepsie** . . . . 3 8a+

9 **Elzevir** . . . . 2 6c+
The extension may be 8b+.

10 **Autodidacte**. 2 7c

11 **Macao** 3 8a

12 **Double nelson** 8a

13 **Clair-obscur** 3 6c
An absorbing voyage with great positions, especially at this grade. There's an in-situ draw to help you strip your clips. *Photo on page 233.*

14 **Nux vomica**. . . . . 1 7c+

15 **Orgao**. 2 7b

16 **Putain de frigo**. . . . . . 2 7c+

17 **Curcao** 1 7b
The bolts are about one metre left of all the good holds, so the line is a bit uncertain. It gets 7b+ in the local topo, which it probably is if you eliminate all the jugs out right.

18 **Sekombien??** . . . . ?

19 **Oh My God!**. 2 7a
A bolt-on hold in a distinctive shape points the way. The extension is 7b+.

20 **Vol de retro sans 02**. . . . 3 7b

21 **La renaissance de harlem** 3 7b+

The distinctive bolt-on on *Oh My God!*

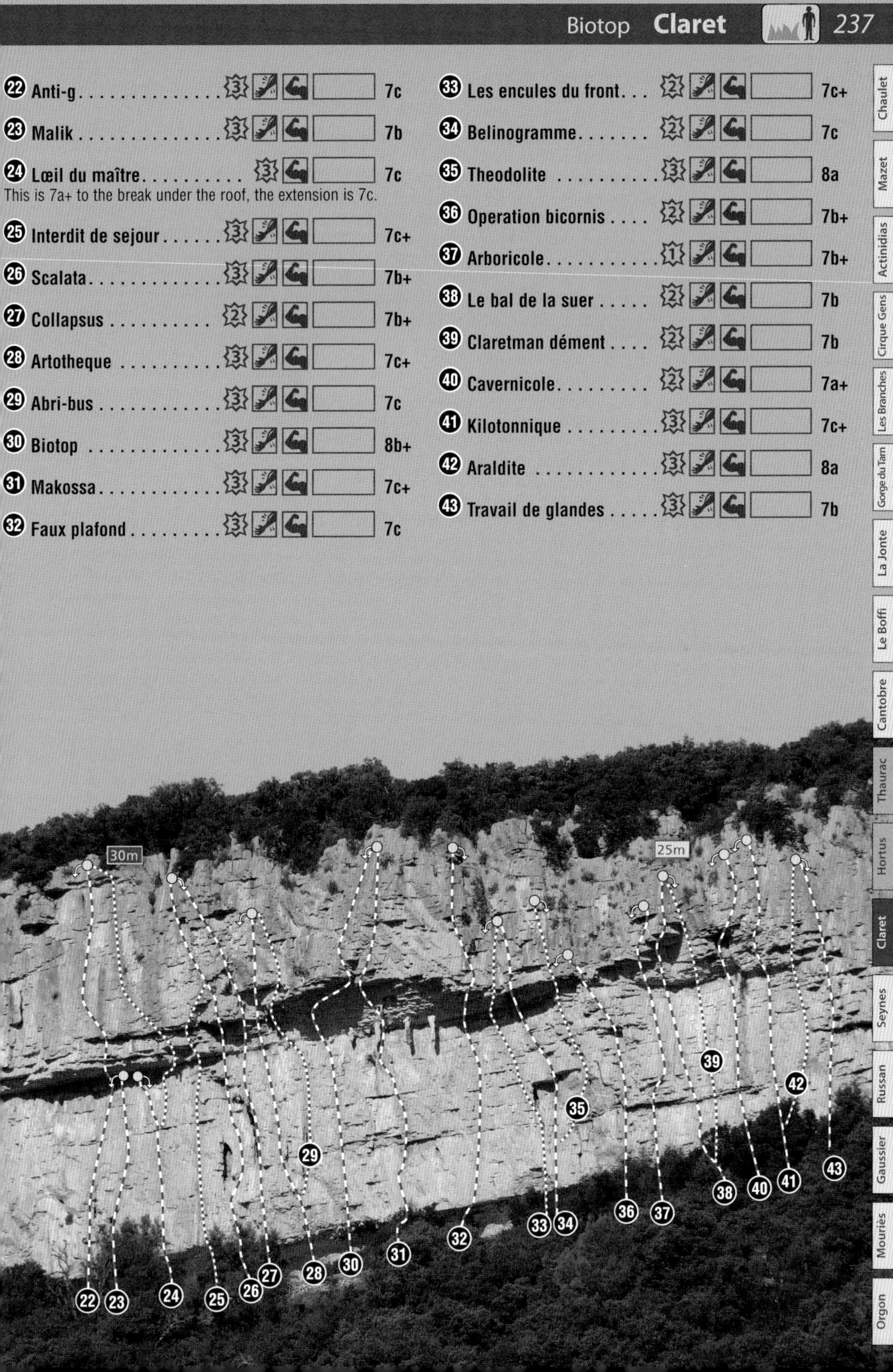

22 Anti-g 3 7c
23 Malik 3 7b
24 Lœil du maître. 3 7c
This is 7a+ to the break under the roof, the extension is 7c.
25 Interdit de sejour . . . . . . 3 7c+
26 Scalata. . . . . 3 7b+
27 Collapsus . . . . 2 7b+
28 Artotheque . . . . 3 7c+
29 Abri-bus 3 7c
30 Biotop . . . . 3 8b+
31 Makossa. . . . . 3 7c+
32 Faux plafond 3 7c
33 Les encules du front. . . 2 7c+
34 Belinogramme. 2 7c
35 Theodolite 3 8a
36 Operation bicornis . . . . 2 7b+
37 Arboricole. . . . . 1 7b+
38 Le bal de la suer 2 7b
39 Claretman dément 2 7b
40 Cavernicole. . . . . 2 7a+
41 Kilotonnique . . . . 3 7c+
42 Araldite 3 8a
43 Travail de glandes 3 7b
30m
25m
22 23 24 25 26 27 28 29 30 31 32 33 34 35 36 37 38 39 40 41 42 43
Chaulet
Mazet
Actinidias
Cirque Gens
Les Branches
Gorge du Tarn
La Jonte
Le Boffi
Cantobre
Thaurac
Hortus
Claret
Seynes
Russan
Gaussier
Mouriès
Orgon

No.	Route	Stars	Grade
1	Awele		7a
2	Belle embolie		7b+
3	L'estouffade	1	7a+
4	Happy Birthday	1	7a
5	Squale	1	7a
6	Black and White	2	7b
7	Houlala	3	6b+
8	Caraïbe	2	7a+
9	Tarif plein ciel	3	7b+
10	Classe économique	2	7b
11	La saison des amours	2	7a+
12	Il fut un temps	2	6c
13	L'appel du bistrot	2	7b+
14	L'excellent toucher vaginal du docteur	3	7b
15	Intervalle lucid		7a
16	Vésanie	2	7a+
17	Le mot du president	2	7a
18	Toussaint louvertude	2	6c+
19	Des vers solitaires in Fred	2	7a+
20	Des margouillats plein les murs	2	6c+
21	Les vignerons de pic	2	6c

Photo on page 235.

Lots of sun · 9 min · Steep

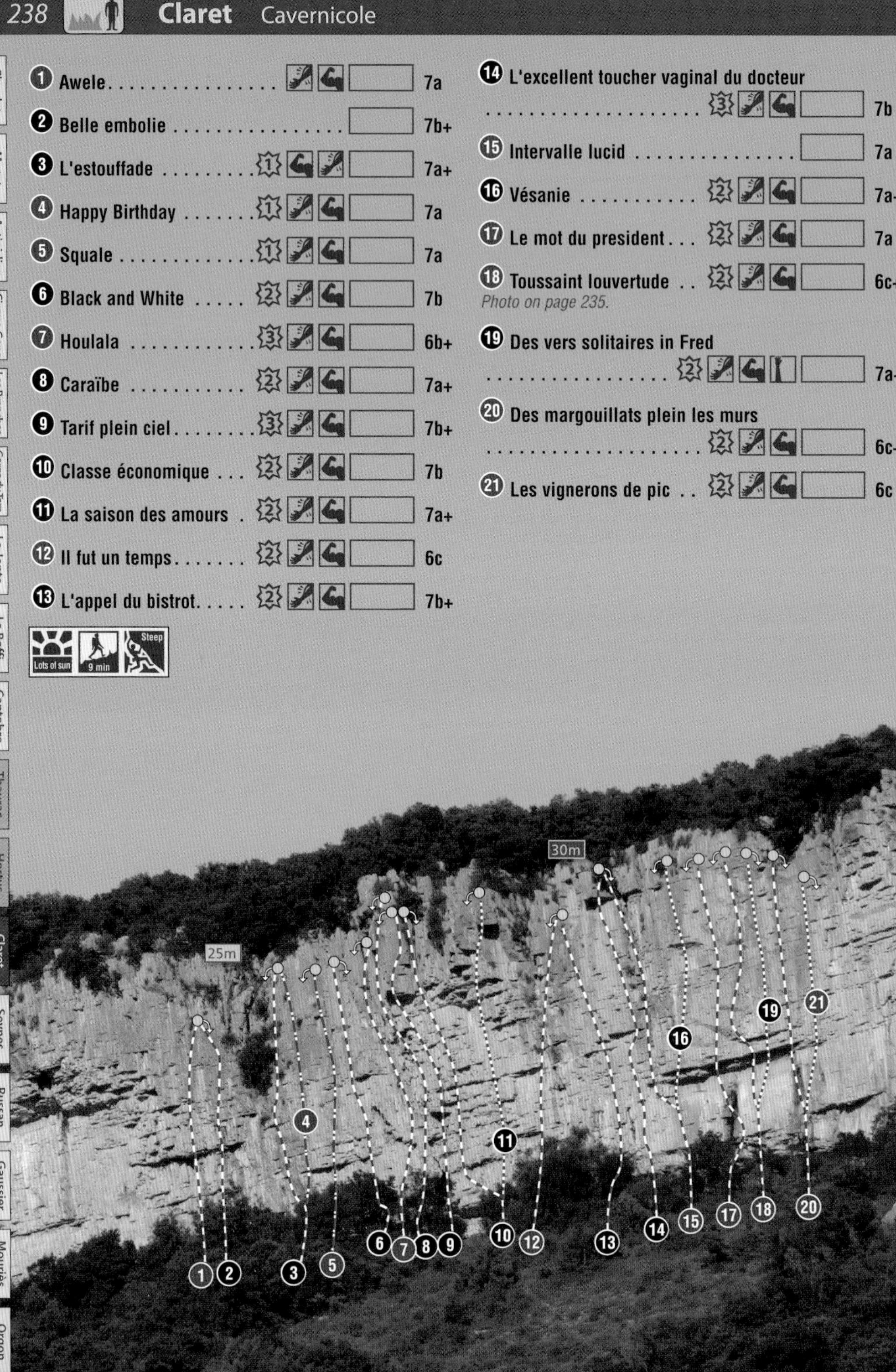

Chaulet
Mazet
Actinidias
Cirque Gens
Les Branches
Gorge du Tarn
La Jonte
Le Boffi
Cantobre
Thaurac
Hortus
Claret
Seynes
Russan
Gaussier
Mouriès
Orgon

22 Zuthôs and pécôs for ricôs .... 3 6c+
23 Tarzoon 3 7a
24 Furia .... 3 7a+
25 Horrible et mental .... 7a+
26 Ttci .... 2 7b+
27 L'abidjanaise 2 7a
28 Chuuut au sol .... 3 8a+
29 Linea 3 7b
30 Amnesie internationale .... 3 7b+
31 Céramic vi 2 7b
32 Faux et usage de faux .... 2 7a+
33 "locos" et cons a la fois .... 3 6c+
34 No Photocop! 2 7b
35 Chronaxie 3 8a
36 Malaga .... 3 7b+
37 Double Penetration (left) 3 7c
38 Double Penetration Direct (right) .... 3 7b+
39 Il est libre max .... 3 7b+
40 Vis comica .... 3 7b+
41 Coït ou double 3 6a
42 Message personnel: "AVFF" .... 2 6b+
43 Trou d'air 2 6c
44 Anastasie 2 6c
45 Somalie .... 2 7a+

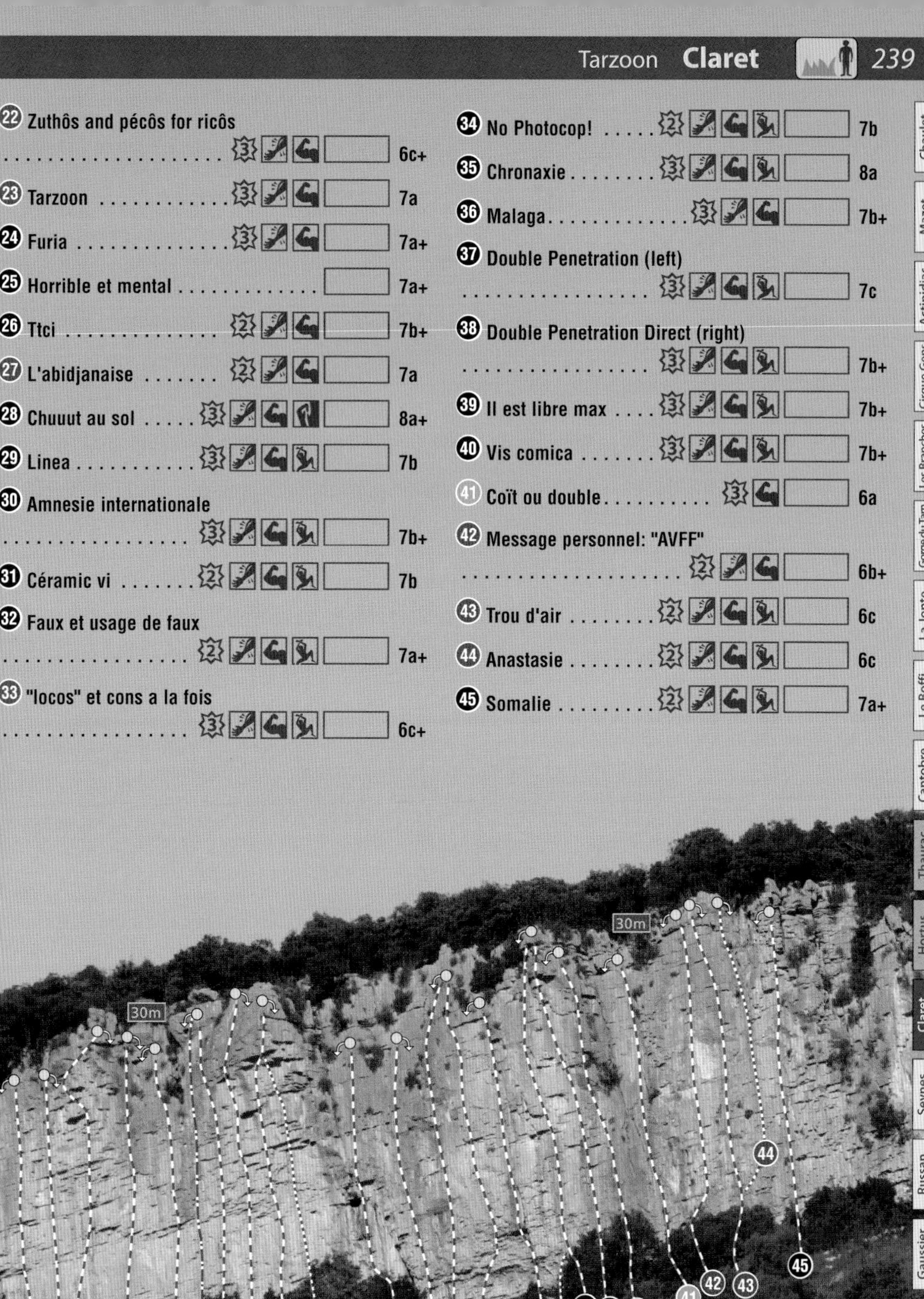

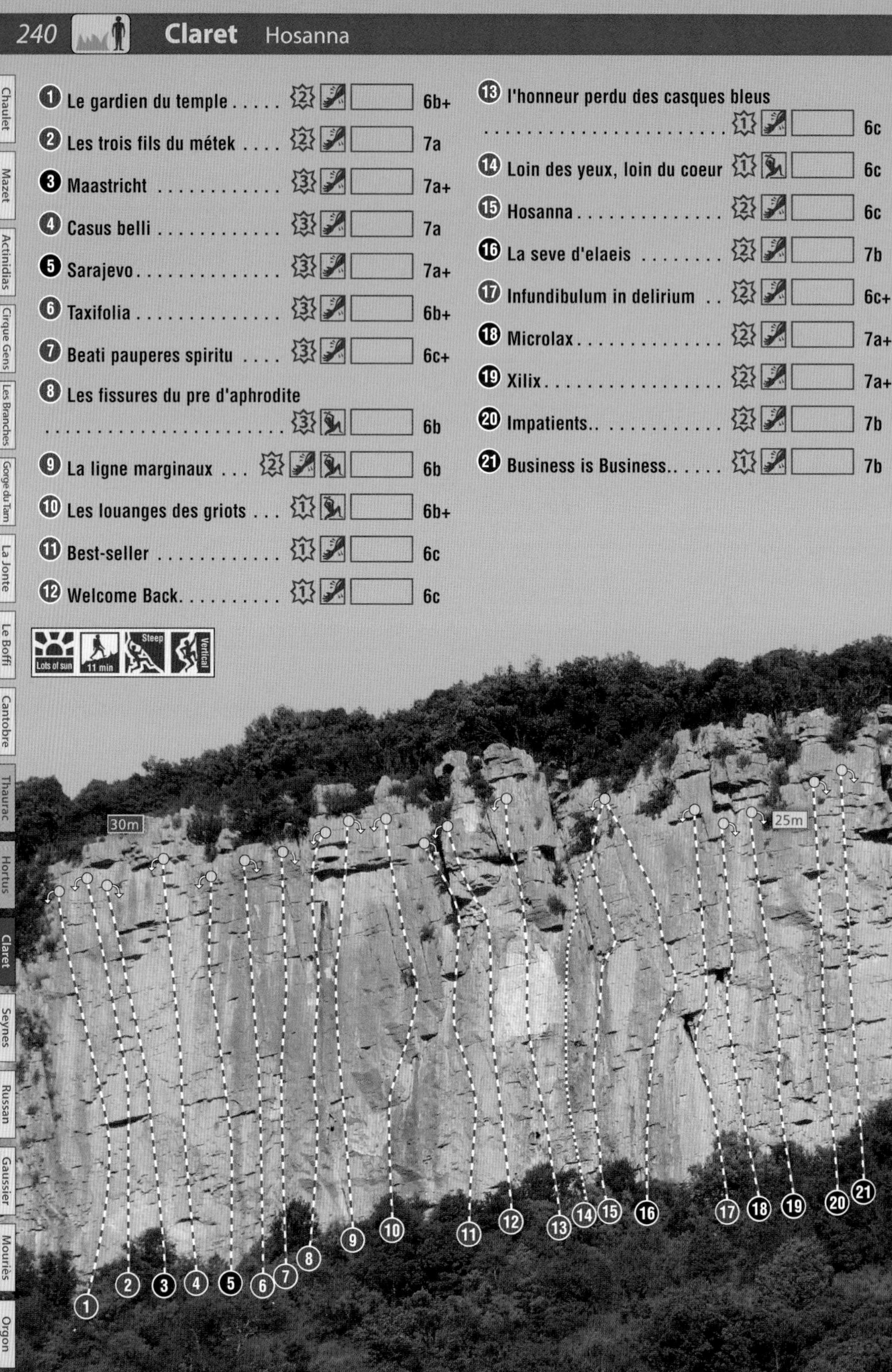

No.	Route	Stars	Grade
1	Le gardien du temple	2	6b+
2	Les trois fils du métek	2	7a
3	Maastricht	3	7a+
4	Casus belli	3	7a
5	Sarajevo	3	7a+
6	Taxifolia	3	6b+
7	Beati pauperes spiritu	3	6c+
8	Les fissures du pre d'aphrodite	3	6b
9	La ligne marginaux	2	6b
10	Les louanges des griots	1	6b+
11	Best-seller	1	6c
12	Welcome Back	1	6c
13	l'honneur perdu des casques bleus	1	6c
14	Loin des yeux, loin du coeur	1	6c
15	Hosanna	2	6c
16	La seve d'elaeis	2	7b
17	Infundibulum in delirium	2	6c+
18	Microlax	2	7a+
19	Xilix	2	7a+
20	Impatients	2	7b
21	Business is Business	1	7b

- 22 Les sujets de sa thèse .... ★1 — 6c
- 23 Le chirurgien de la glotte n'est pas poli .... ★1 — 7b
- 24 Libertaire .... ★2 — 6b
- 25 Africa Unite .... ★3 — 6b+
- 26 United Colours in the World ★3 — 6b+
- 27 Red Red Wine .... ★2 — 6b
- 28 Passage à l'euro ..... ★2 — 7a
- 29 Soweto .... ★2 — 6c
- 30 Rasta Revolution ..... ★3 — 6c+
- 31 Cayenne .... ★3 — 6a+
- 32 La "hugolin" .... ★1 — 6c
- 33 Gandhi, le mahatma ..... ★1 — 6c
- 34 La force de l'ame ..... ★3 — 7a+
- 35 Drole de nuit .... ★2 — 7a+
- 36 Les chants noirs ..... ★2 — 7a
- 37 Cacachouete .... ★2 — 7a
- 38 La came isole .... ★2 — 7a
- 39 Mise en croix .... ★2 — 7a
- 40 Verticalidem .... ★2 — 7a
- 41 Effets de cul .... ★2 — 7a
- 42 Popers .... ★2 — 7a
- 43 Les tueurs de la vache qui rient .... ★2 — 6c
- 44 Peul .... ★2 — 6a+

Beyond Soweto

The crag continues for several hundred metres, and there are plenty more routes ranging from 5+ to 7a detailed in the local topo.

Chaulet | Mazet | Actinidias | Cirque Gens | Les Branches | Gorge du Tarn | La Jonte | Le Boffi | Cantobre | Thaurac | Hortus | Claret | Seynes | Russan | Gaussier | Mouriès | Orgon

Chaulet
Mazet
Actinidias
Cirque Gens
Les Branches
Gorge du Tarn
La Jonte
Le Boffi
Cantobre
Thaurac
Hortus
Claret
Seynes
Russan
Gaussier
Mouriès
Orgon

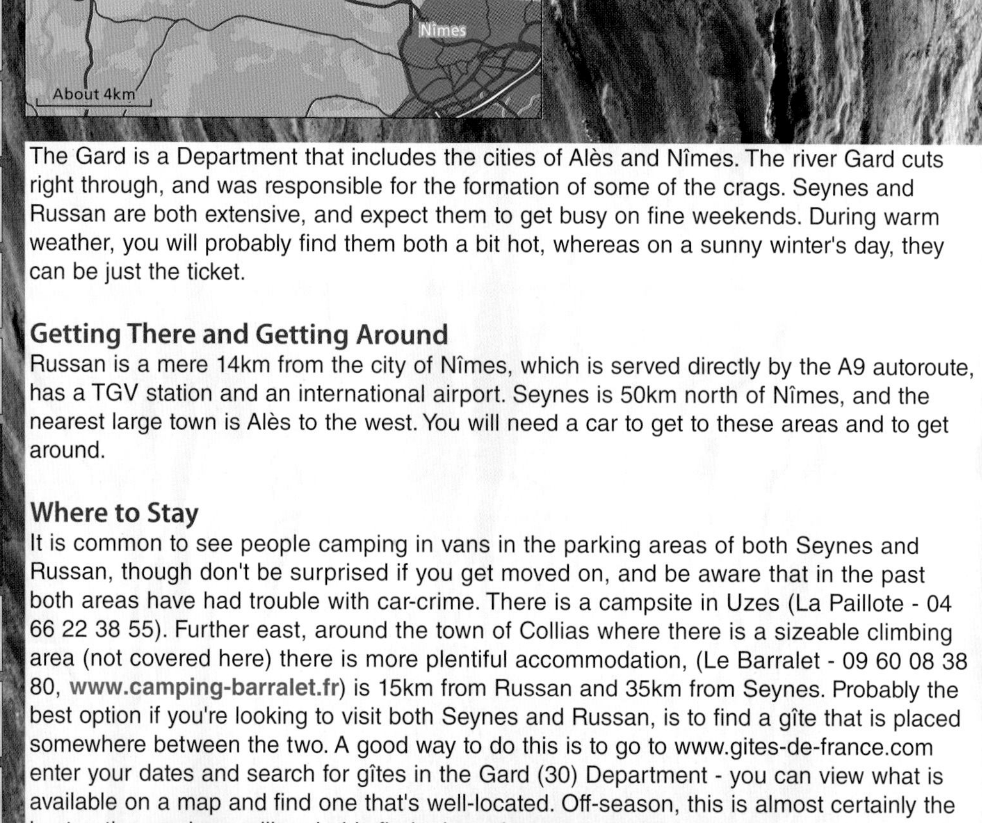

The Gard is a Department that includes the cities of Alès and Nîmes. The river Gard cuts right through, and was responsible for the formation of some of the crags. Seynes and Russan are both extensive, and expect them to get busy on fine weekends. During warm weather, you will probably find them both a bit hot, whereas on a sunny winter's day, they can be just the ticket.

Getting There and Getting Around

Russan is a mere 14km from the city of Nîmes, which is served directly by the A9 autoroute, has a TGV station and an international airport. Seynes is 50km north of Nîmes, and the nearest large town is Alès to the west. You will need a car to get to these areas and to get around.

Where to Stay

It is common to see people camping in vans in the parking areas of both Seynes and Russan, though don't be surprised if you get moved on, and be aware that in the past both areas have had trouble with car-crime. There is a campsite in Uzes (La Paillote - 04 66 22 38 55). Further east, around the town of Collias where there is a sizeable climbing area (not covered here) there is more plentiful accommodation, (Le Barralet - 09 60 08 38 80, **www.camping-barralet.fr**) is 15km from Russan and 35km from Seynes. Probably the best option if you're looking to visit both Seynes and Russan, is to find a gîte that is placed somewhere between the two. A good way to do this is to go to www.gites-de-france.com enter your dates and search for gîtes in the Gard (30) Department - you can view what is available on a map and find one that's well-located. Off-season, this is almost certainly the best option, and you will probably find a bargain.

Unknown climber stretched out on *Ventricule droit* 7a+ - *page 261* - Seynes.

Local Guidebooks

There are many more climbing areas than the two described here, though Seynes and Russan are undoubtedly the biggest and most widely known. The local guidebook **Les Falaises du Gard** covers fifteen areas, as well as more of Seynes than we cover here. You will need to find a climbing shop if you want to get a copy (SOeScalade in Avignon is probably your best bet).

José
p.254
Liason
p.256
Nouveau Monde

Seynes

	No star	1 star	2 star	3 star
Up to 4+	10	15	10	-
5 to 6a+	12	50	37	7
6b to 7a	3	24	46	19
7a+ and up	5	15	40	31

Seynes is a thoroughbred crag of the very highest quality, and although the photos you're most likely to see are of wild, continuous tufa-routes, most of the crag consists of technical climbs taking slabby or vertical grey rock. In other words there is definitely something for everyone.

Approach See also map on page 196

Seynes lies above the D6 that links Alès to Bagnols-sur Cèze. All the sectors are reached by following a track that runs parallel to the D6. Detailed approach descriptions are given on page 248.

Conditions

Facing south throughout, Seynes is no place to be on a sunny summer's day, however, if you find yourself here on a sunny winter's day, you'll quickly go from being snug in a down jacket to smug in a T-shirt. It is worth bearing in mind that Seynes is covered in flow-stone and tufas which will get wet after prolonged or heavy rain, and will take a while to dry out, so if it's been raining, the tufa routes may be impossible.

It's not all overhanging tufas! John Eales enjoying one of the many fine slab-routes to be found at the right side of the cliff.

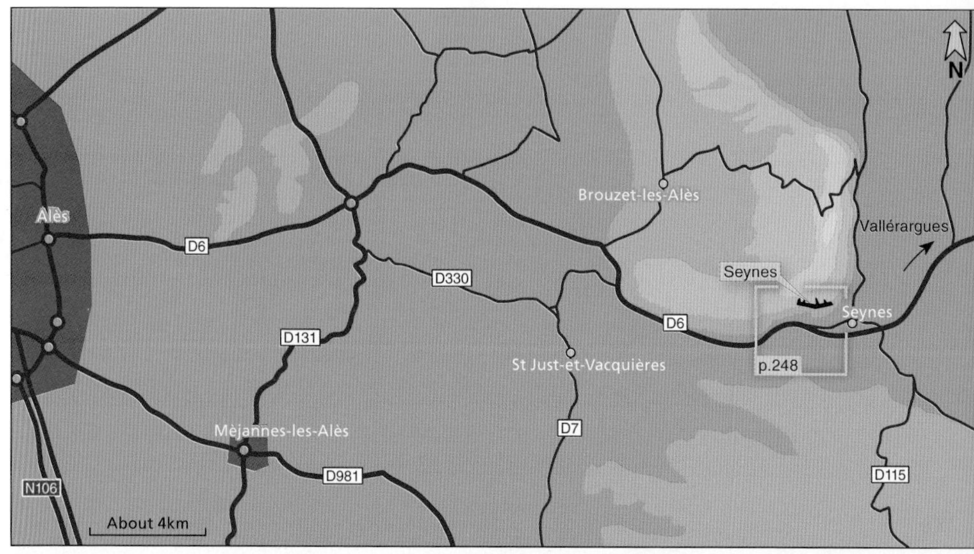

Jonathan Ayrton being eaten by the classic *Le tube neural* (6c+) - *page 261*.

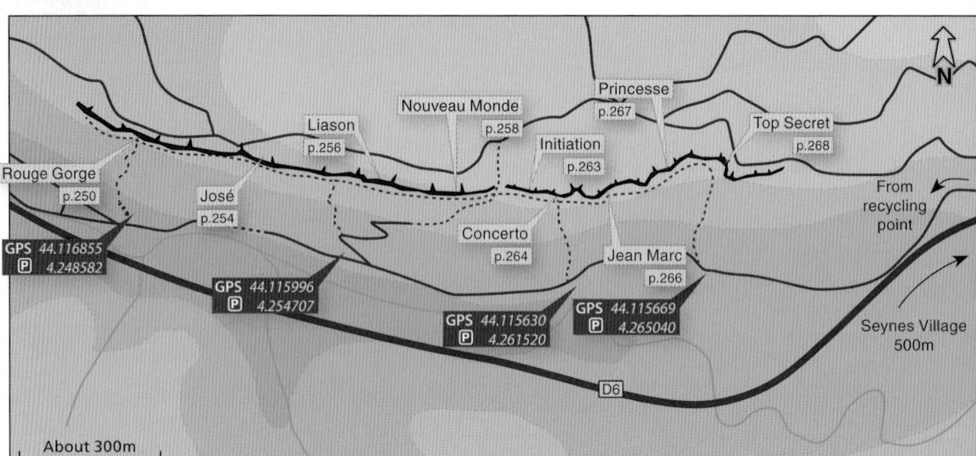

Rouge Gorge

This sector can be reached by walking along the base of the crag from sectors further right. A quicker approach is to pick-up a track from the junction between the A6 and the D7 (to Saint-Just-et-Vacquières). Follow the track parallel with the A6 for 1km until a parking area is reach on the left. Park here and follow a trail up to the crag.

All the following sectors are reached by driving west along the track that runs parallel with the A6. At the junction of the A6 that leads to the village of Seynes (recycling point) take the track leads off in the direction of the cliff and not the adjacent track that leads up the hill. Distances are measured from here.

José

Follow the track for 2km until you reach an extensive parking area at the base of a track leading up towards the cliff. Park here and follow the wide track, at the first switch-back a path leads off to the left, follow this, to the crag.

Liason

Approach as for Nouveau Monde, then follow the track along the base of the crag.

Nouveau Monde

Approach as for José but continue along the switch-back track until it eventually becomes a trail that leads to the base of *Le tube neural*.

Initiation, Concerto, and Jean Marc

Follow the track for a total of 1.5km until you reach a parking area - a trail leads off up the hill to the right - the start of this trail may be marked with large cairns.

Princesse and Top Secret

Drive for a total of 1.2km until you reach a rusting post and trail leading off on the left, just before a bend in the track. Park here and follow a trail off up the hill on the right to all the sectors.

Nouveau Monde
Liason
José
Rouge Gorge
p.258
p.256
p.254
next page

Nouveau Monde - Right
Initiation
Concerto
Jean Marc
p.263
p.264
p.266
p.262

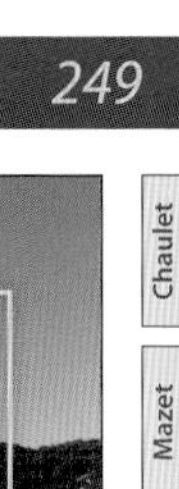

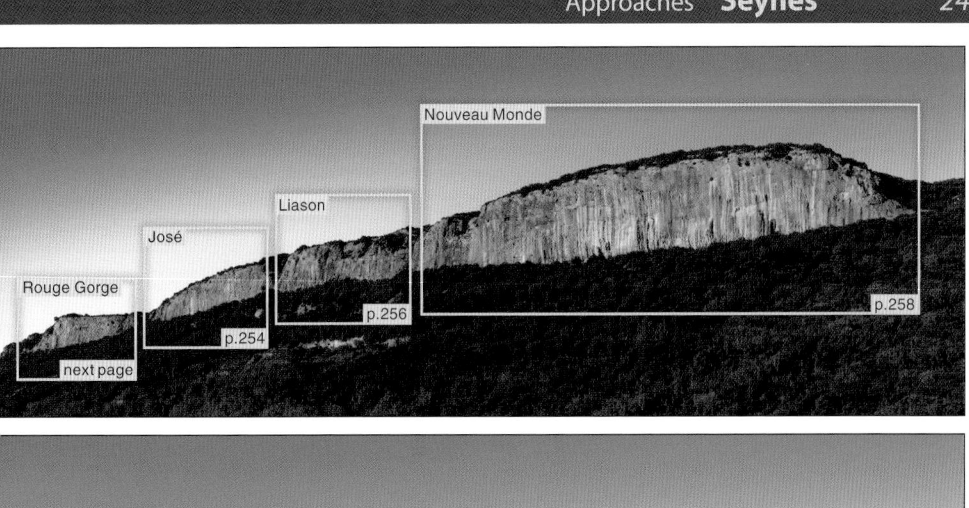

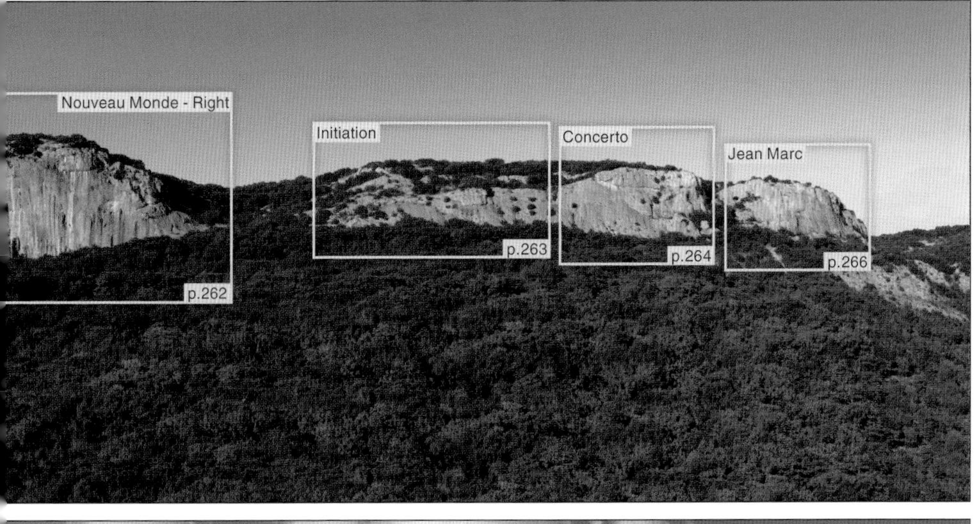

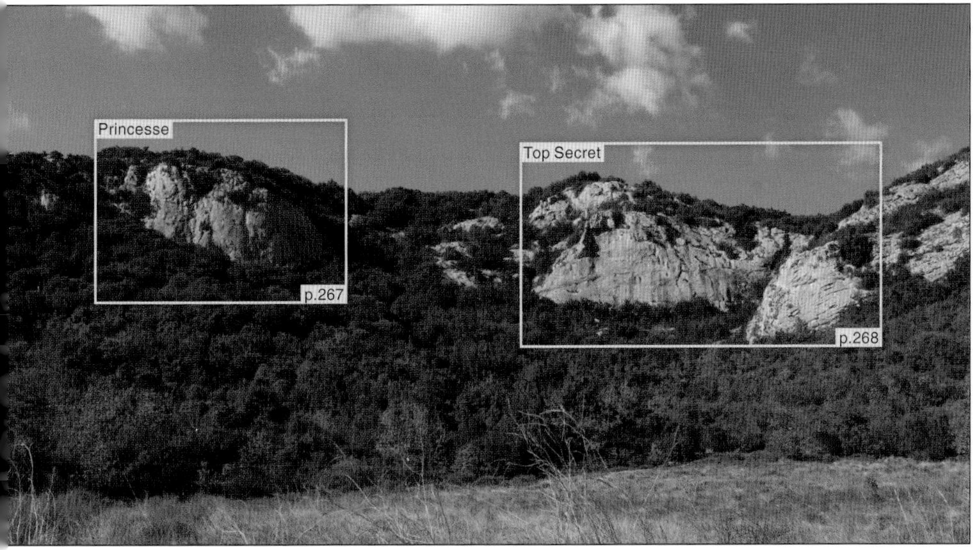

Princesse
Top Secret
p.267
p.268

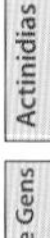

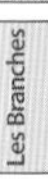

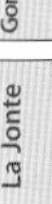

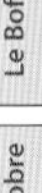

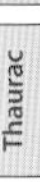

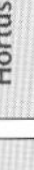

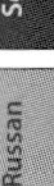

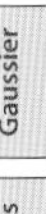

Rouge Gorge

At the extreme left-hand end of the crag is this collection of mostly slabby routes in the lower grades, while not up to the quality of the rest of the crag, the quantity of low grades routes makes this a popular sector.

Approach - See page 248.

1. Excalibur ... 4
2. Stormbringer ... 6b
3. Sébette ... 5+
4. T'es haut Théo ... 5+
5. Verticaland ... 6a
6. Promenons-nous dans les voies ... 5+
7. Et un, et deux, et trois zéro ... 5
8. Sika sinoque n'est pas une sinécure ... 4+
9. Les yeux dans les bleus ... 5+
10. Prises en tete ... 4
11. P'tit bout d'ain ... 4
12. Un ch'ti coin de paradis ... 1 ... 5
13. Et guise et buis ronds ... 1 ... 5
14. Pédale douce ... 1 ... 5+
15. Meije angen et rossignol ... 1 ... 5
16. Une peur bleue comme ces yeux ... 1 ... 5
17. Surprise sur prise ... 1 ... 5
18. Quelle et ses grattons ... 1 ... 5
19. C'est quoi ca...? ... 1 ... 5+

Lots of sun | 10 min | Slabby

20m 30m 32m

1 2 3 4 5 6 7 8 9 10 11 12 13 14 15 16 17 18 19 20 21 22 23 24

No.	Route	Stars	Grade
20	Martin entre en Seynes	1	6a
21	Manhattan	1	5
22	Zen tout est la	2	5+
23	Techicien de surface	1	6b
24	Meme pas peur	1	5+
25	P'tit chamois	1	5+
26	Lou cherche son ann	1	5
27	Le grand meije en lou	1	4+
28	Louis d'or pas	1	4
29	Euro qui comme ulysse	1	4
30	Le bobojaulais	1	4
31	Les 100 balles du docteur	1	4
32	En selle héros	1	5
33	La voie des 3 III	1	4+
34	Pieu main	2	6a
35	El blanco	2	5+
36	El negro	1	6a+
37	El tinto	1	6a
38	Lukas	2	6a
39	Les dix ocelles de la malmignatte	2	6b+
40	La belle rouge	2	7a

Photo on page 253.

No.	Route	Stars	Grade
1	Rubis sur l'ongle	2	7c+
2	Coup de gouze	1	7a+
3	First	2	7b+
4	Batman	3	7b+
5	Red rock blues	2	7c
6	Soescalade	2	7b+
7	Ho! Rage	1	7c+
8	Coup de douze	1	7a+
9	Unknown	1	7b+
10	Unknown	1	7b+
11	Bonne grimpe	2	7c
12	Amézamours	1	7c
13	Toutencamion	1	7b+
14	Lune et toi laid	1	7a+
15	Tarnagas	1	6b+
16	Petit dec	2	6b
17	Lou provecao	1	6b
18	La cagne	2	6c
19	Gargantua	2	6a+
20	Figue molle	2	6b
21	Unknown	2	6b+
22	Unknown	2	6b
23	Belle nuit	2	6b
24	Ciel rouge	2	6b+
25	Riri	1	6a
26	Fifi	1	5+

Lots of sun · 10 min · Slabby · Vertical

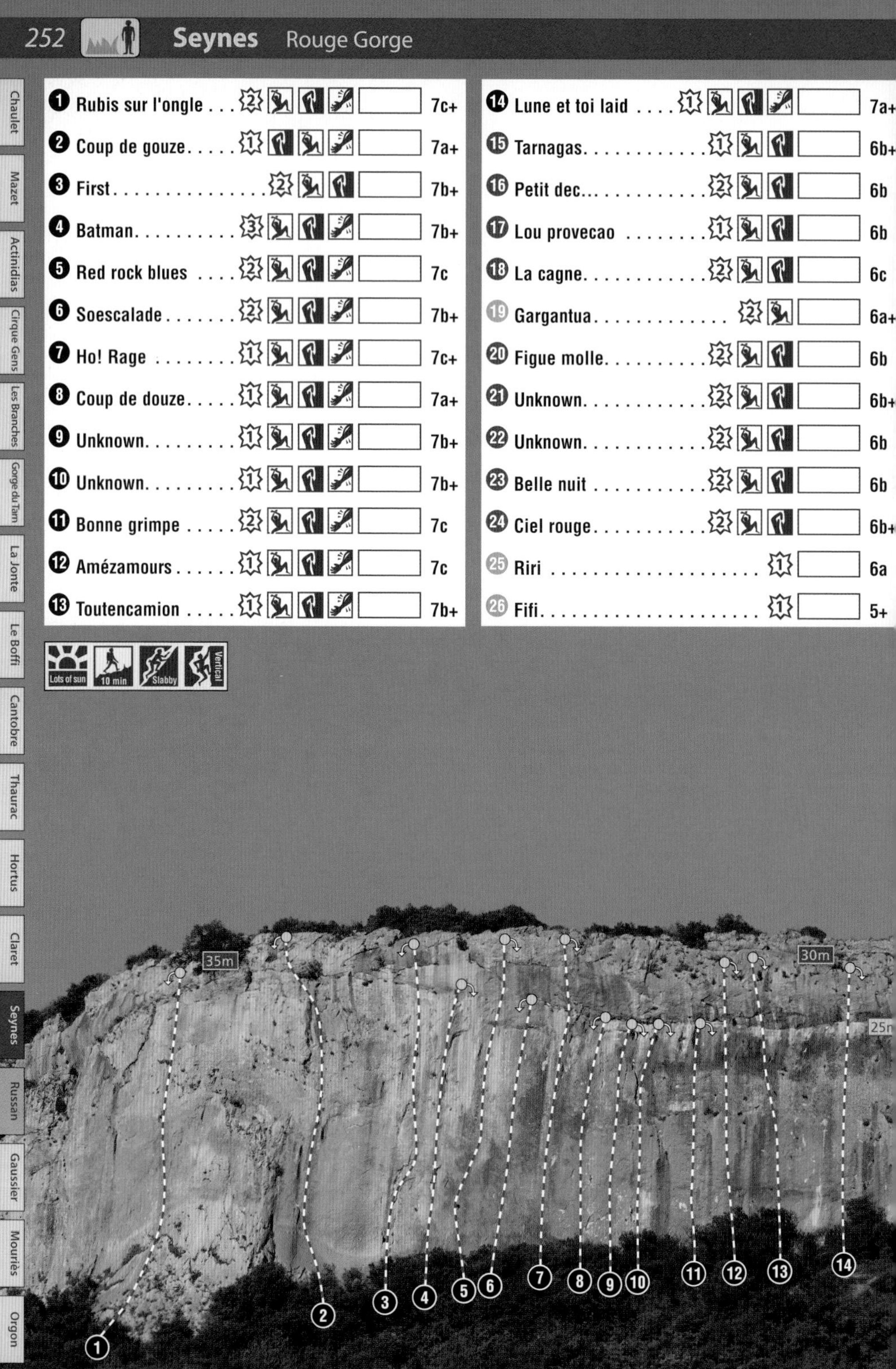

Chaulet · Mazet · Actinidias · Cirque Gens · Les Branches · Gorge du Tarn · La Jonte · Le Boffi · Cantobre · Thaurac · Hortus · Claret · Seynes · Russan · Gaussier · Mouriès · Orgon

Unknown climber on *Lukas* (6a) - *page 251*.

José

An excellent sector with a good number of quality routes on largely immaculate grey rock.
Approach - See page 248.

No.	Route	Stars	Grade
1	Maya	2	6a+
2	Ponch	1	5+
3	Christian sund	2	7a
4	Change rien	1	6b+
5	Sauze qui peut	1	6b+
6	La concubine de l'hémoglobine	1	6b+
7	Vénus	2	7a+
8	Ouais c'est ça	3	7a+
9	Zimbabwe	2	7b
10	Alensund sund	2	7a+
11	Engager vous qu'ils disaient	1	7b
12	Krakow	3	7a

Unknown climber on *Jardin passion* (6b) - *opposite*.

No.	Route	Grade
13	Tokyo Eyes	7a+
14	Mouriés le retour	7c
15	Smoke Addict	7a
16	Pornography	7a
17	Le retour du nettoyeur	6c+
18	La croix et la bannière	7a+
19	La pierrasse	6c+
20	Dégueulante	6c+
21	Unknown	?
22	Chaîne qui brille	6c+
23	Escartefigue	7b+
24	Cassiopé	7b+
25	Bence alors	7a+
26	Si! J'y étais	7b
27	La pureté	6c
28	Le point stop	6c
29	Guernika	6c+
30	Jardin passion *Photo opposite.*	6b
31	Raquette	7a
32	Quel pied!	6b+
33	Finesse	6b
34	José	6a+
35	Shut the Fuck Up	6c
36	In passe!	6b
37	Coulée	5+
38	La première à José	6a

Chaulet
Mazet
Actinidias
Cirque Gens
Les Branches
Gorge du Tarn
La Jonte
Le Boffi
Cantobre
Thaurac
Hortus
Claret
Seynes
Russan
Gaussier
Mouriès
Orgon

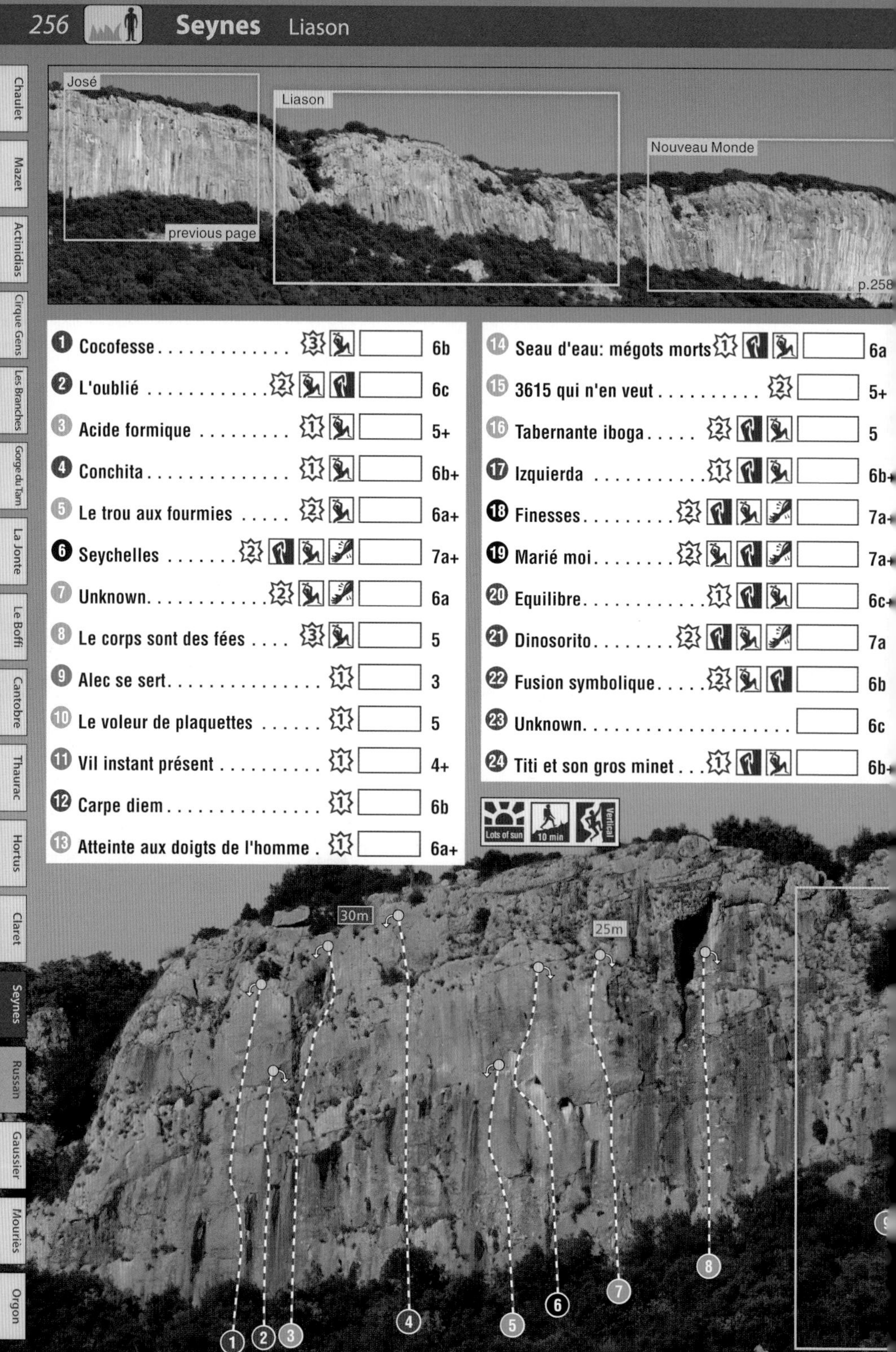

No.	Route	Stars	Grade
1	Cocofesse	3	6b
2	L'oublié	2	6c
3	Acide formique	1	5+
4	Conchita	1	6b+
5	Le trou aux fourmies	2	6a+
6	Seychelles	2	7a+
7	Unknown	2	6a
8	Le corps sont des fées	3	5
9	Alec se sert	1	3
10	Le voleur de plaquettes	1	5
11	Vil instant présent	1	4+
12	Carpe diem	1	6b
13	Atteinte aux doigts de l'homme	1	6a+
14	Seau d'eau: mégots morts	1	6a
15	3615 qui n'en veut	2	5+
16	Tabernante iboga	2	5
17	Izquierda	1	6b+
18	Finesses	2	7a+
19	Marié moi	2	7a+
20	Equilibre	1	6c+
21	Dinosorito	2	7a
22	Fusion symbolique	2	6b
23	Unknown		6c
24	Titi et son gros minet	1	6b+

Chaulet
Mazet
Actinidias
Cirque Gens
Les Branches
Gorge du Tarn
La Jonte
Le Boffi
Cantobre
Thaurac
Hortus
Claret
Seynes
Russan
Gaussier
Mouriès
Orgon

Liason

A varied sector that makes a good location for a group with mixed abilities or enthusiasm.

Approach - See page 248.

Nouveau Monde - Left

The jewel in Seynes' crown with an extensive range of routes of the highest quality, mostly in the higher grades, though with a scattering of very good routes in the 6s that are well-worth seeking out.
Approach - See page 248.

No.	Route	Stars	Grade
1	Homo seynien erectus	2	6a
2	Bingo crépuscule	2	6a+
3	Terre	2	6b+
4	Edune	2	6b
5	Blanche neige	1	7a
6	Congas	1	5+
7	Prends ta brosse!	1	6b+
8	Le zubial	2	7c
9	Cortijo l'extreme	1	8a

Unknown climber on the classic tufa *Le sphynx* (7c+) - *page 260.*

No.	Route	Stars	Grade
10	Trinity	1	7c+
11	Le missionaire du saint éthique	1	8a
12	Mamy de jardin	2	7b+
13	Derniere tentation	2	7c
14	Vipère	3	7b
15	La roche des amants	2	7b+
16	Le rastaquouere au brésil		?
17	La chute du rastaquouere	3	7b+
18	Au nom du pere	3	7a
19	La foire aux slips	2	7b+
20	Première	2	7c+
21	La blondasse	2	7c
22	Un doigt	3	7c

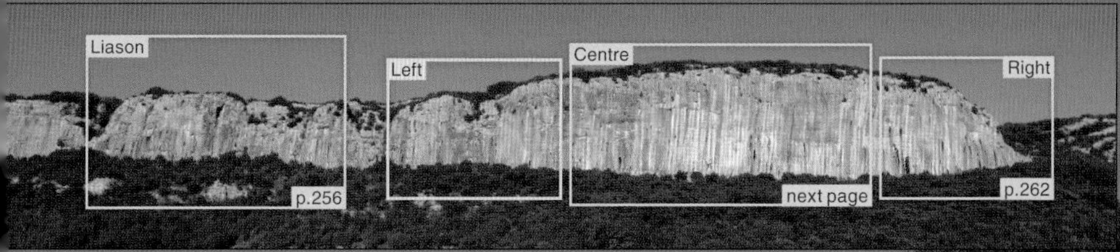

Liason p.256
Left
Centre next page
Right p.262

35m
30m
30m
22m

Chaulet Mazet Actinidias Cirque Gens Les Branches Gorge du Tarn La Jonte Le Boffi Cantobre Thaurac Hortus Claret Seynes Russan Gaussier Mouriès Orgon

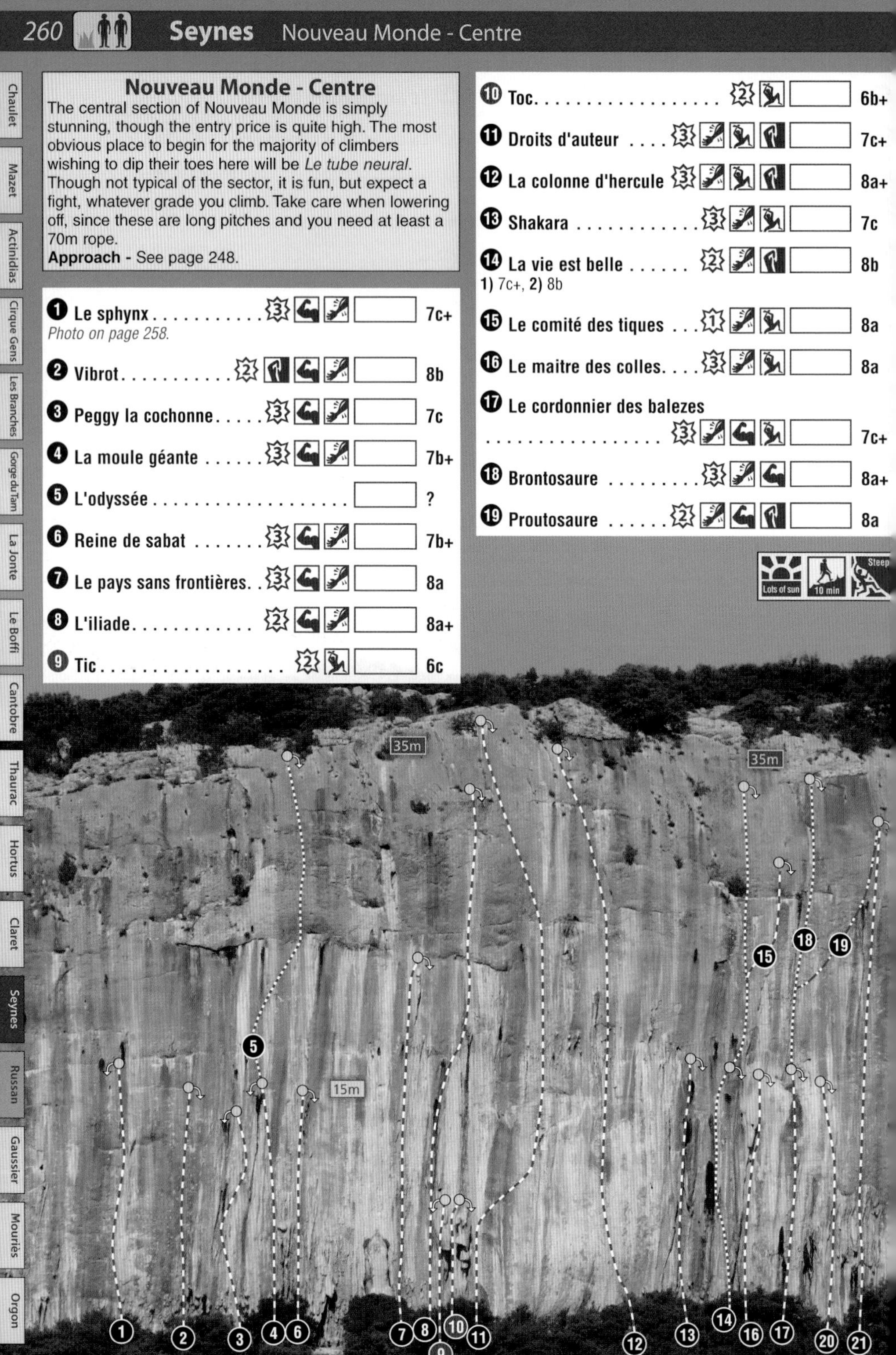

Nouveau Monde - Centre

The central section of Nouveau Monde is simply stunning, though the entry price is quite high. The most obvious place to begin for the majority of climbers wishing to dip their toes here will be *Le tube neural*. Though not typical of the sector, it is fun, but expect a fight, whatever grade you climb. Take care when lowering off, since these are long pitches and you need at least a 70m rope.

Approach - See page 248.

1. **Le sphynx** .... 3 stars — 7c+
   Photo on page 258.
2. **Vibrot** .... 2 stars — 8b
3. **Peggy la cochonne** ..... 3 stars — 7c
4. **La moule géante** ...... 3 stars — 7b+
5. **L'odyssée** .... ?
6. **Reine de sabat** .... 3 stars — 7b+
7. **Le pays sans frontières** .. 3 stars — 8a
8. **L'iliade** .... 2 stars — 8a+
9. **Tic** .... 2 stars — 6c
10. **Toc** .... 2 stars — 6b+
11. **Droits d'auteur** .... 3 stars — 7c+
12. **La colonne d'hercule** 3 stars — 8a+
13. **Shakara** .... 3 stars — 7c
14. **La vie est belle** ...... 2 stars — 8b
    1) 7c+, 2) 8b
15. **Le comité des tiques** ... 1 star — 8a
16. **Le maitre des colles** .... 3 stars — 8a
17. **Le cordonnier des balezes** .... 3 stars — 7c+
18. **Brontosaure** .... 3 stars — 8a+
19. **Proutosaure** ...... 2 stars — 8a

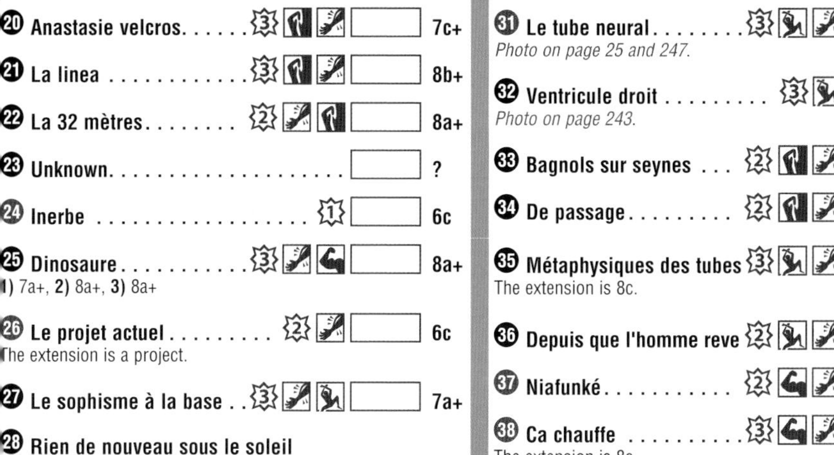

20 Anastasie velcros . . . . . 3 — 7c+

21 La linea . . . . 3 — 8b+

22 La 32 mètres . . . . 2 — 8a+

23 Unknown . . . . — ?

24 Inerbe . . . . 1 — 6c

25 Dinosaure . . . . 3 — 8a+
1) 7a+, **2)** 8a+, **3)** 8a+

26 Le projet actuel . . . . 2 — 6c
The extension is a project.

27 Le sophisme à la base . . 3 — 7a+

28 Rien de nouveau sous le soleil . . . . 2 — 8a+

29 La patience minérale . . . 2 — 7a+

30 C'est lisse hélas c'est là qu'est l'os . . . . 3 — 6c+

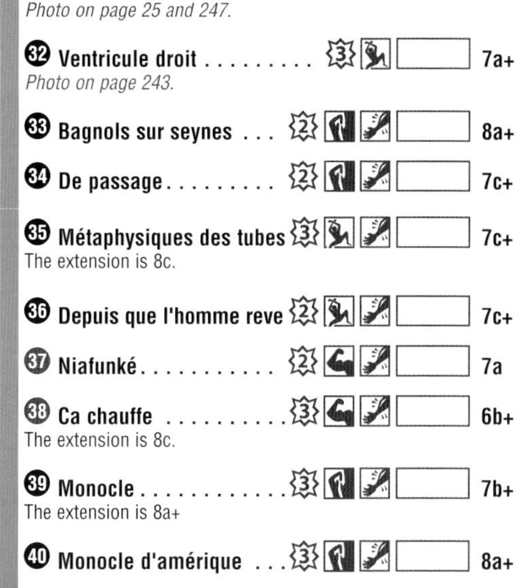

31 Le tube neural . . . . 3 — 6c+
Photo on page 25 and 247.

32 Ventricule droit . . . . 3 — 7a+
Photo on page 243.

33 Bagnols sur seynes . . . 2 — 8a+

34 De passage . . . . 2 — 7c+

35 Métaphysiques des tubes 3 — 7c+
The extension is 8c.

36 Depuis que l'homme reve 2 — 7c+

37 Niafunké . . . . 2 — 7a

38 Ca chauffe . . . . 3 — 6b+
The extension is 8c.

39 Monocle . . . . 3 — 7b+
The extension is 8a+

40 Monocle d'amérique . . . 3 — 8a+

41 Crateres de lune . . . . . 2 — 7c

No.	Route	Stars	Grade
1	Voyage	3	8a+
2	Nieman	2	8a
3	Rage de dents	2	8a+
4	Du rire à l'oubil	3	7b+
5	Grincheux et les deux naines		?
6	Maëva	2	8b
7	L'avant dinosaure	2	7c
8	Masculin féminin **1)** 7a+, **2)** 7b+	2	7b+
9	Jour de fête	3	7c
10	Çà va, çà vient	3	7b+
11	Mat de cocagne	3	7a
12	J'ai recontré des gens heureux	3	6b+
13	Le manége enchanté	2	6c+
14	Farandole	3	6c
15	Brigand d'amour	3	7a+
16	Symphonie de nouveau monde	3	7a
17	Fragment de vie	2	6a
18	Clownerie	1	6b
19	Queenstown	1	5
20	Sale temps les mouches pétent	1	5+
21	Timber	1	5+
22	Jardiniere	1	5+
23	Taisson	1	4
24	La doublure	1	4
25	Le petit grillé	1	4

Lots of sun · 12 min · Steep · Slabby

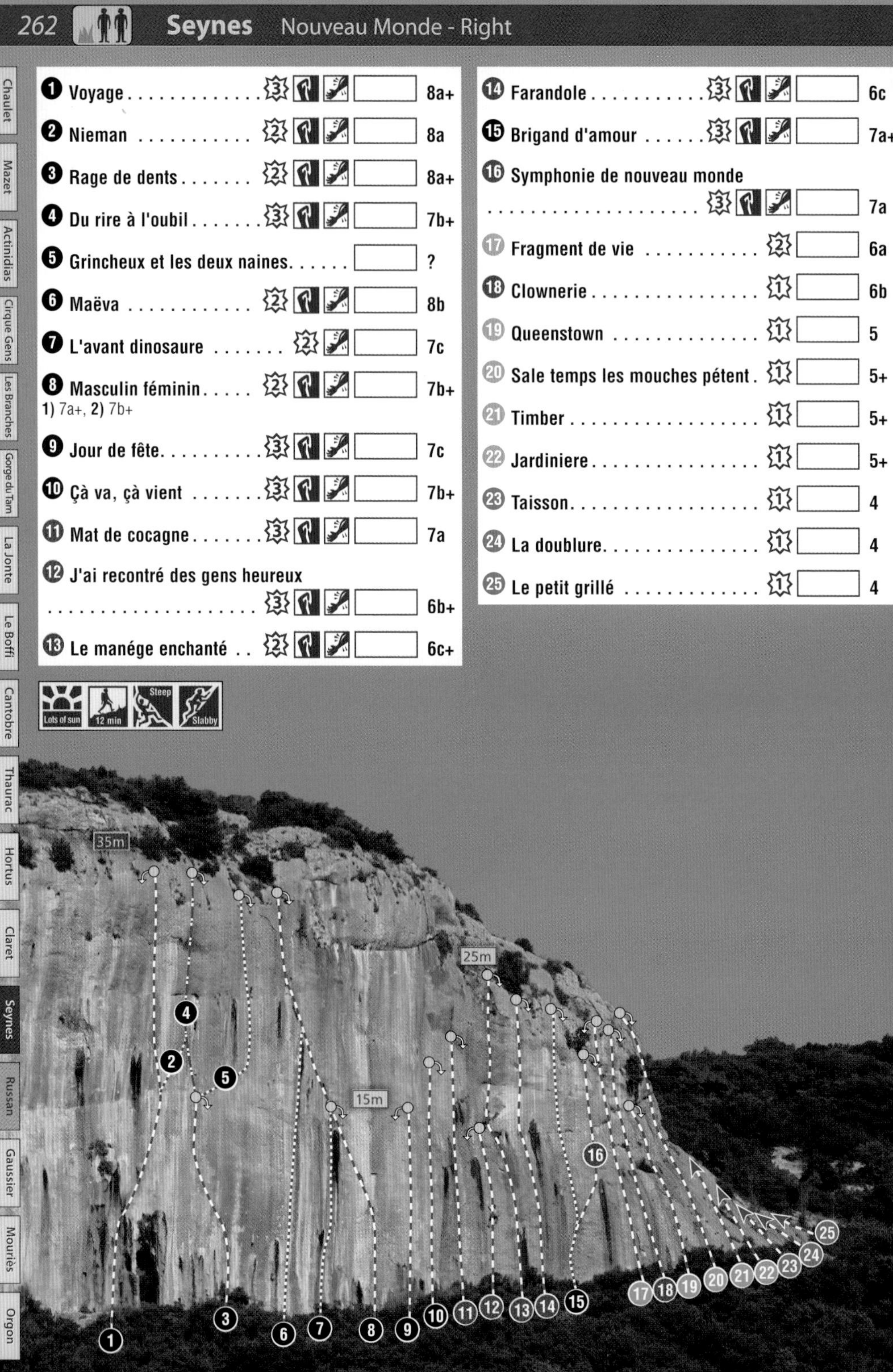

Chaulet · Mazet · Actinidias · Cirque Gens · Les Branches · Gorge du Tarn · La Jonte · Le Boffi · Cantobre · Thaurac · Hortus · Claret · Seynes · Russan · Gaussier · Mouriès · Orgon

No.	Route	Stars	Grade
26	Les agneaux		3+
27	Les jeunes loups		3+
28	Les vieux croûtons		3
29	Les cinq hops	2	4
30	5 ops	2	3+
31	Les cas dopés	2	5
32	Les K hops	2	3+
33	Les ramoneurs	2	4
34	Le rat moine	1	3+
35	Le raieur	1	4
36	Le rateua	1	4
37	Le ratal	1	5
38	Le rat pourri	1	5

Lots of sun · 10 min · Slabby

Initiation

A sector that very much lives up to its name, with plenty of low-angled, low-grade routes to go at.
Approach - See page 248.

No.	Route	Stars	Grade
39	Finalement	1	5+
40	L'encore	1	6a
41	Jeudi	2	4+
42	Surprise	1	4+
43	Les pieds	2	3
44	La pomme	2	3
45	L'iris	1	6a
46	Le cil	2	3
47	L'œil	2	4
48	Variante de l'œil	1	6a
49	Variante à droite	1	6a
50	Serge	1	6c

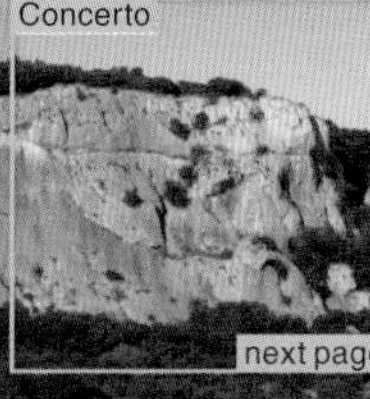

Concerto

Usually a quiet sector with a good range of grades, and some excellent rock.

Approach - See page 248.

No.	Route	Stars	Tick	Grade
1	Marie	2		5+
2	Bonsaï			6a
3	Madame folle dingue			5
4	Docteur cynoque			5+
5	Variante du docteur cynoque			6b
6	Phosphore	2		6b
7	A nous deux	2		6b
8	Vitamine	3		6b
9	Les amants de la déroute	2		6b
10	Symphonie fantastique	2		7a
11	Concerto n°3 en sol majeur	3		6a
12	Un sale dimanche	2		6b+
13	Un dimanche inachevé	2		6b+
14	Un dimanche à la campagne	2		6a+
15	Señoritas	2		6a
16	Promène couillon			6a

Photo on page 21.

Lots of sun
8 min
Slabby
Vertical

	Route		Grade
17	Boulevard unique		6a
18	Rue canot	2	6a
19	Hailey	1	7a
20	C'est à toi	1	7a
21	Day	1	6b+
22	Night	1	6c
23	Départ du fauteuil		6a+
24	Promène couillon II down		4+
25	Promène couillon	2	4+
26	Le fauteuil du roi	2	6a
27	Le fou du roi	2	6c
28	Caresse surplombante	2	7a+
29	Zeste d'amour	2	6b
30	Rêves d'enfants	2	5+

Jean Marc

Another usually quiet sector with a good range of routes taking technical lines up some excellent rock.
Approach - See page 248.

No.	Route	Stars	Style	Grade
1	Cherokee Lane	2		6b
2	L'essentiel *Photo this page.*	2		6a
3	Etroite surveillance	2	Slabby	7a
4	Couleur poupre	2	Slabby	7a
5	Le diable par la queue	1		6b+
6	Apocalypse Rock	2	Slabby	7a
7	Moi roger toi paul	1	Slabby, Vertical	7b
8	Crème renversée aux abricots	2	Slabby	7a
9	Break	2		6c
10	Le rouge et le noir	1		6a+
11	Verdon	3		6a+
12	Plaisir de gourmet	2		6a
13	Crécerelle	1		5
14	Tichodrome			4+

Piers Cuncliffe on *L'essentiel* (6a) - *this page.*

Lots of sun | 8 min | Slabby | Vertical

No.	Route	Stars	Grade
15	Le retour du mouleur	1	6a
16	Le retour des choses	2	6a
17	Tombé sous le charme	2	5+
18	Princesse	2	5+
19	Rencontre fortuite	1	5
20	Les sens en portables	1	5
21	Frisson émouvant	2	5
22	Aimes-moi encore au moins	1	6b
23	Les risques en tous genres	2	6c
24	Environnements professionnel	3	7b
25	Danse érotique	3	6b
26	Les risques inadaptés	3	5+
27	Entraide	1	6b+
28	Décision rapide	1	6b+
29	Jean Marc	2	6a
30	Découverte	2	5
31	Magic light	1	6a+
32	Durite express	1	6a+
33	Durite en rythme	1	6a+
34	Le bonheur retrouvé	1	5
35	L'ultime essai		4+

Lots of sun | 8 min | Slabby | Vertical

20m

Chaulet
Mazet
Actinidias
Cirque Gens
Les Branches
Gorge du Tarn
La Jonte
Le Boffi
Cantobre
Thaurac
Hortus
Claret
Seynes
Russan
Gaussier
Mouriès
Orgon

Top Secret

A friendly little sector with a handful of routes that all start off gently but often have a sting in the tail.

Approach - See page 248.

No.	Route	Stars	Grade
1	Allégresse	2	6a
2	Soupçon	2	6b+
3	Fragment d'universe	2	6b
4	Top rove	3	6a+
5	Top Secret	3	6b+
6	Pharmacie du bon dieu	3	6a+
7	Aphrodisiaque *Photo opposite.*	3	6a+
8	Ici sous le soleil	2	6a+
9	Expert s'abstenir	2	6a+
10	Jalousie	2	6a
11	Inutile d'insister	2	6a
12	Un point c'est tout	2	5+
13	L'entente féminine	1	5
14	Ici gît le dur	1	6a
15	Gigi autonome	1	6a
16	Gigi l'âme rose	1	6a
17	Gigi sans ginette	1	5+
18	Pourquoi pas	1	5

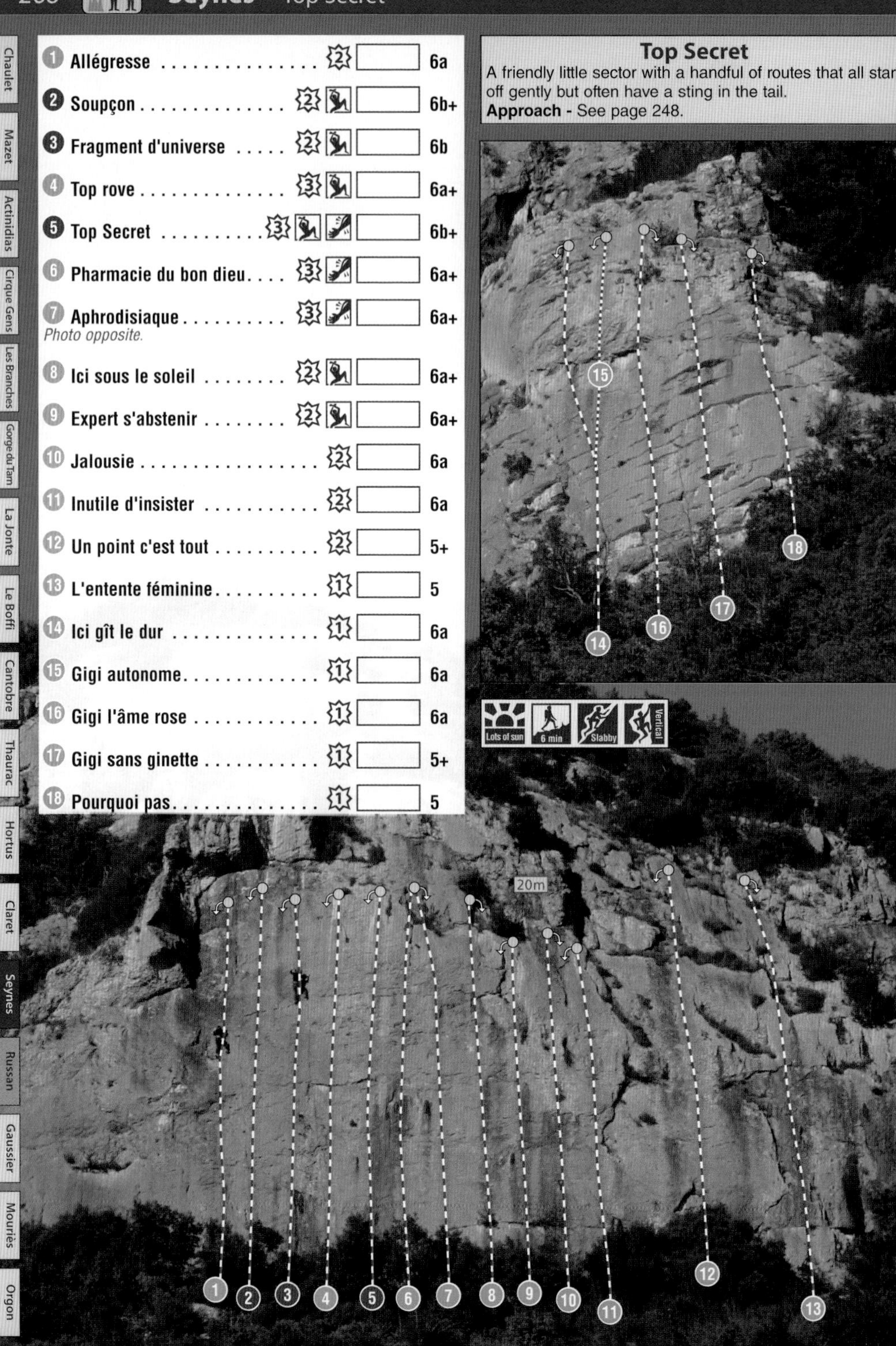

Andy Morris avoiding the wet patches on *Aphrodisiaque* (6a+) - *opposite*.

Rolling Stones
p.274
La Belle Époque
p.276
Sole
Septieme Sceau
p.278
Tenere
p.278
Baisé Volé
p.280

Russan

Lucifer
Piece en Trois Actes
Moi Vouloir Toit
p.281
p.282
p.284
p.285

Russan

	No star	1 star	2 star	3 star
Up to 4+	-	3	-	-
5 to 6a+	6	27	29	8
6b to 7a	4	27	36	11
7a+ and up	10	23	24	28

An extensive area of crags, offering everything from technical grey slabs through to spectacular, overhanging tufas. Like Seynes, Russan is a great winter-sun destination. Although, unlike Seynes, there is a lot more to go at in the 5s and low 6s.

Approach Also see map on page 242

The approach to Russan is not obvious, as you cannot see the crag until you're right on top of it. There is a large roundabout at the centre of the village of Russan, exit this roundabout along Avenue des Sept (passing a bar on your left). Follow Avenue des Sept for 200m, turning right at a colourful selection of signs onto Rue de Castellas. Follow Rue de Castellas up the hill for 500m until you reach a public information sign on the right, and a sign to Las Castellas, which you are going to follow. If you wish to park away from the crag (which does have a bad record for break-ins), it's probably best to park here and continue on foot. Turn left opposite the public information sign onto Chemin Dit des Cabines and continue for another 500m (the road turns to gravel after 100m) until you reach a large parking area on the left. If you park here, you are strongly advised to leave no valuables in your car, leave it so it's clearly not got any valuables in it, and you may even wish to leave it unlocked.
From the parking area, pass around the prominent gate and follow the track for 700m until you reach a fork.

For the right-hand side (looking in) of the crag, take the left fork, and follow the track for a short way past a sign to another fork, take this second fork on the right and continue until a small track leads off to the right (a sizeable tree is on the left). Follow this trail down to the right-hand side of the crag.

For the left-hand side of the crag (looking in), take the right fork and continue for another 600m until you reach a chain across the track. Pass the chain and take a path off to the left after just 30m - or walk a bit further and get a great view of where you're going to be climbing - and follow the track down along the base of the crags.

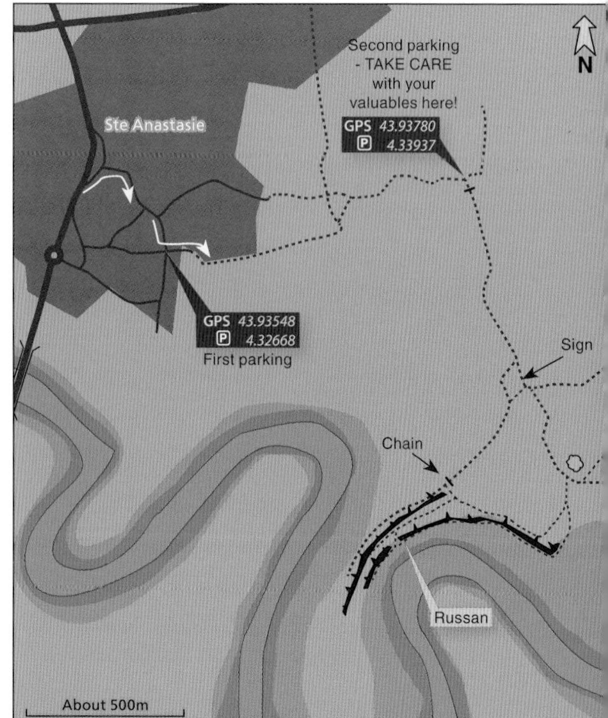

Conditions

Russan is a real sun-trap, shaped like a reflector oven it can offer climbing in T-shirts in the middle of winter when the puddles at the top of the crag are frozen solid - it is a good idea to be prepared for each end of the temperature spectrum if you're visiting in the winter. Though mostly south-facing, the wings at either end offer a little shade at the start and end of the day. If it is warm however, you would be better off climbing elsewhere. The great majority of routes dry very quickly - though the tufas will be dripping for sometime after prolonged rain.

Jonathan Ayrton on *Tamponnoir brisé* (6b) - *page 281*.

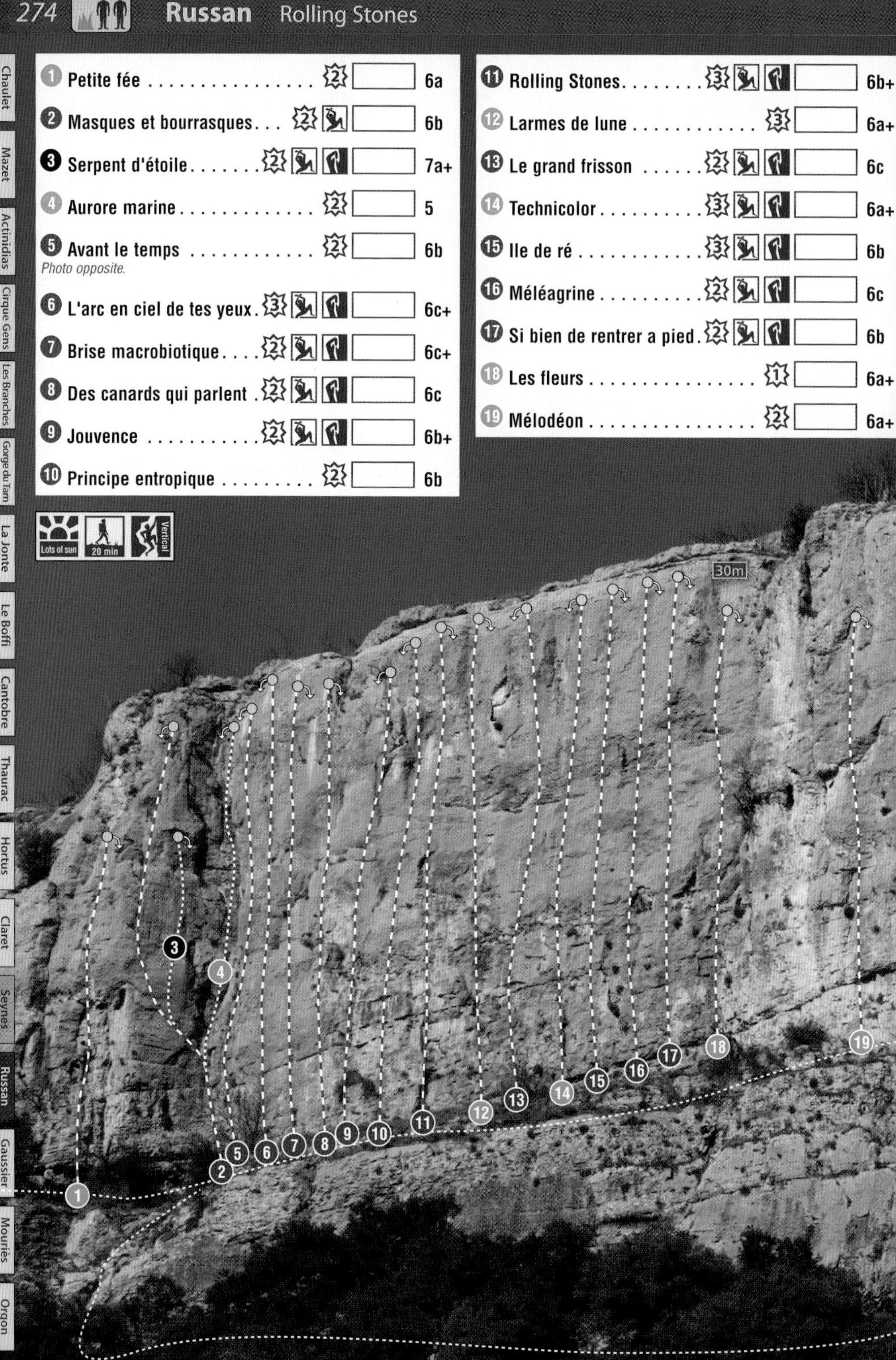

1 Petite fée 2 6a
2 Masques et bourrasques 2 6b
3 Serpent d'étoile 2 7a+
4 Aurore marine 2 5
5 Avant le temps 2 6b
Photo opposite.
6 L'arc en ciel de tes yeux 3 6c+
7 Brise macrobiotique 2 6c+
8 Des canards qui parlent 2 6c
9 Jouvence 2 6b+
10 Principe entropique 2 6b
11 Rolling Stones 3 6b+
12 Larmes de lune 3 6a+
13 Le grand frisson 2 6c
14 Technicolor 3 6a+
15 Ile de ré 3 6b
16 Méléagrine 2 6c
17 Si bien de rentrer a pied 2 6b
18 Les fleurs 1 6a+
19 Mélodéon 2 6a+
Lots of sun
20 min
Vertical
30m

Rolling Stones

An excellent crag with a fine collection of routes mostly in the low 6s, though expect to have to work hard even on the lowest grades here.

No.	Route	Stars		Grade
20	Téléologie	3		5+
21	Nid d'aigle	1		6a+
22	Nooshere	1		6b+
23	Sur la piste de laetoli	2		6b+
24	Mur de poussiere	3		6c+

Adrian Berry on *Avant le temps* (6b) - *opposite* - Photo: Piers Cunliffe

La Belle Époque

A collection of excellent, long pitches, frequently with technical fingery starts that get the crux out of the way and allow you to relax and enjoy the journey to the top.

No.	Route	Stars	Grade
1	Un parfum d'iris	1	5+
2	Les jardins de Babylone	1	5
3	Peau de peche	1	5+
4	Aux sources du bonheur	1	4
5	Avenurine	1	6b
6	Histoires sans fin 1	1	6b
7	Histoires sans fin 2	1	6a
8	Demeure des dieux	1	6b
9	Efflorescence	1	6a+
10	Aegagropile		6a
11	Le sourire du Sphinx	1	6c
12	Oú sont-ils doc	1	7a
13	Rousseline		5+
14	La belle Époque	2	6a
15	De jaspe et d'opale	2	6b
16	Améline mélodie	2	6b+
17	Danse avec les clous	2	6b+
18	Anglypique	2	6c
19	Les racines du ciel	2	6b

Photo opposite. (18 Anglypique)

Lots of sun · 20 min · Vertical

25m

35m

20 **Par-del l'azur des reves** . . . 3 stars — 6a+

21 **Mallefougasse** . . . . 3 stars — 6a+
Can be split at 5+, 6a+

Routes 22 - 25 are reached by climbing Epitome and walking along the ledge.

22 **Vague a lame** . . . . 2 stars — 5

23 **Le grande diedre** . . . . 2 stars — 5+

24 **L'épitre aux clés** . . . . 2 stars — 5+

25 **Ramon** . . . . 2 stars — 6a

26 **Epitome** . . . . 2 stars — 6a

27 **Musique céleste** . . . . . 2 stars — 6a+

28 **Les cavaliers de l'orange** 2 stars — 6a

29 **Nouvelle cosmogonie** . . 2 stars — 6b

30 **La couleur du plaisir** . . 2 stars — 6b+

31 **Alicantropie** . . . . 2 stars — 6a+

32 **Paradis oubliés** . . . . . . 2 stars — 6c+

33 **Avalanche** . . . . 2 stars — 6a+

34 **Dans le sillage de Poséidon** . . . . 2 stars — 6b

35 **Eternal** . . . . 6a+

Unknown climber on *Anglypique* (6c) - *opposite* - Photo: Piers Cunliffe

Chaulet
Mazet
Actinidias
Cirque Gens
Les Branches
Gorge du Tarn
La Jonte
Le Boffi
Cantobre
Thaurac
Hortus
Claret
Seynes
Russan
Gaussier
Mouriès
Orgon

Septieme Sceau and Tenere

Short, pleasant routes on good rock. Approach as for La Belle Epoque, then follow the path on the left between these two sectors. Turn right for Septieme Sceau and left for Tenere.

No.	Route	Stars	Grade
1	Promeneur de minuit	1	7a+
2	La metamorphose de marcisse	1	6b
3	Crepuscule lunaire		6a
4	Layrinthe	1	5
5	Transparence vers le futur	2	6a+
6	Grand large	1	6a+
7	Epitaphe	2	6a+
8	Bactriane	2	6a+
9	Le septieme sceau	2	6c
10	Un autre monde	1	6a
11	Digitaline	1	6a
12	Le principe et la fin	1	6a+
13	Elegie funebre	1	6b

Lots of sun | 24 min | Vertical

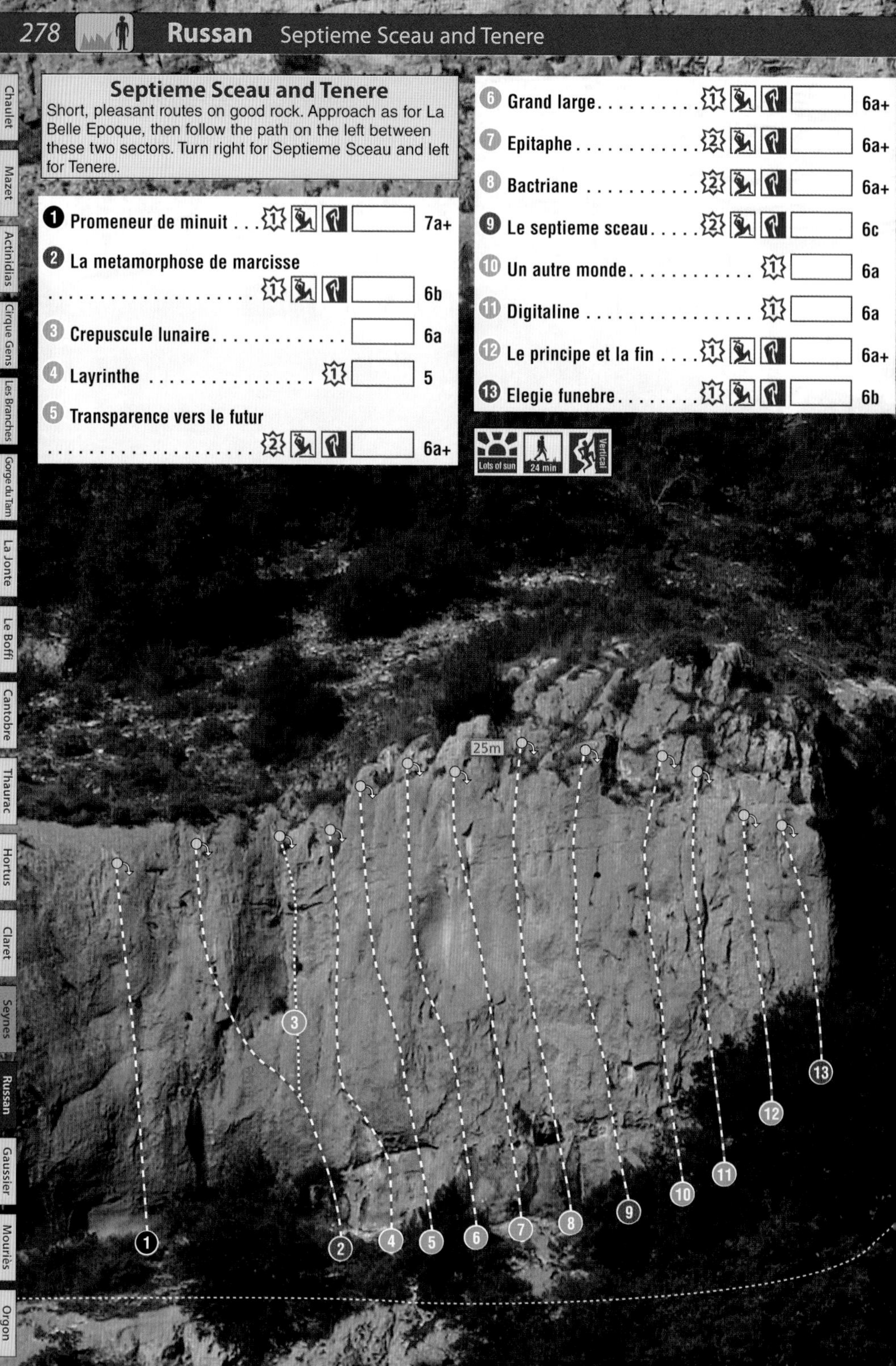

	Route		Grade
14	Alizari		6b
15	Tenere	2	6c
16	Infinitude	1	7a
17	Florilege	2	6b+
18	Barkhane	1	7b
19	Murmure du désert	1	6a+
20	Le penule de foucault	1	6b
21	Antinéa	1	6a+
22	Calme	1	4
23	Rose de sable	1	6a

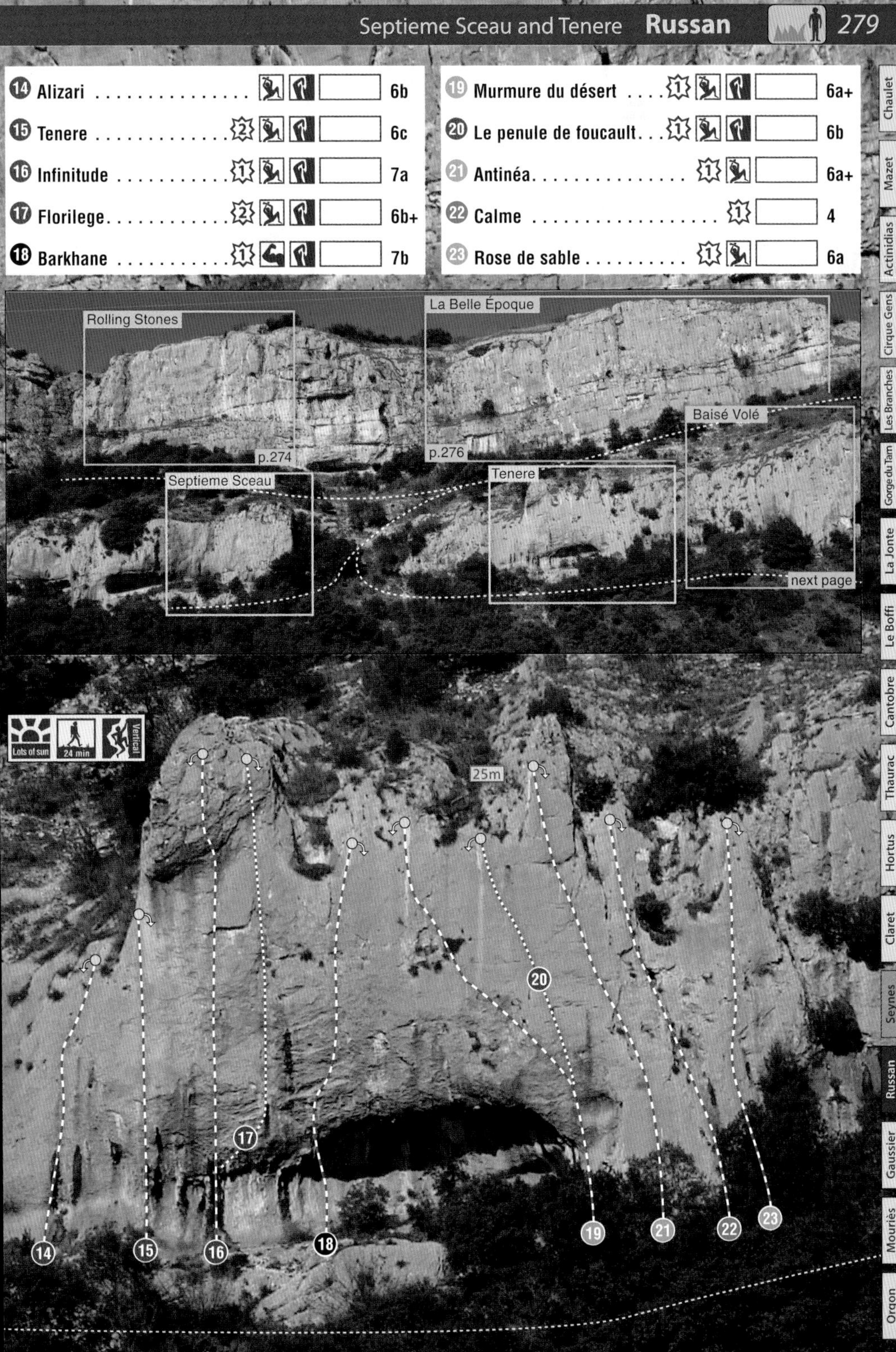

Baisé Volé

A superb expanse of grey walls, offering a fine collection of largely technical and fingery routes. There are a number of good lines following natural weaknesses, but the majority of routes take uncompromising lines up blank-looking walls. On a hot day expect to suffer.

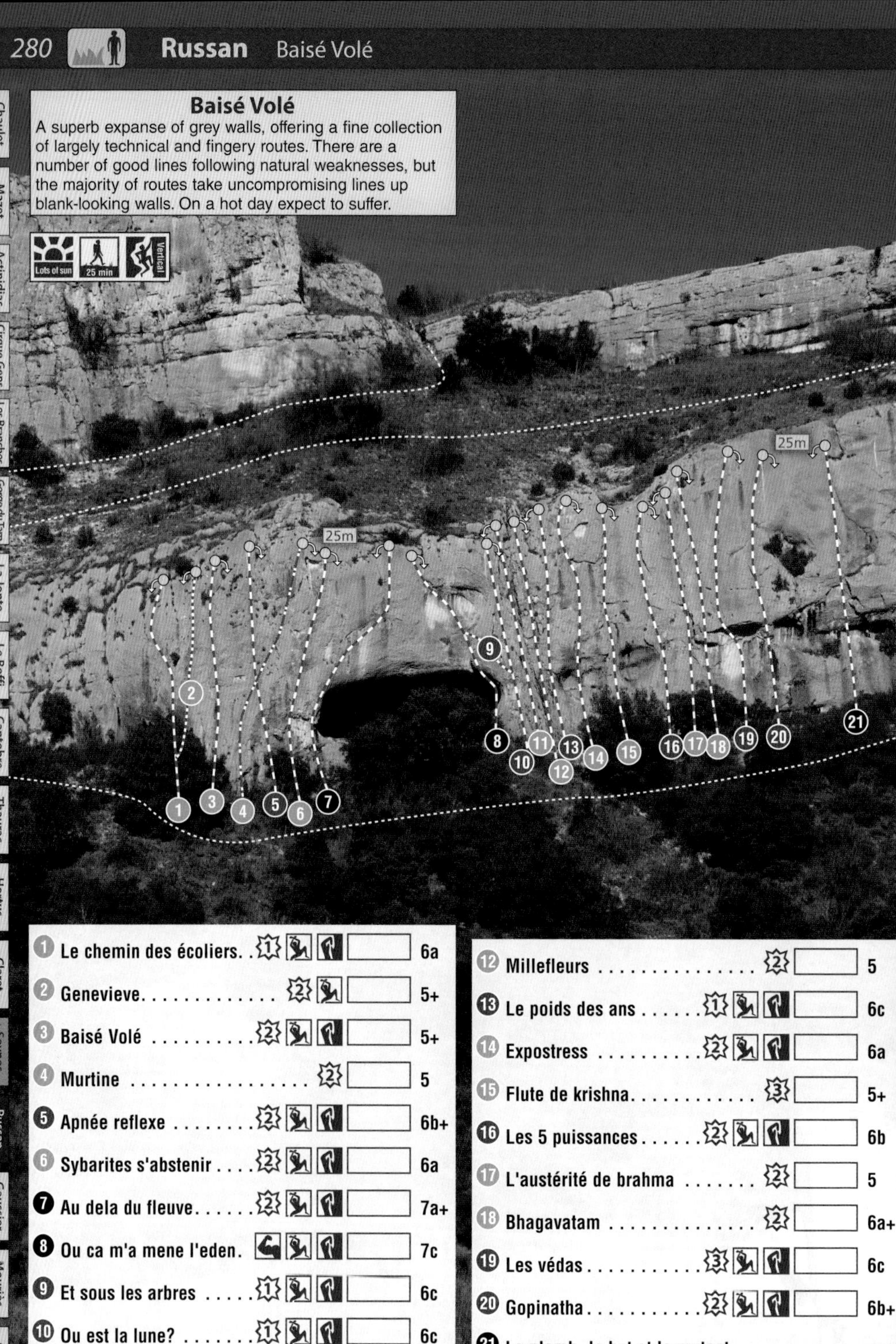

No.	Route	Stars	Grade
1	Le chemin des écoliers	1	6a
2	Genevieve	2	5+
3	Baisé Volé	2	5+
4	Murtine	2	5
5	Apnée reflexe	2	6b+
6	Sybarites s'abstenir	2	6a
7	Au dela du fleuve	2	7a+
8	Ou ca m'a mene l'eden		7c
9	Et sous les arbres	1	6c
10	Ou est la lune?	1	6c
11	14 juillet 1986	2	5
12	Millefleurs	2	5
13	Le poids des ans	1	6c
14	Expostress	2	6a
15	Flute de krishna	3	5+
16	Les 5 puissances	2	6b
17	L'austérité de brahma	2	5
18	Bhagavatam	2	6a+
19	Les védas	3	6c
20	Gopinatha	2	6b+
21	Le plomb, le but et le mutant	3	7a+

Soleil Noir

More excellent routes - the routes around *Celine* are particularly worth seeking out - not too physical, but all very technical. Approach either from the left by walking around, or from the right by abseiling into the big cave (see page 283).

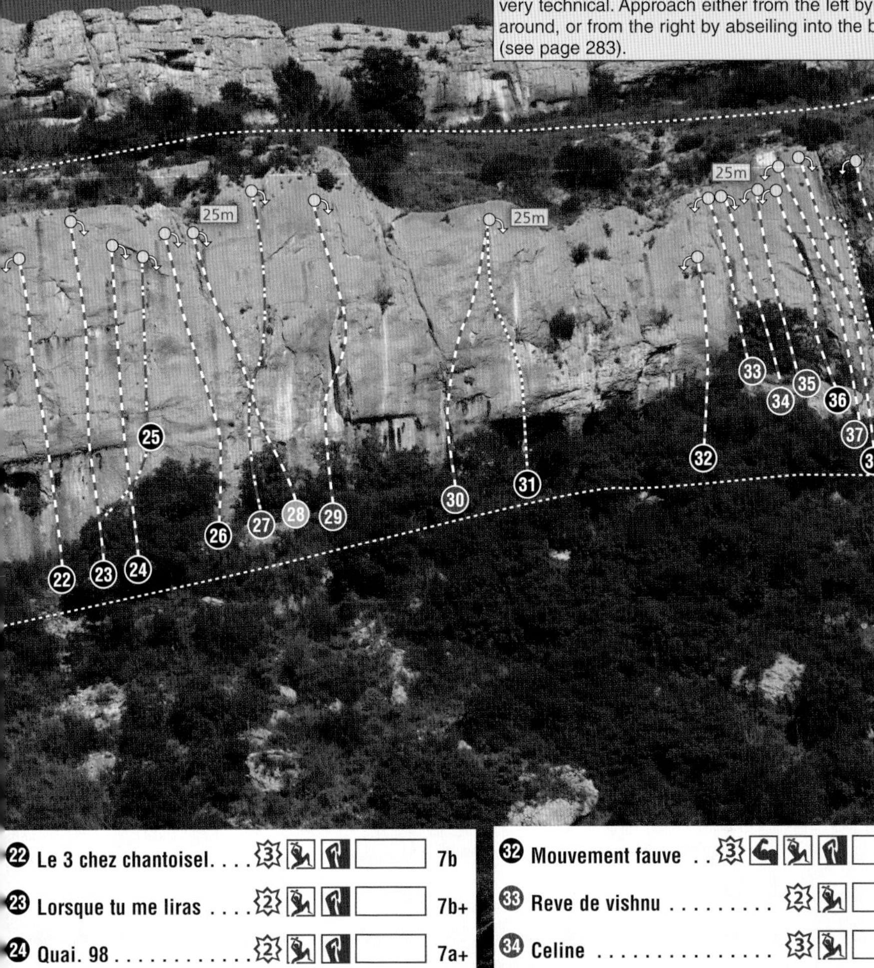

No.	Route	Grade
22	Le 3 chez chantoisel	7b
23	Lorsque tu me liras	7b+
24	Quai. 98	7a+
25	C'est a prendre ou a laisser!	7b
26	Le souvenir, le savoir et l'oubli	7b
27	Saveur du soir	6c+
28	Pulsion d'1 jour	6a
29	Salade de style	6c
30	Soleil noir	7a
31	Canticum sacrum	8b
32	Mouvement fauve	7c+
33	Reve de vishnu	6c
34	Celine	6c
35	Ars longa vita brevis	7a
36	Jalouisies	7a+
37	Oh papé, c'est ugolin!	6c+
38	Laetitia (gauche)	7a+
39	Laetitia (droite)	6a
40	Tamponnoir brisé	6a+
41	Courrier d'autriche	6b+
42	Lumiere du vitrail	7b

Photo on page 18 and 273. (route 40)

Piece en Trois Actes

A very varied sector with the whole grade range covered, through the best routes are all in the higher grades.

No.	Route	Stars	Grade
1	Mauvais gout	2	7c+
2	Danse de siva	1	7b+
3	Mulholland drive	2	8a+
4	Les belles idées de chico mendes	3	7b+
5	Taratata	2	7a
6	Le X	2	6b+
7	Deux temps, trois mouvements	1	6b+
8	Avant leurre	1	5
9	Signé relax	1	5+
10	Double Dose	1	6b+
11	La confrérie du souffle		8a+
12	Serie noire	1	5
13	Zig zag	1	5
14	Bas les pattes	1	5
15	Patou	1	4
16	Urgostyle	1	6a
17	Le temps est assassin	1	7b
18	Longue attente	1	7b
19	Primate égardé	2	6a+
20	Reeves de l'espace	2	7c
21	Hypérion	2	7c+
22	Endymion	2	8a+
23	Check Point Charlie	3	8a+

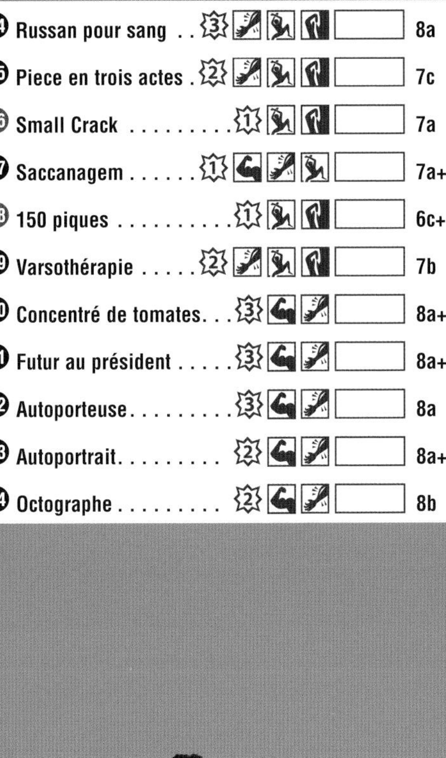

	Route	Stars	Grade
24	Russan pour sang	3	8a
25	Piece en trois actes	2	7c
26	Small Crack	1	7a
27	Saccanagem	1	7a+
28	150 piques	1	6c+
29	Varsothérapie	2	7b
30	Concentré de tomates	3	8a+
31	Futur au président	3	8a+
32	Autoporteuse	3	8a
33	Autoportrait	2	8a+
34	Octographe	2	8b

Chaulet
Mazet
Actinidias
Cirque Gens
Les Branches
Gorge du Tarn
La Jonte
Le Boffi
Cantobre
Thaurac
Hortus
Claret
Seynes
Russan
Gaussier
Mouriès
Orgon

Chaulet
Mazet
Actinidias
Cirque Gens
Les Branches
Gorge du Tarn
La Jonte
Le Boffi
Cantobre
Thaurac
Hortus
Claret
Seynes
Russan
Gaussier
Mouriès
Orgon

Moi Vouloir Toit

An incredible piece of rock that has some neck-straining routes. It also serves well as a quick approach to the neighbouring sectors, via a 30m abseil through the hole.

1 Roubignolles . . . . 3 stars **8b**
Exit through the large hole that is also used to abseil in.

2 Vers la lumiere . . . . 2 stars **6c**
Exit through the small hole - abseil approach (at this grade).

3 Quand tu fumes du shit. . . . . **8a+**

4 Connexion automne-hiver 3 stars **8a+**

5 Moi vouloir toit . . . . 3 stars **8a**

35m

35m

Lots of sun
25 min
Steep

A

Lucifer

Right of the cave, the rock quickly returns to a more amenable angle, and offers up a number of fine, technical routes on fine grey rock.

No.	Route	Stars	Grade
6	Turnoi d'échecs	3	8c
7	Plus x	3	8b+
8	Project		?
9	Gros sexe non désiré	3	8a
10	Les dix mouvements	3	8b
11	Une nympho a vérifier		7c+
12	Rien que pour toi	2	6c
13	Les yeux de Lucifer	2	6a
14	Eclipse	1	6a+
15	Le temps d'un sourire	1	6a+
16	Grain de folie	1	6a+
17	Ergonome	1	6a+
18	Micromicon	1	6b
19	Tagazou	1	6b
20	Temps imaginaire	1	6c
21	Lycaon	1	7a+

Lots of sun | 22 min | Steep | Vertical | Slabby

Maelstrom

A superb collection of classically proportioned hard sport climbs on steep, tufa-covered rock. For many of the focussed, trained, and talented, Russan pretty much starts and ends here.

No.	Route	Stars	Grade
1	Nénni	2	5
2	Orphée	1	6b
3	Régime sensuel	1	7a+
4	Retraite anticiée	1	6b+
5	Encore une fois	1	6c
6	Calgon	2	7a+
7	Arrampicatopitheque	1	6b
8	Karkul	1	6c
9	Samarcande	1	7a+
10	Prudence	1	7b
11	Casamance	3	7b+
12	Tabasco	3	7c
13	Tire-jus	2	7c+
14	Loco motivée		7a+
15	Footoof		6c
16	Quart de siecle	3	8a
17	Macumba	3	7c
18	Maelstrom	3	8a
19	Tractopelle	3	7c+
20	Pink Panther	3	8a+
21	Eau de colonne	3	8a+
22	Pipeline	3	8a
23	Scoliose	2	8a

From mid morning | 20 min | Steep

20m
20m
Bivvi cave - complete with chimney

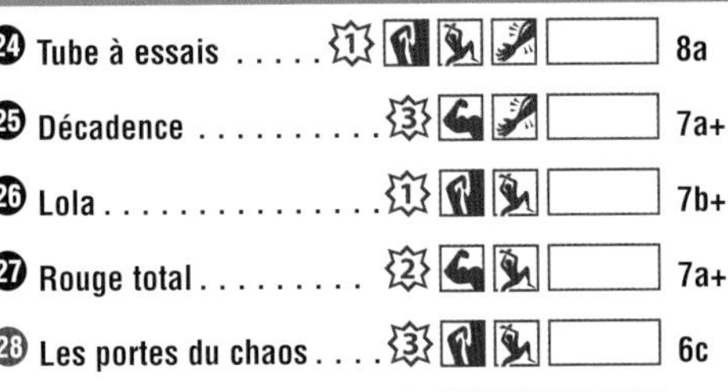

No.	Route	Stars	Grade
24	Tube à essais	1	8a
25	Décadence	3	7a+
26	Lola	1	7b+
27	Rouge total	2	7a+
28	Les portes du chaos	3	6c
29	La forge du diable	2	6c+
30	Attention fragile	1	7a+
31	Zénith	3	6c+

No.	Route	Stars	Grade
32	Prisonnier de l'inutile		7c
33	Oú l'horizon prend fin		7b+
34	Russan avant J-C	2	7c+
35	La ruse du nain ailé	1	8b
36	Unknown		?
37	Incertain voyage		6c+
38	Au seuil de l'univers	2	6a
39	Le cancer infernal de la fuite		8a

Chaulet
Mazet
Actinidias
Cirque Gens
Les Branches
Gorge du Tarn
La Jonte
Le Boffi
Cantobre
Thaurac
Hortus
Claret
Seynes
Russan
Gaussier
Mouriès
Orgon

Babylone

When approaching the crag from the right-hand side, this is the first sector you approach. Mostly short and bouldery, the quality of the climbs does improve a little further on.

No.	Route	Stars	Grade
1	Le blues de camille	2	6b+
2	Acceptez ma légende	1	6c+
3	Les tournesols	2	6c+
4	L'orifice prodigue	2	7c+
5	Babylone	2	8a
6	Vice de pute	1	7c
7	Kitch Lorraine	1	7c+

8 SDF 1 7c
9 Tintin et l'oreille recollée 1 7c+
10 Commedia dell' arquée 2 8a
11 Imboglio 1 7c
12 Haïku 1 8a
13 Petit déjeuner 1 7b
14 Mascarade 1 7b+
15 Tox frot 1 7a
16 Tox frot droite 6b
17 Amuse-gueule 5+
18 Casse-croûte 5+
20m
20m
Chaulet
Mazet
Actinidias
Cirque Gens
Les Branches
Gorge du Tarn
La Jonte
Le Boffi
Cantobre
Thaurac
Hortus
Claret
Seynes
Russan
Gaussier
Mouriès
Orgon

Chaulet
Mazet
Actinidias
Cirque Gens
Les Branches
Gorge du Tarn
La Jonte
Le Boffi
Cantobre
Thaurac
Hortus
Claret
Seynes
Russan
Gaussier
Mouriès
Orgon

Guidebook

Escalade Les Alpilles is a comprehensive guidebook detailing climbing at seven areas within the region, and if you want to explore beyond Mont Gaussier, Mouries and Orgon, you will need to get a copy.

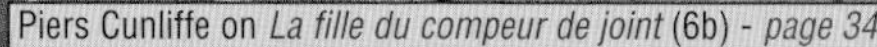
Piers Cunliffe on *La fille du compeur de joint* (6b) - *page 344*.

Half an hour south of Avignon is the Massif des Alpilles. There are a number of climbing area to be found here, all of which are documented in the local guidebook 'Escalade Les Alpilles'. The crags typically consist of ridges of limestone that form clean vertical walls. Being quite close to large population centres, it's no surprise that the crags here have had a lot of traffic over the years - so expect some polish here and there. The area Fontvielle is located in this area, details are not included as there is no access rights to this crag, so it should be avoided.

Access - Fire Risk

The Parc Naturel Régional des Alpilles which contains Orgon, Mouriès and Mont Gaussier has restricted access at times when there is a risk of fire, typically during the summer. There are three degrees of risk: orange (open access), red (open from 6am to 11am only), and black (closed). To find out the current situation check **www.parc-alpilles.fr**. This gives the current access situation for Orgon, Mouriès and Mont Gaussier (Saint Rémy de Provence). Alternatively, if you have not got internet access, you can call 0811 20 13 13. Lighting fires is obviously not permitted at any time of year.

Getting There

All of the areas featured here are easily accessible from the A7 autoroute, the TGV runs direct to Avignon, and a local train service will take you straight to Orgon where you can walk from the station to the campsite, and from the campsite to the Orgon crags. The nearest major airports are Montpelier to the south-west, and Marseilles to the south-east.

Where to Stay

While there are a number of campsites throughout the area, the 'La Vallée Heureuse' campsite at Orgon (**www.camping-lavalleeheureuse.com**) is probably the best place to base yourself if you're looking to sample all three crags. From Orgon, it's only thirty minutes to Mouriès, and twenty minutes to Mont Gaussier, and if you climb at Orgon you won't need to drive at all.

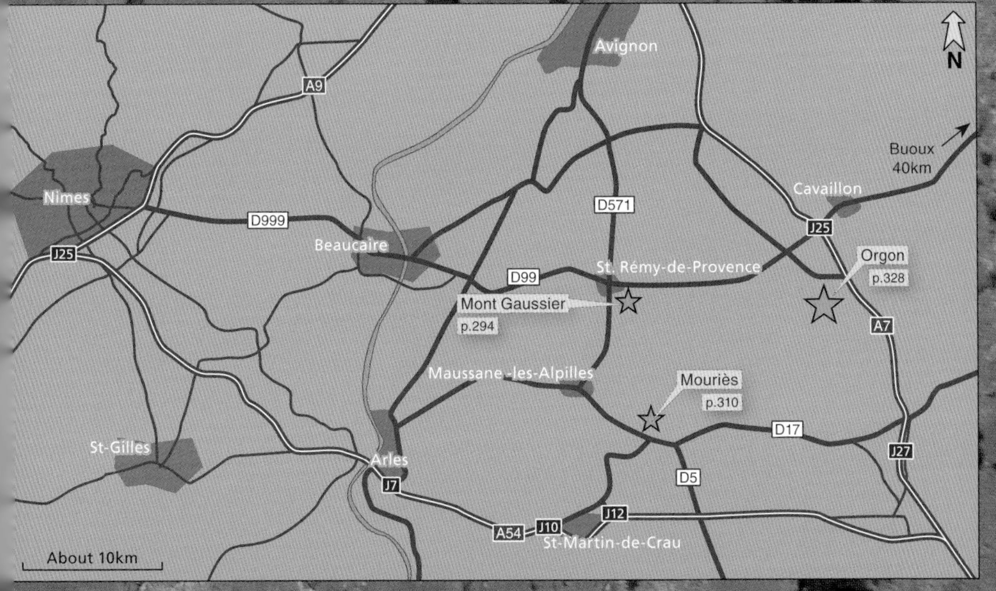

L'Épicerie p.301
Le Trou Souffleur p.302
Le Lit du Monde p.303

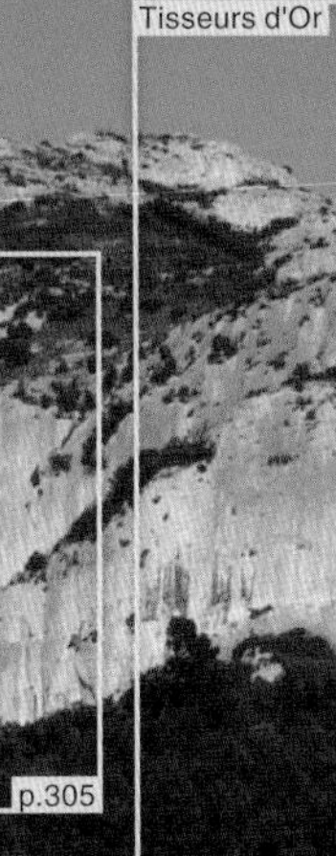

Mont Gaussier

	No star	1	2	3
Up to 4+	-	-	-	-
5 to 6a+	11	11	4	3
6b to 7a	10	15	20	4
7a+ and up	7	6	17	12

Audrey Seguy on *Appel de la forêt* (6c) - *page 305.*

A terrific venue in a superb setting, and definitely worth a day or more of your time. From the steep and powerful routes at Les Abeilles to the super-long mid-grade endurance classics at Tisseurs d'Or, most needs are catered for here. The only short-coming is the lack of good routes in the 5s and below.

Approach Also see map on page 291

Mont Gaussier is just off the D5 - south of the town of Saint Rémy. From the direction of Saint Rémy, head south on the D5 for 2.5km when you reach the first parking area on the left - this is the best place to park for everything from Secteur Route to Le Trou Souffleur. Continuing for a few hundred metres up the road reveals another parking area on the left - this leads to a steep scree-trail to the right hand end of Tisseurs d'Or, and is convenient for all the sectors between Le Lit du Monde and Tisseurs d'Or. A path links all the sectors.

Conditions

The walls generally face west, so get here in the morning if you're searching for shade. Some face south and are winter sun-traps. The more exposed sectors catch the wind.

Secteur Route and Cluckers

A couple of roadside sectors that offer grades not found in great supply at the other sectors of Mont Gaussier.

Approach - For Route, use the first parking, then walk back down the road past the crag and approach from the left. Cluckers is clearly visible from the roadside parking.

No.	Route	Stars	Grade
1	Un olivier argenté		5
2	La vuelta		5
3	La flamenca	1	5
4	Sévillanes	1	5
5	Jim Beam	1	5
6	Enamorado		5
7	Liv or leave	1	6a
8	Au bord de la route	1	6a
9	Tu bloc ou pas?	2	6c+
10	Au pays des oies sauvages	2	6b+
11	Version impimable	2	6a+
12	Ooh bordel route	2	6c+
13	Hi-pote		6a

Alexander Arrizabalaga on *L'enneige* (6a+) - *opposite*.

No.	Route	Grade
14	Les deux potes	5+
15	Madame Denis	5+
16	Coup de calgon	6a
17	L'enneige *Photo opposite.*	6a+
18	Gömböc	6b+
19	Chassé par les requins	6c
20	La guerre des vautors	7b
21	A quand la prochaine?	6a+
22	Gommage de chèvre	7a+
23	Les dents de l'amer	6b
24	Ready for Clucking?	6b+
25	Superpolygone	6b
26	L'investiture	6b
27	L'oral et hardi	5+

Alternoon Roadside Vertical

Sam Harvie testing the bolts on *Topomania* (7a) - *opposite*.

Lots of sun | 4 min | Steep

Les Abeilles

A super sector and bags of fun for those looking for steep power climbing, mostly with the clips in, and you can't complain about the grade progression either: 6a+ > 6b > 6c > 7a > 7b > 7b+ > 7c > 7c+ > 8a > 8a+. Start with the 6a+ and see how far you get ...

Approach - Use the first parking area and following the path. Take a left after just 20m and continue to the crag.

No.	Route	Stars	Grade
1	**Café Gourmand**		6a+
2	**Powerslide**	1	7b+
3	**Topomania** *Photo opposite.*	1	7a
4	**Trou des abeilles**	2	7b
5	**Maxi grip** *Photo on next page.*	3	7b+
6	**L'exploit de jules**	3	8a+
7	**Rattlesnake**	3	8a
8	**L'effet placebo**	2	7c+
9	**Salut le Frankenjura**	2	7c
10	**Le secret de polichinelle**	2	6c
11	**Alix en Provençe**	2	7a
12	**Congé de paternité**	2	6b

Laurent Moseley on the compelling *Maxi grip* (7b+) - *previous page.*

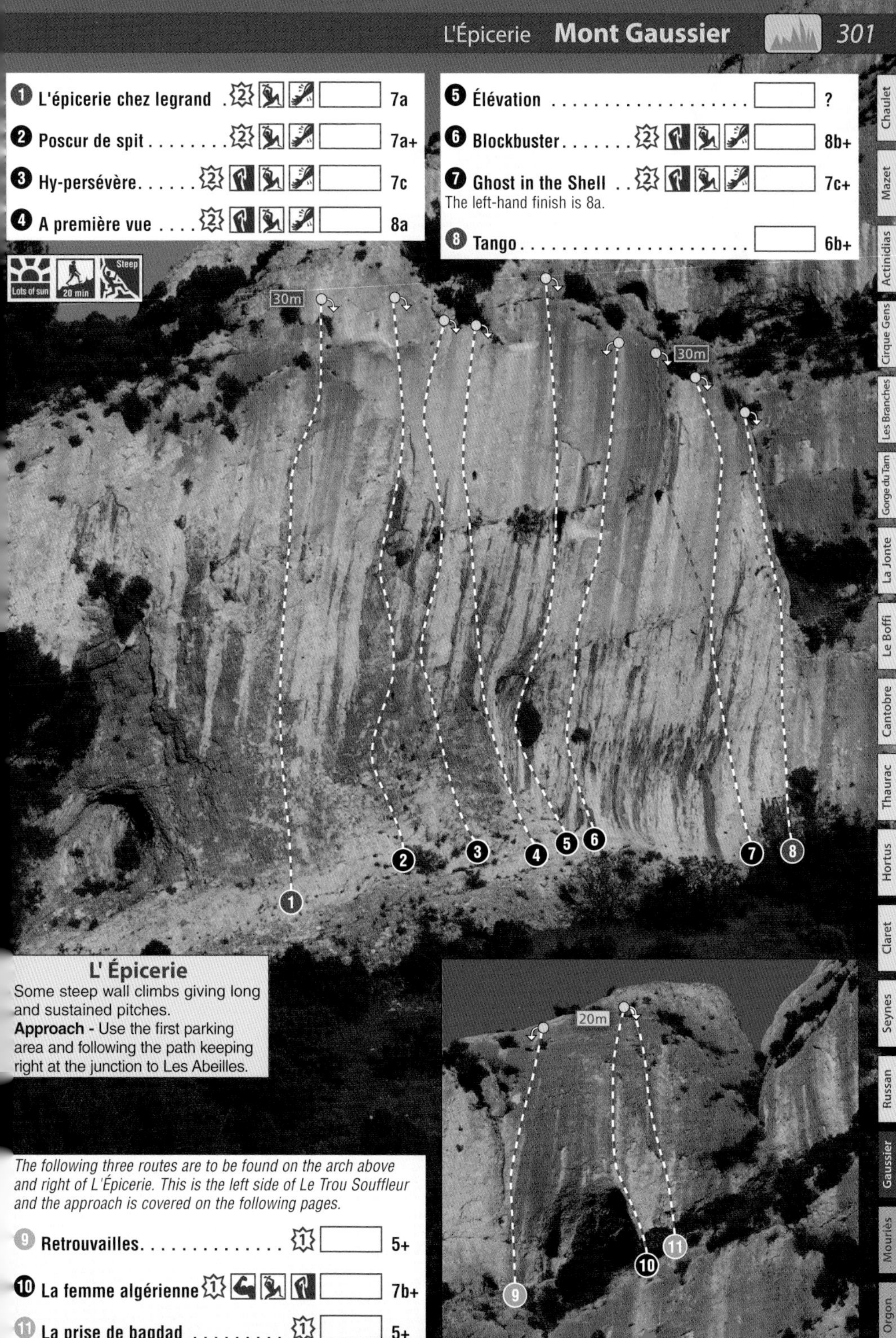

1 **L'épicerie chez legrand** . . . 2 . . . 7a

2 **Poscur de spit** . . . . 2 . . . 7a+

3 **Hy-persévère** . . . . . . 2 . . . 7c

4 **A première vue** . . . . 2 . . . 8a

5 **Élévation** . . . . ?

6 **Blockbuster** . . . . 2 . . . 8b+

7 **Ghost in the Shell** . . 2 . . . 7c+
The left-hand finish is 8a.

8 **Tango** . . . . 6b+

L' Épicerie

Some steep wall climbs giving long and sustained pitches.
Approach - Use the first parking area and following the path keeping right at the junction to Les Abeilles.

The following three routes are to be found on the arch above and right of L'Épicerie. This is the left side of Le Trou Souffleur and the approach is covered on the following pages.

9 **Retrouvailles** . . . . 1 . . . 5+

10 **La femme algérienne** 1 . . . 7b+

11 **La prise de bagdad** . . . . 1 . . . 5+

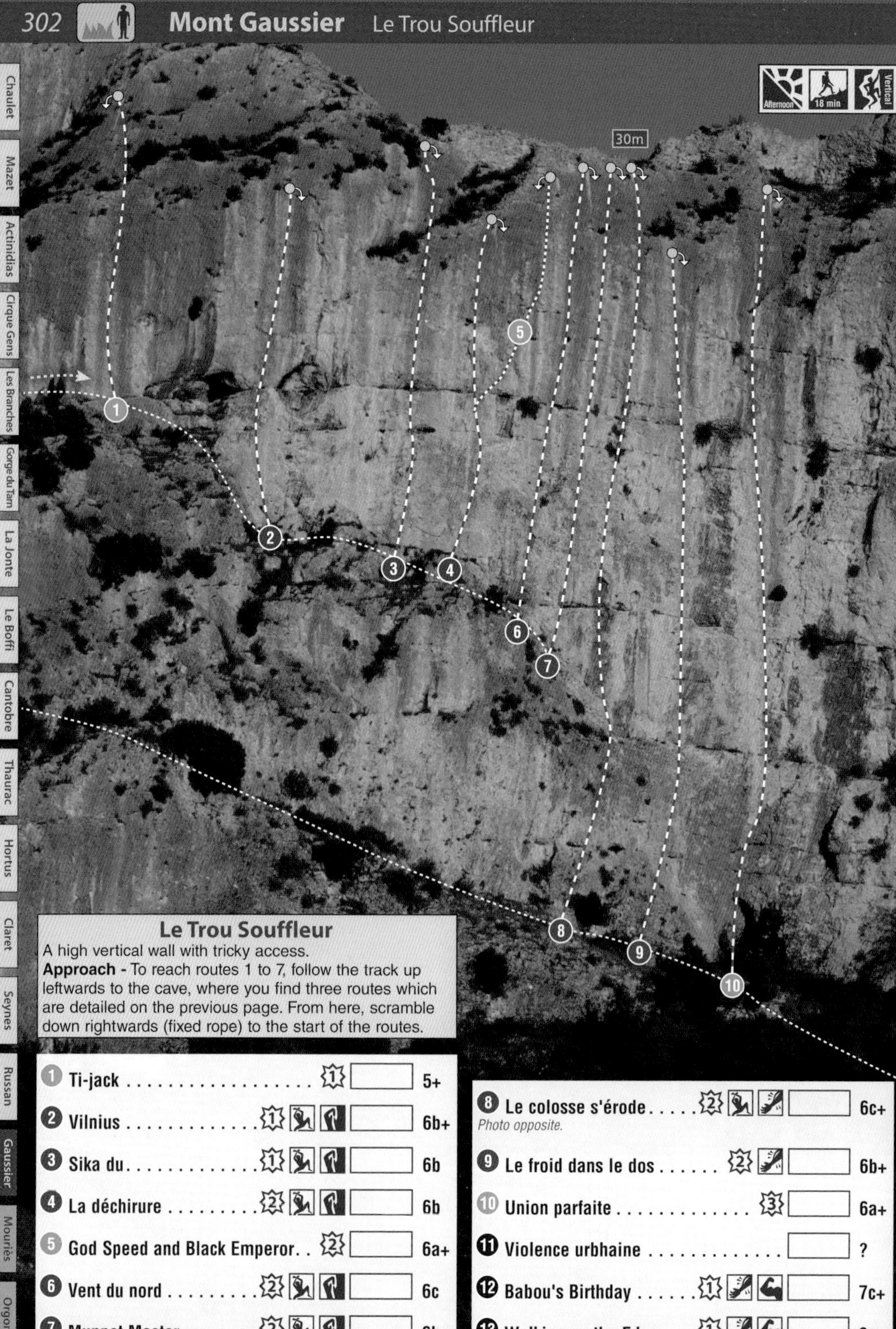

Le Trou Souffleur

A high vertical wall with tricky access.

Approach - To reach routes 1 to 7, follow the track up leftwards to the cave, where you find three routes which are detailed on the previous page. From here, scramble down rightwards (fixed rope) to the start of the routes.

No.	Route	Stars	Grade
1	Ti-jack	1	5+
2	Vilnius	1	6b+
3	Sika du	1	6b
4	La déchirure	2	6b
5	God Speed and Black Emperor	2	6a+
6	Vent du nord	2	6c
7	Muppet Master	2	6b+
8	Le colosse s'érode *Photo opposite.*	2	6c+
9	Le froid dans le dos	2	6b+
10	Union parfaite	3	6a+
11	Violence urbhaine		?
12	Babou's Birthday	1	7c+
13	Walking on the Edge	1	8a

Laurent Moseley on *Le colosse s'érode* (6c+) - *opposite.*

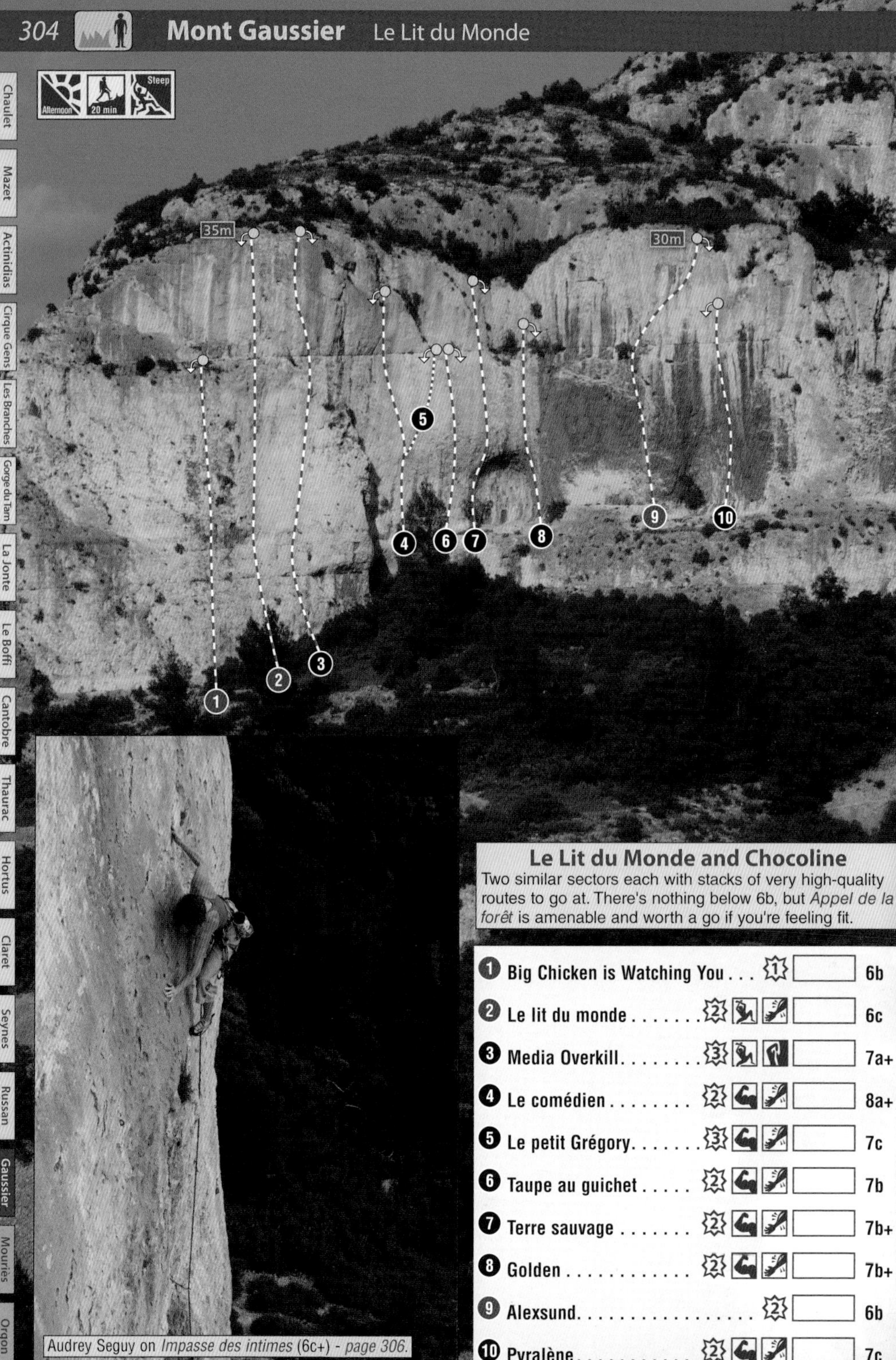

Audrey Seguy on *Impasse des intimes* (6c+) - *page 306.*

Le Lit du Monde and Chocoline

Two similar sectors each with stacks of very high-quality routes to go at. There's nothing below 6b, but *Appel de la forêt* is amenable and worth a go if you're feeling fit.

No.	Route	Stars	Grade
1	Big Chicken is Watching You	1	6b
2	Le lit du monde	2	6c
3	Media Overkill	3	7a+
4	Le comédien	2	8a+
5	Le petit Grégory	3	7c
6	Taupe au guichet	2	7b
7	Terre sauvage	2	7b+
8	Golden	2	7b+
9	Alexsund	2	6b
10	Pyralène	2	7c

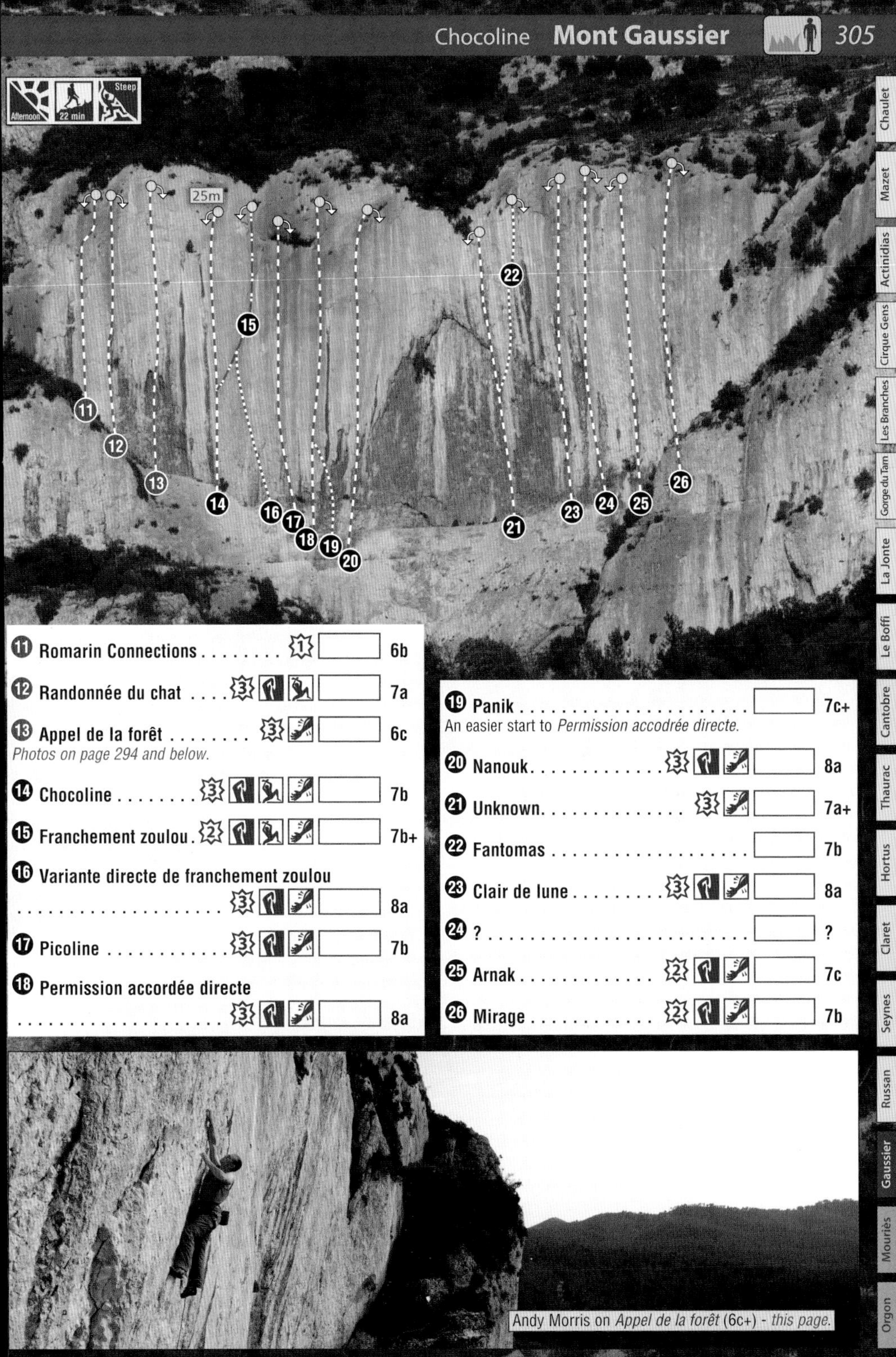

11 Romarin Connections . . . . {1} 6b

12 Randonnée du chat . . . . {3} 7a

13 Appel de la forêt . . . . {3} 6c

Photos on page 294 and below.

14 Chocoline . . . . {3} 7b

15 Franchement zoulou . {2} 7b+

16 Variante directe de franchement zoulou . . . . {3} 8a

17 Picoline . . . . {3} 7b

18 Permission accordée directe . . . . {3} 8a

19 Panik . . . . 7c+

An easier start to *Permission accordée directe.*

20 Nanouk . . . . {3} 8a

21 Unknown . . . . {3} 7a+

22 Fantomas 7b

23 Clair de lune . . . . {3} 8a

24 ? . . . . ?

25 Arnak . . . . {2} 7c

26 Mirage . . . . {2} 7b

Andy Morris on *Appel de la forêt* (6c+) - *this page.*

Tisseurs d'Or

Certainly the main attraction at Mont Gaussier, with lots to go at, and with a wider range of grades than most of the other sectors here. An 80m rope is a good idea, but not essential.

No.	Route	Stars	Grade
1	Le blues de l'ornitho	1	6c
2	Faut pas rêver	1	6b
3	La grand muraille	1	6a+
4	Permanence hebdomadaire	1	6a+
5	Fluide glacial	1	6b+
6	Une rose en hiver	1	6b+
7	La frime	1	6c
8	Tes trente ans	1	6b+
9	Marionette	2	6b
10	Les tisseurs d'or	3	6a+
11	Planète	1	6c+
12	Bien manzé kreol	1	6b+
13	Ça pétille	1	6b+
14	Impasse des intimes	3	6c+
15	Aux quatre vents	3	6b

Route 14: Photo on page 304.

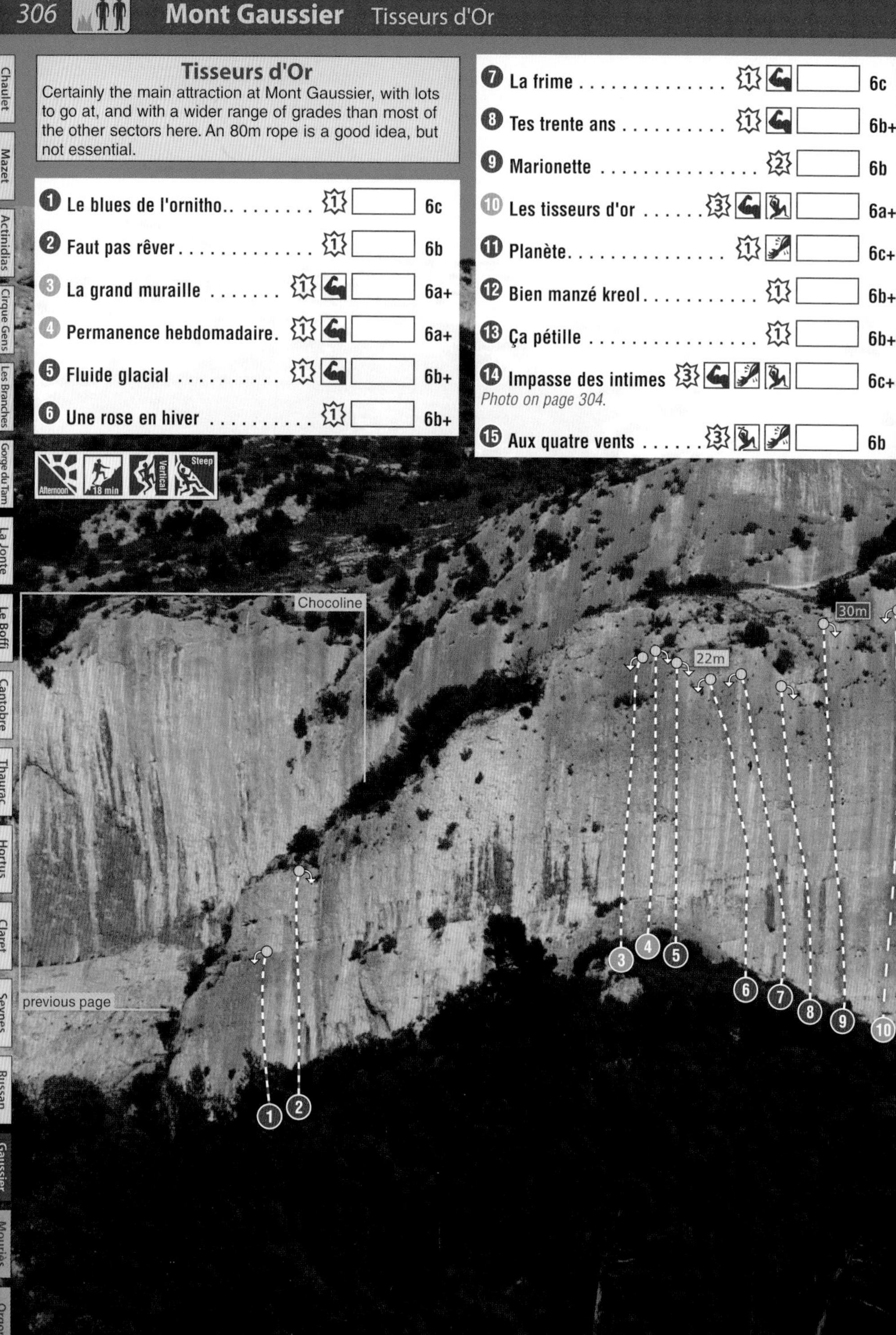

	Route		Grade
16	Cœur de pigeon		6b
17	Les échos		6b
18	Mon gosier en pente..		6a+
19	Viva la vie		6b
20	Lève toi et marche	3	6a+
21	Habitation à loyer élevé		6b
22	Biotope à grimpeur	2	7a+
23	Appel à toutes les stations		7a
24	Ils sont fous ces romains		6c
25	Roules dans la pousssières.		7a
26	Les gladiateurs	2	6c
27	L'amie dalle		6a+
28	Bleu, blanc, vert		6b
29	L'éperon des alpilles	2	6a

Prairie p.312

Mouriès

Mouriès

	No star	1 star	2 star	3 star
Up to 4+	5	-	-	-
5 to 6a+	15	18	3	-
6b to 7a	15	7	18	6
7a+ and up	6	10	15	2

A short, but interesting crag consisting of a kilometre-long fin of rock, with one face pointing north and the other south. The north side is by far the better, and the south face is not covered here. The climbing is mostly technical wall-climbing, with pitches around the 20m length. The crag is very family-friendly, in particular, the Prairie sector at the east end of the crag has a wide, open grassy-meadow at its base - ideal for a relaxed family-day. Many of the easier routes are now quite polished, so expect to have a slippery time on some. The nearest campsite is the Camping Municipal des Romarins in Maussane-les-Alpiles. There are many more further north in Saint-Rémy de Provence.

Approach Also see map on page 291

From the centre of the town of Mouriès (where the Tourist Information office is situated), head north along Cours Paul Revoil - it soon becomes Avenue des Alpilles. Turn left onto Route de Servanes and follow this out of town, passing a turning on the right to the golf course. Soon, the road turns sharp left then sharp right, and in 150m a track leads off to the right to a small car-park. Park here (or on the main road if the car park is full) and follow the track along the base of the north side of the crag to reach the climbing. The first few walls are short, polished, and not included - it gets a lot better further along.

Conditions

Being north-facing, this is a good place to come to escape the sun, and logically, is not somewhere you'd naturally head if it's cold. Consisting of a fin of rock, the routes have no rock above them to cause seepage, and so could be worth a look if it has been raining and other places are seeping. The south side of the fin is not of a similar quality to the north side and it is covered in the local guide.

Piers Cunliffe on *Du brut pour les brutes* (6c) - *next page.*

Prairie

The far end of the crag opens out into a pasture. This is a popular spot for families, though unfortunately the routes are generally quite hard, and the easier ones will probably be in high demand on a warm weekend.

1. **Invitation au voyage** . . . . 1 star — 5+
2. **Quinsi, viens ici** . . . . 1 star — 5
3. **Pilier des mines direct** . . . . 1 star — 6b
4. **Souffle doucer** . . . . 2 stars — 6c
5. **Du rififi sur les alpilles** . . . . 1 star — 6a+
   Requires the odd pull on bolts at this grade.
6. **Vol du nuit** . . . . 2 stars — 7a
7. **L'oreille en coin** . . . . . . 2 stars — 7a
8. **Le pion** . . . . 2 stars — 7a
9. **Brouillard de violence** . . . . 2 stars — 6b
10. **Le mandarin orgueilleux** . . . 1 star — 6b
11. **Vol de jour** . . . . 2 stars — 7a
12. **La saison des amours** . . 2 stars — 7b
13. **Du brut pour les brutes** . . . . 3 stars — 6c
    Photo on previous page.
14. **Du glucose pour noémie** . 2 stars — 7b
15. **Un doux câlin** . . . . 2 stars — 7b
16. **Zoom avant** . . . . 1 star — 7a

Not much sun | 20 min | Vertical

Prairie
20m
10
11
12
13
14
15
16

Not much sun | 19 min | Vertical | Slabby

	Route		Grade
1	Bonjour le soleil	☐	6a
2	Erreur médiatique	☐	6b
3	Quand tu veux, tu démarres	☐	5
4	Via velpa	☐	5+
5	Mefi	☐	4+
6	Unnamed	☐	4+

7 **Tendre douceur** 4

8 **Révolution permanente** 5

9 **Tintin au niger** 5

Both finishes are the same grade.

10 **Le corbeau solitaire** 4

11 **Canyon Street** . . . . 5+

12 **Black Out** . . . . 6a+

13 **A voile et à vapeur** 6c

14 **Divergences** 7a

20m

7 8 9 10 11 12 13 14

1. Prélude à la lune . . . . 5+
2. Quatre pas dans l'étrange . . . . 5+
3. Luigi le moineau 6b
4. Chemin du paradis 6b
5. Bal a nuit 6b
6. Un royaume vous attend 6c
7. BCBG 7b
8. Nuits câlines 7c
9. Les sucettes à l'anis 7a
10. Gloubi boulga 6b
11. Les ours . . . . 5+
12. En voiture Simone 7b
13. Grosse brute technique 6c
14. La ballade d'arlequin 6a
15. Bivouac sur la lune 6c
16. Le sourire des crabes 3
17. Oradour sur glane 6c
18. Michel stupéfiant 6c
19. Expresso Love . . . . 7b+

Not much sun | 19 min | Vertical | Slabby

20m
1 2 3 4 5 6 7 8 9

Then end of a family day-out at Prairie.

1 **Docteur Octopus** 7b

2 **La crise du proprieraire** . 7c

3 **Le cœur est un chasseur solitaire** 8a

4 **Magie Blanche** . . . . 8b+

5 **Dieu ne veut pas mourir** . 7c

6 **Laissez-le dire**. . . . . 7b+

7 **La vie en couleur**. 7a

8 **Charybde et Scylla** 6c
The right-hand finish is 6b+

9 **Saint Firmin** . . . . 7c+

10 **Le fluide enchanté** 8b

11 **Le voyageur imprudent**. . 8a

12 **Et le diable hurla de jolie** 7a

13 **Le temple du soleil** . . . . 7a+

14 **Un monde si noir**. . . . . . 7a+

15 **Rêve de singe** . . . . 7b+

16 **Le vent du nord** 7c

17 **Felicitade** 7c

18 **Le défi générique**. . . . . . 7a+

19 **Les jeux de la tentation** . 8a+

20 **Mourir au hasard** 7c

21 **Métro pour l'enfer** 7a

22 **K.O. en 9 rounds** 7a

23 **Unknown**. ?

24 **Les petites douceurs de la vie** . . . . . 7c+

Not much sun | 8 min | Vertical

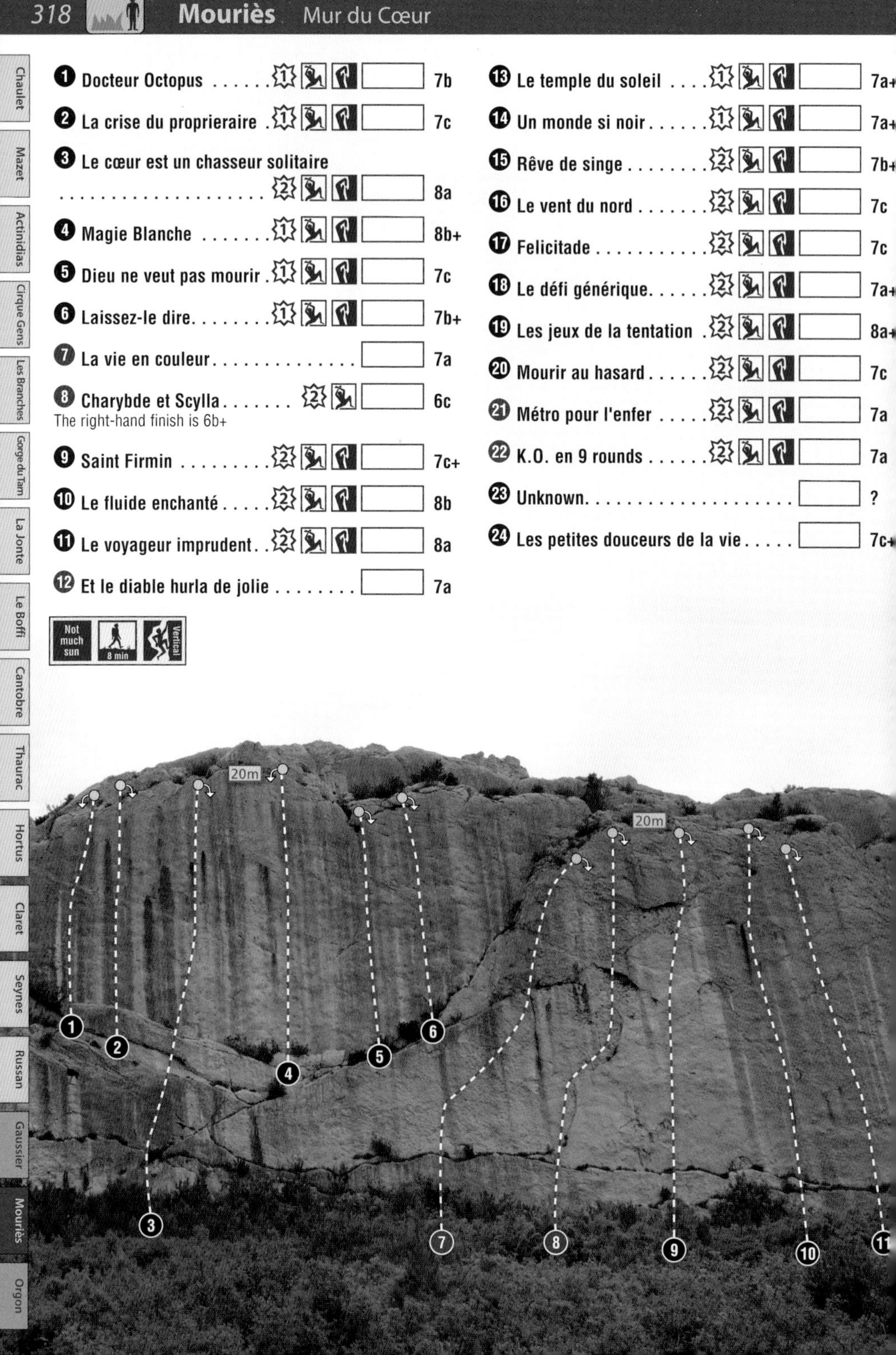

Chaulet
Mazet
Actinidias
Cirque Gens
Les Branches
Gorge du Tarn
La Jonte
Le Boffi
Cantobre
Thaurac
Hortus
Claret
Seynes
Russan
Gaussier
Mouriès
Orgon

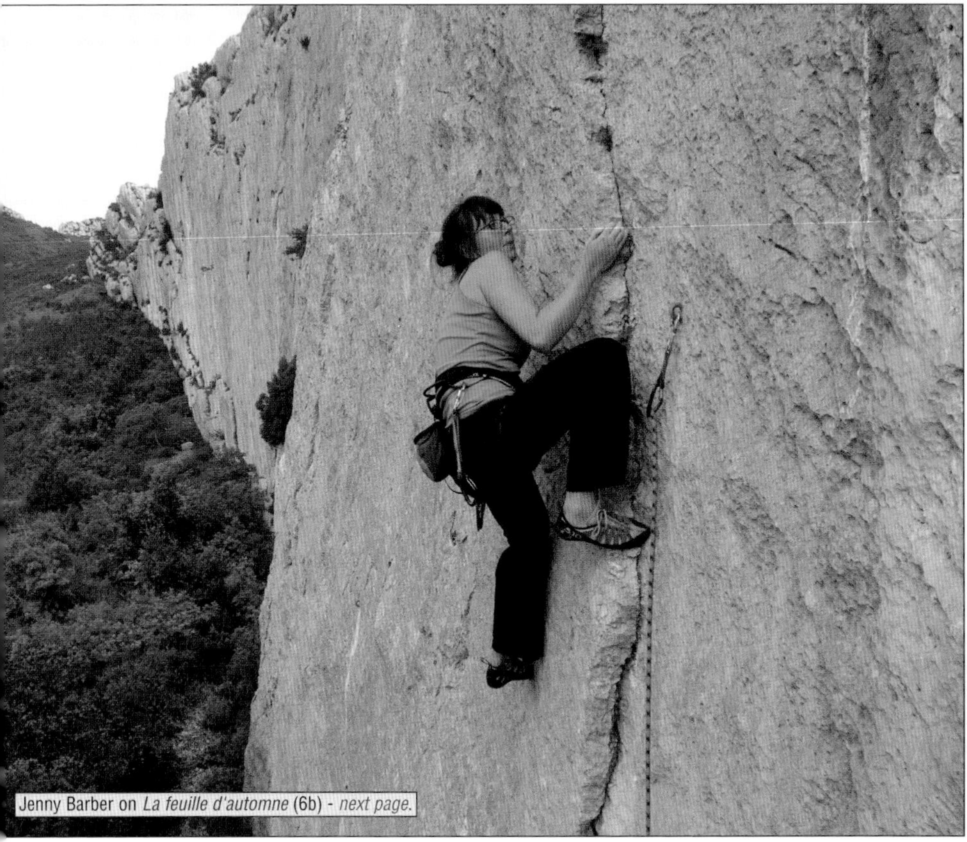

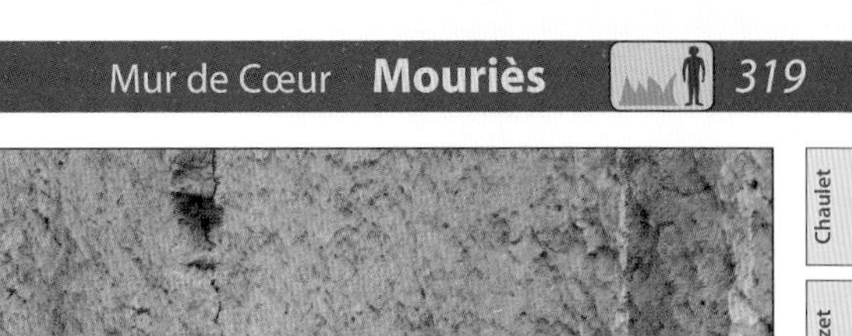

Jenny Barber on *La feuille d'automne* (6b) - *next page.*

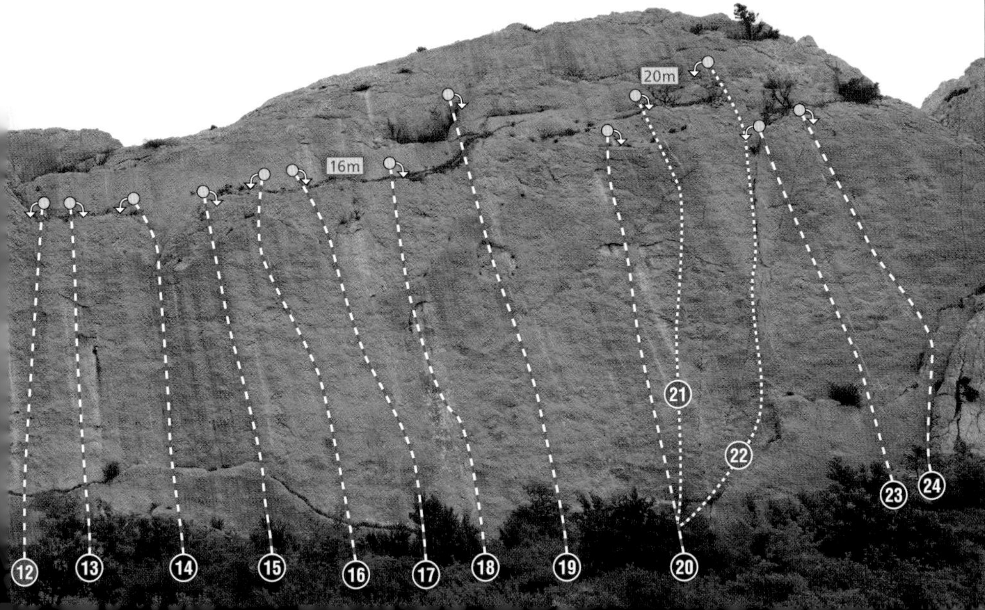

Tranche de Vie

Probably the best wall at Mouriès with stacks to go at in the upper 6s and lower 7s. If you start with *La feuille d'automne* - don't be put off, the harder routes are less polished, and may even feel a bit easier.

No.	Route	Stars	Grade
1	Sans queue ni tete	1	6b
2	Totes griffes dehors	1	7b
3	La feuille d'automne	1	6a
4	5'eme avenue	2	7b+
5	Pour qui sonne le glas	3	6c
6	Pique au vif	3	6c
7	Big-mac	2	7b
8	Au bout du monde	3	7c
9	Ceux qui vont mourir te saluent	3	7b+
10	Super frite	2	7a
11	Chronique martienne	3	7a
12	Tranche de vie	3	6c
13	Bisous dans le cou	2	6c
14	Version integrale	3	6c
15	Coup de pied dans le cul	2	6c
16	Les yeux verts de l'ete	2	6b
17	Sans importance	1	6a+

Route 3: The prominent flake is a great line - but very polished. *Photo on previous page.*

Route 11: *Photo on page 325.*

Not much sun | 6 min | Vertical

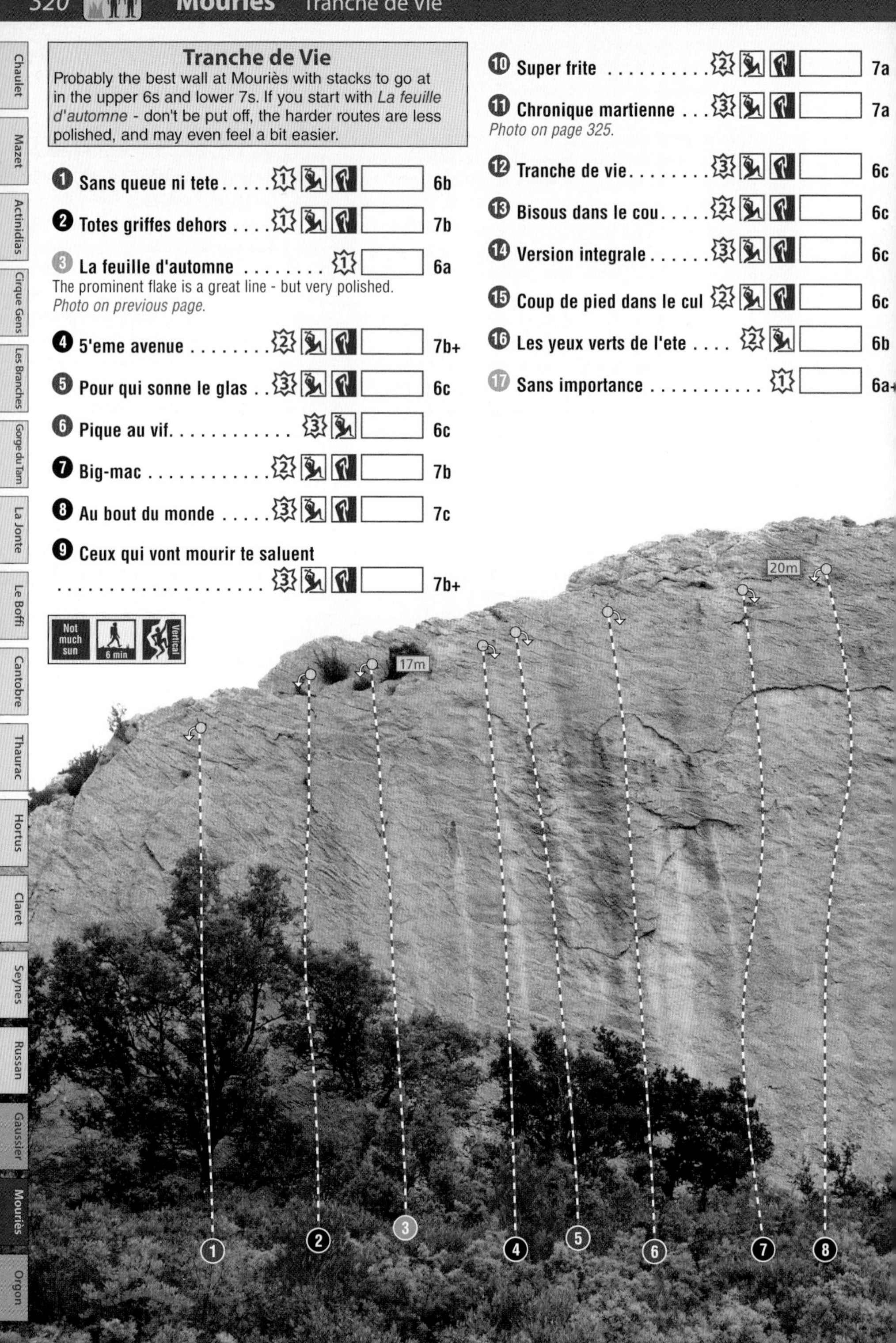

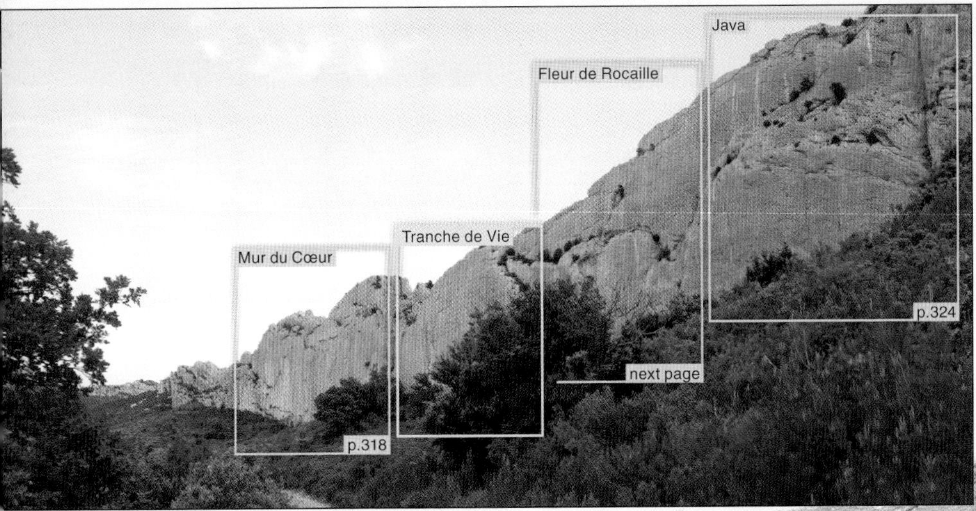

Java
Fleur de Rocaille
Tranche de Vie
Mur du Cœur
p.324
next page
p.318
20m 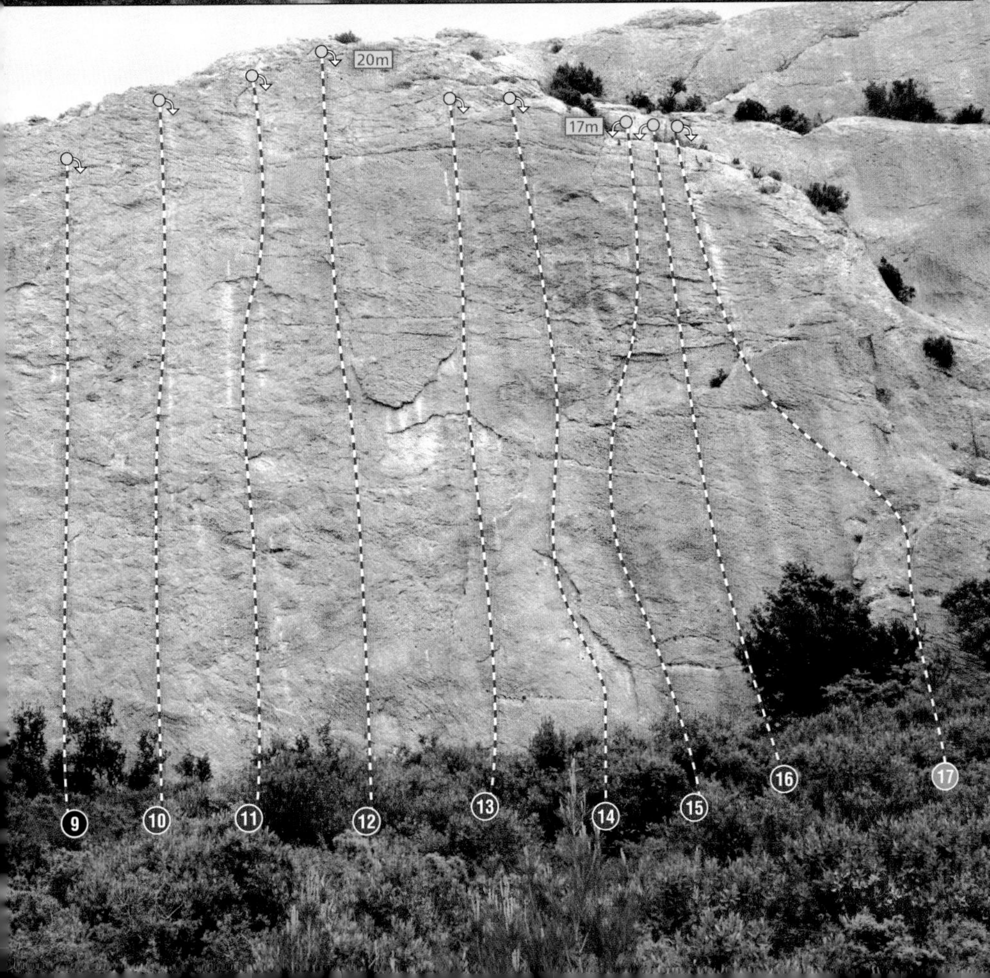
17m
9
10
11
12
13
14
15
16
17

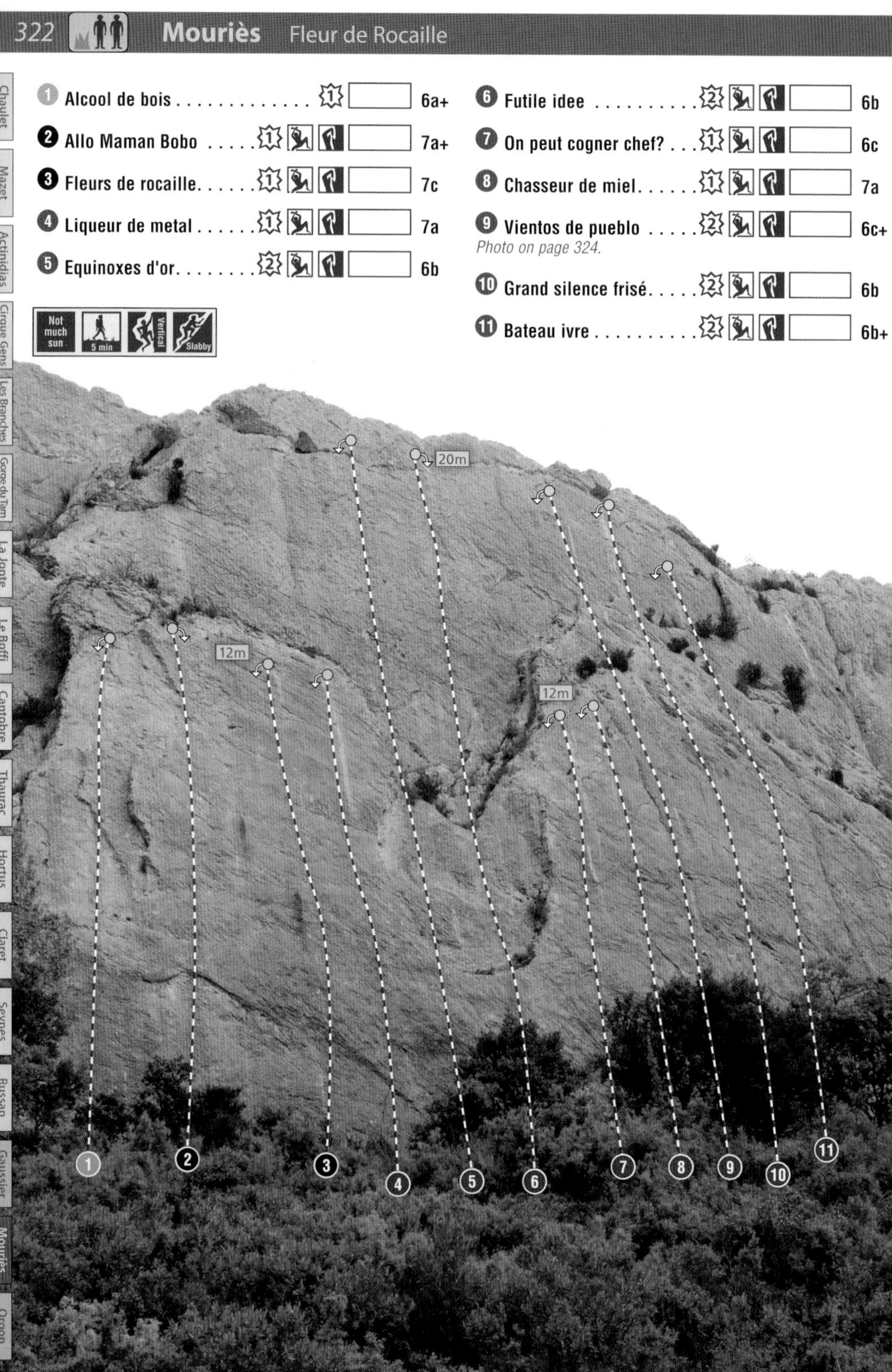
1 Alcool de bois 1 6a+
2 Allo Maman Bobo 1 7a+
3 Fleurs de rocaille 1 7c
4 Liqueur de metal 1 7a
5 Equinoxes d'or 2 6b
6 Futile idee 2 6b
7 On peut cogner chef? 1 6c
8 Chasseur de miel 1 7a
9 Vientos de pueblo 2 6c+
Photo on page 324.
10 Grand silence frisé 2 6b
11 Bateau ivre 2 6b+
Not much sun
5 min
Vertical
Slabby
20m
12m
12m
1
2
3
4
5
6
7
8
9
10
11
Chaulet
Mazet
Actinidias
Cirque Gens
Les Branches
Gorge du Tarn
La Jonte
Le Boffi
Cantobre
Thaurac
Hortus
Claret
Seynes
Russan
Gaussier
Mouriès
Orgon

No.	Route	Stars	Grade
12	**Java du diable**	1	6a
13	**Sentimental bourreau**	1	6a+
14	**Le petit lapin bleu**	2	6a
15	**Je suis une nuit d'ete**	1	6a
16	**La petite demande**		5+
17	**Kazanbur**		6a
18	**Hors la loi**		6a

No.	Route	Stars		Grade
1	Zidi	1		6a
2	Serious moon lite	1		6a
3	Rayons de lune	1		5+
4	Version originale	2		6a
5	Verdure et discorde	2		5+
6	Ouistiti song	1		6a
7	Le berceau du chat	1		6a
8	Deux couettes et des lunettes			6a
9	Sois stage et tais-toi	1		6a
10	Dieux existe	1		5+
11	Je ne suis rencontreé	1		5+
12	La der des der	1		5+

Not much sun | 5 min | Vertical | Slabby

Laurent Moseley on *Vientos de pueblo* (7a) - *page 322.*

Fine sustained face climbing on *Chronique martienne* (7a) - *page 320*.

Pointe de la Découverte
p.336
Babylone
Acteur's Studio
Papy
p.340
p.339
p.338

Orgon

Pte Sikamole
p.334
p.332
Petit Cirque
Pilier Nord
Sentinel
p.342
p.342
Le Grand Cirque
p.344

Secteur du Haut
p.345

	No star	1	2	3
Up to 4+	12	12	1	-
5 to 6a+	27	55	59	16
6b to 7a	7	26	39	8
7a+ and up	6	22	41	3

Mention Orgon to climbers who are reasonably familiar with French climbing and most will assume you are referring to Orgon Canal - a super-steep collection of routes, some of which were once amongst the hardest in the world. This is to mis-judge Orgon almost entirely, as the great majority of the climbing here consists of low- to mid-grade routes on largely slabby or vertical rock. There are, of course, steeper sections, like the Canal, but really there is something for everyone from grade 3 to grade 9. The facts that there is a campsite right in the middle of the place, and that it is so easy to get to, even without a car, make it surprising that it is not more popular than it is.

Approach Also see map on page 291

If you decide to come by train, you will find that a service linking Avignon with Marseilles stops a short walk from the campsite - about as convenient as it gets. If you come by car, exit the A7 at junction 26 (or 25 if coming from the north) and follow signs to Orgon.

Vallée Heureuse

The main road through town is the D7n - locally known as Avenue de la Victoire. Heading east through town, as if to travel south on the D7n, the last right-hand turn before leaving town is Rue Jean Moutte. It is at quite a sharp angle and very easy to miss - look for a sign to the campsite. Follow Rue Jean Moutte - it becomes Route de la Gare and goes past the railway station. After about 800m from the D7n, you will reach a sign to the campsite off to the right, next to a large pond. Follow the road up to the campsite where there is plenty of parking around the entrance. See individual sectors for approaches from the campsite.

Beauregard

You can either approach from the campsite, or you can save a fair walk by navigating the warren of streets to get to the church of Notre Dame de Beauregard (it is a prominent landmark, and well signposted). The road that leads to the church has a sizeable parking area on its right, just before a sharp left-hand bend. Park here, walk up the road and follow the path off to the right after about 25m.

Canal

See page 354 for a detailed approach to Canal sector.

Conditions

The sectors at Orgon as so incredibly varied that it's not possible to give a general indication of conditions - in all likelihood there will be a crag facing the right way with some routes that you'll want to try whatever the time of year.

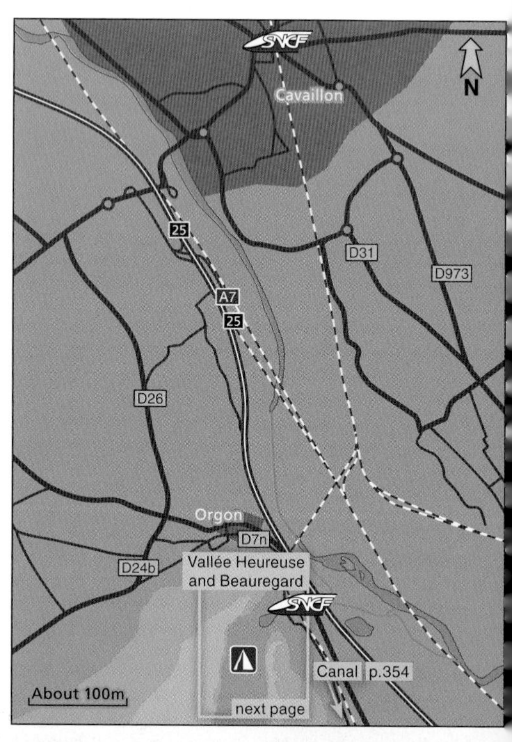

Chaulet
Mazet
Actinidias
Cirque Gens
Les Branches
Gorge du Tarn
La Jonte
Le Boffi
Cantobre
Thaurac
Hortus
Claret
Seynes
Russan
Gaussier
Mouriès
Orgon

Piers Cunliffe on *Sikamol* (6a+) - *page 335* - Pte Sikamolle.

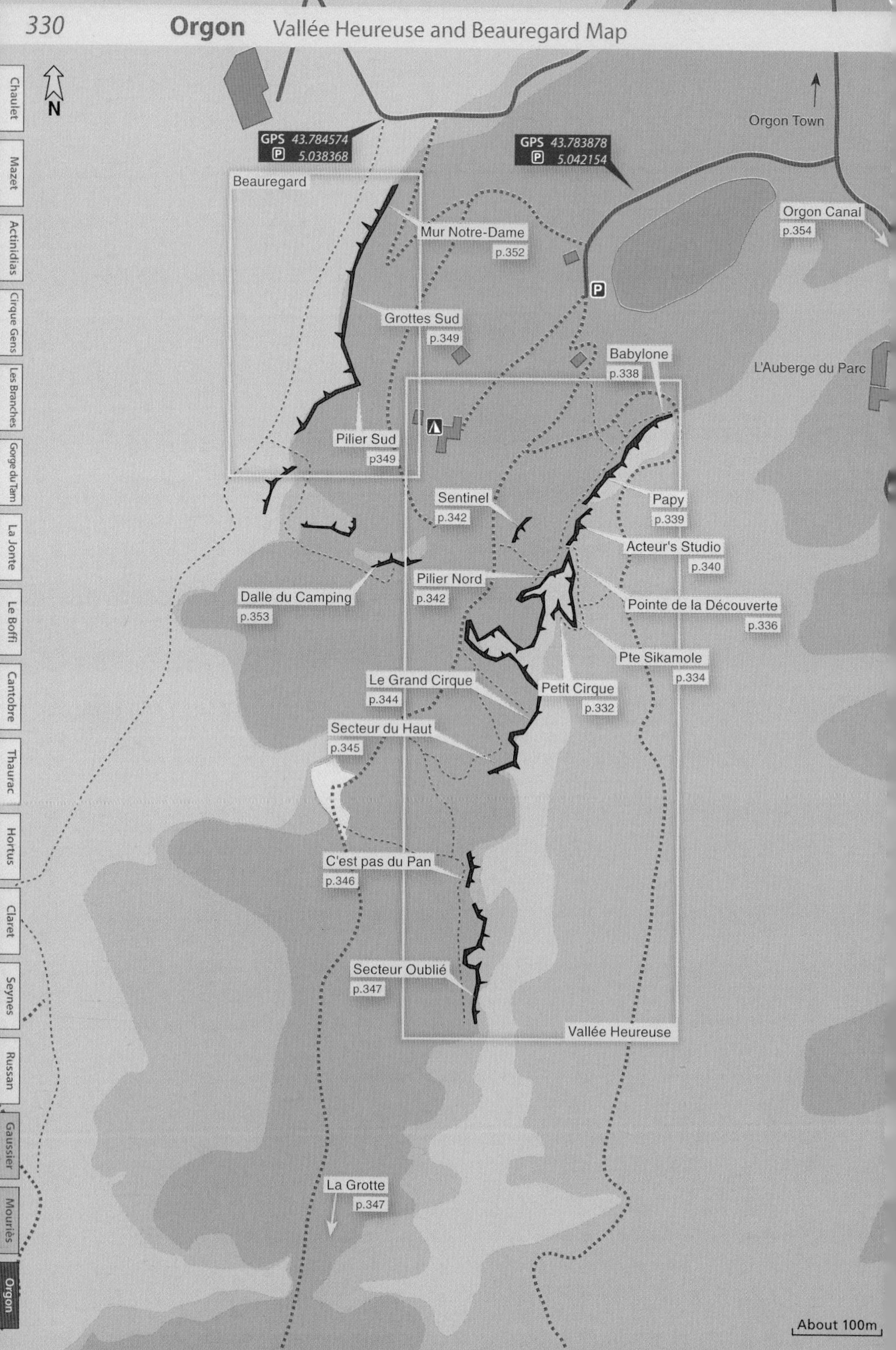
N
GPS 43.784574
P 5.038368
GPS 43.783878
P 5.042154
Orgon Town
Beauregard
Mur Notre-Dame
p.352
Orgon Canal
p.354
Grottes Sud
p.349
Babylone
p.338
L'Auberge du Parc
Pilier Sud
p349
Sentinel
p.342
Papy
p.339
Acteur's Studio
p.340
Pilier Nord
p.342
Dalle du Camping
p.353
Pointe de la Découverte
p.336
Pte Sikamole
p.334
Le Grand Cirque
p.344
Petit Cirque
p.332
Secteur du Haut
p.345
C'est pas du Pan
p.346
Secteur Oublié
p.347
Vallée Heureuse
La Grotte
p.347
About 100m

Piers Culiffe and Laurent Mosely on *Sans nom* (5+) - *page 349*.

Chaulet
Mazet
Actinidias
Cirque Gens
Les Branches
Gorge du Tarn
La Jonte
Le Boffi
Cantobre
Thaurac
Hortus
Claret
Seynes
Russan
Gaussier
Mouriès
Orgon

Vallée Heureuse - East-facing Sectors

While most of the crags in the Vallée Heureuse face west, there are a few good crags on the other side of the ridge that get the morning sun. The rock is of a very high-quality, and they are well-worth a visit. Pte Sikamole and Pointe de la Découvertre are right next to each other, and are clearly visible on the right of the path.

Approach - From the entrance to the campsite (see map on page 330), follow the track that leads from just left (east) of the entrance to the campsite. Continue uphill around the left-hand side of the west-facing crags, then up a pleasant valley with crags on both sides. Pte Sikamole and Pointe de la Découverte are soon visible on the right.

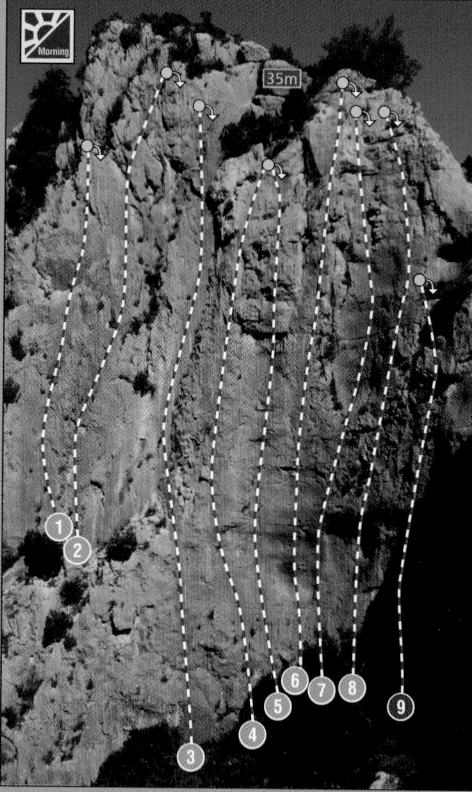

No.	Route	Stars	Grade
1	**Transit**	1	5+
2	**Transat**	1	5+
3	**Zerorama**	3	5+
4	**Gr40**	2	5+
5	**Cav va mieux en le disant**	2	6a+
6	**Bolino and co**	2	6a+
7	**Chevre chaud**	1	6a
8	**Tresor cache**	1	6a+
9	**Bossa nova**		6c

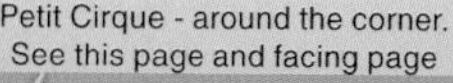

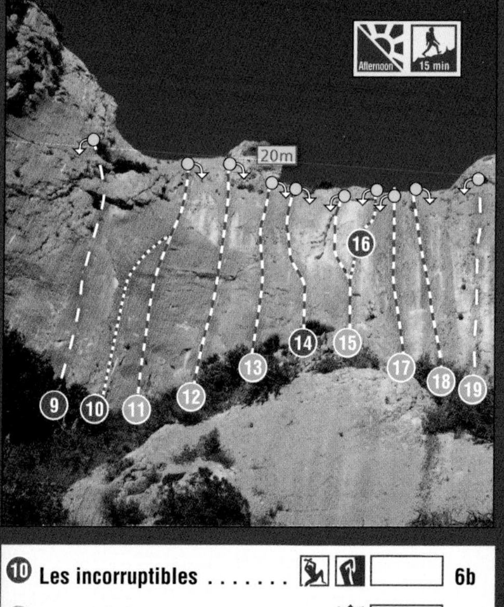

Petit Cirque

A small but pleasant amphitheatre of rock. Take care at the base as a slip could lead to a rapid descent of the crag below - Cash Cache (which is not detailed here).

Approach - To reach Petit Cirque, approach as for Pte Sikamole and continue around the left side of the crag. Go through a notch, and you will find yourself at the right-hand end of the cirque. A chain is in place to descend to the routes.

No.	Route	Stars		Grade
10	Les incorruptibles			6b
11	Self Control	3		5+
12	La decouverte	2		5+
13	Une journeée bien remplie	2		5+
14	Declic	2		6b
15	Coup de vent	2		6a
16	Chute d'humeur	2		6b+
17	La raison du plus fou	2		6a+
18	Shop-suey	2		6a
19	Les glaces a l'eau	2		6a
20	L'art d'oublier	1		5
21	Fleur de mai	1		6a
22	Curieux mec-up	1		6b
23	Les jardins du casino	1		4+
24	Titouli			4+
25	Culture Club			5
26	Nuit des thes			5
27	Par ici la sortie			5

Pte Sikamole

A great wall with technical routes up a shield of excellent rock.

Approach - See page 332.

	Route		Grade
1	La prise de parole		3+
2	La junior	1	4
3	Le recommencement	1	4
4	Fatima la douce	2	4+
5	Poussiere d'ange	2	5
6	Deuxieme couche	2	6a
7	Sikamol *Photo on page 329.*	3	6a+
8	Menuett/msaunt?	2	6a+
9	Belahouab	3	6a
10	Grand Large	3	6a+
11	Symphonie fantastique *Photo this page.*	3	6b
12	Acca	2	5+
13	La barriere	1	5+

	Route	Grade
14	Rien a voir	7b
15	Laisse Madeleine	6b
16	Theorisque	5+
17	La colo	4+
18	Sauf conduit	5

Laurent Moseley on *Symphonie fantastique* (6b) - *this page*

Pointe de la Découverte

A collection of short routes in a fine position.

Approach - See page 332.

	Route	Stars		Grade
1	Objecteur de confiance			3+
2	Gamaelic			5+
3	Le detournement			4+
4	Gromu gros bras			5
5	Toxicodendron	1		6a
6	Fan la bise	1		5
7	Tele-dimanche	2		6a+
8	Marie lou danse reggae	2		6a
9	Amazonia *Photo opposite.*	2		6a
10	Tutor Show	1		6a
11	Pilier du mistral	1		5
12	Au son du fifre	1		4

Unknown climber on *Amazonia* (5+) - *opposite*.

Babylone and Papy

These sectors are next to each other.

Approach - Follow the main track up from the campsite, a path leads off to midway between the two crags. Alternatively continue a little further and a short path takes you straight to Babylone.

No.	Route	Stars	Grade
1	**Cybersex**	1	6b
2	**Frerot, j'ai rate le train**	1	6b+
3	**La goutte**	1	6c
4	**Vieux bonhomme**	2	6b
5	**La sieste** 1) 5+, 2) 6a+	2	6a+
6	**Canard a la horst**	1	6a
7	**Fun board** 1) 6b+, 2) 6a	1	6b+
8	**La nuit du sphynx**	1	7c+
9	**Gros deguelasse le retour**	1	7b+
10	**Babylone** A hold is broken - so this may be harder.		7a+
11	**Culture Rock!**	1	6b+

No.	Route	Stars		Grade
12	Cocktail	1		5+
13	Lunettes noires	2		5+
14	Nuits blanches	2		6a
15	Oublier	1		5+
16	Dix ans plus tard	1		5+
17	Panorama	1		6a
18	Gaviscon	3		6a
19	Abus dangereux	3		5+
20	Papy fait de la resistance	1		5+
21	Combat des chefs	1		6a+
22	Trans europ express	1		6a+
23	Projection privée			6a
24	Surboum chez les soviets			5+

Chaulet
Mazet
Actinidias
Cirque Gens
Les Branches
Gorge du Tarn
La Jonte
Le Boffi
Cantobre
Thaurac
Hortus
Claret
Seynes
Russan
Gaussier
Mouriès
Orgon

Acteur's Studio

A short crag, but the routes can pack a lot in.

Approach - Walk along the base from Papy. You can also approach from the other side of the ridge by walking around from Pointe de la Découverte (see page 336).

Afternoon | 10 min | Vertical

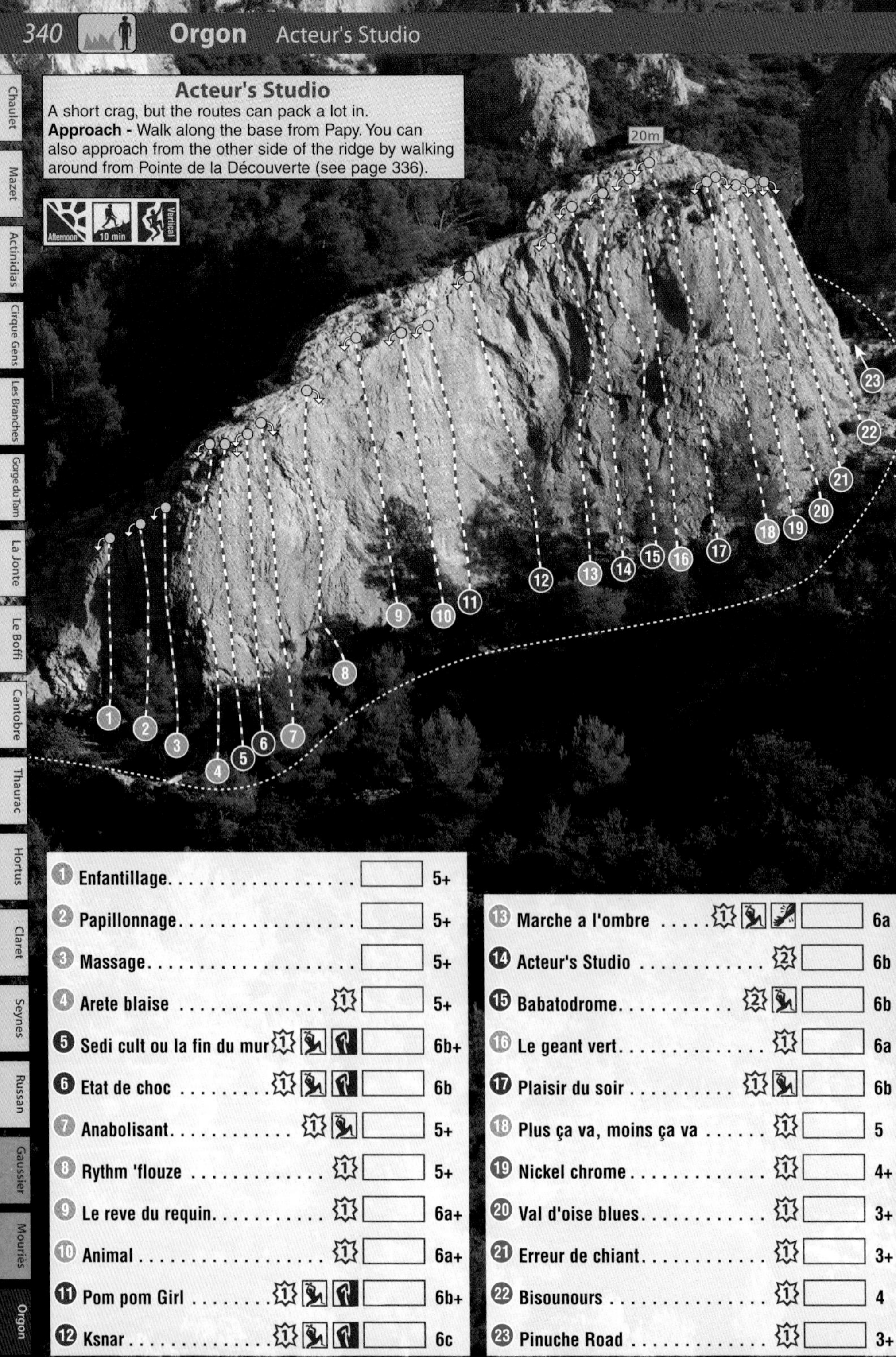

No.	Route	Stars	Grade
1	Enfantillage		5+
2	Papillonnage		5+
3	Massage		5+
4	Arete blaise	1	5+
5	Sedi cult ou la fin du mur	1	6b+
6	Etat de choc	1	6b
7	Anabolisant	1	5+
8	Rythm 'flouze	1	5+
9	Le reve du requin	1	6a+
10	Animal	1	6a+
11	Pom pom Girl	1	6b+
12	Ksnar	1	6c
13	Marche a l'ombre	1	6a
14	Acteur's Studio	2	6b
15	Babatodrome	2	6b
16	Le geant vert	1	6a
17	Plaisir du soir	1	6b
18	Plus ça va, moins ça va	1	5
19	Nickel chrome	1	4+
20	Val d'oise blues	1	3+
21	Erreur de chiant	1	3+
22	Bisounours	1	4
23	Pinuche Road	1	3+

John Eales on *Royal zouc* (5+) - *page 350* - Mur du Six.

Chaulet
Mazet
Actinidias
Cirque Gens
Les Branches
Gorge du Tarn
La Jonte
Le Boffi
Cantobre
Thaurac
Hortus
Claret
Seynes
Russan
Gaussier
Mouriès
Orgon

Sentinel and Pilier Nord

The Sentinel is an impressive free-standing rock. Behind it is Pilier Nord, which only has a few routes, but some are very good.

Approach - Walk along the campsite's perimeter path. The Sentinel will be clearly visible on the left, 50m after the barrier. Pilier Nord can be reached by following a (vegetated) path around the right side of Sentinel. Alternatively Pilier Nord can be reached by walking across from Acteur's Studio (page 340) or from Pointe de la Découverte (page 336).

Unknown climber on *Bonne pioche* (6a+) - *this page.*

No.	Route	Stars	Grade
1	**Le délire de l'indien**	1	6c
2	**Faut con's concerte**		4
3	**La grotte diabolique**		5+
4	**Rita la folle**	1	6a
5	**Grosse fatique**	1	6b
6	**Rien à cirer**		6a+
7	**Body Board**		7a
8	**Waïkaloa**	2	7a
9	**Prêt à porter**	2	6b
10	**Olfactive**	2	7a+
11	**Les filles de maint'nant**	3	6c
12	**L'autre route du soleil**	3	6b+

The following three routes are to be found on the Sentinel.

No.	Route	Stars	Grade
13	**Gaucho**	2	6a
14	**Sentinel**	2	6b
15	**Bonne pioche**	2	6a+

Photo this page.

The small pinnacle below and left (facing the crag) of Sentinel has two routes - both are 6a.

Le Grand Cirque

A superb crag, one of the best at Orgon with soaring lines up immaculate rock.

Approach - Walk along the campsite's perimeter path, 30m after passing a stone obelisk on the right a path leads up to a minor crag (Satellite). Follow the path close to the rock and after a little jungle bashing it will deliver you to the centre of the crag.

1. **Doumé, Pierre, Stéphane, et pas les autres** ... 5+
2. **Téléthon 94** ... 5
3. **Spaghetti Bolognèse** ... 5+
4. **Parfum exotique** ... 1 star ... 5
5. **Nuit de chine** ... 5
6. **La course du temps** ... 1 star ... 6a+
7. **Cosyrock** ... 3 stars ... 5+
8. **Rêve d'altitude** ... 2 stars ... 6a
   1) 5+, **2)** 6a
9. **Pulp Fiction** ... 2 stars ... 7a+
10. **Consultant clandestine** ... 2 stars ... 7a
11. **Ganja** ... 2 stars ... 7a
    1) 7a, **2)** 6a+
12. **Terrific Jessie** ... 3 stars ... 6a+
    1) 6a+, **2)** 6a
13. **Ceil noir sur la banquise** ... 2 stars ... 7a
14. **La fille du compeur de joint** ... 3 stars ... 6b
    Photo on page 290.
15. **La balance** ... 3 stars ... 6b+
16. **Command pernod** ... 2 stars ... 7a
    1) 7a, **2)** 6a+
17. **La route du rhum** ... 2 stars ... 6b
    1) 6a, **2)** 6b
18. **Crème caramel** ... 2 stars ... 6a+
19. **Robin des bras** ... 2 stars ... 5+
20. **Voie de la rénovation** ... 2 stars ... 5+

Afternoon | 12 min | Slabby | Vertical

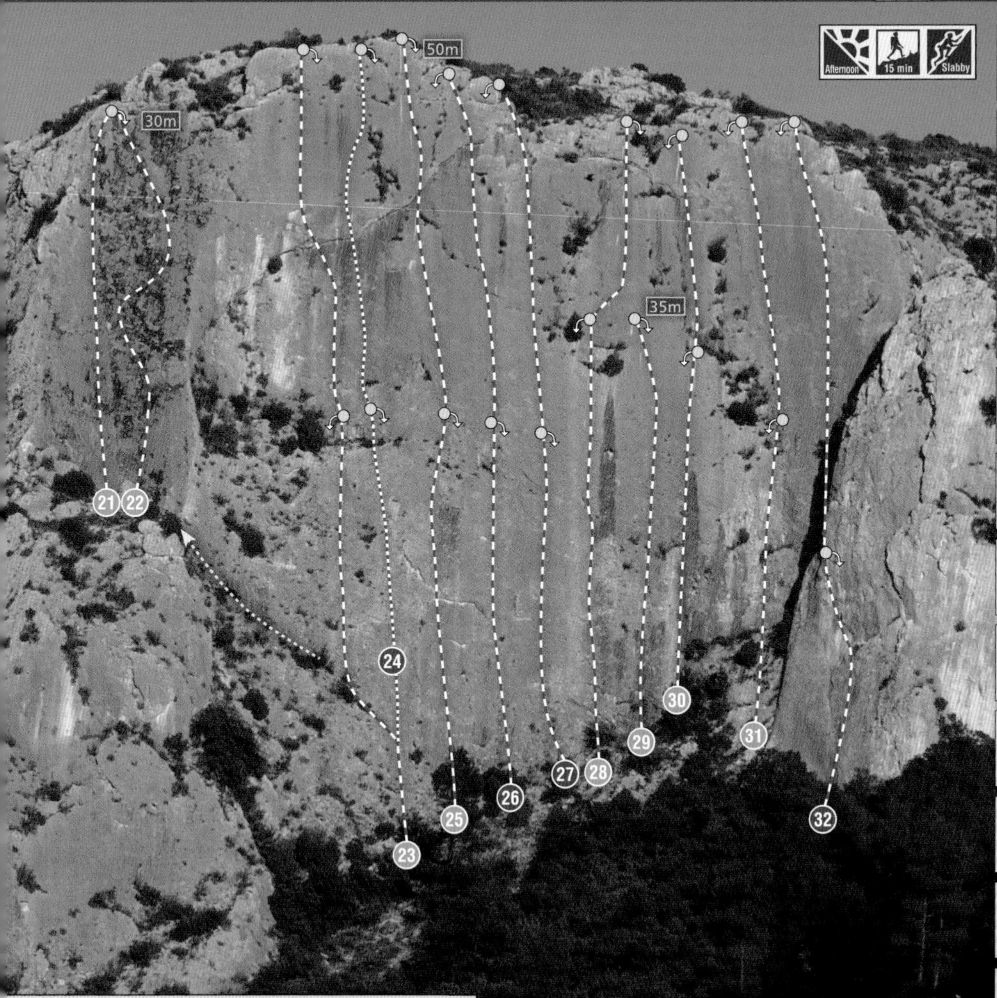

Afternoon | 15 min | Slabby

30m | 50m | 35m

Du Haut

Another superb piece of rock with plenty to go at.
Approach - Walk along the campsite's perimeter track, the path leads off opposite a very large pinnacle on the right side of the track. Where the path splits, take the left fork. Alternatively, a path leads off from the start of the path to Le Grand Cirque. See opposite page.

No.	Route	Stars	Grade
21	**Drôle de zèbra**	2	5+
22	**Fleur de Pierre**	2	6a
23	**Plein ouest** **1)** 5+, **2)** 6a+	1	6a+
24	**Eau de gamme** **1)** 6b, **2)** 6a+	2	6b
25	**Incontinence** **1)** 5+, **2)** 6a+	1	6a+
26	**Des larmes ou des mots** **1)** 6b, **2)** 6a	2	6b
27	**Odd fellows local 151** **1)** 6b+, **2)** 6b+	3	6b+
28	**Mille et un pétards sous la tête** **1)** 6a+, **2)** 5+	2	6a+
29	**Métissage**	2	6a+
30	**Happy Birthday** **1)** 6a+, **2)** 5+	1	6a+
31	**La rose et le lilas** **1)** 6a, **2)** 6a+	2	6a+
32	**Cul et chemise** **1)** 6b, **2)** 6a+	3	6b

C'est pas du Pan

An isolated sector consisting of a superb steep slab, it is well worth the effort of the approach as the rock is perfect. Approach as for Secteur du Haut, but follow a vague and quite vegetated trail off to the right after about 50m.

No.	Route	Stars		Grade
1	Mauvaise troup	1		6a
2	Prise au vent	2		6b
3	Le fruit défendu	3		6a
4	Les shaddoks	3		6a
5	C'est pas du pan!	3		5+
6	Ticket pour un aller retour	2		6a+

Afternoon · 20 min · Slabby · Multi-pitch

Secteur Oublié

In the unlikely event of Orgon getting crowded, this is where to head to avoid them. Follow the track along the east side of the campsite all the way past it and you will find the crag on your left.

7 **Le nettoyeur** . . . . {2} ☐ 5+
1) 5, **2)** 5+

8 **Le crépuscule sur les falaises** . . {2} ☐ 5+
1) 5, **2)** 5+

60m · 40m · 7 · 8

La Grotte

The furthest crag at Orgon has a rather specialised offering - just three hard routes. Follow the track along the east side of the campsite, past Secteur Oublié and you find the crag on your right after about 1km.

Morning · 20 min · Steep

about 1km

9 · 10 · 11

9 ? . . . . {1} 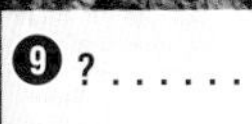 ☐ 8a

10 ? . . . . {1}  ☐ 8b

11 **A l'abri des renards**. . . . {1}  ☐ 8a

Directly opposite the Vallée Heureuse crags is another group of walls. This time shady in the afternoon, sunny in the morning.

Approach Also see map on page 330

The approach via the road to Notre Dame de Beauregard is covered on page 328. To approach from the campsite below, locate a rough track leading up the hill following the right-hand perimeter of the campsite. Where the track turns back on itself you are directly below Les Grottes. A number of short trails connect the track with a path that follows the base of the cliff.

Sam Harvie on *Sur le fleuve amour* (7b) - *opposite* - Photo: Piers Cunliffe.

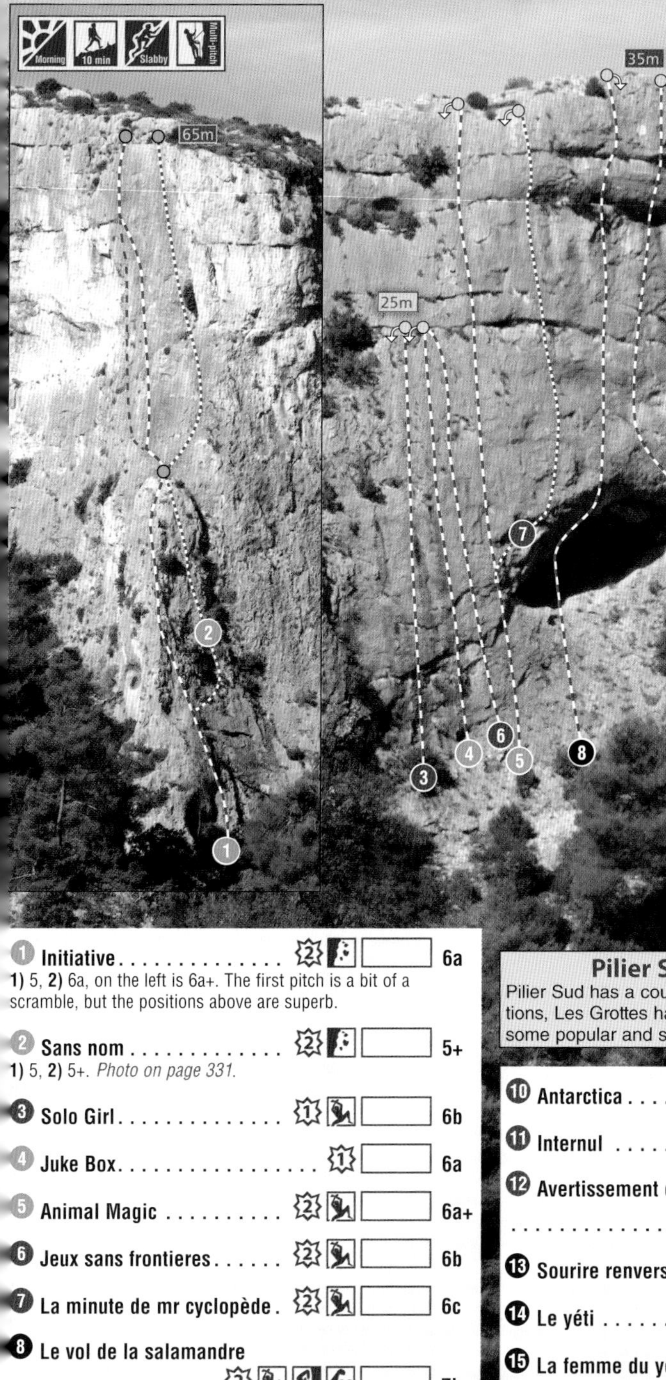

1 Initiative . . . . 2 stars 6a
1) 5, **2)** 6a, on the left is 6a+. The first pitch is a bit of a scramble, but the positions above are superb.

2 Sans nom . . . . 2 stars 5+
1) 5, **2)** 5+. *Photo on page 331.*

3 Solo Girl . . . . 1 star 6b

4 Juke Box . . . . 1 star 6a

5 Animal Magic . . . . 2 stars 6a+

6 Jeux sans frontieres . . . . . . 2 stars 6b

7 La minute de mr cyclopède . 2 stars 6c

8 Le vol de la salamandre
. . . . 2 stars 7b+

9 Unnamed . . . . 2 stars 7b+

Pilier Sud and Les Grottes

Pilier Sud has a couple of two-pitch routes in fine positions, Les Grottes has a mix of excellent face-climbs and some popular and steep jug-hauls.

10 Antarctica . . . . 2 stars 7a

11 Internul . . . . 6c+

12 Avertissement de conduite
. . . . 2 stars 6c

13 Sourire renversant . . . . 2 stars 7b+

14 Le yéti . . . . 2 stars 7c+

15 La femme du yéti . . . . . 2 stars 7b

16 Sur le fleuve amour . . . . 3 stars 7b
Photo opposite.

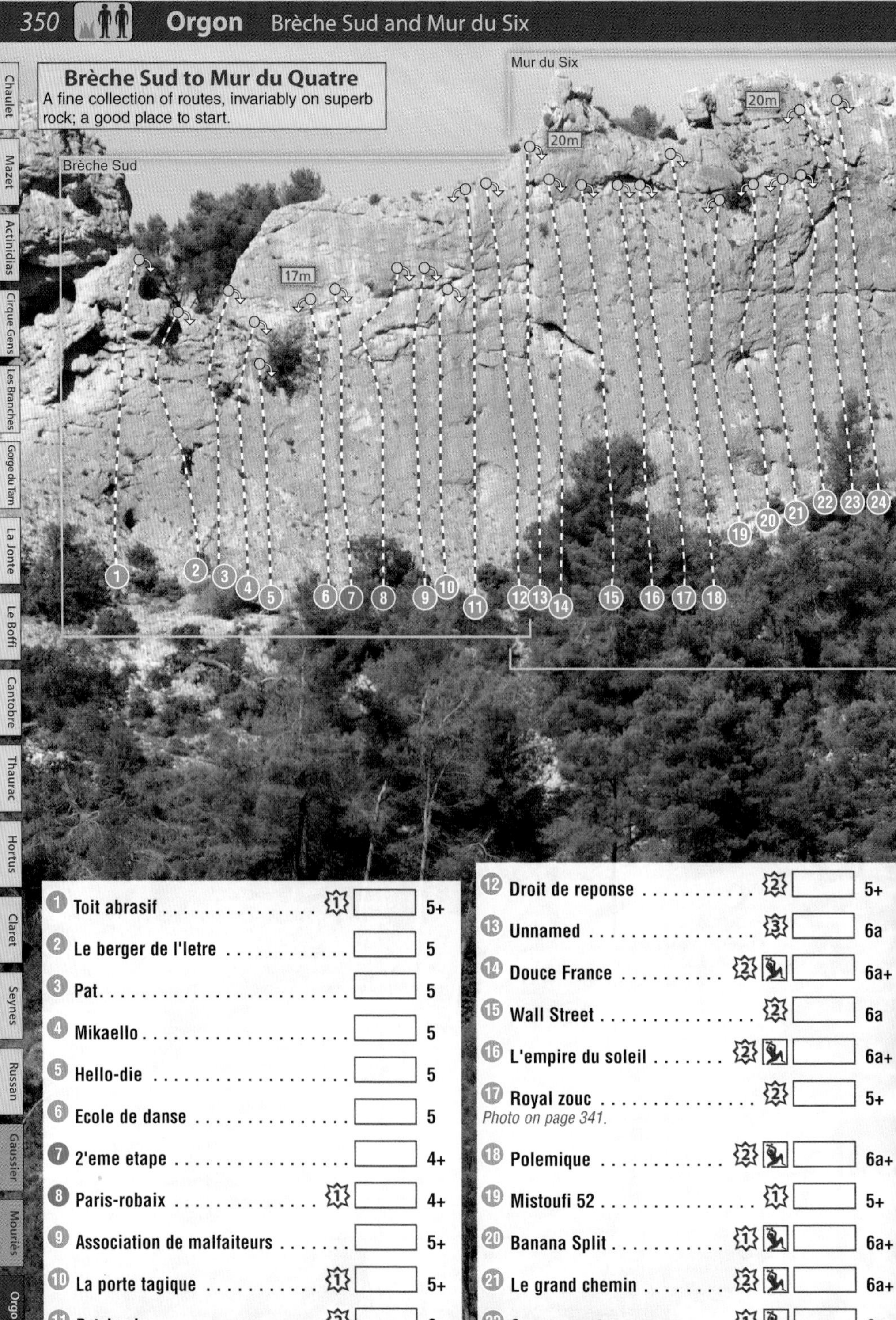

Brèche Sud to Mur du Quatre

A fine collection of routes, invariably on superb rock; a good place to start.

No.	Route	Stars	Grade
1	Toit abrasif	1	5+
2	Le berger de l'letre		5
3	Pat		5
4	Mikaello		5
5	Hello-die		5
6	Ecole de danse		5
7	2'eme etape		4+
8	Paris-robaix	1	4+
9	Association de malfaiteurs		5+
10	La porte tagique	1	5+
11	Patchanka	2	6a+
12	Droit de reponse	2	5+
13	Unnamed	3	6a
14	Douce France	2	6a+
15	Wall Street	2	6a
16	L'empire du soleil	2	6a+
17	Royal zouc	2	5+
18	Polemique	2	6a+
19	Mistoufi 52	1	5+
20	Banana Split	1	6a+
21	Le grand chemin	2	6a+
22	Seance nocturne	1	6a+

Photo on page 341. (Royal zouc)

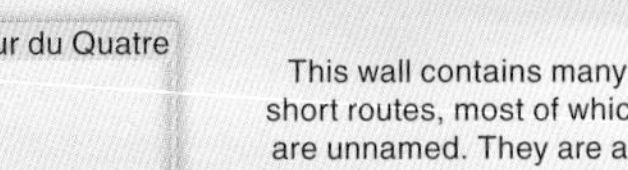

20m

Mur du Quatre

15m

15m

This wall contains many short routes, most of which are unnamed. They are all grade 4 or easier.

No.	Route	Stars	Grade
23	Chic planete	2	6a+
24	Saison du plaisir	3	6a
25	Ze rien compris	2	6a+
26	Ze gaivota	2	6b
27	L'amazone	1	6a+
28	Carrefour aux oies	2	5+
29	Farol da guia	1	6b
30	Les demenageurs	2	6a
31	Lisboa City	2	6a+
32	Vent du soir	2	6a
33	Jardin sauvage	1	5+
34	La cloture	2	5
35	L'heure de s'ennivrer	1	5
36	L'araignee	1	4+
37	D-lyre	1	5+
38	A.B.C+	1	5
39	Rock in Chair		4+
40	Top camembert		5
41	Pipine		4+
42	Mamour		4+
43	Méloman		5

Mur Notre-Dame

The first crag you reach when approaching from above. The routes on the right-hand side are all quite hard, but things ease off rapidly as you walk further on.

No.	Route	Stars	Grade
1	Les jardins	1	5
2	Bonne fete	1	5
3	Petite canaille	1	5
4	Germanofolie	1	5
5	Radioactive	1	5
6	R.F.M.	1	6a
7	Absence de malice	1	6a
8	Guele de bois	2	6a
9	Rock 'n' Roll!	2	6a
10	Surprise de vue	2	6a+
11	Coproduction	2	6b+
12	Autoproduction	2	6c
13	La frite mysterieuse	2	6c+
14	Machin dur	2	7a+
15	Machin mou	2	7a+
16	Pink Floyd	2	7b+
17	Cure de sommeil	2	7a
18	Reve de pierre	2	7b
19	Rolling Stones	2	7a+
20	Genesis	1	6b+
21	Antidope!	1	6b
22	Fait d'hiver		6b

Dalle du Camping

Technical routes up some very good rock, unfortunately the approach is a bit of a pain - it is possible to get there from the campsite if you're staying there, by a bit of an earthy scramble. The official approach is to walk along the east side of the Beauregard crags, passing several short sectors until it is possible to pass through around the side of Pilier Sud. Follow a poor trail off to the right. The trail drops down behind a crag and eventually delivers you to the left side of the sector. See map on page 330.

No.	Route	Stars	Grade
23	Levèvre-utile	1	6c
24	L'amoire à gruyère	2	6c
25	Les valseuses	2	6b
26	La religieuse	2	7a
27	Plein sud	2	6b
28	Le petit forestier	2	6c
29	Aux frais de la princesse	3	7b
30	Aux toute beauté	3	6c+
31	Inoxydable	2	6b
32	Tontons flambeurs	3	6a+
33	Attaque frontale	3	6a
34	La vallée heureuse	2	6b+
35	Crévoux express	2	7b+

A very impressive crag with plenty of steep and lengthy routes, and a surprising number of slabby lower-grade routes too. The style of the harder routes resembles indoor climbing.

Approach Also see maps on pages 291 and 328

To get to the Canal sector for the first time, we recommend approaching via Orgon. First of all follow the directions in the introduction to Orgon to get to the pond below the entrance to the campsite. Rather than turning right towards the campsite (signed Camping de la Vallée Heureuse), continue on Rue de la Gare, past the entrance to l'Auberge du Parc, and after just 100m turn right into a large area of rough open ground. Head to the opposite side of the area, cross the canal, and follow the track that runs parallel to the canal. After about 800m you will notice the crag on your right. Continue to find plenty of parking spaces at the side of the canal, just below the steepest part of the crag.

Conditions

The steep areas will naturally seep after rain, but are very sheltered. The slabby walls dry quickly after rain. The crag faces east, and gets morning light, though heavy tree cover ensures you're never going to see much sun if you're climbing on the left side of the crag.

Tom Kendall being keenly observed on *Les deux flans* (5+) *page 365*.

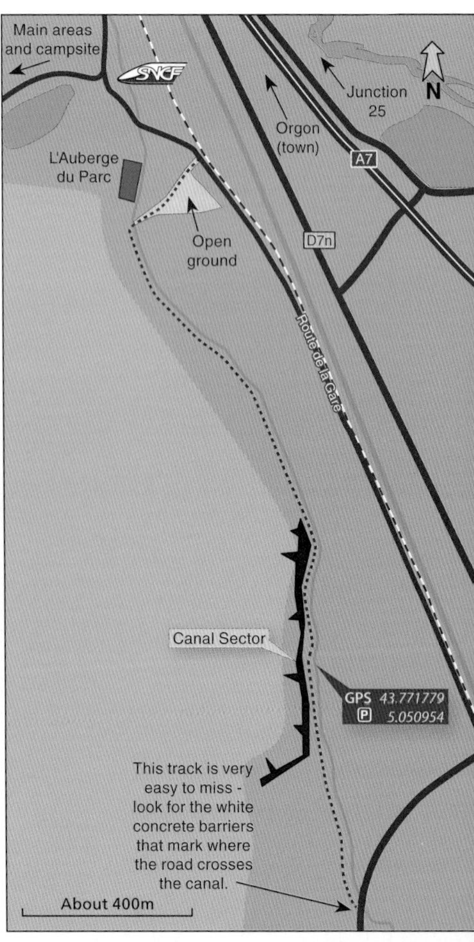

1 L'ami jean-mi	2	7a+
2 Univers en expansion	2	7a+
3 Génération résine	1	7c+
4 La qualième dimension	1	7a

Morning
Roadside
Steep
35m
35m
1
2
3
4
5
6
7

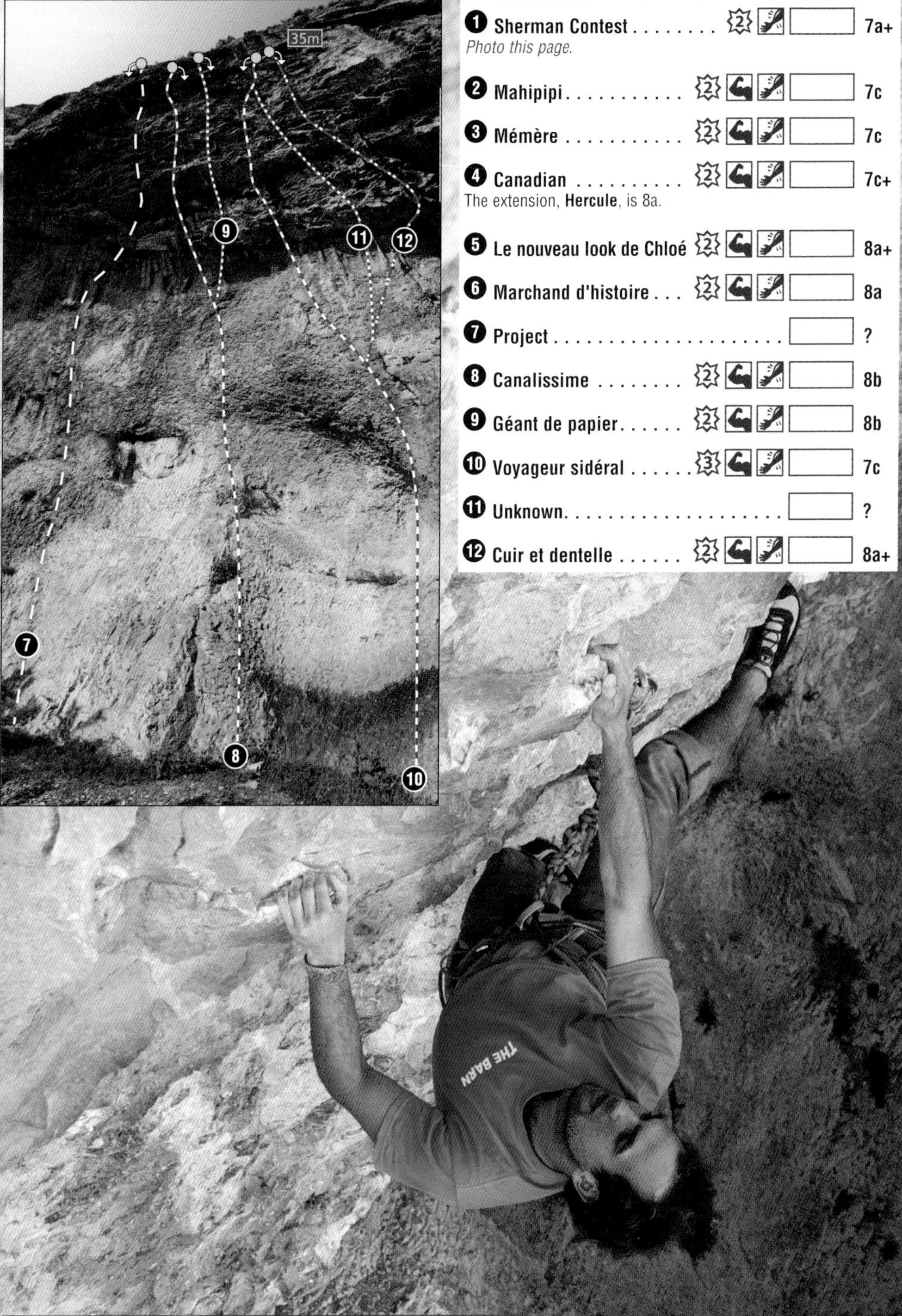

	Route	Stars	Grade
1	**Sherman Contest** *Photo this page.*	2	7a+
2	**Mahipipi**	2	7c
3	**Mémère**	2	7c
4	**Canadian** The extension, **Hercule**, is 8a.	2	7c+
5	**Le nouveau look de Chloé**	2	8a+
6	**Marchand d'histoire**	2	8a
7	**Project**		?
8	**Canalissime**	2	8b
9	**Géant de papier**	2	8b
10	**Voyageur sidéral**	3	7c
11	**Unknown**		?
12	**Cuir et dentelle**	2	8a+

Laurent Moseley on *Sherman Contest* (7a+) - *this page.* Photo: Piers Cunliffe

Chaulet
Mazet
Actinidias
Cirque Gens
Les Branches
Gorge du Tarn
La Jonte
Le Boffi
Cantobre
Thaurac
Hortus
Claret
Seynes
Russan
Gaussier
Mouriès
Orgon

Canalissime

Though chipped, glued and polished, the routes at the left end of the Canal sector take on an amazing piece of rock and enjoying one often feels like a guilty pleasure. It should be obvious from the condition of the first few metres whether the route is seeing much traffic. Spotting chalk on the holds is no indicator of popularity - they never really get wet.

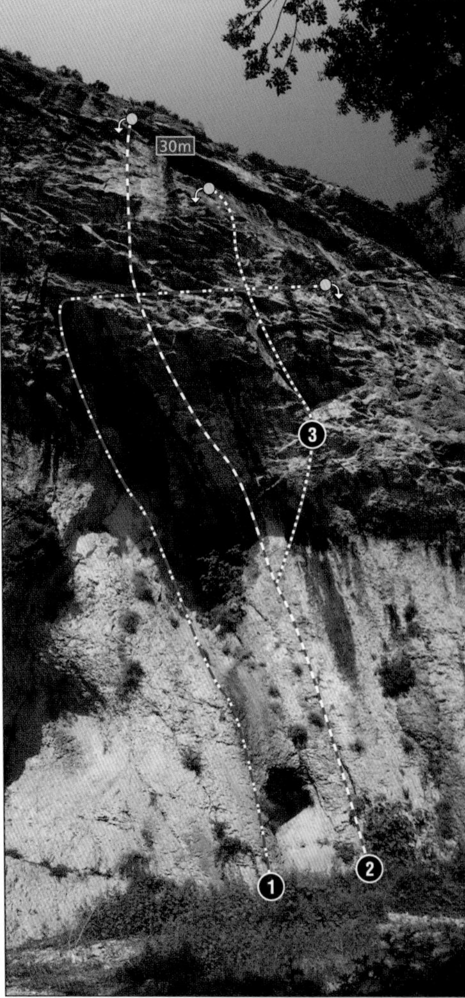

No.	Route	Stars	Grade
1	Lutinerie		7c
2	Injustice	1	8c
3	Le mimis	1	8a+
4	Monk	1	8a+
5	Unknown	2	8a
6	Gosse de riche		?
7	Cœur de loup	2	7c
8	Cacou	2	7c+
9	Biceps mou	2	8a+
10	Le bus des déctman	2	8a
11	Fleur de grisou	1	7c+

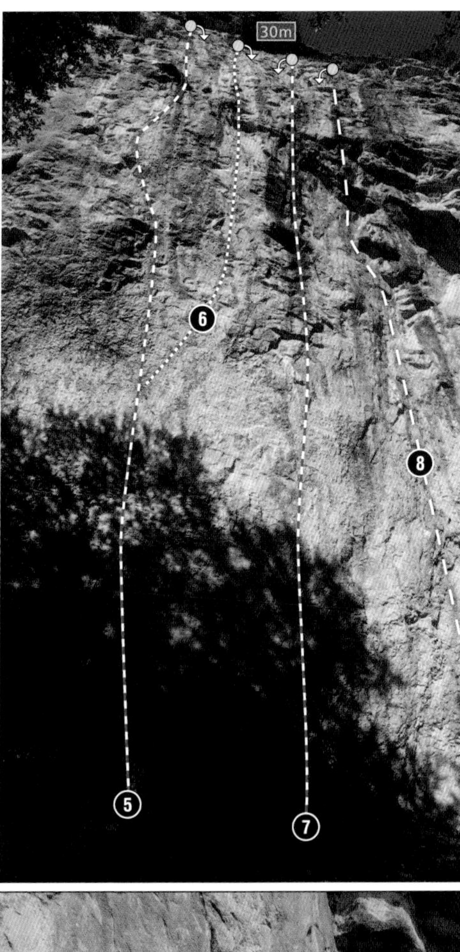

Piers Cunliffe on *Benjamin Digoudi* (6a+) - *page 362*.

Chaulet
Mazet
Actinidias
Cirque Gens
Les Branches
Gorge du Tarn
La Jonte
Le Boffi
Cantobre
Thaurac
Hortus
Claret
Seynes
Russan
Gaussier
Mouriès
Orgon

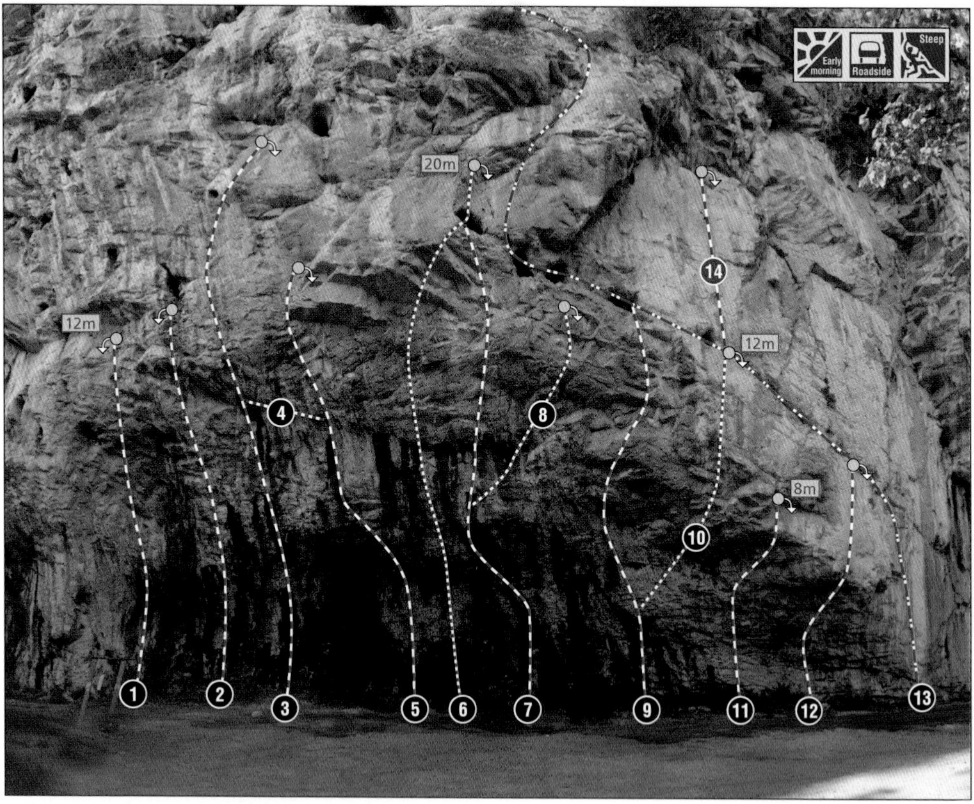

Bronx

For a while, this sector held some of the hardest routes in the world, and made Orgon a well-recognised name. The routes are still there, and the clips are still in, but the slide into obscurity is well under-way. Get strong, pay it a visit and feel the history.

1. Basamba . . . . 8a+
2. L'irrévérence. . . . . 8b+
3. Macumba Club 8c
4. La connexion. . . . . 8c+
5. Bronx . . . . 8c+
6. Sachchidanandah. 9a
7. Fox et methews . . . . . . 8b+
8. Diesel 8b
9. Tourneboule . . . . 7c+
10. Moulino 7c
11. Famille daube 7c
12. Parcours santé 7c
13. Tarte a la crème / atmosphere 7b
    1) 7a+, **2)** 7b.
14. Squeletor nous gonfle . . . . 6c+
    Start as for *Tarte a la crème/atmosphere.*
15. Petite mimie 6b
16. Super mamie 6b
17. Gazouillis . . . . 7a+
18. Bourinos. 7b
19. Le monde es fou . . . . . 7c+
20. Melusine . . . . 6c+
    1) 6c+, **2)** 6a+

Early morning
Roadside
Vertical
35m
20m
20
16
17
18
20
13
15
19
Chaulet
Mazet
Actinidias
Cirque Gens
Les Branches
Gorge du Tarn
La Jonte
Le Boffi
Cantobre
Thaurac
Hortus
Claret
Seynes
Russan
Gaussier
Mouriès
Orgon

Frank Loessner on *Minederien* (4+) - *page 365.*

No.	Route	Stars	Grade
1	**Antonin paysan du causse**	2	6c
2	**Morgane**	1	7a+
3	**Changer tout** — There is an unknown variation finish to the left.	1	7a+
4	**Lisa**	1	7b+
5	**Bebe chanteur**	1	7c
6	**La black music**	1	7b
7	**En catimini**	1	7a+
8	**Calinas feutres**	1	7a
9	**Les menthes sauvages** — **1)** 7a, **2)** 7a+	1	7a+
10	**Benjamin Bigoudi** — *Photo page 359.*	2	6a+
11	**La jument de fernand**	2	6c
12	**Les caillons bleus**	1	6c+
13	**Gris souris**	2	7a
14	**Patchouli Tea** — **1)** 6b, **2)** 6c	2	6c
15	**Pousse au reve**	2	6b
16	**La siesta a l'ombre**	1	7a
17	**Calinette**	1	7a+

Tchao

The left-hand side carries on the theme of the main crag but thing get quickly more friendly as you work rightwards finishing with some pleasant slabby routes.

Early morning
Roadside
Vertical
15m
1
2
3
4
5

1. Voyage en mappe monde . . . . . ① 7a
2. Histoire d'un jour . . . . ① 6c
3. Tchao . . . . ② 6b
4. Mort au cons . . . . ② 6a+
5. Chichipan . . . . ② 5+
6. Les deux flans . . . . ① 5+

Photo on page 354.

7. L'espagnol . . . . ① 5
8. Lettres majuscule . . . . ① 4+
9. Canelle . . . . ① 5+
10. Pattes de mouches . . . . ② 6a
11. Arc-en-ciel . . . . ② 6a

There are three more lines just off the topo:

12. La fée du marais . . . . 5+
13. Pipi au lit . . . . 4+
14. Minederien . . . . 4+

Photo page 362.

Mountain Rescue

Dial 112 - Ensure you have details of your location and what the incident involves. This number works on any mobile on a French network.